B separates hey (the people) from us
                    (intellectuals)
agonistic crit.s 216

Intellectuals in Power:
A Genealogy of Critical Humanism

15^{00}

PAUL A. BOVÉ

Intellectuals in Power

A Genealogy of Critical Humanism

COLUMBIA UNIVERSITY PRESS
NEW YORK

Library of Congress Cataloging-in-Publication Data

Bové, Paul A., 1949–
Intellectuals in power.

Bibliography: p.
Includes index.
1. Criticism—History—20th century.
2. Literature—Philosophy. 3. Humanism in
literature. I. Title.
PN94.B68   1985   801'.95'0904   85–17486
ISBN 0–231–06011–4 (alk. paper)

Columbia University Press
New York   Guildford, Surrey
Copyright © 1986 Columbia University Press
All rights reserved

Printed in the United States of America

Designed by Ken Venezio

In Memoriam
Mario Bové
(1921–1985)

Contents

Preface   ix

Acknowledgements   xix

1. Mendacious Innocents, or the Modern Genealogist as
   Conscientious Intellectual: Nietzsche, Foucault, Said   1

2. A Free, Varied, and Unwasteful Life: I.A. Richards'
   Speculative Instruments   39

3. The Last of the Latecomers (Part I): The Critical
   Syntheses of Erich Auerbach   79

4. The Last of the Latecomers (Part II): Humanist in
   Conflict   131

5. Intellectuals at War: Michel Foucault and the
   Analytics of Power   209

6. Critical Negation: The Function of Criticism at the
   Present Time   239

Notes   311

Index   331

Preface

This book has its origins in my attempt to prepare to write a
history of the institution of academic literary criticism. Such a
project, I felt, could only follow an investigation into how
others have thought about cultural and intellectual institutions. With the help of grants from Columbia University and
the American Council of Learned Societies I set out to read
more consistently in the work of intellectual historians, critical historians, and ideological critics of the state-related apparatuses of our culture. In the process, it quickly became evident
that the writings of these theoreticians, critics, and historians
were themselves historically situated acts understandable only
as events within networks of discourses, institutions, and politics. But it also became clear to me that their relation to the
state did not and could not, in itself, account for the specifics
of their functions. At the same time, it became more and more
striking how resistant most traditional humanistic and belletristic forms of literary critical or theoretical activity are to
admitting any involvement of criticism or theory with specific
forms of power, politics, desire, or interest. Yet it seemed increasingly apparent that there was no way to understand the
past and present social and cultural role of advanced literary
education and criticism except by trying to see it as situated
within an entire range of discourses and institutions whose
own metier is power and interest.

Such a project, I felt, had to be somewhat different from most
past ideological critiques of literary study, such as John
Fekete's *The Critical Twilight*.[1] At least as Fekete carries it
out, ideology critique remains too abstract; that is, it operates
at too high a level of generality to catch the specifics of par-

ticular material and discursive situations. For example, as admirable as Fekete's few suggestive pages on I. A. Richards' relation to functionalism might be, they do not bring us very far in understanding the position of functionalism or Richards' adaptation of it in the postwar crisis. In his much more empirically materialist study, *The Moment of 'Scrutiny'*,[2] Francis Mulhern shows in greater detail how deeply inscribed within the politics and culture of England's crises Leavis and his friends really were. In a manner I find more valuable than Fekete's, Mulhern also outlines for us many of the affiliations of *Scrutiny* with other artistic and political discourses and consequently helps us to see how *Scrutiny* stood in relation to the other empowered discourses, practices, and ideologies of its period.

As valuable as such contributions might be to grasping the ideological and political function of "Eng. Lit.," especially in Great Britain, it seems important to try to accomplish at least two other goals in any consideration of the institution: first, to place the leading figures of our profession within a partial genealogy of their discursive and nondiscursive practice and, second, to attempt to show how positioned, indeed, how responsive to their historical position, those we have come to think of as greater critics, like Auerbach and Richards, might be. The second is the more important of these goals. The first is merely a way of understanding that the positioned nature of critical practice is what must be studied because this allows us to see that such positioning defines, limits, and enables critical action.

To try to carry out this entire project would have made an already overly long book impossible. I have compromised on trying to illustrate the historically positioned nature of the critic. I have only suggested some of Richards' historical interrelationships in an attempt to indicate a bit about his critical function within humanism and the American and English academies. I offer a more nearly full account of the material genealogy of critical humanism in chapters 3 and 4 in which I examine Erich Auerbach in terms of both the German humanistic tradition before and after World War II, as well as the

American academic construction of Auerbach's reputation following his emigration to this country. I show that he was conscious of his historical position and of the value and power of
the critical tools he had available.

Chapter 4 shows how he deploys the resources of critical humanism for quite specific historical purposes and precisely in
response to the position in which his genealogy and modern
history place him; it also illustrates how his humanistic genealogy restricts his work. In other words, I hope chapter 4 suggests the complexity of his critical position: while his
humanism compels him to the magnificent struggles against its
degradation that make up his postwar essays, it also inevitably
catches him up in its own defining contradictions.

Not until the end of his career, however, do we see Auerbach
prepared to admit—and he experiences this as a defeat—that
his humanism not only cannot but perhaps should not be re-
stored. In the genealogy I reconstruct, Auerbach becomes central to our critical history precisely because his work makes
clear that critical humanism is a situated historical practice
enacted within a set of power relations found in discourse,
research, and intellectual interest. Furthermore, as I argue
throughout, Auerbach brings us to the point where we cannot
but conclude that critical humanism can no longer function
legitimately as the toolbox of oppositional intellectual practice: Auerbach's failed struggle to restore it is evidence of its
illegitimacy, and his final gestures beyond it point to the need
for a nonhumanistic critical practice. This in turn takes us to
figures like Edward W. Said and Michel Foucault, who
embody both the strengths of a politically progressive critical
humanism and the most concerted and rigorous effort to think
against it.

It is, of course, a cliché that Foucault is an "antihumanist";
that is, in the reductive sense that most reactionary critics give
to the term, Foucault is perceived simply as being opposed to
"man" and wanting to replace "man" and his historical works
and values with some equally reductive concept such as "language," "discourse," or "power." Yet Foucault is an "antihumanist" in a much more complex sense which, I would argue,

traditional humanists must obscure precisely because he concerns himself with the materiality of humanistic practice. Foucault's work is antihumanistic in its struggle against the *material* consequence of the cultural and political institution of the will-to-knowledge of humanistic practice and values. That such values and practice are dependent on and in turn support these concrete materialities is what humanists tend to deny, or when they admit them at all, do so only to insist on their "pragmatic rationality."[3] Traditional or conservative humanists insist always on subordinating the role of power, interest, and politics to some more assuring notion of "reason," "communication," or "practice."

Unfortunately one cannot argue, in advance, against all possible forms such claims might take. As Stephen Jay Gould once remarked of reactionary theories of biological determinism, each time you cut one down another springs up somewhere else. I realize, too, that general arguments against such conservative intellectual practice are not adequate or fully convincing, because they always allow a hostile reader to deny the point of the argument by making the easy reviewers' claim that something is left out, that the picture is biased or incomplete. In a moment of intellectual honesty, Auerbach once warned his critics that they should not assume he had not read materials simply because he did not have room to treat them in his work. His general arguments were based on this often unwritten understanding of the entire field he studied. I would make a similar claim here, and I make it as a way of disarming, in advance, the conservative humanistic response that "things are more complex" than I make them seem. I have tried to handle this antagonistic response by combining both general and specific analyses in this book.

I hope I have given some sense of the range of this genealogical configuration of critical and traditional humanism by studying the institutional and discursive project of Richards' "practical criticism." This essay does not pretend to the degree of historical completeness necessary to demonstrate the complex position of Richards' works. Nor is this a "balanced" essay; it makes no attempt to catalogue much that is admirable in

Richards: my goal is to focus attention on the darker side of Richards' critical project while allowing his other admirers to develop the resources his work has left them. Our sublime critical masters need less implicitly imitative explanation.

Indeed, I am more interested in understanding how such figures as Auerbach come to occupy their masterful position in our pantheon. Chapter 3 is an attempt to trace the material process by which a profession forms its heros. It is also an attempt at a partial material analysis of the sort that might show the specific operations of power within our institution and how they interact with larger discursive and nondiscursive positions. My aim all along is to help the profession confront the materiality of its practices and institutions, to recognize how it operates, and to call into question the secular humanistic rhetoric that makes a self-understanding of the profession materially difficult to achieve.

As I argue throughout, the present configuration of critical practice is politically and socially unsatisfactory; indeed, it is often irresponsible and reactionary: it supports the worst elements of an imperialistic and repressive society while justifying itself under the sign of "liberal humanism," of "litterae humaniores." Not until the profession begins to see through the discourse of humanism and to understand some of the material functions of the institutions it embodies as these relate to the hegemony can criticism begin to wrest the knowledge-producing apparatus away from the interests it now serves.

But my real concern throughout the book is with the critical intellectual. I take it that Edward Said has produced the most powerful model of oppositional critical practice within the American literary academy. In large part, Said's project results from his organic relationship to an oppressed and homeless people, which, in turn and reciprocally, explains his passionate response to Auerbach's work. Said, therefore, appears frequently in this book because his position reveals what a critical humanism is capable of when it sets out to fulfill its progressive secular potential. For that very reason, it is also essential to take Said's work as a test case, as a "limit," in other words, of what is possible within and as a result of humanism by an oppositional figure who has learned many of the lessons of Auerbach's efforts and has absorbed the most advanced oppositional work of his day. Those interested in the role and function of the critical intellectual today should ask this question when they read Said: how can such a redoubtable humanist function as an oppositional critic? And we should not look for the answer in some discussion of ideology or history of ideas. We should look instead to what is central to all of Said's work, the function of the will in critical intelligence, which appears not only in his writing but which he attempts to embody in his discursive and nondiscursive practice. As I see it, Said is important to the history of modern criticism in the United States precisely because in his work the question of the critic as intellectual, as positioned "subject-function," emerges as central to all the various critical practices that make up the modern institution.

I show that at least since Kant's *Anthropology* secular critical humanists have willfully represented themselves as essential to the progress of the "species" and have done so in images that present them as "leaders," as "representative" or "sublime masters." We see this figure emerge, for example, in Kant's image of "the ill-natured men" who redeem our race as lawgivers and scholars. We can follow this figure to the complex set of images that the professional academics deploy in their self-justifying apotheosis of Auerbach. Indeed, as I suggest in chapter I, this image of the leading intellectual is so powerfully inscribed within secular humanism, that even oppositional critical genealogists, like Nietzsche and Said, find themselves inscribed by it and enfiguring their critical, intellectual norms within it. This repetition is of concern because when its consequences are worked out even in part, they suggest limits to the politically progressive aims of oppositional humanistic practice that need to be modified.

I would argue more specifically that these limits involve perpetuating the institutional privilege of leading intellectuals with consequences that can be dangerous for all those struggling for greater self-determination in our society and in other cultures. I have been able only to suggest why and how this is so: a more detailed materialistic demonstration of these relations that might consider, as Said has in part done,[4] the complex interactions in any given instance of the role of intellectuals in dealing with other peoples or in representing groups here at home—minorities, women, gays.[5] As I work out this particular version of the genealogy of the modern intellectual's various positions, I take Said to be the fulfillment of one dimension of critical humanism that essentially represents the critic as will capable of negation.

At the same time, I take Marshall Hodgson, the late Chicago orientalist, as the most nearly complete example of the other crucial strain of critical humanism, that which abandons the critic's responsibility to negate for a more "positive" oppositional practice, comfortable with the idea of reforming the institutions of secular humanism and insistent upon their value for producing magisterial monuments of humanistic generosity that preserve the values of past and other cultures. Reading Said and Hodgson together reveals how they complement each other and how they are rooted in a common genealogy of humanistic discourses and practices.

I argue that this humanistic genealogy of traditional and oppositional intellectuals alike is what must be seen as the problem for critical practice. We may have many possible options for dealing with our political situation, but as long as we are positioned within the institutions of that humanism, I see two primary ways to proceed. First we must support politically progressive work within humanistic categories; it makes a difference, for example, if the critical institutions are reformed along the lines Said might like[6] or if it is turned further in the service of the ruling interests by following the course recently proposed by Walter Jackson Bate.[7]

I also argue that a greater difference could exist if the oppositional critic's inscription within humanism, as this appears in the reiterated figure of the leading intellectual, gave way to antihumanistic practice. We have no clear idea of what that would look like. We see gestures made toward moving away from humanism's dominance even in such redoubtable humanists as Auerbach. Foucault, of course, has made such a project his life's work, hence his central place in this book. Unfortunately his early death will slow the work that needs to be done.[8]

Foucault's challenge to the self-justifying histories of the-human sciences is not the only thing that is important. His critiques of whiggish histories of prisons and medicine are essentially attempts to delegitimate the institutionalization of secular or anthropological humanism and its dominant figure, the representative intellectual and his discourses. Foucault's idea of the local or guerrilla struggle of the "specific" intellectual is not simply a challenge and an attempt to replace the so-called "universal" intellectual. It is rather a way to authorize and legitimate the intellectual's antihegemonic practice without reinscribing it within the representative figure—no matter whether that takes on the attributes of the humanistically "universal" type—à la Croce—or the professionally leading type, as Auerbach was made to do in America. Foucault's work is important in this book, at least, because he helps us see what the figure of the "master" involves and how to try to avoid it. In "Powers and Strategies," for example, he discusses the function of the figure of the "master" in analyses of power. I have shown throughout how humanism, except in its most oppositional forms, refuses to pose the question of power except to deny it.

In chapter 3, I outline how the figure of Auerbach as "master" is created by the American critical academy and how this is possible only by virtue of the inscription of that figure within the defining and enabling discourses of humanism and its institutions. In other words, one might say that I have tried to work out the consequences of Foucault's comment that "The notion of 'love of the master' . . . is a certain way of not posing the problem of power, or rather of posing it in such a way that it cannot be analysed."[9] Indeed, I ask what might be the consequences in general for an oppositional intellectual practice that depends on some version of the sublime master figure as it derives from critical humanism. The point of studying Auerbach at length is precisely to show how humanism carries itself to its own exhaustion. My aim, in a sense, is to be convincing about humanism by following Auerbach's movement toward a nonhumanistic stance. Purely external attacks on humanistic institutions can be too easily dismissed; I hope that a detailed reading of Auerbach's (failed) struggles to revivify it will suggest how fruitless and inappropriate further attempts at its restitution might be. Auerbach's inventiveness seems to have exhausted historical humanism's resources in an attempt to restore them.

I must insist that this book should not be taken as "antihumanistic" in the sense of denying the value and achievement of the work of writers like Richards, Auerbach, Hodgson, and Said. On the contrary, it is necessary to preserve the critical impulses of their work over and against the reactionary cries of those who caricature the work of Foucault, for example, as merely fanciful, indulgent, or bourgeois. Of course, this genealogy would have looked different if other figures had been treated. Trilling, Arnold, Raymond Williams, and Louis Althusser come to mind as forming another possible configuration around similar issues. Or R. P. Blackmur, Henry Adams, and the critics of American literature suggest a third. The point is not that this genealogy is exclusive or exclusionary; it is rather an attempt to get a handle on the present by trying to suggest its history. Foucault's writings insist that the genealogical intellectual's work must be useful to others as they do whatever it is they do to reconfigure power, to struggle "against" power wherever they are. Intellectual work, the "truth" of scholarly production should thus be put in the service of political struggles for self-determination. I make no excuse then for the "incompleteness" of this book, especially in light of my discussion of the synoptic drives of a Richards or of Auerbach's hopes for syntheses. If only this book can be of some use to those who hope to modify the profession of critical scholarship and teaching, it will have served its purpose.

Acknowledgments

It is impossible to name all the individuals who have helped or in some way supported me in this project. The list would be embarrassingly long. Some special friends from Pittsburgh must be mentioned, though, because without them the book might not yet be finished: Mary Louise Briscoe, Steven Carr and Jean Ferguson Carr, Jane Feuer, Jim and Peggy Knapp, Marcia Landy, Alexander Nehamas, Dana Polan, and Mariolina Salvatori. In New York, Karl Kroeber has read much of the manuscript and has offered fine advice. During my time at Columbia, Edward Said stimulated my thinking about the matters I deal with here, and Barbara Jetton provided an important critical skepticism that made the book better than it would have been.

Various parts of this book have been presented as lectures at many universities, conferences, and symposia. I thank the organizers for their kind invitations and the audiences for their helpful questions and comments. I want particularly to thank Kathleen Woodward for providing me with an opportunity to clarify my sense of the differences between Michel Foucault and Edward Said. The American Council of Learned Societies allowed me to take a year off from teaching when it was essential to get this project under way, and the University of Pittsburgh has been generous in its research, secretarial, and summer support. I express my gratitude to William Germano, the editor-in-chief of Columbia University Press, for his patience during a difficult time and for his continually sound advice.

Parts of chapters 1 and 6 have been previously published in somewhat different form in *boundary* 2 and *SubStance*. I thank the editors for permission to republish these chapters.

I must give special acknowledgment to a close group of intellectual and personal friends who make up the editorial staff of *boundary 2:* Jonathan Arac, Joseph A. Buttigieg, Margaret Ferguson, Michael Hays, Daniel O'Hara (who was especially helpful in the difficult matter of naming this text), Donald Pease, William V. Spanos, and Cornel West. Together and individually they represent the best that the profession has to offer. They provide irreplaceable support and help keep me from the worst of errors.

For all that Carol Mastrangelo Bové has done to make this book possible, I offer it to her. It is small recompense for tolerance, generosity, and love.

I

Mendacious Innocents, or the Modern Genealogist as Conscientious Intellectual: Nietzsche, Foucault, Said

> We have never sought ourselves—how could it happen that we should ever *find* ourselves?
> —Nietzsche, *On the Genealogy of Morals*

> And I am not a demigod,
> I cannot make it cohere.
> If love be not in the house
> there is nothing.
> —Ezra Pound, Canto 116

This is a book about some of the political possibilities open to the humanistic and oppositional intellectual who practices his or her critical skills within the discourses and institutions that have constituted the traditions of high intellectual literary scholarship. In this Chapter I begin to study the interrelationships between individual critical projects and the discursive space in which they operate. I suggest something of how individual scholars such as Erich Auerbach, Marshall Hodgson, and Edward W. Said are empowered and defined by the tradition of humanistic and oppositional critical practice in which they work. I contend throughout this book that even the most revisionist, adversarial, and oppositional humanistic intellectuals—no matter what their avowed ideologies—operate within a network of discourses, institutions, and desires that, as we can see especially well in the most sublime and powerful of critical projects, always reproduce themselves in essentially antidemocratic forms and practices.

This is not meant to be a comprehensive text. Not only do I not examine all of the humanistic figures I believe belong within this tradition, but also I give practically no attention to the various alternatives that might be located within certain feminist and minority studies and writings. My aim is rather to uncover certain operations within the high intellectual humanistic critical discourse and the limits it imposes on the antihegemonic figures who try to work from within it.

I am at pains to insist repeatedly that two things must be kept in mind. I am not suggesting that all critical projects are always and everywhere the same; essential and politically crucial distinctions must be made between any number of critical discourses and practices. Indeed, as I argue at length in chapter 6, a critic should never lose sight of the politically positive possibilities of even the most bourgeois and humanistic projects; in that direction lies ahistorical misunderstanding and the fulfillment of Nietzsche's nihilistic nightmare. Yet critics must also try to move away from the oppositional humanistic tradition because it unavoidably leads to antidemocratic positions. To show that this is the case, I trace a genealogy of some adversarial humanists to show that the structures of modern critical discourse and its institutionalization often inhibit self-determination.

I pursue this investigation by focusing on the way in which the figure of the masterful or leading intellectual is repeatedly reinscribed within the major works of what Marshall Hodgson calls "greater scholarship." Throughout critical humanism, no matter the critic's ideological commitments, scholarly work unavoidably repeats and reproduces this antidemocratic structure precisely so that the critic can gain the authority needed to be heard, to have an effect in bringing about the most progressive results.

In this chapter, I focus on the representation of the intellectual within genealogical writing and research, in part to show that I am aware of my own participation in this essentially white male set of family relations. No one should assume that I am trying to position myself—or anyone else—outside the network of authority and representation I am describing. More importantly, though, I focus on genealogical research because, despite its awareness and its adversarial intentions, it repeats the structures I want to elucidate and in a strange way helps to make my point about the difficulty of evading them. Indeed, in the works of Nietzsche, Foucault, and Said, I believe we see how the value and limits of genealogical struggles within and against this set of institutional and discursive conditions form a countertradition paradoxically dependent for its own authority on the hegemonic humanistic discourse. Essentially, despite the attempts by Nietzsche and Foucault to undermine the major formations of humanistic practice, especially by questioning the status of the metaphysical subject and so the figure of the masterful intellectual, their alternative practices cannot entirely avoid reproducing the tradition they hope to deconstruct; comic parody in the play of style and the creation of anonymous research projects do not either exhaust or avoid the complexity of what Foucault calls "finitude" and what Kant calls "anthropological humanism."

I begin my discussion of these issues in this chapter with a brief look at Ezra Pound's Canto XIII. I hope that Pound's representation of these problems of authority and repetition, of competition and power, will give some theoretical sense of the structure I am laying out in much of this book.

II

Ezra Pound's Canto XIII is a montage of figures of history, writing, influence, and creativity—all of which are organized into a complex representation of power and authority.[1] This Canto opens by positioning the figure of the revisionist, Kung, within a topography symbolically burdened by the concrete and historical institutions that "represent" the past and extend its influence into the present. They represent the power of the dynastic to shape intellectual and cultural actions through and in the repetition of certain patterns of struggle for identity and authority—patterns reproduced even, or most especially, by those successors who hope to mark their difference from the dominant forms of the present, from the forms their precursors have helped to sustain:

> Kung walked
>> by the dynastic temple
>>> and into the cedar grove
>>> and then out by the lower river. (p. 58)

Kung's passing by the temple suggests not only that the relationship between the master and his tradition must be seen in positional terms within a site that defines the possible forms of that relationship but also that these terms apply to the revisionist, as well as to the hegemonic, intellectual. There is, in other words, a seemingly permanent bond between the master and the embodied past.

In fact, this image suggests much of what the rest of the Canto explores: modern intellectuals (perhaps all successors) repeat the dynastic patterns that they hope to transcend in revisionist acts meant to establish their own authority and priority. The pattern of repetition is not, however, important, only for the individuals involved; rather, the poem is concerned with something of much broader social and cultural significance: the structures of power reproduce themselves by making it seem that the only possible way to reform or overthrow them is by revising them in an act of repetition. Often this reproduction occurs as a result of mistaking the critic/scholar for an orginary figure—how could the critic/scholar be anything else, if he or she is, or is to become, a master? By becoming aware of the reproductive effect of repetitive variation, we can see the critic/scholar as a function of discourses that usually have as their effect—and as their necessary humanistic condition of existence—obscuring the functionality of their practitioners.

In Canto XIII, this entire complex of constitutive relationships appears in a dramatic figure of self-authorization:

> And "we are unknown," said Kung,
> "You will take up charioteering?
>> Then you will become known,

> "Or perhaps I should take up charioteering, or archery?
> "Or the practice of public speaking?" (p. 58)

Should the poet represent himself publicly and so pursue authority and become "representative?" Kung's successors hope to find their own authority by troping upon his mastery: for Tseu-lou, " 'I would put the defenses in order' "; for Khieu, to put the province "in better order than this"; for Tchi, in "a small mountain temple" to maintain " 'order in the observances, with a suitable performance of the ritual' "; and, finally, for Tian the lute-player, to sing Haiku-like painted images. These are all turns on Kung's figure of "being known": the military, that is, the defensive or anxious; the domestic, that is, political or economic; the religous, that is, the conservative and mythic; and the aesthetic, that is, the apprehensive and fragile.

> And Thseng-sie desired to know:
>   "Which had answered correctly?"
> And Kung said, "They have all answered correctly,
> That is to say, each in his nature." (p. 58)

Each ephebe's trope competes against the predecessors' authority: the continuing presence of the predecessor keeps the ephebe unknown. Furthermore, each successor's trope competes for survival and pride of place with the others. Yet, not so ironically, they ask the father, Kung, for approval. On the one hand, they are asking for the father's blessing, the right, like Jacob to inherit the estate—the father is the guardian of the position they hope to occupy and cannot inherit unless they fulfill their training; and so, on the other hand, and more importantly, they are asking for confirmation that they have conducted themselves properly. They can succeed only if, in fact, they have understood the "rules of the game" and have carried out decorously the function reserved for them as the elected heirs of the masterful figure.

At times, Pound's poem seems to propose an alternative to this seemingly ubiquitous structure of power and repetition that carries out cultural reproduction. But the alternative is itself a repetition of the structure it seems to displace. In fact, it is perhaps the most seductive variation on that pattern and perhaps even its most dangerous.

Kung's response to Thseng-sie's question introduces a new

theme to the poem. This is a theme of quietism, of tolerance, of removal from the world of power and competition, of superior humanistic understanding that transcends the limited struggles of the ephebes. Kung's response suggests that tolerance and openness, that standing aside from the arrogant imposition of order upon the historically real might be the way to break with the repetitive order of empowered and empowering institutions that form his ephebes' actions and language.

Kung refuses to judge among the ephebes: "And Kung smiles upon all of them equally" (p. 58). This gesture could be read as signifying Kung's acceptance of the relative value of each trope, which would, in effect, be to authorize the competition. But as an alternative, Kung's smile might be more tellingly read as an attempt to authorize a noncompetitve ethos. When read this way, Kung's gesture marks his refusal to reenter the domain of competition, which for his followers is the only real site where their practice can be meaningful. Kung refuses to choose among the transumptive responses to his original question about being "known" and thereby seems to step out of the entire competitive network of cultural, institutional, and discursive competition for mastery. Kung's gesture highlights how his ephebes cultivate merely the newest version of an earlier dynastic metaphor—which they represent as infertile and bankrupt—to trope against it and so establish their own legitimacy: they will rule the country *better* and make sure the rituals are carried out.

Kung's attempt to produce a noncompetitive alternative to his own historic relationship to the dynastic is emblematic of the effort made by revisionists who are aware of the problematic nature of the power structures in which they are inscribed. Kung's noncompetitive alternative takes the form of "character." "Character" is a figure of strength and openness; it is the Keatsian ability to tolerate the potentially warring tropes of the revisionist ephebes without choosing any one among them as representative, as a master trope:

> If a man have not order within him
> He cannot spread order about him;
> And if a man have not order within him

> His family will not act with due order;
> > And if the prince have not order within him
> He can not put order in his dominions.
>
> . . .
>
> > "Anyone can run to excess,
> > It is easy to shoot past the mark,
> > It is hard to stand firm in the middle." (p. 59)

Kung's desire is for a form of noncompetitive authority that avoids the excesses resulting from the dominance of any one trope. Such dominance, Kung sees, means a struggle for closure that is another way of saying that becoming a masterful representative involves a dedifferentiation of history and social order. Noncompetitive authority would mean resisting the seduction of a hypertrophied trope, of what Edward Said would call "dogma."[2] In a statement that uncannily foreshadows the position Auerbach comes to late in his career, Kung insists that the achievement of mastery is possible only at the cost of closure and dedifferentiation. He hopes to transform the dynastic figure of power into a trope of discontinuous historical narration that implicitly recognizes the limits of power/knowledge to represent the real:

> "And even I can remember
> A day when the historians left blanks in their writings,
> I mean for things they didn't know,
> But that time seems to be passing. (p. 60)

This refusal of continuous narrative is not just a defense of Pound's own technique of spatial superimposition. The discontinuity of metonymy represents the turn away from the presumed force of closure unavoidably involved in achieving authority. Kung would have it not that the form of power is reorganized but that power itself is displaced by tolerance and generosity—the values of "character." The endless displacement of one variation by another would, presumably, be itself displaced once and for all by the movement to another structure, another possibility; yet the inescapable question remains by what authority this change will occur. How to achieve the final displacement? For Kung, not surprisingly, the answer seems to lie in the aesthetic possibility of expressing desire, in another variation of the Paterian sublime:[3]

> And Kung said, "Without character you will be unable to
>   play on that instrument
> Or to execute the music fit for the Odes.
> The blossoms of the apricot
>   blow from the east to the west,
> And I have tried to keep them from falling." (p. 60)

That Pound could find in the figure of Mussolini the incarnation of this aesthetic desire suggests its contradictory position: to impose the representative figure who will establish the final displacement. The real historical version of this quasi-religous, utopian aesthetic vision uncovers its dependence on power and coercion to end the dizzying and repetitive struggles of dynastic inheritance. This would seem not the path to follow in walking by the temple. The competition cannot be so easily avoided—all our best critics tell us this—but Pound and others also reveal, in no matter how distorted a fashion, the real human desire to get beyond it. Kung's concern that struggle brings closure and dedifferentiation is valid, but difference and the ability to tell the stories of the different must ironically be won in competition with those who would preclude them. The new burden is to struggle for openness with the weapons that seem to have only the power to establish closure.

The point not to be forgotten, I think, is that closure and dedifferentiation seem to be absolutely dependent on the inscribed figure of the sublime representative intellectual, of the most masterful opponents. Above all, Kung's mystification of power—the suggestion that it can simply be turned from in a trope of generosity and openness—that most sublme of seductions, must be avoided. Above all, we must suspect so-called "pluralism" of sharing in the same mystifications that befell Kung. In fact, and not surprisingly, we can end by seeing that Kung's pluralistic claims authorize his own position: a figure of "character" whose delegitimation of all conflict precludes the ongoing intellectual and political struggle of marginal groups and individuals for their own identity and their own difference from and within the dynastic. The figure of character carried the master to his sublime fulfillment: the embodiment of newly retrieved and privileged knowledge ("'I can remember'"), lifted above the dirty competition of political struggle among the ephebes and their world. Kung's terms may embody an appropriate desire; his appropriation of them for his own authority, however, simply reproduces the very structure he claims to try to end.

III

In *On the Genealogy of Morals*,[4] Nietzsche reproduces a composite figure of the genealogical intellectual that, even more nearly fully than Pound's poem, highlights the major features of the structure I am discussing. Although far from the beginning of this tradition, Nietzsche is an appropriate starting point in trying to understand it. His work and authority have created some of the chief weapons of Modern and Postmodern oppositional writing and, as Daniel O'Hara has suggested,[5] the shape of his career prefigures those of many writers coming after him.

Nietzsche's speculations on the nature of genealogy are inseparable in this work from his analyses of asceticism and nihilism. Even though it is not genealogy as a "method" that interests me, it is impossible not to consider the idea briefly as a way of approaching the figure of the genealogist.

The *Genealogy* ends with a reprise of a motif made central earlier in Nietzsche's performance:

> We can no longer conceal from ourselves *what* is expressed by all that willing which has taken its direction from the ascetic ideal: this hatred of the human, and even more of the animal, and more still of the practical, this horror of the senses, of reason itself, this fear of happiness and beauty, this longing to get away from all appearance, change, becoming, death, wishing, from longing itself—all this means—let us dare to grasp it—*a will to nothingness*, an aversion (*Widerwillen*) to life, a rebellion against the most fundamental presuppositions of life; but it is and remains a *will*! . . . And, to repeat in conclusion what I said at the beginning: man would rather will *nothingness* than *not* will. (*GM*, 162–63)

In the struggle against all forms of ascetic nihilism, genealogy is a powerful weapon. As historical research it highlights and disentangles a skein of documentary and cultural traces of how the present was formed. It leads to a kind of "self-understanding" that, if you will, comically deflates the great humanistic visions of a Humboldt or Kant. I argue in chapter 6 that for anthropolgical humanists the human sciences are essential to cultural development because they interpret the record of past and present human action and discover there the "message" that will guide humanity toward its species fulfillment in some distant future. Nietzsche's *Genealogy*, however, tells a different story of the intellectuals' involvement with history. Like the humanist, the genealogist also writes of the past—but with a concern for the present, not the willful shaping of the future—and sees in it a record of struggles that have left their marks in documents and institutions. As we shall see, Kant had much the same sense of history but found ways to insist that reason, benevolence, and providential order inhere in all actions and struggles.

Throughout Nietzsche's writings, the critical intellectual appears in the figure of a genealogist.[6] This figure is represented dramatically as always concerned with the material configurations of power, with the possibility and legitimacy of certain tropes and interpretations, and with the concrete human effects of such power structures. In addition, within the figure, this concern always rests upon and emerges from the genealogist's superior understanding of the implications of these structures of power for human life and culture.

Nietzsche outlines this figure at the end of the *Genealogy* in terms borrowed from Byron. The Nietzschean genealogist always has a heroic nature—even though usually tinged with a mock-heroic irony: alone and for the first time he dares or risks a confrontation with the powers of the dynastic order to demystify them according to his own lights: "let us dare to grasp it," he writes. The point is, of course, that the "powerful daring" of the genealogist's demystification should render the previously authoritative interpretation inoperative or impotent: "We can no longer conceal from ourselves."

Nietzsche's figure is not unlike Pound's Kung: both assume

authority to displace the structure, which itself has made possible only an endless and undesirable succession of displace-
ments. And in both cases the problem is the same. The
genealogist's act gains its legitimacy from a claim to special
knowledge and concern. In making that claim, though, the
genealogist repeats the pattern of repetitive displacement
within humanism, the authority of which itself rests on the
superior knowledge and interpretative power of its leading or
representative intellectuals. This representation of the genealogist is, then, thoroughly inscribed within the tradition it
hopes to refute; it cannot be otherwise. Nietzsche's great
strength is in both letting us see that and in allowing us to
know we must do the best with what we have. Yet we must be
aware of how this genealogical variation can, in itself, have
politically undesirable consequences. Its reassertion of the intellectual's leading role in cultural formation and the control
of knowledge is precisely one of the problematic consequences
limiting the genealogist's ability to help in the development of
participatory democracy.

Although I am not concerned to argue the philosophical or
ideological correctness of Nietzsche's comments on asceticism
and nihilism, I do want to draw attention to one tactic basic to
his argument and assumption of authority. In Nietzsche's story
the ascetic ideal is completely dominant and dynastic. "Philosophers," like himself, those who have not succumbed to nihilism, are truly rare and, submerged in their libraries, are also
truly marginal. Are genealogical scholars, though, not themselves in danger of succumbing to an image of the intellectual
that Nietzsche makes seem tempting and romantic: the isolated, struggling, heroic, oppositional figure rising above and
against the treacheries of the past and present? Is it not one of
Nietzsche's ironies that critical humanists find his analysis
convincing because the role of the marginal intellectual is itself increasingly attractive and empowering to those who either deny the scholar's social function or hope to avoid its
responsibilities—perhaps by exploiting their own privileged
"difference"? I ask these questions not to deny the effect this
image has had and continues to have in reactivating critical

intelligence; the point is rather does not this intelligence itself belong to an easily defined "countertradition" whose major tropes, in anticipation, encode both the activities and authorizing self-representations of all critical humanists?

One of the primary tropes of this tradition is struggle or "agon." Nietzschean genealogy is always revisionist and so competitive or "agonistic." In his work, the "agon" appears as itself something won by struggle with and against a metaphysics that obcures the realities of power and will:

The two *opposing* values "good and evil" have long been engaged in a fearful struggle on earth for thousands of years; and though the latter value has certainly been on top for a long time, there are still places where the struggle is yet undecided. One might even say that it has risen even higher and thus become more and more profound and spiritual: so that today there is perhaps no "*higher nature*," a more spiritual nature, than that of being divided in this sense and a genuine battleground of these opposed values. (*GM*, 52)

The genealogist is not only aware of the ubiquity of struggle and fights to bring it into the open, but also the genealogist is the site of such struggle: he is the place in which the dynastic order meets its limit and where struggle can indeed be continued. The genealogist is always, in other words, part of the dominant order and is affected by it, but he is also always unique in his difference from and superiority to those others who have given their assent to the dominant order. One might say that this internal division allows the genealogist to write the history of the present as a battle for the present and not the future or the order of the past. Foucault perhaps develops this dimension of Nietzsche's thought more thoroughly than anyone else.

The hallmark of genealogical work is that it struggles to establish itself as a powerful alternative to the dominant forms of knowledge production and to the social role knowledge occupies in relation to power and the possibility of continuing human life. In Nietzsche's text, this particular struggle is central. In fact, Nietzsche defines "science" as the modern avatar of asceticism precisely in order to open a space in which genealogy and the genealogical figure can battle for authority. Nietzsche understands that genealogical practice can gain power only as it is materially embodied in discourse and only as it then replicates itself in more genealogical research and struggle. His goals are, from the start, as it were, to change the intellectual's affiliation with humanistic science and to reorganize critical production for nonnihilistic, that is, nonhumanistic ends.

Nietzsche's particular problem, once he adopted this strategy, was to differentiate genealogy from science, especially the humanistic sciences. Nietzsche's solution, though, poses its own problem, namely, the threat of paralyzing critical intelligence in an abyss of duplicitous reflection.

The differentiating movement necessary to separate science from genealogy first appears as a radical skepticism: "Presuming that everything man 'knows' does not merely fail to satisfy his desires but rather contradicts them and produces a sense of horror, what a divine way out to have the right to seek the responsibility for this not in 'desire' but in 'knowledge'!" (*GM*, 156). Kung's position reflects the struggle between what one desires and the dynastic traditions that try to end those desires. Kung's "solution" would preserve the desire but in a way that restores the dynastic. Nietzsche, too, would preserve the prior reality of the desire and looks to the other term in the problem for a solution: knowledge. The ascetic ideal that has become the tradition of humanistic knowledge authorizes always and everywhere the production of more knowledge as a way to understand the past and present as, in Kant's terms, a guide to the future and the species' fulfillment. How then can genealogy, so manifestly the production of more "knowledge," not share from the beginning in the dynasty it hopes to end?

Nietzsche's solution to this problem is the play of style, whose effect and value he explains and defends in his claims for comedy's subversive powers.[7] He hopes to put the abysmal possibilities of the duplicity of science and genealogy to work for him: "the ascetic ideal has at present only *one* kind of real enemy capable of *harming* it: the comedians of this ideal—for they arouse mistrust of it" (*GM*, 160). In other words, while producing "new knowledge," genealogy assigns it another value and challenges the value of knowledge in the humanistic tradition. As Foucault puts it, "Genealogy is history in the form of a concerted carnival."[8] In other words, genealogy does not just produce "new knowledge"; rather it repositions the role of knowledge production in our culture, and it does this by casting doubt on the value and desirability of "knowledge" as it functions under the sign of "will to truth" within the humanistic project, that is, as it is presumed to "assure" liberty, progress, and human fulfillment.

In a comedy of duplications, then, in which Nietzsche does the best with what he has, genealogy should not be paralyzed but empowered:

all great things bring about their own destruction through an act of self-overcoming. . . . And here again I touch on my problem, on our problem, my *unknown* friends (for as yet I *know* of no friend): what meaning would *our* whole being possess if it were not this, that in us the will to truth becomes conscious of itself as a problem? (*GM*, 161)

There are then some not so apparently compatible features to the Nietzschean genealogist: formidably learned scholar, committed to the revision of the role of knowledge in the present, heroic in his isolation—yet also always an ironist practicing the strategy of comically subverting the ideal.[9] Various versions of this figure appear in the works of all Nietzsche's genealogical successors and other sorts of oppositional critics who owe much of their authority to Nietzsche's practice of radical critique.

Nietzsche's most important gift to his heirs is his allegory of the origins of a genealogist's "difference." This story must also be read as an ironic account of all versions of "originality" in the complex history of western philosophy and religion. But despite the irony, this passage in which Nietzsche reflects on the mystery of his own "difference" at the "origin" of his identity reinforces an unavoidable claim at the heart of all oppositional, and certainly all genealogical, work: a claim to insight which no self-irony can finally dismiss because such claims are at the heart of all intellectual practice, even that of the (ironical) negation of knowledge and the will to truth. Nietzsche's version of this trope appears in the "Preface" of 1887:

Because of a scruple peculiar to me that I am loathe to admit to—for it is concerned with *morality*, with all that has hitherto been celebrated on earth as morality—a scruple so entered my life so early, so uninvited, so irresistibly, so much in conflict with my environment, age, precedents, and descent that I might almost have the right to call it my *"a priori"*—my curiosity as well as my suspicions were bound to halt quite soon at the question of where our good and evil really originated. (*GM*, 16)

This passage can be read as a parody of a scene of instruction like those we have seen in Kung's exchange with his ephebes. Nietzsche's "scruple" is a perfect figure of the dominant trope which Kung's response tells us must be avoided. Since it is the condition for knowledge produced by the scholar-critic, it is, indeed, the mark and origin of his "identity."

But Nietzsche's version of this master trope of all critical revision is not simply a parodic repetition. His irony also makes this "identity," like the trope upon which it depends, a function of the material operations of a tradition within textual production. In other words, this "scruple," like all the other tropes it represents, exists nowhere but within the complex network of research, individuation, self-representation, and interest which are made up by the dynastic forms of humanistic discourse and the institutions in which they are embodied. But within this complex the intellectual appears as a self-generated origin, unaccountable in scientific or causal terms. Above all, though, these apparently self-enclosing "origins" obscure the intellectual's position as a function of transsubjective realities.

The genealogist, unlike other intellectuals, however, is doubly "privileged"—and so perhaps doubly deluded. Given his difference within the hegemonic order, he appears as even more "original" and more "self-identical" than the dynastic intellectual: for the genealogist, all ideas intersect with each other and, above all, grow out of the integrated life of a philosopher, of the man who lives the scruple of his project—who, we might say, metaphorically *becomes* his own origin. The following parodic expression of Schopenhauerian euphoria represents this doubling:

That I still cling to them today, however, that they have become in the meantime more and more firmly attached to one another, indeed entwined and interlaced with one another, strengthens my joyful assurance that they might have arisen in me from the first not as isolated, capricious, or sporadic things but from a common root, from a *fundamental will* of knowledge, pointing imperiously into the depths, speaking more and more precisely, demanding greater and greater precison. For this alone is fitting for a philosopher. We have no right to *isolated* acts of any kind: we may not make isolated errors or hit upon isolated truths. Rather do our ideas, our values, our yeas and nays, our ifs and buts, grow out of us with the necessity with which a tree bears fruit— related and each with an affinity to each, and evidence of *one* will, *one* health, *one* soil, *one* sun.—Whether *you* like them, these fruits of ours?—But what is that to the trees! What is that to *us*, to us philosophers! (*GM*, 16)

Nietzsche's play of styles creates multiple self-representations or "masks" that, opposed to philosophically traditional forms of knowledge production, are complex and should be read with the same attention to context and irony as any high modernist literary text. It is dangerous to decontextualize or overvalue any one passage in his work; one runs the constant risk of incompletion and distortion. If I seem to do so here, it is only because I take this ironic, self-engendering representation of identity to be somewhat paradoxically fundamental to the elaborate Nietzschean play of styles.

Unity of purpose underlies the differences Nietzsche creates, represents, and deploys in his struggles against ascetic nihilism. Genealogists always need to believe that such unified purposes are possible, though in the best of cases they greet the notion with skepticism.[10] Even if discovered only in retrospect, as Nietzsche discovers his "after the fact," as it were, in his late authorial reconstruction of 1887, such willed purpose has become essential to oppositional intellectual practice, which often has no other source for its authority but the critic's own self-confirming project. The genealogist need not, as it were, actually hold that his or her identity exists in a world "beyond" the project; Nietzsche's image of willed purpose makes no claim for either the extratextual existence of that unity or, romantically, for writing as the liberal process of producing a "self." His retrospective discovery of "oneness," of the submerged unity of his project, undermines the authority of the metaphor of organic wholeness precisely by using it as a "post-hoc" representation of the belatedness of self-knowledge.

Willed purpose is, then, a trope for the production of texts and for the essential agonistic component of all genealogical research. Disconnected from the dynastic forms of humanistic disciplines—as Nietzsche separated himself from philology—this figure authorizes and sustains the genealogist's project: not romantic self-making but ironic self-authorization marked everywhere by signs of its own "non-originality." And what else should we expect from the genealogist, who Nietzsche tells us is obsessed by the power, obscurity, and ubiquity of documents. At best, the Nietzschean genealogist is the hero of the bibliographical archive. So, according to Nietzsche, a genealogist of morals must not gaze into the blue sky for essentialist answers to the problem of origins. He should resign himself to another color: "namely *gray*, that is, what is documented, what can actually be confirmed and has actually existed, in short, the entire long hieroglyphic record, so hard to decipher, of the moral past of mankind!" (*GM*, 21).

Nietzsche's text develops this gray figure's inevitable fate: heroic repetition. The genealogist painfully and endlessly unearths and reinterprets texts and relationships between texts and other institutions long unavailable to "official" history. Such research struggles not only to say what the hegemonic order does not want said but also strives to change the way of saying to one which that order cannot tolerate. (Of course, given the adaptability of our culture, which Nietzsche could not quite have foreseen, there may be no such way of saying which cannot be tolerated.) Not just the hidden patterns newly discovered, but antidynastic, antihumanistic ways of saying become the genealogist's project and willed purpose.

Despite the apparent similarity between the genealogist's task of "unearthing" what has been left untraced in the archive and the hermeneut's task of recuperative reinterpretation, the real differences between them should not be blurred. The genealogist does not "rediscover" in the sense of "un-covering" more "authentic" meanings obscured by the sedimented history of official interpretation. On the contrary, rather than engage in this idealistic practice, the genealogist tracks down the materially lost and displaced texts that have at best left a trace of their existence in the official archive. Often this archive is a set of canonical texts and interpretations whose material institutionalization as some version of the "great tradition" has actually supressed almost all record of the existence of these other documents and the network of cultural and social order that they helped to constitute.[11] The consequence of such canonization is that we look at our history as being orderly tradition, as made for us—as we shall see Kant explicitly argue—by great men whose works alone are of value. It obscures the effects of transubjective discursive and institutional realities and closes off access to the anonymous operations of "ordinary" contributors to culture and to the limits they impose upon the so-called "men of genius." It hinders the development of other sorts of research and critical tools that might help us understand the actions and contributions—benevolent and otherwise—of those actions and events not central to the humanistic dynasty.

Heroic repetition is the milieu and form of this willed purpose. Intellectual sublimity is purchased at a very high but self-satisfying cost: "distress, want, bad weather, sickness, toil, solitude." But since that which does all but kill us always strengthens us, in the Nietzschean scheme of things, this cost assures the marginal agonist of sublimity and reward:

Fundamentally, one can cope with everything . . . born as one is to a subterranean life of struggle; one emerges again and again into the light, one experiences again and again one's golden hour of victory— and then one stands forth as one was born, unbreakable, tensed, ready for new, even harder, remoter things, like a bow that distress only serves to draw tighter. (GM, 44)

Except in such self-representations, the sublime genealogist achieves no final apotheosis in Nietzsche's revision.[12]

Drawing strength from this image's promise of a victorious aesthetic integrity, the genealogist, nonetheless, can only (but must always) reemerge, renewed, to pursue an always delayed final achievement. How, then, does the genealogist find strength to go on, to emerge "again and again into the light"? Even though genealogists have only one "golden hour of victory" that echoes and repeats itself in every passing moment, each resurfacing spirals toward sublimity; each repetition of the victory tightens and increases the sinew-like strength of this genealogist who takes aim at the present order of things. It is always the genealogist's fate to oppose the sciences of man that have sickened him with "man" and have brought about "man's" near destruction. Although modern antihumanistic ideology often appears as aestheticism, it paradoxically rests upon a hope that some human works, not yet destroyed in advance by "Judea," might justify the genealogist's project. The genealogist never sounds more like a humanist than when voicing this most antihumanistic desire:

> But grant me from time to time—if there are divine goddesses in the realm beyond good and evil—grant me the sight, but *one* glance of something perfect, wholly achieved, happy, mighty, triumphant, something still capable of arousing fear! Of a man who justifies *man*, of a complementary and redeeming lucky hit on the part of man for the sake of which one may still *believe in man!* (*GM*, 44)

Perhaps the obvious needs to be said. The genealogist is that "man" and is thus a self-confirming figure: the marginalized hero preserving struggle, the appreciation of beauty and justice (in a way I will show implicates even Chomsky and Said), and establishing the limits of the dynastic. In this passage, Nietzsche revises what we shall see is Kant's insistence on the assurance of the species' perfection; in Nietzsche, any one instance of beauty in a humanistic world is only a lucky hit, an act of chance, an instance of a marginal survival of life itself. To genealogists who have such glimpses belongs the authority to carry out the "transvaluation of all values." In Nietzsche's work, a composite figure of the sublime "artist-philosopher-saint" not only has these glimpses but also is itself one rare occurrence of that accidental perfection—brought once more into the world by Nietzsche's works. Here we again see Nietzsche repeating his "scrupulous" insistence on the mysterious unaccountability of the marginal oppositional figure.

The genealogist is, as it were, a powerful synechdoche of this composite trope—powerful because it represents the sublime victory of the so-called "marginal" intellectual over the nihilism he identifies with his own marginality. The irony is that Nietzsche's figure makes this rhetoric of marginality so readily available, it inaugurates so powerfully a tradition of opposition, that the genealogist becomes, as a result, a domestic figure of sorts in modernity. Akin in training and values to the leaders of the authorized disciplines of the hegemonic culture, the genealogist is a transformation of his enemy: he problematizes knowledge in a carnival of "truths." The genealogist is not outlandish but subversive and different. Most importantly—as the myth of self-creation goes—his strength depends on his vision of himself, which he must successfully disseminate—as a predecessor of the perfect man.

In fact, the Nietzschean version of this figure has had a maieutic effect on later radical intellectuals such as Said and Foucault. Nietzsche has sketched a face with familiar and useful features: the "disinterest" of the scientist, of the defender of the modernist ideal of nihilistic asceticism, but a face crinkled with a wise and deadly smile that marks it as that of a "co-median of this ideal." Seriousness, anger, personal interest—all of these Nietzsche sublimates to produce this ideal. Without the comedy, "genealogy" would be science or pointless excess.

IV

Nietzsche's critique of "science" is a critique of anthropological humanism. His aim is to empower genealogy by disclosing, genealogically, the comic falsifications and dangerous foolishness at the engendering source of humanistic disciplinary knowledge—as this is repeatedly reasserted to maintain that knowledge's position in the hegemonic class and gender-based order. In the *Genealogy*, this complex struggle involves degrading the authority of "the origins," "the subject," and "the tradition." Above all, though, as an attempt to authorize genealogy—which is willed purpose—Nietzsche must subvert the authoritative humanistic claims for the benevolence of reason—Kant's "pragmatic gift"—and the separation of truth and the will.

Nietzsche's tactics involve showing the operations of violence and power in the formation, maintenance, and functioning of the humanistic commitment to its versions of "truth" and "reason." The subject he considers as a way of establishing his critique is the humanistic confusion between "origin" and "purpose" in punishment:

The worse man's memory has been, the more fearful has been the appearance of his customs; the severity of the penal code provides an especially significant measure of the degree of effort needed to overcome forgetfulness and to impose a few primitive demands of social existence as *present realities* upon these slaves of momentary affect and desire. (*GM*, 61)

Violence exercised by powerful individuals and institutions gaining their authority—this structure produces a social order that defines its own high ideals by obscuring the memory of its cultural and intellectual practices' associations with power:

With the aid of such images and procedures one finally remembers five or six "I will not's," in regard to which one had given one's *promise* so as to participate in the advantage of society—and it was indeed with the aid of this kind of memory that one at least came "to reason!" Ah, reason, seriousness, mastery over the affects, the whole somber thing called reflection, all these prerogatives and showpieces of man: how dearly they have been bought! How much blood and cruelty lie at the bottom of all "good things!" (*GM*, 62)

Humanism always obscures the "origins" and persistence of reason in violence by idealizing the origin and by claiming—as we shall see in Kant—the sublime redirection of all violence and power as its own contribution to the species' "self-overcoming" fulfillment. Ironically, of course, as Nietzsche argues, humanism can end violence—but only by ending the race:

A legal order thought of as sovereign and universal, not as a means in the struggle between power-complexes but as a means of *preventing* all struggle in general . . . would be a principle *hostile to life*, an agent of the dissolution and destruction of man, an attempt to assassinate the future, a sign of weariness, a secret path to nothingness. (*GM*, 76)

Naming and arresting this process requires the genealogist, who alone can do the necessary violence to reason's claims. Breaking the circle of identity formed by confusing "origin" and "purpose," Nietzsche shows, restores the violence of the origin, of the differences between "interpretations," or different "knowledge-functions," and so releases "truth" into the site of will, power, and struggle. Nietzsche's powerful cata-

chresis—peace assassinates life—is the *locus classicus* of genealogical comedy. The "creation" of "objects" by interpretations,
the subduing of people by "representatives," the complicity of
causality and reason with nihilism, the role of chance in the
transformational events of history, the conflicts of interpretations, the denial of "proper meaning" to the event as a sign—
all these and more, in a Nietzschean sense, make possible the
work of genealogists like Foucault and Said.

V

An important question nags at Nietzsche's claim that the
Genealogy authorizes a figure of intellectual work essential to
the tradition of adversarial or oppositional criticism: Is
Nietzsche not the most powerful demystifier of the idea of the
subject? How then can his work authorize such a subject-based
practice? In brief, of course, the answer is that the will constitutes the critic function without restoring the priority of the
subject as origin. In fact, though, the question cannot be and
has not been so easily settled. As we shall see, Foucault and
Said have developed Nietzsche's figure in two different ways,
each of which has its own strengths and weaknesses. I will only
sketch some of their differences in this chapter and extend my
analysis in the final chapters.

This entire problem of authorization can perhaps best be discussed as it might appear in a summary of my comments so far:
genealogy is itself an institutional discursive representation of
the leading intellectual, which always implies the question of
the individual's (the "subject's") relation to those larger systems of representation of which genealogy is a part. Nietzsche
problematizes the question in rejecting the subject as part of
his turn against metaphysics:

A quantum of force is equivalent to a quantum of desire, will, effect—
more, it is nothing other than precisely this very driving, willing, effecting, and only owing to the seduction of language (and of the fundamental errors of reason that are petrified in it) which conceives and
misconceives all effects as conditioned by something that causes effects, by a "subject," can it appear otherwise . . . as if there were a
neutral substratum behind the strong man, which was *free* to express

strength or not to do so. But there is no such substratum; there is no "being" behind doing, effecting, becoming; "the doer" is merely a fiction added to the deed—the deed is everything. (*GM*, 45)

About this passage and its relation to the history of philosophy, books have been written.[13] Let it suffice to say that this passage at least revises Hume and Kant.

In this passage, Nietzsche poses a unique problem for the tradition of genealogical research: we notice that he does not *eliminate* the subject from the range of concerns of genealogical research or from genealogical rhetoric. He tries instead to reposition the term as a social reality constituted by will and authority, no longer as a given origin or ground. "The deed is everything" means that power creates reason, judgment, intention, causality—not that the "subject" does not "exist." The question then becomes: how does the "subject" come to exist in its various forms. Foucault's studies of clinics, prisons, and sex offer one scenario for understanding the "subject's" constitution. In genealogical work after Nietzsche, then, the "subject" is always a sign for a configuration of forces, discourses, interests, and institutions that can be genealogically analyzed.

Two separate constituents appear in Nietzsche's project for genealogical criticism: will and anonymous discourse. Said's work emphasizes the possibility of developing critical negation and critical consciousness by radically extending Nietzsche's emphasis on the will. Foucault pursues a dream of subjectless research projects. He hopes to turn away from all ideologies based on the priority of the subject's authority. Since all such ideologies always assign leading roles to the intellectual, Foucault's aim is to produce procedures that help others, wherever they may be struggling, to get a grip on the power-knowledge complexes of transsubjective, discursive, institutional, and hegemonic social configurations. In other words, Foucault's project has at least two goals: to avoid assigning the intellectual a leading role and so to challenge humanism's hegemony and to produce theories and research methods, as well as new forms of knowledge, which might be useful to others engaged in their own confrontations with the dynastic forms of power throughout our culture.

Foucault articulates this project in *The Order of Things:*

Can one speak of science and its history (and therefore of its conditions of existence, its changes, the errors it has perpetrated, the sudden advances that have sent it off on a new course) without reference to the scientist himself—and I am not speaking merely of the concrete individual represented by a proper name, but of his work and the particular form of his thought? Can a valid history of sciences be attempted that would retrace from beginning to end the whole spontaneous movement of an anonymous body of knowledge? . . . I do not wish to deny the validity of intellectual biographies, or the possibility of a history of theories, concepts, or themes. It is simply that I wonder whether such descriptions are themselves enough, whether they do justice to the immense density of scientific discourse, whether there do not exist, outside their customary boundaries, systems of regularities that have a decisive role in the history of the sciences. I should like to know whether the subjects responsible for scientific discourse are not determined in their situation, their function, their perceptive capacity, and their practical possibilities of creation by conditions that dominate and even overwhelm them.[14]

An essential part of this project[15]—which will grow to become its dominant part later in Foucault's work—is the critique of the figure of the traditional representative or leading intellectual as this appears in the guise of either the disciplinary specialist or of the man educated in *culture generale*.

In Foucault's analyses of modern history, the leading intellectual has always had a double existence. The various forces of discipline and punishment that shape subjectivities throughout that society also form the intellectual; in addition, though, the leading intellectual is specially determined by the disciplinary operations of the particular discourses and institutions in which he or she has been trained and practices. This particular secondary determination is what gives the leading intellectual a unique role in the extension and development of a disciplinary society. The leading intellectual is essential to the reproduction of the disciplinary apparatus and to the dynastic formations' application of power upon the subjugated.[16]

Consequent upon his critique, Foucault thinks it necessary to radicalize Nietzsche's sense of how interpretation or will to power sustains humanism and leads to nihilism.[17] In one of his most extreme moves, Foucault turns away from interpretation altogether. It simply is absent from his major texts. Foucault accepts the identification of interpretation and will to power and concludes that no matter how oppositional or demystifying hermeneutic practice might be in intent, it always proceeds by trying to regain access to what has been repressed or mistaken; in other words, like humanism itself, even violently suspicious interpretation aspires to recover what is fundamentally always already known—even if it has also always been forgotten. No matter how "successful" such recuperations might be, Foucault will not credit their adversarial claims: involved in a repetitive return they belong to the pattern of metaphysical humanism that takes "man" and his works as the object and subject of power-knowledge and so strengthens its operative dynasty. One might reverse the usual stress contemporary criticism gives to Nietzsche's insight and insist, with Foucault, that all will to power must be interpretation.

Adversarial interpretation and Nietzschean genealogy both emerge from or depend on the given authority of the critical subject. Nietzsche's genealogist gains power as a sublime figure, a privileged consciousness and stylist whose "demystified subjectivity" is nonetheless merely an (inadequate) catechretical "difference" from that of the dynastic. Foucault's significant contribution to oppositional genealogy is his turn from that apocalyptic redemptive stress Nietzsche places—even in parody—on the figure of the genealogist as the midwife of the perfect man, as the surety of the future. What follows from this turn—and this is of great importance to criticism—is the inevitable deauthorization of interpretation as the primary form of critical work and the problematizing of the subjectivity of the critic and of the *oeuvre* as the givens of critical study.

Rather than the authority and allure of the *amor fati* for the heroic marginal genealogist, Foucault proposes a depersonalized "research strategy" that would enable genealogical research and its oppositional tactics.[18] His aim is to develop a tool that can be made available and might produce results helpful to others in their own struggles. I shall say more about this part of Foucault's apparently anarchic project in the final chapters.

While Foucault generally asks the same sort of questions

Nietzsche does about power and discourse, he tries to put forward some authoritative but nonauthorial procedures to come to grips with the issues they raise:

A whole set of assessing, diagnostic, prognostic, narrative judgements concerning the criminal have become lodged in the framework of penal judgement. Another truth has penetrated the truth that was required by the legal machinery; a truth which, entangled with the first, has turned the assertion of guilt into a strange scientifico-juridical complex.[19]

But in one move Foucault both rejects humanism's self-justifying liberalism and refuses the authority Nietzsche's figure of the sublime genealogist might afford his critique of humanism: "one runs the risk of positing as the principle of greater leniency in punishment processes of individualization that are rather one of the effects of the new tactics of power . . ." (DP, 23). This passage points, at least implicitly, to the conjunction of Nietzsche's critique with its liberal humanistic opponent.

Foucault argues that intellectuals should be on guard against becoming agents furthering the disciplinary processes of individualization, as well as the socializing practices of the individual humanistic disciplines—a convergence some of whose effects I hope to at least sketch in my comments on I. A. Richards in chapter 2. "I simply intend," Foucault writes,

to map on a series of examples some of the essential techniques that most easily spread from one [disciplinary institution] to another. These were always meticulous, often minute, techniques, but they had their importance: because they defined a certain mode of detailed political investment of the body, a new 'micro-physics' of power. (DP, 139)

Foucault's value, in part, consists of his thinking rigorously the Nietzschean representation of the anonymity of power and its consequences for liberal humanistic practice. But as I shall show, Foucault's radical antihumanism blurs important differences within various humanistic oppositional practices.

VI

Said's recapitulation of Nietzschean genealogy[20] insists, like Foucault's, on the materiality of representation: there is nothing "so innocent as an 'idea' of the Orient." Yet unlike Foucault, Said does "believe in the determining imprint of individual writers upon the otherwise anonymous collective body of texts constituting a discursive formation like Orientalism" (*O*, 23). Said's belief results in the rather Auerbachian "high intellectual" or "canonical" aura of some of his major works: essays on Massignon, Gibb, Swift, Conrad, etc. In other words, despite the prominence in Said's *oeuvre* of studies of anonymous discourses and institutions,[21] his most powerful theoretical and genealogical achievements center on the study of canonical "authors," a fact that, in part, makes possible Said's continuing distinction within literary criticism.[22]

The problematic nature of the "author" rarely leads Said away from critical tactics that themselves rest upon the presumed coherence and identity of the "subject." He rarely analyzes in any detail the constitutive material and institutional realities in which these "authors" work. As a result, when Said claims that individual writers modify the tradition, he is, like Eliot, whom he follows on this, weekly echoing some form of a "genius" or "great man" theory of history. I want to suggest now and develop later the idea that this focus on canonical authors, in fact, limits Said's work by requiring that he ground his claims to the importance of criticism on the privileged nature of critical "consciousness." As we have seen with Nietzsche and Pound, there are great difficulties involved in any attempt to account for the appearance of such presumed-to-be "privileged" critics. As we shall also see, Auerbach's discussion of Vico falters on the same issue: the claims that Said and Auerbach both make for the historical unaccountability of the so-called initiatory and "negative" consciousness of such magisterial intellectuals, for their "difference" from both the anonymous workers in the field and the leading hegemonic intellectuals, is merely a hard-to-recognize form of ahistorical idealism.

By examining Said's difference from Foucault, we can get a clear sense of the nature and importance of his project, especially as this emerges from *Orientalism* to the late essay, "Secular Criticism."[23] In this chapter, I shall only begin a discussion of Said by commenting on his differences from Foucault in *Orientalism*. In the last chapters, I shall extend the analysis and discuss Said's later essays and the implications that his very powerful project have for all adversarial critics.

While it might be acceptable to say that Gramsci's theory of the intellectual has had an influence on Said's thinking about the importance of individual authority and the personal experience of the critic, one might more aptly suggest that Gramsci simply provides Said with another figure to articulate what has always been an important aspect of his own critical project:

> The starting-point of critical elaboration is the consciousness of what one really is, and is 'knowing thyself' as a product of the historical process to date, which has deposited in you an infinity of traces without leaving an inventory . . . therefore it is imperative at the outset to compile such an inventory. (O, 25)

As Said's quotation from Gramsci suggests,[24] he does not want to see the genealogical critic as a metaphysical subject or as some version of the Nietzschean perfect man's apocalyptic and redemptive heroism. In context, this quotation from Gramsci implies that the major *critical* failure of orientalists is that they have not examined their own place within a material and institutional network of texts, desires, politics, and sexual fantasies. Over and again Said has functioned as the conscience of critical humanists, reminding us repeatedly of the need to be careful in our complicity with forms of power and oppression that we do not understand because we have abandoned the critical reflection that would alone protect us from the worst consequences of the dogmatic institutionalization of our practices and discourses.

Orientalism, then, has at least two functions that I consider central to all contemporary critical practice: to produce an inventory of orientalism that shows it is indeed part of a system of power whose effects are highly undesirable and seemingly contradict orientalism's humanistic ethos and, by so doing, to show that the skills of the *critical* humanist, especially the literary intellectual, can be adopted to a consideration of what Said calls the "worldliness" of texts as systems of representation and as agencies of power. *Orientalism* is, therefore, both an inventory of how the Western intellectual has come to be in the service of the hegemonic culture[25] and an example of how critical humanists might become oppositional intellectuals as well.

Said's work shows that literary critics have at their disposal, as part of their training and tradition, a set of critical tools that might well be adopted to adversarial purposes. In *Orientalism*, for example, Said himself uses T. S. Eliot's notion of "Tradition and the Individual Talent" and I. A. Richards' metaphor of the "balanced compass" to great political and theoretical advantage. Indeed, Said no doubt means his ability to turn these most mandarin of figures to his radical purposes to validate his claim that individual authors can be thought of as making a difference within the determining pattern of a discourse.

Yet Said's use of these figures poses a question similar to those I have already raised about Pound and Nietzsche: to what extent does the use of such traditional figures—no matter the ends—in turn determine their user. In *Orientalism*, some of the consequences of this question for critics appear most plainly in Said's discussion of the nature of representation and of the effects that individual writers may have on discursive systems:

What this must lead us to methodologically is to view representations (or misrepresentations—the distinction is at best a matter of degree) as inhabiting a common field of play defined for them, not by some inherent common subject matter alone, but by some common history, tradition, universe of discourse. Within this field, which no single scholar can create but which each scholar receives and in which he then finds a place for himself, the individual researcher makes his contribution. Such contributions, even for the exceptional genius, are strategies of redisposing material within the field; even the scholar who unearths a once-lost manuscript produces "found" text in a context already prepared for it, for that is the real meaning of *finding* a new text. Thus each individual contribution first causes changes within the field and then promotes a new stability, in the way that on a surface covered with twenty compasses the introduction of a twenty-first will cause all the others to quiver, then to settle into a new accommodating configuration. (*O*, 272–73)

Scholars familiar with Modernist criticism will, of course, see that Said has adopted Eliot's model of tradition and Richards' model of poetic discourse. What are some of the implications of his usage?

First we can say that it is consistent with Said's own theory:

he comes to a critical occasion prepared with the tools of the field that, among others, have created the possibility for his own action. He deals with the problem of the individual's relation to the existing discourse in Anglo-American terms, in part, to offer an alternative to what he will later describe as Foucault's quietistic sense that individual authors can have little direct effect on power and have little responsibility for confronting it. Secondly we can say that this is an effective strategy because it dramatizes the failure of humanistic literary criticism to make use of its own resources—as Said does here—for something other than either mandarin or professional writing bound by disciplinary norms. All in all, this is quite a remarkable passage.

Yet there are those nagging questions that Said's own theory raises so insistently: Where is the revisionist intellectual in all this? How is the oppositional critic being positioned by these tools he employs so cleverly? Has the critic done the full inventory needed to use these tools with such relative confidence? Has the critic thought through the implications of the position he describes and accepts?

These questions must be considered in light of Said's attempt to relegitimate critical practice at a time when its belletristic and diacritical modes seem particularly complicitous with forces of imperialism and domestic repressive tolerance.[26] The attempt is paradoxically conservative because it does not emerge from or base itself on the full inventory Gramsci's own text calls for. More specifically, Said does not work out the elaborate relationships of literary criticism and critical humanism with orientalism. Consequently, his text often points to instances of where he is unavoidably and necessarily—despite his magisterial powers of self-criticism—reproducing what he must think of as unacceptable aspects of critical humanism's discursive universe.

In the passage I have just quoted, we can see how this happens. To the degree to which *Orientalism* succeeds in revising critical practice—and it has to a great extent—to precisely that degree Said is like the twenty-first compass. In other words, we must read this passage for the image of the critic that appears in it (no matter Said's wish on this point) because it is "about" both representation and the critic's relation to those systems. It is about how the powerful critic[27] modifies the context by working within it, but that merely means it is about how the critic changes the representation of the critic within that broader universe of intellectual representation.

What does this mean in the case of this passage from Said? As the twenty-first compass, Said *or any other magisterial intellectual* modifies and perpetuates one central component of humanism: the sublime role of the leading—even if adversarial—intellectual whose work is able both to shake the order of forces and make possible a new accommodation—an intellectual whose image as the empowered revisionist alone is attractive and authoritative within the otherwise anonymous network of discourse and representation. Strangely, then, it is Said's relegitimation of critical humanism within the academy that, despite its most radical claims (later I will argue *because* of them), reminds one of the self-exiled, isolated genealogist of Nietzsche's work. Said's image of the twenty-first compass, borrowed as it is from one of the originary figures of academic literary criticism, despite its mundane and mechanical appearance, is not so distant from the heroic Nietzschean figure of the genealogist or, indeed, from Kung's ephebes' project of "being known." Nietzsche and Said are both renegades from a discipline they try to redeem by transcending. Both employ the philological and critical resources of their disciplines combined with essential borrowings from related fields to organize an oppositional practice and an adversarial figure in the modern West.

I hope it is clear that I have made these comments about *Orientalism* precisely because it carries antihegemonic critical practice further in our academy than any other work has. For that very reason, however, we must consider some of the limits up against which Said's work so paradigmatically brings all adversarial criticism. The basic question might be put too simply: how complete an adversarial practice can a critic represent when the weapons deployed are those enabling figures basic to the origins and perpetuation of the dynastic discourses against which the oppositional critic always struggles? Said's work suggests this is an impossible dilemma; like Nietzsche, but in a different way, his work implies we must do the best with what we have since we cannot afford the political quietism that seems to be its alternative. Yet, over and again, Said's work suggests the inadequacies of Nietzsche's endless irony. But in turn, Nietzsche provides a curious view of Said's claim: Nietzsche always reminds us that ascetic nihilism constantly extends its hegemony under the guise of responsibility and morality.

Said's use of Richards illuminates the danger of both positions: no matter whether irony or responsibility underlies the disruptive presence of the twenty-first compass, all such disruptions of the unified discursive field can be "accommodated." No matter how ironic or politically directed, then, adversarial critics practicing within the field of critical humanistic discourse, their texts suggest, cannot make more than an incremental difference within that field and can distance themselves only minimally from an essential part of the hegemony they oppose. Indeed, their attempted differentiation, which is revision set within the complex figure of the leading intellectual, falls victim to that discourse's strategy for self-preservation.[28]

We can learn a great deal about the possibility of critical humanism from *Orientalism* precisely because by employing literary criticism against an adjacent discourse—indeed, they are at times the same!—Said reveals precisely the family resemblance that cannot be effaced or avoided whenever literary studies are used as weapons in the critique of adjacent humanistic disciplines. This resemblance must be accepted as inevitable by critical humanists, exploited where possible, learned from always, and resisted everywhere. Such resistance will be the key to politically significant local intellectual struggle. (I should perhaps add in anticipation of my final chapters that it is precisely this sort of resistance that involves Foucault's work and obviates, in part, Said's charge that he underestimates the importance of resistance in his theory of power.)

One conclusion of Said's work may be that the critical humanist must be seen to be impossible.[29] *Orientalism* makes clear that, in Nietzsche's terms, the West's representation of itself is a bizarre conceit. But does it not also suggest that the figure of the oppositional critic may be as well? Nietzsche cautions against all such cunning and suspicion like that which Said displays: "All science has at present the object of dissuading man from his former respect for himself, as if this had been nothing but a piece of bizarre conceit" (*GM*, 155–56). Perhaps the most important consequence of *Orientalism* is that it exhausts the respectability and efficacy of critical humanism. Nietzsche would laugh at such a thought, but in so doing he would escape the hidden dangers of such a challenge to critical humanism—a challenge that might assassinate us all by treacherously drawing us further into the ubiquitous web of Western nihilism. Foucault and Said are surely aware of the dangers and so are Nietzsche's true heirs. Consequently, they share in the strangeness of his final paradox: "the ascetic ideal is an artifice for the *preservation* of life" (*GM*, 120).

VII

Let me attempt to summarize a few of the implications of the genealogical model as I have discussed it so far so that the direction of the rest of my analyses may be clearer. I shall return repeatedly to the issues I can only sketch out here.

Above all, critical humanists should be concerned that Nietzsche can establish the power of his critique of ascetic humanism only by constituting himself, the prototypical modern critical intellectual, as a sublime figure. Indeed, the *Genealogy* suggests that he must do this in an attempt to fend off the effects of ascetic humanism and its institutions, particularly philosophy and philology. But Nietzsche's adoption of this tactic, his movement toward the sublime figuration of the critic, enacts for us the inscription of both dynastic and oppositional humanists within a larger pattern of authority that depends on the ideal of the leading intellectual cast as a heroic practitioner come down from the mountain. Nietzsche is, of course, a parodist of this ideal, who makes clear how foolish but unavoidable is the competition for cultural authority that circles around the success and power of different versions of the leading intellectual. My point, however, is that such parody is not, in itself, an adequate response to the situation this insight creates for the intellectual. *Both* forms of foolishness are nihilistic and their political consequences are antidemocratic and unacceptable. Nonetheless, one must be prepared to admit that within an ascetic humanistic intellectual structure it is better politically to compete to acquire such authority for progressive purposes than to abandon the position of authority to the reactionary figures within dynastic power.

In short, Nietzsche does not so much prescribe a set of possibilities for intellectual oppositional practice as he does lay out for us the site on which it must be performed. In fact, he inventories the various intellectual and discursive tools available for the struggles to oppose and to take power. Granted that the nihilism of ascetic humanism is to be resisted, granted in addition that such resistance requires struggling against the cultural institutions that sustain and disperse it, nonetheless, the comic resources of irony and research Nietzsche makes available to the opposition are tools of dubious value to be taken up warily and employed for specific purposes against the hegemony. The duplicity of these "weapons" is that they both define the topography of the terrain of the dynastic structure and are, at the same time, the only resources for redefining that terrain.

Nietzsche's greatest weakness (as it may also be Foucault's on another level) is the conclusion that he draws from this insight and that he embodies in the play of styles. For Nietzsche, all forms of humanistic intellectual practice are too much determined by their nihilistic associations. As a result, for Nietzsche, none of them can make (or mark) any serious or significant human difference. For us, the problem is that such a position paralyzes the powers of judgment necessary to discriminate the material results of different forms of intellectual practice. In fact, the threat of paralysis and failure of judgment that results from this indiscriminate condemnation is the greatest burden Nietzsche leaves for all who take him and his work seriously. In a sense, as I show in the final chapter, Nietzsche is simply carrying on one of the two major traditions of post-Kantian humanistic work, that one most readily identified with Hölderlin's protests against the death of the gods. If this is true it signifies that Nietzsche's own nihilism—and that of those who operate within the tradition he highlights—is itself a consequence of being constituted within the genealogy of ascetic humanism. Nietzsche's despair of humanism, then, is humanism's despair of itself—a confession of painful self-betrayal repeated in the pathos of Auerbach's greatest accomplishments.

Foucault's great importance consists precisely in his attempt to develop a critical and scholarly alternative to the authority and power of asceticism and disciplinary humanism without, like Nietzsche, replicating so very much of the structure he hopes to challenge. Central to this project, as I see it (and as I develop it throughout this book), is Foucault's renunciation of the figure of the "leading" or "representative" intellectual. He is critical of this figure in its chief modern versions: as sublime "hero" and "savior" of a culture or as a "masterful" leader of a discipline. Foucault understands the cost of adopting any version of this figure—even for the seemingly most progressive political ends. (I shall be at pains to develop this point in distinguishing Foucault and Said.) Foucault lets us see that these costs are not only the destruction of the scholar's critical role but also the always present antidemocratic threat to "subjugate" the other. The events of May 1968 and Foucault's research into prisons, asylums, and schools, as well as into sexual discourses and practices, bring him to his special project: developing cultural and intellectual devices to serve others' struggles for political decentralization and self-determination.

Foucault's critique of the subject has a political rather than a metaphysical burden. Putting aside the various post-Nietzschean versions of the "heroic" intellectual as a way of legitimating critical practice is a consequence of displacing the "subject" from its constitutive role as both the object and subject of humanistic scholarship. Specifically, Foucault shows us, intellectual work is not and should not be read as the product of an "originary author," no matter how subtly that figure is hedged. Intellectual production is anonymous, the function of discourses, desires, and institutions that have a history, a certain set of affiliations to the hegemonic order, and that, above all, sustain the existence, in representation, of the "subject as origin." It is precisely the complex interweavings of this self-legitimating practice (in all the senses of "self" here) against which Foucault struggles. His works, like Nietzsche's, are constituted by the critical elements of the counterhumanistic tradition within humanism itself, by Nietzsche's ironizing of them, and by the peculiarities of recent history's demonstration of the terrible dangers of concentrated political and cultural power. As a result, these genealogies outline the constitutive forces that make up not only the subject but also the ideology and institutions that legitimate those forces as "given." The "positive" contribution Foucault makes to this project is his practice: scholarly, critical work whose authority is not dependent, in any direct figuration, on the image of the heroic and sublime master in any of its prescriptive or leading forms.[30]

The crucial difference between Said and Foucault over the role of the author takes such extended form in their works that, at least for my purpose in this book, one can say that between them they define the problem facing humanistic intellectuals today: Said insists on the political necessity of critical consciousness as the ground for justice in the world; Foucault hopes to challenge the very priority of the subject precisely because its continuation as the ground of critical opposition inscribes too much of the genealogy of ascetic humanism and so, doubling back upon the critical intellectual, blunts his or her activity. As I see it, these two very strong positions bring critics to a difficult set of judgments: they both require not only that we see practice and theory as specific and situated—discursively and culturally—but also that we find precise and definite ways to evaluate the relative political efficacy of various forms of opposition as these exist in humanism and as they either signal the need to escape it or try, as in Foucault's case, to destroy and go beyond it.

There seems to be no doubt that most forms of what I shall

call variously "ascetic" or "anthropological" humanism as it is inscribed within the practice of the human sciences, particularly the humanities, and especially literary criticism, make culture and discourse an inhibition to self-determination.[31] Yet, at the same time, one must concede and identify the powerful progressive elements within certain humanistic practices, such as Said's. I shall be at pains to show, especially in the case of Auerbach, how the very powerful weapons of humanistic scholarship can be made to operate for progressive and humane purposes; at the same time, I shall show how they delimit such action and how, in fact, they do so precisely because they are involved, as Auerbach discovered, with some of the darkest aspects of modern history. Given the different configuration of political and cultural forces in the U.S., Foucault's broad condemnation of all humanistic rhetorics and practices should not be uncritically adopted. Some effort must be made to make more precise judgments than Foucault's discourse sometimes allows, judgments that will permit us, as we must, to acknowledge and support those forms of skeptical, oppositional humanism directed toward political self-determination.

2

A Free, Varied, and Unwasteful Life:
I. A. Richards' Speculative Instruments

> It is so necessary and so difficult to secure a stable and
> general system of public behaviour that any means
> whatsoever are justifiable, failing the discovery of bet-
> ter.
> —I. A. Richards, *Principles of Literary Criticism*

The history of the institution of the critical study of English
and American literature in the university has never been given
the detailed analysis it requires. Books have been written recording the rise of English studies, but they have been primarily chronicles of events and personalities. Stephen Potter's
The Muse in Chains and E. M. W. Tillyard's *The Muse Unchained* are the two best known of these books, but they are of
interest primarily as documentation of what went on in England and not as analyses of the causes, effects, and structures of
the institution.[1] Nonetheless, we are very much dependent on
these books and others like Babbitt's *Literature and the American College* to understand the articulated reasons for English
study, as well as to find the unarticulated interests underlying
the foundation of the critical discipline. The genealogy of the
profession can be traced out in part by studying the metaphoric
representations of "Eng. Lit." and "the critic" as they develop
in these texts.

A full analysis of this genealogy that would bring us from the beginnings at London University in the middle of the last century to the various experimental actions of the 1960s through to the preternaturally complex textual practices of the present—such a study is, of course, a book-length project.[2] I focus on one figure in that genealogy—I. A. Richards—because of his importance to all literary study in English. In fact, as far as I can tell, he, more than any one else, deserves the title "father" of academic criticism. Yet, of course, as soon as I name Richards "father" and write him into a genealogical relationship, I am required to speak of his ancestors and contemporaries and to insist that because of and despite his great inaugural contributions to the discipline of criticism inside the university, Richards' "originary" actions are radically circumscribed by discourses and institutions enabling and limiting his practice. In many ways, he is the right man in the right spot. He appears at precisely the historical moment when academic criticism is struggling to be born; in a sense, if Richards had not existed, the university system and the culture that supports it would have been forced to invent him.

I intend very briefly to survey the emergence of literary study in the university before addressing the problem of Richards himself. I shall only highlight the story as I draw it from Potter and Tillyard, and, in fact, since I will be moving toward Richards, I shall take Cambridge English as my example. This means, of course, that much of the most interesting material regarding such questions as Richards' relationship to syndicalism, feminism, and the collapse of liberalism must be suspended, along with the affiliative importance of eugenics and anthropological functionalism.

In 1908, when he went up to Cambridge, Tillyard writes, "no one dreamt of associating literary criticism with the courses in English" (MU, 13–14). Since Cambridge was heavily under German influence, literature was an adjunct of philology. Potter recounts the external pressures that arose in the society of the nineteenth century—usually utilitarian pressures—to teach English language and literature in the universities to help train young men for careers. This pressure first had its effect in the provincial universities, in extension lecturing, where Churton

Collins made his reputation, and then in London. Oxford University finally "fell," to use his metaphor, when Sir Walter Ralegh was appointed Professor of Eng. Lit. in 1904, eleven years after a Final Honors School in English Language and Literature had been approved. Cambridge, however, was the last to fall; in 1910 the King Edward VIIth Chair in Literature was endowed—and promptly filled with a philologist who obligingly died the next year. Quiller-Couch was finally appointed to the position because of his political support of Asquith's Liberal party in Cornwall. In fact, he was appointed over Grierson, the Donne scholar. As this sketch suggests, at the moment of its birth, "Eng. Lit." had strong connections to the world of journalism, amateurism, and impressionism—all traditions against which practical criticism felt it necessary to rebel.

The significant date, though, in this history, as in so much else of Modern studies, is 1917—World War I. Tillyard tells us that English studies "began a new kind of life as soon as the first world war ended." Students and teachers "knew that they were doing something fresh" (*MU*, 11). Tillyard records his own personal experience as typical of those students and young intellectuals interested in literature at that time. He felt very attracted, he tells us, to the best emotional criticism of the previous thirty years, yet "I craved something that stuck closer to the texts and that sought to give reasons for a literary effect" (*MU*, 88–89). Potter describes the general scientific tenor of the age as one of the pressures on the university to introduce the critical study of English. Not only were Latin and Greek, to say nothing of Anglo-Saxon, not "useful," but also they gave no scientific access to the essential moral, semantic, and emotional aspects of literature. They felt that philology only danced around their borders.

In terms of the larger genealogy I am sketching, Potter and Tillyard's evidence of the spread of discipline and "scientism" into the study of language and literature should be seen as part of the dominance of secular or anthropological humanism. There are many ways to recreate this genealogy, but throughout I shall in large part follow Foucault in describing the rise of the sciences of "man" as a material reformation of culture in which "man" and "his" works and discourses become the sole guarantee of the future and the sole reservoir of value and meaning. The human sciences are the endless commentary on both of these constituted objects. Potter's summary of the pressures on the universities to take on literature, so to speak, as the object of a disciplined investigation marks not just the replacement of a gentlemanly student body by a more middle-class professionalized one, nor just a change in the social understanding of literature as a means of cultural legitimation— although it surely is both of these.

In addition, what we see reflected in Potter and Tillyard is the expansion of the disciplinary society by the inclusion of literature into the realm of "objects" constituted by a rigorous method that, in studying literature and by training and examining its students, can provide infinite amounts of knowledge and discourse about not only the works being read but also about the readers themselves. Nietzsche insists that the humanities, in their pursuit of "truth," are involved in an infinite and regressive process of interpretative commentary and that this process is an instance of the "will to power." Indeed, "will to power" and "interpretation" are synonymous in Nietzsche. Extending this regressive process to the "critical" study of literature simply fufills the ethos of humanism: to an infinite future "man" can endlessly comment on the reconstructed past, listening for its secret, which it promises but in fact it will never tell us even in an infinite future.

"Literary criticism" becomes established as a legitimate institution precisely because it is, from the beginning, inscribed within the materially effective and expanding discourses of the humanistic hegemony. I submit that Richards and "practical criticism" come to serve precisely this function: extending the humanistic, anthropological impulse across a spectrum of human activity never before made part of the endless process of making culture in the power of coming to know it. I. A. Richards fits rather nicely into the demands of the age as Tillyard reflects them. He offers a critical and pedagogical method based on an awareness of the latest science and yet he also hopes to "save" literature from the scientific reductionism broadly felt by poets and litterateurs to threaten civilization after the war.

I would say that one of the keys to Richards' success, that is, his ability to institutionalize "practical criticism," is to be found just in this combination of science and poetry. As I show later, anthropological or secular humanism branches in at least two directions: the positive line, which celebrates the humanist's scholarly abilities to produce knowledge and shape institutions for the purpose of making a career while "perfecting the species," as Kant might put it, and a second branch, perhaps best typified by Hölderlin in his "Empedocles" or by Erich Auerbach in his extraordinary postwar essays on Pascal and "Weltliteratur." This second is a tradition of lament and caution, as well as of celebration and imagination. It upholds the "literary" as a replacement for the religion lost in the death of the gods and as protection against the destructive forces of modernization, of science, and of professionalization. Yet, and this is the paradox that lies at the heart of literary humanism, to save literature and culture the critic/teacher attempts to institutionalize and disperse what he sees as a redemptive ideology and practice. Invariably, as with Richards, this involves professionalizing literary study and expanding the sociocultural force of secular humanism even while appearing intent on resisting it. Richards' work paradigmatically develops the empowered cultural, discursive, and institutional resources of both offshoots of secular humanism—the positive extension of knowledge and its productive apparatus and the antisecular "values" and other reactionary desires of the antimodernist.

As a result, the most important aspect of Richards' work is that he directly brings about the establishment of literary criticism of English inside the university as a cultural force and institution. Tillyard says rightly that the great critics like Dryden did not have "the least notion of English as an academic subject . . . " (*MU*, 22). Its direct ancestry begins with Skeat, Ward, Furnivall, and the other nineteenth century scholars. Yet, despite this nineteenth century explosion in literary scholarship, as late as 1883, the examination for the Modern Languages Tripos at Cambridge did not include a question on English. After the war and the coming of Richards, however, the outlines of the institution as we now know it began to emerge: English is detached from its subservient place to the classics; college-trained graduates teach English in the public schools—something that Babbitt and Tillyard both think is a mistake; scholarships are offered in English Studies; admission examinations are set at college; research is encouraged; and publication marks the rise of professionalism. The various professional organizations are founded by 1925, as well as the major bibliographies. Running as the connecting thread through much, if not all, of this institutional activity is I. A. Richards' "invention" of "practical criticism." Tillyard tells us it filled the need all felt at Cambridge for close textual study; it provided the only adequate means of examination in literature—both for degrees and scholarships (the explicatory question was made obligatory at Cambridge after *Principles of Literary Criticism* appeared and while Richards was preparing *Practical Criticism*).

Practical criticism was seen as the best way to discipline not only the student but also the "man"—the references are always male despite both the large number of women students and twenty years of militant feminist agitation in the U.K. "Discipline," it turns out, was the key word to the founders of our "discipline." "By learning the solid things," Tillyard writes, "and not the languages men would fit themselves for careers in business and the public services, and something would be done to breakdown the insularity of most educated Englishmen which the war had revealed" (*MU*, 59). (Note the class shift in this rhetoric.) But in keeping with Richards' profound interest in Bentham and Mill, the utilitarianism Tillyard describes also has higher motives: "And we thought that if a man entered his subject in this way," that is, first through the classical languages and then through practical criticism, for discipline, "he could learn to deal with the experience of life better than if he had been trained to accumulate the facts of vowel-changes . . . . He ought to be able to judge of a situation on its true qualities rather than be tempted to meet it on some preconceived plan which might be far from fitting it" (*MU*, 83).

"Practical criticism" legitimates humanism; it produces pragmatic men who will guide the species—even those parts of it that were not consulted. The sublime romance desires underlying this figure of the well-educated Englishman become completely overt when Tillyard euphorically describes the mood of Cambridge between 1917 and 1929: "The mood of lively young men, not at all well instructed, free to range and revel in a fresh and little explored province where charms on every side provoked exploration" (*MU*, 96). No wonder he (like his heirs) grows so sad at the inevitable professionalization of English studies! But I suggest that even these blissful titilating moments at the scene of instruction are much more contradictory, less laudable, and certainly more self-interested than Tillyard recalls.

I have begun with this sketch and variation on Tillyard because I would like to approach I. A. Richards' complex discourse by considering its originary status. I stress that before Richards, academic criticism of English literature did not exist as a discipline in English and American universities. There were other studies of language and literature in the universities—even at Richards' own Cambridge—but in almost all of these other "fields" the study of English literature existed, not as a separate discourse and discipline, but rather as an accidental accretion, an essentially marginal product of philology, history, language study, classics, and aesthetics. No less a student of Richards than Muriel Bradbrook, whose own studies of the Renaissance have been initiatory, says: "*Principles of Literary Criticism* introduced the collaborative yet selfcritical examination of English literature which justified it as a discipline."[3] Furthermore, William Empson, undoubtedly Richards' most accomplished student, defends his former professor against charges of an unliterary concern with "ethics" by saying that "indeed, the whole of 'Eng. Lit.' as University subject badly needs to be returned to the Benthamite position" espoused by Richards.[4] And even as strenuous a critic of Richards' utilitarianism as W. K. Wimsatt admits, even while disagreeing about the ethical dimension of literary criticism, "that there is probably more of Richards than of any other critic in the founded antecedents, the essential substrate of [this] essay."

The debt of the New Critics to Richards has been so frequently rehearsed that perhaps we no longer adequately attend to the initiatory functions played by both his discursive and nondiscursive practice (such as his adoption of his students' "protocols" as evidence for critical theory; I will return to the significance of the protocols). As Bradbrook's comment makes clear, it is the peculiar power of Richards' practice that made possible literary criticism as a collaborative enterprise, that is, as a discipline. In the process of modifying Richards' theory of value, Wimsatt acknowledges the continuity of his discourse and his project with Richards': "Polysemism, ambiguity, irony or inclusiveness, the poem's verbal independence of author's plans and motives, the multiple (yet coalescing) relations of language to emotion—these are the matters all more or less sagely, even triumphantly, expounded by Richards in various places. They too must be assumed if the present argument is to proceed."[5]

As a founding act, Richards' discourse occupies a place in what he himself calls a "chaos of critical theories." The nineteenth century's investment in the wealth of language study expanded its domain while fragmenting its classical unity in the field of representation.[6] In the guise of many, often conflicting species, language insistently questions its own legality as tender for the circulation of ideas, feelings, and experiences. It is no longer backed by the full faith of a discourse inscribed within representation. In the nineteenth century's overheated linguistic economy, the sign is not a successful balance between its face value and exchange value. The classical theory of the sign had required, as Foucault points out, that "the sign, in order to function, must be simultaneously an insertion in that which it signifies and also distinct from it. For the sign to be, in effect, what it is, it must be presented as an object of knowledge at the same time as that which it signifies" (OT, 60). The intersection of words and representation had not only "provide[d] a spontaneous grid for the knowledge of things"

(*OT*, 304), but also it had represented language as unity and transparency.

Sociological analyses of the eighteenth century have shown the unity of the classical field of representation to be disrupted by a multiplicity of social and economic causes: demography, reorganization of the means of production, threats to the stability of the legal and familial authority of paternity and filiation. To these disruptive forces, Foucault's archaeology adds other marks of discontinuity fragmenting the classical grid: the disruptions of general grammar by the attention to inflection, of the analysis of wealth by the figure of labor, and of life by the organic metaphor of depth. In an attempt to "manage" this "disorderly" apparatus, new disciplines reorganized knowledge in fields like economics, biology, medicine, and psychology. But this new knowledge expanded the areas that reciprocally generated more knowledge and thereby reinforced the power and authority of the entire system.

Significantly, the circular way in which knowledge, proliferating in an ever-expanding number of disciplines and creating a need for its own ongoing extension and perpetuation, left language itself as the only resource common to all other disciplines not only assured the centrality of investigation into language by philologists, logicians, and grammarians but also prevented a unified conception of or function for language from appearing. The organic, evolutionary metaphor of the nineteenth century represented language as historical and particular. Moreover, unlike the positive human sciences, which often dream of reducing language to its universalizing qualities through definition and designation, the "authors" of antipositive, often antihumanistic, critical texts, such as Kierkegaard, Marx, Nietzsche, and Pater, were supremely aware that all linguistic cognitive productions are marred in their processes and results by the special uncertainties of language itself: its historical burden, its epistemological duplicities, its sociological determinations, its polysemous ambiguities, and its inability to produce determinate meaning. And, moreover, they show us not only that the human sciences are inscribed within a place where the market for their knowledge is bound by language but also that literature, in reaction, defines itself as a special use of language beyond reference, knowledge, and communication that must deploy and profit from the mysterious multiplicity of language's inflationary proliferation.

Foucault and others argue that Mallarmé's coining of an impersonal poet writing about nothing, limning only the Word itself in its "enigmatic and precarious being" (*OT*, 305) represents the modern literary strategy to reunite language to itself, to let language reappear in all its plentitude. Yet Foucault himself is not certain of the historical emergence of this desire. It is indeed unclear how far and if Anglo-American high modernism, even in the international style of Pound, Eliot, and Joyce, can be defined as an extension of Mallarmé's project. What is clear, however, is that I. A. Richards and a great deal of Anglo-American academic criticism practiced after him as a discipline, that is, as an accumulative, cooperative project for the production of knowledge, the exercise of power, and the creation of careers, emerges with a degree of self-consciousness from this nineteenth-century problematic and furthermore that it attempts in its own ways to rebalance what it sees as the disorderly functions of language, to reestablish a linguistic unity through and in a positively productive academic critical discipline that, somewhat belatedly, affiliates itself with and at times tries to master the other positive disciplines such as economics, psychology, medicine, and anthropology. Richards urgently senses that the inflation and differentiation of languages and language study is a threat to a balanced, sane, and healthy civilization. To balance the complex machine of language he initiates a realignment of elements of critical method, rhetoric, and practice with the hope of changing the existence of literature as a special sphere of language unavailable to disciplined study.

Ogden and Richards present *The Meaning of Meaning* as a specific response to this proliferation and inflation.[7] Richards makes clear in its "Preface" that he sees this linguistic upheaval as a historical and class problem: the breakdown of elite bourgeois culture's class distinctions, roles, and responsibilities following World War I threaten the stability of civilization and require the development of disciplinary techniques to assure that these new students are "equipped" to deal with matters no longer in the hands of the gentlemanly elite. Richards senses that the prognosis for controlling what he sees as the potential breakdown of culture in the modern world is not good. The "chaos of critical theories" Richards hopes to correct is only one sign of culture's illness. In *The Meaning of Meaning* Richards suggests that the proliferation of disciplines in modernity is itself a symptom of a disease caused by an inadequate theory of language. In fact, the symptoms dialectically aggravate the disorder: the seemingly endless differentiation of knowledge into new fields not only does not generate *one* adequate theory of language but also, in fact, often harmfully puts mistaken theories into play—and thereby further obscures the need for one *correct* theory of language as representation. In a telling passage, Richards draws an analogy between his own historical period and England, the entire West, on the one hand, and the decline of Athens and the plague during the Peloponesian war as it is told by Thucydides. The point for Richards here is that Thucydides' history acutely identifies the cultural decay of established morals brought about by the war and plague with the decadence of the plain sense of language, of its agreed upon ability to refer.

Richards goes on to make clear (*MM*, 19) that in what he thinks is a similar historical situation a technique for controlling words and meaning is needed, not a new system of language. This is a crucial belief because Richards is knowingly inserting his discussion of language into the problem of power and authority as a way of preserving "reason" and "sanity." The needed control can be provided only by the materialization of a theory of definition that would unfailingly define the referent in any context. A theory of definiton must, in turn, be derived from a theory of signs that cannot be developed from introspection (because this always leads to solipsism) but must rather be developed from the empirical observations of others. Richards' fascination with empiricism remains a necessary element of his method and theory throughout his career even though it is at times less important to him than it is in the 1920s. The "others" to be observed in *The Meaning of Meaning* are, of course, other thinkers about language and ordinary language situations. In *Practical Criticism* and *Interpretation in Teaching*, the "others" will be his student protocol writers. But his constant desire is always to find a mode of ordering that guarantees communication and saves culture by assuring a high degree of effective organization of knowledge and experience.

That this is so in *The Meaning of Meaning* can be seen in a brief examination of his comments on Saussure. Richards disagrees with Saussure's theory of semiology because Saussure, first, "invented" *la langue* as the object of linguistics (an unfortunate choice for invention since Richards identifies it as the realm of "linguistic convention," of "fixed meaning," that is, as the opposite of his own theory of contextualism), and secondly, he disagrees with Saussure because semiology neglected "entirely the things for which signs stand . . . ." So while the contemporary French school—epitomized by Derrida and Foucault—appreciate Saussure's work because his theory allows them a way out of the traditional Western insistence that there be a necessary relation between words and things— one need only think of Foucault's ironically entitled *Les mots et les choses*—Richards represents him as caught within a symbolic system he doesn't comprehend. By inventing the object of investigation, Saussure abandons the possibility of scientific verification altogether (*MM*, 6). Most important, the loss, in Saussure's model, of the assumed necessity of referentiality minimizes, for Richards, the possibility that language can indeed, in its contextual grammar and semantics, immediately organize and reflect the structure of knowledge and experience.

Richards tells us at the beginning of *The Meaning of Meaning* that all previous attempts to solve the problem of the relationship between words and things have failed. Put more precisely, he feels that no other theories can account for the evident meaning and communication that does occur in social exchange because none begin from an understanding of the contextual nature of all articulation—and context here includes language and action. But the one hope for curing mo-

dernity's disease Richards senses in the very symptom of the
demise of its cultural order: in the modern world, because of
the mad proliferation of knowledge, the need to overcome the
past's failures in aligning words and things in a transparent
language thematizes the relationship between things and
words as *the* modern problem of knowledge, judgment, and
culture. The tryanny of this problem threatens Western civilization. But whereas others, like Saussure, and later Foucault,
think of this tyranny as unavoidable—one cannot escape the
fact that the semantics of one's system are only a reflection of
its syntactical rules—Richards actually believes that an adequate theory can be achieved by simply not making conceptual
mistakes. From his point of view, all other theoreticians make
errors that can be avoided.

The Meaning of Meaning places Richards in the genealogy of
humanism and sets out some of the major strategies of his entire intellectual career. Two points are especially noteworthy:
Richards' insistence on the need to produce a single theory
of language that will provide a *unitary* explanation of all
linguistic and literary phenomena typifies humanism's inability to tolerate difference. As we shall see, even the most
complex historical humanists, like Auerbach, assume a proprietorial relation to what they believe is a unitary object of
study, no matter whether that might be the history of literature
or the "nature" of language. Essentially, humanism, as I shall
suggest is clearly the case with Richards, is an exclusionary
practice that at best is pluralistic in its self-justifications but
rarely in its practice. Marshall Hodgson is a case in point, as we
shall see. Equally important, though, is Richards' insistence
that this unitary theory of representation will not only control,
manage, or in some other way displace all other competing
theories of language but also call a halt to such competition
completely.

In this attitude, Richards is like Kung. What is central, however, in this gesture is how it reveals Richards' willingness to
engage in struggle in order to gain and maintain the priority of
his "interpretation." Indeed, Richards soon comes to learn that
such a victory cannot be just a matter of rhetoric and theory

but must involve pedagogy and institutional "reform"; that is, it must involve authority as well. As critic, theoretician, and educational reformist, Richards must be an astute institutional politician and tactician. His self-justification is that the other theories of language, by their very existence in a competitive struggle, are a threat to civilization. His own contextualism is so necessary and "correct" that it justifies his figure of the critic as representative intellectual leading others from what he sees as their self-threatening behavior to a more sane and balanced world. Richards, in other words, epitomizes himself as the sublime intellectual leader whose privileged insight grants him special authority and legitimacy to speak for others in whatever he takes to be their own interests.

The same image of the critical intellectual appears in Richards' empiricism. Contextualism requires a theory of signs that can be derived only from a study of others. As I shall show, Richards enacts the position of the sublime master teacher, of the leading humanistic intellectual, in his practical and theoretical extension of disciplinary power in which students and others become "readers" who are the subjugated objects of study. Practical criticism creates "readers" as such an object for critical investigation and critical training. The entire project of creating a sane and balanced world resting on the theory of contextualism depends on the critic's assuming the role of scientific investigator of "reading" and "readers" in order to systematize and correct the practice. In addition, of course, this extension of discipline has important social effects of individuation, normalization, and exclusion. At the heart of the project, however, lies the arrogant figure of the leading intellectual whose authority, interacting with that of the institutions and discourses in which he practices, legitimates the disciplinary extension of humanism in an essentially antidemocratic process of subjugating people within categories of social being constituted by the discursive and nondiscursive practices of humanism.

In the process of training teachers and readers, Richards proposes the extension of discipline not to "repress" difference, which seems, to him, unfortunately prevalent in the postwar world of a failed liberal and imperialistic "consensus." We must remember that Richards' immediate "modest" aim was simply to train the newly emergent groups who would be assuming power and responsibility. The university's English school was a way, not of exactly eliminating their differences or of homogenizing them out of existence—although there was much of that attempted—but of assuring that those differences could be controlled by being integrated within an appropriate set of legitimate values. The way to accomplish this was through the disciplinary training in practical criticism. We can say specifically that practical criticism was meant to manage the experience of literature above all, and by closing down the "difference" between literary and other experiences, by insisting on the appropriateness of "literary critical" training to a better understanding and constitution of "life" and "society," it was also meant to manage larger forms of sociocultural and political difference between men and women, various classes, and competing ideologies and nations.

The great failure of this project lies in its textualization of nonliterary reality. In other words, Richards' attempt to close the difference between literary and nonliterary experience had, in fact, the opposite result from what we might think he meant it to have. That is, what we might call "reality" became "literary." The textualization of the nonwritten is not the invention of structuralism or deconstruction.

No matter how "revolutionary" practical criticism may have appeared to its early student practitioners tired of or bored with the dull exhaustion of earlier less rigorous forms of literary study, it is fundamentally conservative, even reactionary. That it is so despite (or because of) Richards' intentions is only further evidence for my contention that he is not an originary subject but a subject function of structures in which he exists and by virtue of which he produces.

Practical criticism is conservative in that it takes its values from the literacy of high culture and hopes to inscribe those values within the new students coming to university. Practical criticism finds its social legitimation in this "educative" function—hence Richards' stress on value, which allows it to carry out certain of the enculturating functions, on a different social level, as the old classical education had done. Practical criticism is conservative also in the way it manages difference: it excludes, includes, and individualizes. It make a hierarchy of the "individuals" it helps to form and judges their value in terms of how well these "students" have internalized the processes and values of practical criticism.

At this point we can see some of practical criticism's affiliations with functionalism.[8] In addition we can see that Richards had no sense of profound social or political change or crisis. His grasp of political issues was usually quite abstract. Like many functionalists, he appears to have felt that the social and cultural order simply needed some modification to be returned to proper working order. Indeed, he acted as if he believed that minor changes were all that were possible or desirable since the alternatives were Bolshevism or other forms of extremism. Practical criticism is an attempt to manage and correct these problems through the agency of cultural institutions. It is also an attempt to institutionalize practical criticism as a "system-regulating" cultural apparatus that would ensure the constant readjustment of the social order whenever it lapsed from its ideal state. It is essential to Richards' position, however, that he cannot acknowledge—if he in fact understood it to be the case—the role of power and politics in the establishment of the institutions he helped promote.

I want to argue that his project failed because it did not and could not—as a humanism—acknowledge its own complicity in power. Instead, it attempted to achieve its political and cultural aims by representing reality as "text" that could be modified, not by the operations of politics and power, but by the reasoned realignment of social misunderstandings made possible by contextualism. Richards effectively effaced culture's and criticism's relations to power and politics. A careful reading of practical criticism and of its American New Critical variant would show that they "textualize" or "poeticize" reality as a strategy for management. That is, practical criticism believes it can be successful if it can establish that reality is like a modernist poem: complex, ambiguous, interrelated, but "orderly" and finaly "static" in its "organic" interrelationships. The poem and reality are both systems whose workings can be understood only on the model of the sublime intellectual's complex sensibility or reading skills. If reality is out of whack, if the system needs to be restabilized, only those whose training in discrimination allows them to understand how the system should work will be able to rebalance it. Quite literally, then, practical criticism is a pedagogy and theory intended for the maintenance and management of the status quo.

Why do I consider this a failure? Because it is a betrayal of criticism to the forces of hegemony? In fact, because it buttresses the hegemony by being an extension of the hegemony's use of the forces and institutions of intellectual and specifically humanistic discourse and practice. No strong oppositional practice can emerge from such a strategy, not only because it "wasn't meant to," or because it was inculcated with the wrong class values, but because it is unaware of its own position in a network of discourses and institutions whose fundamental reality is power and politics—precisely the one reality Richards will not discuss. Indeed, the great success of practical criticism and its academic successors has been to obscure the interrelationships between criticism and power and to inhibit the critical investigations into criticism's own position within the empowered network of knowledge production and its relation to the dominant forces in American culture. Moreover, practical criticism cannot be the ground for an oppositional intellectual practice, because it must trivalize history if it hopes to minimize the importance of change so that it can manage and perhaps even encourage the forgetting of social and gender difference. Essentially, it reduces what might be the complex function of modernist literature to an ahistorical training school for teacher education in cultural management and, in so doing, has a great success: it extends the very social modernity whose bureaucratic scientism and anomie it claims to reject. The desire to modify consciousness to perceive higher values and to discriminate among distorted and clear communications—this training of consciousness, this privileging of the so-called "individualized consciousness" above all is at the very heart of disciplinary subjugation.

The ruling interests cannot be threatened by this textualiza-

tion of reality, because it trivializes critical practice. By remov-
ing history from study and by aiming to reduce social changes
and contradictions to "manageable" problems on the model of
unstable "ambiguities" and "ironies" that can be contained by
a strong contextualized reading, practical criticism cannot
challenge the uneven balance of power in an exploitative society. It inhibits criticism from having a share in such a subversive process. For Richards, social crises are "curable." There is
no antihegemonic or antihumanistic potential in this deployment of criticism's resources. For them to be progressively deployed, their place in the current relations between the
dominant forces in our society and the discourses and institutions that produce and regulate knowledge would first have to
be analyzed and changed.

II

What is at stake in Richards' work is absolutely fundamental:
the proliferation of disciplines and differentiation of knowledge produces a whirlwind of fragmentary images of man, modernity, knowledge, love, and history. Why is this so? Because,
as he sees it, each of the various disciplines that produces its
own knowledge, its own images projected as the results of its
own research, does not contribute to one "synoptic view."
Knowledge is striated because, especially within the human
sciences, each discipline produces it only according to its own
particular semantic rules. To use the pseudo-scientific legalis-
tic rhetoric of Richards we might say that the "truth" produced
by each discipline is only a "law" reflecting the internal syntactical rules of the particular discipline. Richards' aim was to
unify all disciplines on one theory of linguistic practice, on one
universal syntactical and semantic model of referentiality that
would overcome this proliferating differentiation. A unifying
common ground for all knowledge not only would allow one
discipline to communicate with the other—thereby bringing to
a halt the solipsism of the disciplines—but also would ensure
that the knowledge produced by each and all would actually
pertain to a unified reality.

Note that as Richards saw it the postwar proliferation of decision makers brought about the failure of the last socially unified defense against the fragmentation of culture resulting from the burgeoning of knowledge. The unity assured by a culture inculcated with the shared ideology of the Victorian and Edwardian elite no longer endures; it can neither withstand the threat to its own supremacy nor tolerate the world of differentiation and fragmentation, of relevancy and immiscibility, which its collapse leaves exposed. In response to this challenge, Richards develops his theory. His microscopic actions in the field of criticism must be seen macroscopically if they are to reveal their significance. Like other symbolic acts they are overdetermined. They generate their meaning out of their own syntactic laws, but these laws themselves have social effects and emerge from social and discursive pressures. They are, in other words, tactics and functions. Richards' theories and actions insist on their modernity, yet when looked at carefully, we can see that they try once more to resuscitate the image of the dead father.

In his studies of power, *Discipline and Punish* and *The History of Sexuality*, Foucault reminds readers that any concatenation of forces on any level, any particular nexus, has an interest in self-preservation.[9] What can sometimes be deceiving in the history of systems of knowledge is that this self-preservation often takes the form of "reformation," of "re-formation." A given nexus will try to arrest the movement of forces by struggling on the local political level to maintain, legitimatize, and reshape the particular concatenation. This phenomenon appears as repetition (*HS*, 85, 93). This idea is certainly relevant to a reading of Richards. Not only is he immediately indebted intellectually to many writers, some of whom I shall name, and not only is he actively trying to revive the ideology of a society born in the past and dying in his present, but also his practice actually revives some very old phenomena that become essential to his project. For example, the attempt to recentralize authority must be kept in mind when we see Richards reviving the lecture as a pedagogical device in literary study and turning it into a theatrical event, especially in the courses in "practical criticism," where his judging, joking, exciting, articulate presence directs students to a method of self-discipline. In the same way, the origins of bourgeois ideology in the eighteenth century must be recalled when we see that some of the instructive technique of practical criticism methodologically renews the eighteenth century's methods for teaching children how to read.[10]

Because a look at the genealogy of some of Richards' actions and theories suggests that they are large repetitions of fundamental humanistic phenomena, one must be careful to insist that, as originary as Richards' actions are, they are not "original," that is, they in no way mark a complete break with his intellectual or social inheritance; they are rather a curious repetition of it.

Richards is aware of the genealogy of several of his most important notions on language, civilization, and criticism. His acknowledged forefathers range from Plato to Bentham, Coleridge, and Mill, and they include as well G. F. Stout, James Ward, and William James in psychology, along with Sherington on neurology. Among his contemporaries who provide him with a field in which to display his ideas one thinks instantly of Eliot, Ogden, James Wood, Mansfield Forbes, G. E. Moore, Clive Bell, Roger Fry, and others from whose works Richards derives a complete set of counters and weights to align the communicatory and organizing aspects of language.[11]

Yet, truly, the space in which Richards produces his major documents for his immediate and successive audiences exists in a larger frame, in an entire network for gathering and distributing—might one say producing?—positive knowledge on all the subjects related to "man" as an object of knowledge and power that as disciplines form the human sciences. Richards' work emerges only inside this vast network and exists only as a realignment of tropes, figures, and techniques already present in that mesh of forces. Like all producers of positive knowledge his products do not emerge sui generis. What this implies for Richards and the literary criticism that inherits his strength is that this critical activity of analysis, interpretation, and precise description of which we are so proud and in which we are so adept is itself a technology for the *persistent disciplining of society through knowledge about man and his works*. In Richards' case, it is a disciplining that occurs primarily by reducing the ways of enfiguring language and poetry to one recurrent, practical exercise in contextualism in order, as Richards would put it, to "cure" Western man's loss of his willful ability to reharmonize the mental machine that organizes life and experience by judging relevancy according to an accepted norm.

Whereas Richards and his progeny consistently represent themselves as opposed to the division of labor, the fragmentation of man and knowledge, the dominance of will over reason, and the threat to freedom from totalitarianism in politics and ideas, their very procedures, we discover, being no more than a part of the larger disciplinary configuration they so deplore, only naively extend the power of this configuration. We rediscover, in other words, Nietzsche's insight that morality and immorality are reversible. By making available a certain positive knowledge of the nature and experience of literature and the culture that manufactures and sustains it, this criticism trains minds along accepted lines of thought, idealizes certain abstract conceptions of language, and prevents anything else from being done. In other words, by elaborating what seem to be contradictory lines emanating from humanism, Richards helps to disperse into literary, critical, and educational institutions the unacceptable practice—often denounced in theory—of subjugating people to the human sciences and those whose interests they serve.

A full examination of the network of figures and forces with which Richards and modern Anglo-American criticism is affiliated awaits a larger project.[12] Yet one can see in a shadowy and schematic way how Richards realigns certain elements of critical and aesthetic discourse to transform it into a humanistic discipline. His basic strategy for eliminating the "waste" and "chaos" of previously "inefficient" speculations on literature and language is to collapse the distinction both between the aesthetic object and the subject on the one hand and between aesthetic experience and all nonaesthetic experiences on the other hand. This collapse, which he defends at some length in

his utilitarian reconsideration of Coleridge,[13] results from a
series of mediations by positive, largely psychologistic figures
that demonstrate the necessary sensual, perceptive activity of
the subject in constituting the object, as well as from a neo-
Kantian insistence on the role of the imagination in synthesizing the spatiotemporal aspects of "objects" and the "world."

Put more precisely, Richards takes up the central authorized
critical figures of "organism," "subject," and "experience" to
fashion an approach to literature that crosses out what he sees
is its somewhat uncanny uniqueness while saving it as a way to
redeem ourselves:

> The aesthetic mode is generally supposed to be a peculiar way of
> regarding things which can be exercised, whether the resulting experi-
> ences are valuable, dis-valuable or indifferent. . . . What I wish to
> maintain is that there is no such mode. . . . But, [Richards goes on] a
> narrower sense of aesthetics is also found in which it *is* confined to
> experiences of beauty and does imply value. And with regard to this,
> while admitting that such experiences can be distinguished, I shall
> be at pains to show that they are closely similar to many other ex-
> periences, that they differ chiefly in the connection between their
> constituents, and that they are only a further development, a finer
> organization of ordinary experiences, and not in the least a new and
> different kind of thing. (*PLC,* 10)

Those experiences we call "aesthetic" in this acceptable
sense are merely more highly organized, more complex versions of one fundamentally identical kind of human experience. Richards makes this move to displace the aesthetic from
what he claims was its own uniquely uninterpretable realm to
a nexus of "ordinary experiences" in order to bring literature
into the space of analysis, which itself rests on an assumed
supply of shared experiences, what Richards calls a "close natural correspondence between the poet's impulses and possible
impulses in his reader" (*PLC,* 20). Literature can be spoken of;
it is no longer "ineffable." That is to say, once literature joins
the circulation of ordinary experiences it becomes an object of
knowledge that can be "disciplined." No longer an ineffable
experience, the encounter with art can be documented and
explained. In other words, as I read this passage, Richards'
tactic is to bring literature into the realm of commentary as

human science so that it can be established as an effective
material institution to "educate" the minds, bodies, and souls
of its students. I am suggesting that Richards is a function of
the dominant impulses to bring all experience into subjugation
by the powerful, positive institutions of secular humanism.
The fact that it sometimes trains or makes possible its own
opponents does not weaken my point since it is precisely my
claim, as I shall extend it in later chapters, that oppositional
critics exist in this same network. Furthermore, it seems not to
have been Richards' intent to produce his own opposition. His
goal was normalization.

Once it is seen in such a context Richards' thematic focus on
value also appears as primarily a practical instrument for furthering the availability of literature and readers as objects of
investigation. He subdivides the "full critical statement" into
two parts: comment on the "technique" of poetry and comment
on its value as an experience. Only the latter type of remark
can be called "critical." Although Richards would have it that
"value" can be explained psychologically without ethics, politics, or metaphysics, "value" must be seen to have been for
Richards and his heirs simply another discursive tool by which
knowledge can invest in the human being's mind as the object
of investigation most likely to repay interest—and, hence, it is
self-burdened with ethical, political, and metaphysical implications. The "proper critic," Richards contends, is not concerned with a poem "as such," but with its *effect*. This
distinction is what makes possible the surprising remark by the
essentially sympathetic Murray Krieger that Richards' criticism lacks any fully developed theory of the medium of poetry,
language itself.[14] For Richards, all statements about texts are
only ellipses for statements that "such-and-such" objects cause
"such-and-such" experiences, depending on the individual and
other circumstances (*PLC*, 13). Since language is no longer
transparently representational, since it no longer actually designates, it assumes instrumental value as a stopgap and short-
hand substitute for precise statements regarding experience
(*PLC*, 14). And as such an instrument, language can communicate only because the mind itself has evolved through "natural

selection" as an "instrument for communication." Those best suited by evolution are those best able to form an experience for communication; hence, not only Richards' frequent repetition of Shelley's comment that "Poetry is the record of the best and happiest moments of the happiest and best minds," but also his valorization of the critic's judgment of the more successful modes of organization reflected in poetic language (PLC, 17). Hence also Richards' minting of a double-faced coin for critical practice: on one side, there is both the poem to be analyzed as a mode of organization of the impulses of experience and there is the critical interpretation, the protocol to be analyzed; on the other side, both of these are to be judged as evidence of the way the mind—that organizing communicator of experience—can be disciplined and corrected. In all of these claims we see how Richards' discourse depends on and extends a deeply inscribed figure of the sublime, representative, or leading intellectual who, in an ahistorical process of "natural selection," is best able to communicate—that is, to send and receive—and to judge the value and sanity of others' attempts. What could be more "natural" for the "elect" but to educate others in their own best hopes and skills?

Richards' work extends all of these traditional elements of humanism to produce a new phenomenon for investigation: man as reader, as psychic, linguistic storehouse, as an inexhaustible supply of experience and responses to experience to be analyzed and judged. The new factor in the realignment of criticism that precisely makes the latter a human science is the "reader," not as a passive recorder of a communication, not as the subject, who, through reading, relives a romance of mind and imagination, not even as an Arnoldian humanist whose fine sensibility returns over and again to touchstones of high art and good taste, but a "reader" as a data-producing entity, yielding up, however willingly, documents as an end result of its activity, which makes criticism as a discipline possible.

The data produced most directly, in the case of Richards, are, of course, the famous "protocols." The word itself is interesting. Etymologically, the term refers to the first sheet of a papyrus role bearing the date of manufacture; so, it is something like our own copyright page. Even more primitively, it means to glue together, a sense relevant indirectly to Richards' own synoptic desires. Of course, the term has a diplomatic sense in which it means either the agreed upon understanding of a treaty or other text, or it refers to the immediate, first draft of a later text. "Protocol" though also refers to a strict code of etiquette and precedence. Given this much information, one could, if one wished, deconstruct the term and Richards' project.

But the practice the term describes is more interesting than the deconstructive play of the figure. Fundamentally, the protocol is a descendant of religious "confession" from the Middle Ages that was transformed into sex therapy in the nineteenth and twentieth centuries. Not only is "confession" perhaps the finest overall figure for the general process that Foucault describes as modern man forming and altering himself through self-knowledge in the human sciences, but also specifically, the protocol-confession is a perfect emblem for Richards' project in criticism. About the confession, Foucault writes:

> The confession is a ritual of discourse in which the speaking subject is also the subject of the statement; it is also a ritual that unfolds within a power relationship, for one does not confess without the presence (or virtual presence) of a partner who is not simply the interlocutor but the authority who requires the confession, prescribes and appreciates it, and intervenes in order to judge, punish, forgive, console, and reconcile; a ritual in which the truth is corroborated by the obstacles and resistances it has had to surmount in order to be formulated; and finally, a ritual in which the expression alone, independently of its external consequences, produces intrinsic modifications in the person who articulates it. . . . What secrecy it presupposes is not owing to the high price of what it has to say and the small number of those who are worthy of its benefits, but to its obscure familiarity and general baseness. . . . the agency of domination does not reside in the one who speaks (for it is he who is constrained), but in the one who listens and says nothing . . . in the one who questions and is not supposed to know. (HS, 61–62)

The study of literature, according to the principles of close reading or practical criticism, forms the subject. The method produces the being needed by the method for its results to be possible and validated. Without the students to teach, the project fails. At the least, one can say that this modification of the subject that Foucault describes occurs because of the kind of reading methods Richards advocates. It is not the comments on the protocols that affect the students but, as Bradbrook and the others make clear, the guidance that introduces them to the general project. The students, whether their readings are "correct" or not, are trained in forming complex judgments; moreover, they are trained to accept the ideological notion that such judgments and the training they require are "good." No doubt, such training has a reformative influence. Students can be taught, at Cambridge, in the 1920s, to overcome poor personal and cultural habits of reading and writing. They can learn to exclude the personally idiosyncratic; that is, they can learn to make themselves available for correction. The effect of this maneuver, Richards claims, is to guarantee "value," which comes to be established on the basis of the (unequal) bond between teacher and student, between protocolist and reader. Moreover, the student comes to accept the revelation of his intimate relationship to the poem. In its place a new "intimacy" or "consensus" emerges among reader, teacher, other students, other teachers, etc.; that is, through this procedure, which is an operation of power, all who participate directly or indirectly should become part of the sane, general pattern of communication that Richards desires.

At this point, a cogent objection could be made to this reading of Richards. Someone could say: but doesn't this process of normalization you are describing apply only to the bourgeois culture and power? A response would indicate that in some ways Richards *must* first address the bourgeoisie because his project is a recuperative one designed to return the unified age of bourgeois ideology that has been sacrificed by capital in its advanced stage. But perhaps, for now, more to the point, is the idea that what Richards is doing initially is not attempting to subjugate the other in the mold of the classical bourgeois, but rather that he is actively engaged in the defense of the "self." First, a reordering and reaffirmation of the bourgeoisie and then, tactically, the spread of this order and unity to the others, those newly judging millions who so worry Richards in *The Meaning of Meaning*. Also, one must not underestimate the role of pleasure in this story. The bourgeoisie appropriate the pleasure of reading, of extending their own mental and emotional limits, in this new formation of power Richards projects.

In an even more speculative mode, one might argue that the university's adoption of these new techniques of intellectual power and self-gratification mark the turn of capitalism from military to industrial and cultural imperialism. Historically, it coincides with the decline of the British Empire and the reduced importance to the imperialist element of capitalism of those positive sciences Said has identified in *Orientalism*.[15] Certainly, within a given culture, though, it is clear that the expansion of the model Richards develops is an act of first excluding and then including other classes of people whose own most pressing interests and needs might not be adequately addressed by an analysis of the various types of ambiguity in Donne's "Anniversaries." There can be no doubt though that all of these things are in various degrees implicit in Richards' sense of the relation between power and knowledge.

For example, in the introduction to *Practical Criticism* Richards writes:

I have set three aims before me in constructing this book. First, to introduce a new kind of documentation to those who are interested in the contemporary state of culture whether as critics, as philosophers, as teachers, as psychologists, or merely as curious persons. Secondly, to provide a new technique for those who wish to discover for themselves what they think and feel about poetry (and cognate matters) and why they should like or dislike it. Thirdly, to prepare the way for educational methods more efficient than those we use now in developing discrimination and the power to understand what we hear and read. (*PC*, 3)

Although it would seem to some that the documentary technique of explication, the production and feedback of the "protocols," and the measurement and judgment of degrees of justice in the protocol writers' comments are only "natural" teaching devices and neutral instruments in training and evaluation, it is well to remember always that these practices did not exist in the critical study of literature in English departments in universities until Richards introduced them and remember also that no instrument is neutral. Moreover, Richards is quite clear that his technique is not only judgmental but also executive: we are to develop our discriminations; this technique for discrimination should effect change in individuals through education and thereby in culture as a whole. Such desires to improve life by gaining control over nature, consciousness, and will through knowledge—knowledge and the means to produce it; in this context, these are power—is an inheritance from Bacon's humanism and, therefore, should be recognized as a historically bound project whose historicity and ideology gain a certain amount of invisibility and credibility by sharing in a central and perhaps still dominant tradition. It also gains credibility by being one among many technologies of power/knowledge in the post-Renaissance West.

Richards' discursive and nondiscursive practice emerge as equivalent dimensions in the constitution of the critical pedagogical discipline. In both areas he denies the uniqueness of literature by a method that draws the experience of literature into a common, well-illumined space where it becomes available for professional analysis. The configuration of "value," "law," "judgment," "relevance," "sanity," and "health" repeatedly reattaches the experience of literature to all other experiences and repeatedly raises the figure of the reader as proof—if only we would study the reader—of the impossibility of a unique aesthetic experience. Richards offers A. C. Bradley as the finest defender of "poetry for poetry's sake." According to Bradley, the literary experience "'is an end in itself, is worth having on its own account, has an intrinsic value.'" In this view only poetry adequately represents itself and represents nothing besides: "'But its ulterior worth neither is nor can determine its poetic worth as a satisfying imaginative experience; and this is to be judged entirely from within'" (PLC, 56). Poetry, thus, rules itself and remains always immediate to itself; no valuable experience of poetry is ever separable from poetry. Bradley so circumscribes the will in the act of judgment that it can only accept or deny the poem as immediate experience but in no significant way analyze or judge it (the anomaly is, of course, that in his critical practice Bradley does indeed analyze and judge).

Richards' comment on Bradley is both enabled by and directed toward the experience of the reader. He disagrees with Bradley's sense that judgment is imminent to a text: "As a rule we have to come out of it in order to judge it, and we judge it by memory or by other residual effects which we learn to be good indices to its value." Judgment occurs when the mind's experience of the text is mediated not only by memory but also by the already formed "indices" of value, based presumably on past, practiced responses to experiences, which measure, not the poem, but the reader's response. Indeed, Richards perceptively indicates that judgment itself cannot occur in an immanent experience of the text, because judgment is a contextual, cognitive act of the will relying on accumulative repetition: "In . . . judging [a poem], however, its 'place in the great structure of human life' cannot possibly be ignored. The value which it has is dependent upon this, and we cannot judge that value without taking this place, and with it innumerable ulterior worths, into account. It is not that we shall evaluate it wrongly if we neglect them, but that evaluation is just this taking into account of everything, and of the way things hang together" (*PLC*, 57). Thus, the figure of the reader and his repetitive experience of understanding and judging disrupt the aesthetic system in which poetry represents itself, and only itself, to itself and in itself; it is interrupted by making poetic experience available to judgment. Throughout Richards' career the "reader" and its various cognates—student, teacher, translator, cybernetics engineer—all appear in order to extend the range of critical analysis across broader and broader systems of human activity, until it sets itself up as the mediating dialectic of a program of "Universal Studies," and it becomes a measure for all political, cultural, and intellectual method.

Richards' "Principles" and "Practice" of criticism not only make man as reader available for analysis as a means and object of discipline, but also, by pursuing a balanced harmony of experience in perception and communication, they normalize individuals through comparison (see, for example, the comparative evaluations in *Practical Criticism* and *Interpretation in Teaching*), and they do this paradoxically by creating different individuals precisely through comparison and isolation.

That is to say, this technique produces multiple individuals among whom discipline allows us to discriminate so that teachers and students can struggle for identity in sameness. This identity is produced by the practical effect of the authority that judges "sane" and "normal" from "insane" and "unself-conscious" responses, but identity—which is like "sameness"—is produced even more fundamentally by the praxis that incorporates all the individuals within one modality of organization and one set of criteria for judgment. Bradbrook and others at Cambridge and Harvard testify to the embarrassment of having one's protocol selected by Richards at the front of an overly crowded lecture hall as an example of a fault in discrimination, of an error in understanding, or a violation of a necessary awareness of conventions in literature. Foucault, writing of the classical period's educational method for punishing the "shameful class" in French schools, offers a comment that I think both adequately represents the nature of Richards' achievement and suggests another aspect of his genealogy: "The perpetual penalty that traverses all points and supervises every instant in the disciplinary institutions compares, differentiates, hierarchizes, homogenizes, excludes. In short, it *normalizes*. . . ." Foucault, of course, has shown that this power to discipline by means of the norm is part of an ordering extension of disciplinary power: "It is an apparatus that must be coextensive with the entire social body and not only by the external limits that it embraces, but by the minuteness of the details it is concerned with" (*DP*, 213).

If it is not yet clear that Richards' criticism exists within this broadly humanistic pattern of reharmonizing imbalance by discipline, a cento of some of his guiding metaphors might make things clearer:

[Literature] serves . . . as an eminently suitable *bait* for anyone who wishes to trap the current opinions and responses in this middle field for the purpose of examining and comparing them, and with a view to advancing our knowledge of what may be called the natural history of human opinions and feelings . . . . In part then this book is the record of a piece of field work in comparative ideology. But I hope . . . to make some suggestions towards a better control of these tricksy components of our lives. . . . For normal minds are easier to "follow" than diseased

minds, and even more can be learned by adopting the psychologists' attitude to ordinary speech-situations than by studying aberrations. . . .
Our present technique for investigating opinions must be admitted . . .
to be woefully inadequate. Therefore, the second aim of this book is to
improve this technique . . . . When the first dizzy bewilderment has
worn off . . . it is as though we were strolling through and about a
building that hitherto we were only able to see from one or two distant
standpoints . . . . It is as a step towards another training and technique
in discussion that I would best like this book to be regarded . . . .
something like a plan of the ways in which likely ambiguities of any
given term or opinion-formula radiate will make itself apparent. . . .
Ambiguity in fact is systematic . . . . Something comparable to a
"perspective" which will include and enable us to control and place
the rival meanings that bewilder us in discussion and hide our minds
from one another can be worked out. (PC, 6, 7, 9, 10)

Richards metaphorically sums up his representation of criticism: "It follows that criticism itself is very largely, though not
wholly, an exercise in navigation." And he goes on to define
"navigation" as "the art of knowing where we are wherever . . .
we may go" (PC, 11).

This nexus of metaphors of control, system, training, archi-
tecture, and analytic perspective—what Jonathan Arac in his
study of Dickens calls "overview" and Foucault calls "panopticism"—is typical of Richards.[16] It not only makes eminently clear the New Criticism's indebtedness to Richards, and
how he can be called metaphysical and logocentric, but it also
suggests that literary criticism, as training in interpretation
and discourse, is not as innocent a procedure as some would
like to pretend. Richards and his heirs—those who are teachers
and critics of literature and language—produce enormous
amounts of knowledge regarding texts and minds; they certainly announce themselves to be motivated by the highest
ideals and often succeed in defending "reason" and "high cultural values" by training discrimination. Indeed, in "Notes Toward an Agreement Between Literary Criticism and Some of
the Sciences," Richards argues for the high purpose of criticism
against the encroachment upon its area of study by sociology,
psychology, linguistics, and anthropology: "Literary Criticism," he writes, "as guardian Study most widely responsible
for maintaining the art of choice—that exercise of personal

freedom—protests in the name of all the humanities against the attempted usurpation" (*SI*, 12).

The further we follow Richards in his career, the more we see him leaving the realm of literary criticism for pedagogy modeled on the techniques of criticism. And his general project becomes more overtly and totally, as he describes it, "to secure the uniformity which social life requires. . . . to attain maximum satisfaction through coherent systematization . . ." (*PLC*, 42). In effect, from the late forties on Richards elaborates the powerful desires represented by the basic metaphors of his earliest texts. Having gone from a rhetorical insistence on repetition as a tool for training in communication and discrimination to practicing it in "Basic English" and other pedagogical devices, he also repeats his earlier demands for an economic harmony of individuals on not only the personal and societal but also the universal level. Criticism as the means to balance yields to a new avatar of discipline called variously the "synoptic view," "dialectic," or "universal studies." In an important, comparatively late variation on an old theme, Richards suggests that the central result of the synoptic view would be a defense against the "everyday triumphs of methodical comparison [which] are sucking the lifeblood out of everything with which man has endured and endeavoured and protested in the past" (*SI*, 111).

What Nietzsche might call Richards' monumental and antiquarian historicism is not of primary interest here but rather the result and nature of the "synoptic," especially as it articulates the general project of contemporary literary humanists and orients us toward Erich Auerbach's much more profound struggle to deal with the consequences of this totalizing dream: "We would have *authority*: an authority which would have behind it *all* that man knows in *all* his modes of knowing and *all* that he would will to become through *all* his quests for being. [It] could gain our complete consent, could be wholly persuasive, because it would unify us" (*SI*, 112). Richards' dream here is apparently not only for a method to master all other methods but also for a total and closed system of knowledge powerful enough to overcome political, ideological, and intellectual dissemination and differentiation. (What contemporary "humanistic" critics sometimes call "consensus.") It would be inappropriate, and perhaps off the point here, to criticize Richards for believing naively in the efficacy of knowledge and education. Such a criticism of the liberal point of view would be a cliché and would miss the more important aspect of Richards' belief. Might we not, rather, see here, in this statement from *Speculative Instruments*, the fulfillment of the disciplining society's intention? Can we not hear in this a foreshadowing of what Foucault in *Discipline and Punish* calls the "micro-physics" of power? And are we not also compelled to confront the awful uncertainty in the rhetoric of this most redoubtable liberal humanist: shall we admire his illustrious dream which has so many fine forebearers and heirs or shall we doubt the totalitarian potential behind his rhetoric of "authority" and the "all"? Might not the realization of the humanistic dream lead simultaneously to its destruction? Auerbach certainly came to see this destruction was inevitable.

Richards is himself aware of the inherent dangers of the "all" associated with the synoptic; often in his writing he signals that modern man unrhythms his harmony in a wasteful confrontation with variety. Reading and understanding have grown difficult, he feels, because laws for judging the relevancy of data are lacking but can hopefully be made up by criticism. To discipline one's discrimination is, for Richards, to judge relevance, that is, to judge inclusion or exclusion as the fate of a datum or subject. And, of course, "to discriminate" links within itself not only the metaphor of decision and sifting but also the judging by knowledge. What is excluded as irrelevant by a discipline is designated as "criminal"—*discernere* and *cerno* are the same at their roots. Discrimination normalizes not only by homogenizing and categorizing but also by eliminating and excluding those factors that wastefully "unbalance" the "delicate harmony" of the mind and society, as the case may be. Discrimination, then, as Richards teaches it, in a sense creates not only the criminal but also the uncanny and the irrelevant, to be dealt with by either exclusion or incorporation and domestication. In fact, one might say that the uncanny, as that which is "irrelevant," which can *negate* the harmonious balance of the mind and the body politic, is a negativity created by what Richards and others (as we shall see in chapter 5) call "justice" and is designated as the "uncanny" because discipline requires its existence as the defining horizon of its own "field." For Richards, this is preeminently the case in his attack on psychoanalysis and the importance of the unconscious:

Whatever psycho-analysts may aver, mental processes of the poet are not a very profitable field for investigation. They offer far too happy a hunting-ground for uncontrollable conjecture. . . . Very likely, the unconscious processes are more important than the conscious, but even if we knew far more than we do about how the mind works, the attempt to display the inner working of the artist's mind by the evidence of his work alone must be subject to the greatest dangers. . . . The difficulty is that nearly all speculations to what went on in the artist's mind are unverifiable, even more unverifiable than the similar speculations as to the dreamer's mind. (*PLC*, 20–21)

Richards hopes that his recurrent use of metaphors of economy, judgment, will, and immanence will write out of the critical discipline the deferred disruptive psychoanalysis of "truth" because it threatens the critical project: "among all the agents by which 'the widening of the sphere of human sensibility' may be brought about, the arts are the most powerful, since it is through them that men may most cooperate and in these experiences that the mind most easily and with the least interference organizes itself" (*PLC*, 102). To include the "irrelevant" is to suffer from "the law of diminishing returns." The criminal element may be pathogenic, but it is certain that it makes the individual and society "unable to reorganize" and "incapacitated for most of [life's] possible enjoyments" (*PLC*, 39). The Richardsian *good* has always been *the highest good for the highest number*: "That organization which is least wasteful of human possibilities is, in short, the best" (*PLC*, 39).

What this stress on an efficient unitary organization amounts to is such a powerful form of management that it effectively supresses difference: the difference of women and minorities, for example, from the high-cultural norms of white, Anglo-Saxon sublime critics. As we shall see, even Auerbach with his enormous powers of historical analysis and human sympathy found it extremely difficult to admit into his scholarship any real gender or sexual difference. Humanism and its representatives must produce unitary structures since secular humanism exists, as I show in chapter 6, to totalize all human experience within its own categories especially as these have come to serve the interests of those in dominant social and cultural positions. We shall see, for example, that with Kant humanistic intellectuals establish a relationship with given power structures that almost mandates the intellectual management of difference and blocking of democratic self-representation and self-determination. "Practical criticism" is part and parcel of this politically unacceptable process. In Richards' terms, anything that is different is "uncanny," "unbalanced," and "wasteful." Unfortunately, such claims implicate practical criticism as forms of sexism and racism.

For example, the social and cultural political equivalent of the exclusion of the "uncanny" as a means toward a just society reveals how ethnocentric Richards' rhetoric is and how, as Edward W. Said might put it, he is inscribed within an imperialist culture and is, unwittingly, a weapon of that culture.[17] For Richards finds the collapse of will and standards in Western culture can be at least partially accounted for by the unsettling of our stable, unified tradition by a barbarically prolific set of other cultures, rhetorics, and political realities. It is interesting, in the following quotation, to see both just how abstract Richards' grasp of the historical event he is describing truly is, as well as how powerful the "language," "discipline," "stability" network of figures remains:

Possibly, even probably, the difficulties of reading justly are increasing. Within a well-defined tradition the items and the patterns they enter are fewer and clearer than amid *the frothy emulsion of hitherto immiscible cultures* in which today we live and move and aspire to win some being. Our novel acquaintanceship with the untraditional past and with oddities of thought and feeling from other cultures is unrhythming, it may be, the heart of our mental and moral security. (*SI*, 101; my emphasis)

Richards' entire career, up to and including his powerful book on the Greeks, the Bible, and Dante, entitled simply

Beyond,[18] has been an attempt to initiate a counterpractice that would prevent this unrhythming. I hope that what we have seen to this point suggests why his strategies are unacceptable.

Moreover we should see that Richards, while the initiator of a discourse, is not himself an origin. It is important to recognize that his work is an elaboration of both trends in humanism and that, as such, it is contradictory, self-sustaining, and often repressive. Indeed, no matter how "benevolent" or "well-intentioned" a figure like Richards might be, the most important caution a critic can adopt is to examine his position within discourses and institutions that in very large part delimit and enable his work—which is, in these terms, a means of extending and redirecting formations of power in culture. Foucault is the theoretician of all this, especially in his essay, "What Is an Author?".

An artist, for example, can be a founder of a line or tradition if something the artist does is modified—even in as complex a way as Harold Bloom shows occurs in the interrelationships between poets.[19] A scientist, however, no matter how great his discovery, no matter how effective that discovery might be in displacing or modifying previous knowledge—the relation between Einstein and Newton is a perfect example here—sees that his "founding act is on an equal footing with its future transformations. . . . In other words, the founding act of a science can always be rechanneled through the machinery of transformations it has instituted."[20] Yet the initiators of a discursive practice, such as political economy, psychoanalysis, and literary criticism, take on the status of origins inside the discourse they have founded. That is to say, even though the great originator cannot predict or prevent the future often heterogeneous transformations of the discourse that will occur— such as Marx's transformation of Smith and Ricardo—nonetheless he remains the designated source inside the discourse to which all returns must be made. Yet even here Foucault finds (somewhat paradoxically from any traditional point of view on origins and authorities) that the initiator of a discourse functions as origin precisely because of a fundamental lack, absence, or omission in the discourse that is actually constructive precisely because it is not correctable. "In effect," Foucault writes, "the act of initiation is such, in its essence, that it is inevitably subjected to its own distortions, that which displays this act and derives from it is, at the same time, the root of its divergences and travesties."[21] This omission is not supplementable, because it does not arise from outside but rather from inside the discourse, and while it is true that it can be regulated, especially in an act of return, its peculiarity consists precisely in the way in which it is itself the original and its later transformations.

Genealogically this means that the heirs of Richards and the practical institutionalization of secular humanism are unavoidably inscribed within its figures and must return to them even in an attempt to revise or escape them. As we shall see, we can try to do only two things: carry out as progressive a deployment of its resources as possible and hope as well to develop whatever antihumanistic gestures we can discover about us. Essentially, though, this genealogy must be continually analyzed and critiqued because it implicates all of us.

What I would like to suggest briefly is this: modern Anglo-American criticism, at least in one of its major articulations, is from its origin contradictory, bound up with and a servant to forces it doesn't understand, doomed often to replicate the "enemy" it attacks. In fact, it has effectively coopted critical activity into a network of power and an economy of discipline. Until very recently the tradition of Anglo-American criticism has been defined by Richards and others like Empson, Wimsatt, and Bradbrook who, even in their disagreements with Richards, nonetheless operate within the space opened largely by his work. This is important precisely because these critics have been as much as anyone models of critical accomplishment, admired for their erudition, dedication, and brilliant analytic and theoretical contributions to scholarship.

While it is true that the influence of this group and tradition has begun to decline recently with the coming of poststructuralism and psychoanalysis into criticism, attention to Richards' work is not merely a matter of historical interest. His tradition is still powerful and it remains true that it defines the space into which the more recent critical procedures have entered in the United States. And this tradition will have some effect on how these procedures are shaped, used, and perhaps even distorted to "fit" the Anglo-American scene.[22] In other words, this tradition of criticism and pedagogy partially explicated here in the figure of Richards is a powerful tool in the hands of those whose interests it embodies; it can inhibit countervailing work. Richards is like other humanists in being blind to the dependency of the authority of "reason" and "man" on specific configurations of power. As John Fekete reminds us, Richards' criticism is a capitalist bourgeois reification of literature and culture—and he is absolutely correct.[23] One can see this in the way, Richards, offering his synoptic view to mediate diplomatically between East and West does so, very naively, and at the height of the Cold War, on the basis of a liberal humanism and in the name of "democratic pluralism." Unfortunately, Richards' blindness is not just his own nor is it merely political in a narrow, partisan sense. Rather it stands as the perfect emblem of the divergences and travesties of the desires of modern criticism that has made possible its going on.

Very briefly, I have wanted to say not only that Richards' strategy to reestablish the harmonious world of liberal bourgeois humanism at the very moment when advanced Western capitalistic societies were destroying that ideologically comfortable and illusory social order fails, as it must, since literary criticism cannot reverse history, but also that it actually has become part of the disciplining machine of that advanced capitalist society. The effect of the institution of criticism, as Richards found it, and we perpetuate it, is to individualize persons by measuring them against a series of norms. In its attempts to suppress difference it tries to prevent people from seizing their own destiny; that is, humanistic criticism does not help people, as John Brenkman puts it, "to claim the articulation of their own demands and requests."[24] We and our institutions hinder "others" and "ourselves" in attempting to articulate a concrete reaction against the hegemonic discourse and practice of Western disciplining capitalism.

Always already coopted by the discipline that claims them, they are—we are—to various degrees instruments of the absorption, exclusion, and impersonal power of the disciplines. In the name of justice—claiming Plato as an ancestor—and of humanity—invoking Bacon—we train in order to control and be controlled; we disguise power with ideals, and we remain only instruments of a history we rarely try to question or to understand.

3

The Last of the Latecomers:
The Critical Syntheses of Erich Auerbach

Although contemporary literary critics and theorists write a great deal about Auerbach, often under his influence, and always admiring his achievement, they give surprisingly little attention to the cultural and political roots of his work. This lack of attention is rather ironic given Auerbach's emphasis on historical research and the historical disposition of most of his ablest admirers.[1] In fact, as far as I know, none of Auerbach's commentators gives much attention to the influence of early twentieth-century German intellectual and cultural discourse on his work. Others matters concern his critics. They often emphasize Auerbach's tragic exile in Turkey and his later emigration to the United States, in order to give pathos to their account of his achievements. I suggest that we might better appreciate Auerbach's project of writing "a synthetic history-from-within" (PW, 12) if we consider it, at least in part, within its own academic cultural context. In so doing, we might better understand why theorists admire certain aspects of Auerbach's work, and we might also better judge the continuing value of the type of critical intellectual he represents.

In addition and from a different perspective, it might be possible to write a substantial critical history of postwar American criticism by studying the responses to Auerbach's work. In essence, such a dual project would have to be a tale of two cultures, of the one that shaped Auerbach's project and of the

other that welcomed and made it exemplary. Also, it might not
be difficult to show that for a long time, the second culture, at
least as reflected in the writings of some of its ablest critics,
often not only misunderstood basic things about Auerbach's
project but also disapproved of it. Above all, we would see that
American critics have too little investigated the conditions for
Auerbach's production, except in the most abstract terms concerning historism, philology, or relativism. The reasons for this
omission might themselves be suggestive. It seems that until
quite recently many of our leading critics perceived Auerbach's
interests, goals, and procedures as in general so admirable, so
magisterial, and so resonant—providing them with so many
useful theoretical and critical insights and methods—that
Auerbach became an unexamined representative of our own
institution.

In order to begin to write a critical history of our own recent
critical past, it might be useful to test the following hypothesis
to see what it may reveal about critical practice and critical
authority: let us say that Auerbach occupies a place in the
critical academy that both makes possible certain critical operations and legitimates certain critical values while, at the
same time and for the same reason, his institutional position
restricts our investigation into his, and so our own, critical,
intellectual, academic, and political past.

Two results might be hoped for from testing this hypothesis:
first, we might gain some further insight into how the academic critical institution establishes, preserves, and dissemi-
nates authority; and, second, we might glimpse some of the
desires, needs, values, and interests that, in part, motivate and
are reflected by the professional process of establishing Auerbach's institutional authority. Such results might tell us something about ourselves, our practice, and our institution.

Auerbach is representative for those American critics and
students of literature who believe in the enduring cultural importance, not just of literature, but of critical, humanistic
scholarship in an age of need. Auerbach functions as a fantas-
tic resource for American critics and theorists; his primary
function is not as a philological model but as a sign that in an

antihistorical, antihumanistic age of relativism, mass-cultural leveling, and the increasing irrelevance of writers and critics, it is not only possible for critics to perform opportune and important acts, to construct monumental synthetic texts in the face of massive specialization, to invent new techniques for dealing with changed cultural conditions, and to do all this out of the unique intellectual and existential experience of the individual scholar, but also, in so doing, to relegitimate cultur-ally a certain image of the responsible and responsive au-thoritative critical voice.

Since I cannot confront all these issues, I focus my discussion on the key term "synthesis" in Auerbach and in some few of his forebears and heirs. Following Auerbach's own methodological recommendations, I hope that a discussion of this term will lead to a consideration of some of the needs, interests, and structures of our critical institution. Although I attempt to mark the limits of the figure of the critical intellectual legiti-mated by Auerbach, himself, and by our American appropria-tion of him, I do not mean to be at all dismissive or unsym-pathetic; on the contrary, Auerbach's work reminds us of the moral stature of humanistic scholarship in an age of crisis, and his specific scholarly achievements make possible some of the most important, historically aware critical activity in the con-temporary academy. I also hope it is clear that my partial invo-cation of a less than flattering political context at the origins of Auerbach's work is not derogatory, not is it meant to imply, in any way, that his work is determined by external events. What is at issue here is a certain mode of recent (and perhaps still current) critical practice that, by its very achievement—along with changes in social reality and ways of thinking about intel-lectual practice—helped to problematize itself.

II

"Synthesis" plays a central role in Auerbach's work. Not only *Mimesis*, but "Philology and *Weltliteratur*," as well as the methodological introduction to *Literary Language and Its Pub-lic in Late Latin Antiquity and in the Middle Ages*, argue that modern scholarly work is excessively specialized and that some new mode of synthetic thinking and writing must be developed to prevent hermetic sterility. Dante, Balzac, Zola—all the heroes of *Mimesis*—attempt synthetic projects.

Auerbach might be asked several questions about this key element of his thinking: for example, what is "synthesis" in theory and practice; how does this term come to be central to his thought; to what extent is his own work a successful synthesis; how does he recommend syntheses should be achieved; and why are they valuable? We might also ask how American literary critics receive his ideas about "synthesis;" what contribution these ideas and their reception make to Auerbach's position; and what the legacy of these ideas is to contemporary critics and theoreticians.

The method of testing this hypothesis or offering tentative answers to these difficult questions should not be abstract or ahistorical. The figure of "synthesis" and its variants such as "unity," "wholeness," and "individuality" have force as a result of being part of the specific political and cultural struggles of Weimar, a force in part appropriated, distorted, and redeployed by the equally specific institutional structure of American literary study. This force derives from the inscription and deployment of these key terms and, *mutatis mutandi*, the weight of their traditional value, within discursive political systems that form one of the many important battlegrounds of cultural change and social struggle. Consequently, to avoid any mystified idealization, which ascribes weight to these terms "in themselves," that is to say, as "subjects," rather than as "predicates" of human activity, the structure of desire, interest, and power organizing (and organized by) the discourses circumscribing these terms must be outlined in part.

There are at least three crucial elements: first, Auerbach's textual representation of his work, his intellectual ideal, and his goals and values; second, the way in which the Weimer professoriat, of which Auerbach is part, deploy the discourses of the *Geisteswissenschaften* and their remaining authority to relegitimate their own position within modern culture; and, third, how the American academy appropriates Auerbach, his

work, and the authority of his discursive tradition, transforming them in the process to legitimate the institutional structure
of literary criticism. Such a recontextualization of Auerbach
evinces the implication of intellectual discourse and practice
within a network of interest and power and suggests that scholarly authority often depends on irrational social, institutional,
and discursive configurations of power and will.

Attempting to outline the implications of the Weimar professoriat's class interests in discursive and social authority or
the power mechanisms of the American profession's institutionalized desire for legitimacy and strategies for reproduction
does not involve describing the totality of economic and social
forces of the two different cultural moments that Auerbach
links. Indeed, since the work of Lukacs and other leading theoreticians of the totality is intertwined in the complex genealogy of Weimar, social struggle, and the professionalization of
critical practice, it would be inconsistent to adopt a theoretical model of the totality without first, as it were, describing
how it might be implicated in the very power structures under
consideration. That is, theories of the totality and accompany-
ing notions of mediation might inhibit insight into the specif-
icities of the literary critical practices under study (by seeing
them as only a small part of a larger whole). Moreover, since
they are part of the object under investigation (insofar as they
are elements of the Weimar struggle and the academic professions), deploying them might needlessly distort the attempt to
understand some of the tactics and forms of power and desire in
the institution of criticism. Furthermore, to the degree that
theories of the totality are taken up by "oppositional" intellectuals when their place in the genealogy of power structures
has not been first understood, these intellectuals run the risk
of being part of political operations of power of which they
disapprove.

It is not yet clear to what extent the adoption of an "oppositional" ideology and practice *within* the discursive and
institutional confines of academic critical study "makes a difference," that is, is likely to bring about changes in the structures of power and authority or their mechanisms for reproduc-

tion. While differing practices do *make* a difference, the limits of power, interest, reward, and desire within the profession—in which *all* practitioners must survive (or thrive)—narrowly circumscribe their effects on the profession. Theories of the totality imply a perspective detached from such narrow institutional constraints, yet to the degree the institution and its genealogical burden circumscribe them as well (and I realize I am, in part, begging the question), the more insistent becomes the need to describe some of the mechanisms of the profession and its transformative genealogy, to suggest how they make possible and restrict both the orthodox and the oppositional projects of our recent past.

Auerbach's concern with his own "recent past" underlies the final chapter of *Mimesis*, an important essay for understanding Auerbach and neglected for too long because of his commentators' easily understood fascination with his brilliant studies of earlier eras. In "The Brown Stocking," Auerbach analyses the fictional techniques and goals of modern realists like Woolf, Proust, and Joyce to dramatize what he sees as their shared cultural crisis and to suggest the similarities of his philological solutions to this crisis with their fictional ones:

> the great exterior turning points and blows of fate are granted less importance [than in 19th century French realism]; they are credited with less power of yielding decisive information concerning the subject; on the other hand there is confidence that in any random fragment plucked from the course of life at any time the *totality of its fate* is contained and can be portrayed. There is greater confidence in *syntheses* gained through full exploitation of an everyday occurrence than in a chronologically well-ordered total treatment which accompanies the subject from beginning to end, attempts not to omit anything externally important, and emphasizes the great turning points of destiny. (*M*, 547–48; my emphasis)

Auerbach insists again and again that the problem of modernity is not simply that synthetic value-laden world-views break down but also that the carefully cultivated humane European impulse to produce them—from Dante to Zola—especially in inclusive, chronological, scholarly, and literary narratives, flounders in an age of too much information, too much specialization, too much change, and too little ambition to

produce stable syntheses. Auerbach's response to these problems is to abandon standard philological methods of exhaustive
research in order to free himself from the burden of excessive
knowledge—while, of course, in Turkey denied access to it—so
that he might begin to accommodate himself and his valued
discipline to modern conditions:

It is possible to compare this technique of modern writers with that of
certain modern philologists who hold that the interpretation of a few
passages in *Hamlet*, *Phèdre*, or *Faust* can be made to yield more, and
more decisive, information about Shakespeare, Racine, or Goethe and
their times than would a systematic and chronological treatment of
their lives and works. Indeed, the present book may be cited as an
illustration. (*M*, 548)

Auerbach remains committed to the need for synthetic
knowledge and, above all, to the need for new techniques to
produce it. He has a strong sense of the modernity of his project
and, prefiguring many of his critics, of the "fictional" status of
Mimesis.[2] The basic similarity between modern writers and
modern philologists (other than Auerbach, only Spitzer readily
comes to mind as an example) is "the consideration that it is a
hopeless venture to try to be really complete within the total
exterior continuum and yet to make what is essential stand
out" (*M*, 548). Rather than be "swamped" by his material,
Auerbach proposes a certain musical method. If he could have
employed traditional research methods, the results would have
been indirectly proportional to the effort: "the *motifs* which
direct my investigation, *and for the sake of which it is written*,
would have been completely buried under a mass of factual
information which has long been known and can easily be
looked up in reference books" (*M*, 548; my emphasis).

Whereas Auerbach's lament suggests how the very weight of
culture can be an inhibition to writing,[3] it is also a specific sign
of his reaction against the progressive professionalization and
specialization of the *Geisteswissenschaften* and of the consequent loss of authority that they and their practitioners suffer
in their struggle with unjust states, capitalists, communists,
and forceful irrational ideologues for legitimacy and leadership, especially in Weimar, but throughout the modern world.

One purpose of the method he adopted in reaction is to let "what is essential stand out," to let *Mimesis'* motifs, "for the sake of which it is written," appear clearly. Auerbach touches on a problem that remains crucial for us: modern professional scholarship obstructs and obscures synthetic visions and threatens to deauthorize, perhaps even to silence, the voices of those few who are still capable of inventing syntheses to illuminate our past and so make it our legitimate inheritance. Auerbach's reflections suggest how professionalized production often establishes protocols for its own existence that hope to deny any authority or effect to synthetic intellectual production and so hasten the cultural amnesia and fragmentation of modernity. This professionalization further undermines the cultural, moral, and political leadership of the "synthetic" intellectuals who, in an age of their own cultural and ideological hegemony, deploy the *Geisteswissenschaften* both as signs and means of maintaining their authority, especially vis-à-vis the state. Auerbach, and many other Weimar humanists, resist specialization, which they see as the cause of their loss of leadership, in other words, of their growing impotence in the face of alternate claims to authority within the society. Excessive specialization in professionalized production, for Auerbach, is the exact material, intellectual, and institutional equivalent of the somewhat less definite spiritual and cultural disorder of modernity.

Auerbach's attempt to derive authority from modern writing's use of certain musical techniques and from its position as heir to the development of realism in the West is a political act designed to make syntheses possible once more, to prevent the anomie and irrationalism of cultural fragmentation, and to establish the cultural leadership of the new "synthesizers," the elite, modern humanistic intellectuals. Auerbach seems affected by an illusion common among Weimar intellectuals that innovations in the humanities might vitiate the loss of their authority. At the end of *Mimesis*, Auerbach sadly portrays the illusory nature of this belief, as well as some of its consequences. Nonetheless, the Weimar dream to relegitimate the humanists' leading role motivates in part his vision of "modernistic" synthesis.

The works of the modernists become a resource for Auerbach because, as he sees it, they both begin from a common awareness of the impossibility and undesirability of producing totalizing syntheses of the kind created by Dante and Zola or dreamt of by philologists and philosophers and they realize the need to use whatever reduced synthetic possibilities modernism makes available to comprehend a world of overly abundant experience. Whereas the modern writers' materials are the rush of contemporary experience, those of the philologist are the equally overwhelming plentitudes of history-as-text. Having abandoned all encyclopedic ambitions, modernists try to report on a few events or moments "with reasonable completeness." The model for such reporting is that "order and interpretation of life which arise from life itself." This model first appears in *Mimesis* as the highly individualistic attempt of each person to order his or her life as a unity, "with the result," as Auerbach contends, "that our lives appear in our own conception as total entities—which to be sure are always changing, more or less radically, more or less rapidly, depending on the extent to which we are obliged, inclined, and able to assimilate the onrush of new experience" (*M*, 549).

Auerbach not only contends that modern fiction and scholarship firmly root interpretive processes in individual attempts to make experience cohere but also wants to claim that individual idiosyncrasies need not unduly affect the truth claims that are the outcome of such processes. For Auerbach, the process of self-making is universal and so, whereas the fictional and scholarly methods grounded in this process depend on the talents and strengths of the individual, their results are in no way "merely subjective" or without truth value. The "fictional" nature of these methods does not deny them power to produce knowledge:

As opposed to this [traditional philological method] I see the possibility of success and profit in a method which consists in letting myself be guided by a few motifs which I have worked out gradually and without a specific purpose, and in trying them out on a series of texts which have become familiar and vital to me in the course of my philological activity; for I am convinced that these basic motifs in the history of the representation of reality—provided I have seen them correctly—must be demonstrable in any random realistic text. (M, 548)

This method is fully analogous to the universal process of self-making and of self-comprehension that Auerbach postulates: texts (or experience) come to him, presenting evidence of some repetitive or analogous patterns (motifs) that are at first seemingly undirected; he reflects upon and clarifies them and then tests them to see which elements of texts (or experience) they will illuminate and unify. On this model, the interpretative devices, the motifs, emerge from the material they allow the self to organize. For this reason, Auerbach implies, if the critic perceives the patterns correctly, then the illuminating and illuminated order is not simply a function of a "reader's" will; rather it is a function of the "conjugal" relation of the material (which, paradoxically, by virtue of its self-presenting, mediating motifs, now becomes immanent) and of the predisposed, tactful perception of the reader.

Since these basic motifs, produced in this conjunction, are, in part, a function of the trained but historical subject and scholar, they cannot be and are not offered as "objective" or "scientific" totalizing mechanisms. Rather, Auerbachian synthesis is historical and perspectival since the "tempo" of the twentieth century is such "that synthetic and objective attempts at interpretation are produced and demolished every instant." Indeed, even this process is so rapid it "could not be surveyed as a whole" (M, 549). In scholarship and fiction, the modernist response to this tempo is to devise methods to reflect "multiple consciousness." The techniques of To the Lighthouse should be those of modern philology as well: to represent "not one order and one interpretation, but many, which may either be those of different persons or of the same person at different times." This technique results in "a synthesized cosmic view" that is "at least a challenge to the reader's will to interpretive synthesis" (M, 549).[4]

Auerbach's methodological response to modernity (and, as he sees it, that of his "affiliated" realists) is a development of the perspectivist tendencies of his historicist training and commitments. This is clear in the way he enfigures and authorizes his own position: as a modern, the modernist perspective on history he provides in *Mimesis* must be seen as emerging from his period's dominant "forces" and needs; in other words, as Auerbach presents *Mimesis* to us it is itself a historical work, elucidating the main historical forces of modernity while also exemplifying and gaining authority from them. As a modern philological text, *Mimesis* coalesces with those epoch-making "forces" and "tendencies" that appear in and define the period's realism, that is, its ability to produce a new sort of synthetic knowledge and value. Since these "forces" and "tendencies" alone define the synthetic possibilities of the modern period, *Mimesis* not only gains authority by revealing them to us but also gains persuasive power by showing us it shares self-consciously in them, that is, by strategically deploying the "forces" it discovers in its own behalf. And, of course, success in this project is the highest guarantee not only of *Mimesis'* truths but also of its own exemplary value. The open, tactful, and learned critic hears, tests, and validates the only motifs for producing synthetic knowledge and value the modern age provides. (And in the process, he substitutes persuasion for reason.)

Mimesis must be read, then, as an engaged history of the present meant to intervene authoritatively in modernity: organizing past representations of realism genealogically it hopes to make sense of the present as an heir of predecessors whose genetic continuity with the present is outlined historiographically by the very motifs perceived and tested by Auerbach, the modern perspectivist. In the process, Auerbach accomplishes three necessarily intertwined objectives: first, he demonstrates that, beginning with the meager resources of modernity, historical and cultural synthesis is possible; second, as a result, he provides an alternative to sterile, fragmenting specialization by revealing in his own synthetic work the residual possibilities to be found in the epoch-making forces of modernity for constructing unifying perspectives on history and modernity; third, and unavoidably, that is, as both a condition and consequence of the first and second, he gains authority for his own supremely informed and efficacious ideal of intellectual work. The repetitive analogies that proliferate in Auerbach's discussion support this claim. Just as the modern realist organizes from his or her perspective the fragments of already partially ordered consciousness according to whichever motifs suggest a unity both between and among the fragments and also their own integral realities, so the modern philologist, dealing with texts that, in and by virtue of their periods, already have, as it were, their own concept of reality, discovers overarching, synthetic motifs that, emerging from the present, not only tell his history but also say something about its own defining modern forces and tendencies.

Not surprisingly, then, given both the history Auerbach tells and the stylistic analyses of Woolf he carries out, the modernist synthetic methods and models appear as essentially individualistic and, likewise, their practitioners appear as anxious about and in pursuit of their own authority. Auerbach opens this part of his discussion by noting what he calls "a transfer of confidence" wherein, for modernists, great external events, such as war and revolution, reveal very little about the reality of the subject. In discussing Zola, for example, he contends that it is impossible to understand *Germinal* apart from class war but that World War I is not immediately relevant to an understanding of *To the Lighthouse*. Auerbach postulates this privatistic modernist ascesis throughout his discussion of his own method; yet, as he himself acknowledges, the great forces of industrial and social modernization unavoidably not only modify philology and the place of European culture in world history but also may even destroy them. How, then, from Auerbach's perspective, can these reduced and privatized methods based on individualistic values and reality hope to comprehend and effect world history?

One answer to this question lies on the very surface of Auerbach's texts. By virtue of having written this perspectival history of the present cultural crisis, and, indeed, as a condition of its production, he not only understands but also represents the shifting cultural forces between periods that bring about the modernist ascetic mode of individualistic synthesis. As a modernist, he both exploits these techniques as the condition for synthetic, antiprofessional work of any kind and experiences and reflects upon their limits and consequences. His modernistic pessimism means not only that Western culture and *"Weltliteratur"* will end in an indiscriminate mass leveling but also that, as he sees it, uniquely placed at the end of Western history and armed with the period's only effective synthesizing devices, he and other masters of Western culture who understand its crisis will alone be able to write even these perspectival interpretative synthetic histories. Auerbach evinces for us the belief that, in a transitional social moment, these histories may have an effect on cultural practice.

By recalling the diversity of national literatures and the variety of human experience it contains, Auerbach hopes to maintain contact with a rich tradition of individual responsibility for both self- and culture-making that defines for him the post-Dante West.[5] As a humanist, Auerbach believes in the educational efficacy of past cultural models as a reservoir of types of human behavior, but, above all, he believes that the humanistic project in which humans take on the burden of their own fate and the defense of their own values is historical, fragile, and endangered. It is testimony to his faith in literature and humanistic criticism that he feels their (perhaps too belated) preservation can make some difference to the postwar crises of superpower rivalry and global modernization. Not incidentally, this response to what is, for Auerbach, little less than a modern eschaton uniquely positions a certain elite group of academic humanistic intellectuals as the last reservoir of value, knowledge, mastery, and method in this moment of terrible crisis. One cannot, I suppose, disagree with the realism of Auerbach's contentions. Indeed, the number of those capable of such synthetic procedures dwindles down to a very precious few.[6]

But even for this few, the "authority" of their syntheses becomes inescapably an issue by virtue of the very method that makes them possible. Indeed, the problematic authority of such syntheses is a subissue of the problem of radical relativism implicit in historism, and as such, it must be solved or the strategy in which intellectuals deploy it will fail. Historism cannot ground the elite intellectuals' claims to legitimacy if its pledge to produce even "perspectival" truths founders on the appearances of subjectivism, willfulness, and irreconcilable relativism. Historism should, after all, as Auerbach and others hope, overcome the fragmentation and anomie typical of modernity and recenter authority in those intellectuals who see the necessity for a unified culture and try to produce it.

In *Mimesis*, Auerbach essentially accepts Friedrich Meinecke's arguments defending historism's claims to truth.[7] He agrees with Meinecke that the close study of culture discloses not only what is absolutely unique and individual to each period but also what are the most profound, concrete, and "universally valid" of history's epochal "inner forces." In other words, underlying all change for these German historists, but visible only in particular appearances, is the rational meaning of history.[8] This perception leads to an understanding of the historical nature of the present and to a desire to understand its "depths and inner structure" by studying "their origins and . . . the direction taken by their development" (*M*, 444).

But how can historists assume that procedures employed in such study are not willful and so distorted or accidental? Auerbach's attempt to ground the results of such research involves two moves: first, like Meinecke, he takes the position that it is possible to *intuit* the universally valid but *partial expression* of values and truth in each period and in the "genetic" development of history (*M*, 446); second, like the modern realist he postulates, Auerbach asserts he will not "impose upon life . . . an order which it does not possess in itself" (*M*, 548); that is, as suggested above, the ordering principles or motifs must emerge from the inner forces and materials that present themselves to the author as interpretative devices. Yet *Mimesis* also reflects Auerbach's concern that, given the modern loss of a Goethean belief in absolute values that had, as Meinecke argues, grounded historism, these partial syntheses might appear will-

ful, relativistic, or idiosyncratic. They might have no legitimate authority and find no acceptance as partial but accurate
and self-revealing perspectives on history and the truth. But, to
elaborate further on what I have already suggested, Auerbach
finds in the historical necessity of modern methods, and their
results, sad confirmation of their validity. In the process of
recording modern life, Auerbach writes:

something new and elemental appeared: nothing less than the wealth
of reality and depth of life in every moment to which we surrender
ourselves without prejudice. To be sure, what happens in that moment—be it outer or inner processes—concerns in a very personal way
the individuals who live in it, but is also (and for that very reason)
concerns the elementary things which men have in common. It is precisely the random moment which is relatively independent of the controversial and unstable orders over which men fight and despair; it
passes unaffected by them, as daily life. The more it is exploited, the
more the elementary things which our lives have in common come to
light. (M, 552)

This is an extremely powerful and moving expression of the
humanistic vision of universal humanity: modern writing
grounds human value in the commonalities of everyday life.
This view appears to be a recasting of the Vichian insight that
man makes history and society and himself in it and so can
understand not only them but also himself as their maker.
Within his generally pessimistic view of the possibilities for
Western humanism, Auerbach evinces for a moment the hope
that the daily world of private and public ordinary experience
can provide, even in a massified society, a ground for humanistic values and a realm of individual responsibility and authority. In the gently limned figure of a quotidian world, Auerbach
approaches the beliefs of other modern theorists who, like Max
Horkheimer, find and try to support whatever elements of human existence remain outside the reach of any all-embracing
state ideology: Hitlerism, Soviet dogmatism, or New Deal neo-
capitalism. For Auerbach, however, this positive possibility for
human liberation is ontological, not social; it is the timeless
ground of common human experience throughout history that
provides the substratum of value and meaning that ultimately

authorizes his ability to perceive partial truths mediated by immanent motifs and genetic research. Yet, even so, one must recall that for Auerbach this modern achievement is itself an ascesis or an alienation of the public sphere from world history. This ascesis means that all fictional and scholarly approaches to and representations of reality must be, in the modern world, a function of a subject's openness to and struggle for knowledge and truth.

For this reason, among others, the relativistic legacy of historism, which often saps its authority, is not so easily overcome. The comparative optimism of this position cannot survive its own consequences. Auerbach must sadly admit that the truth of the present moment is that this ontological commonality of men is being collectivized:

In this unprejudiced and exploratory type of representation we cannot but see to what an extent—below the surface conflicts—the differences between men's way's of life, and forms of thought have already lessened. . . . Beneath the conflicts, and also through them, an economic and cultural leveling process is taking place. (M, 552)

At this point in the text and the history it tells the project of *Mimesis* is nearly complete. Having earned its authority by discovering what lies beneath the surface of the modern period by applying its realistic motifs, it shows itself to be inseparably a part of the very process it describes. By having continually probed how the mixture of styles makes possible the increasing seriousness of Western representations of everyday reality, by having insisted on the development of Western history as a series of discoveries (in response to external events) of methods for progressively disclosing the reality of ordinary experience, and by having adopted a powerful variant of the modern realism that culminates the genetic process he studies, Auerbach appears within his own text and its "history" as a contributor to this leveling process despite his own contrary intention to preserve the memory of cultural and human diversity. Of course, on many levels, Auerbach's project is successful; because of him, for example, we can see Dante as other than, but yet also as part of, ourselves and our own human experience. In other words, Auerbach tries to make us aware of our cultural position and shared human nature by reconstructing both our canon and our history, which has brought us to this situation.

In a very real way, he is uniquely placed. Unlike a formalist or deconstructor for whom the historical variety and specificity of texts are less important than their "rhetoricity"—these would be examples for Auerbach of (perhaps) unconscious levelers—Auerbach is still ideologically committed to the idea that historical diversity is the realm of meaning and that humane life requires the transformation of knowledge about the past into lived experience (*Erlebnis*) of the West's ability to record and transmit its own historically achieved potential to humanize its civilization in the daily task of making culture. Yet, as a historically aware modern, Auerbach realizes he is only in a very limited way able to bring about this transformation. The devices he must employ (what others are available?) are themselves modernist and, so, ironically, as likely to aid in the leveling of human life as to recall its diversity. In "The Brown Stocking" chapter of *Mimesis*, Auerbach says of Woolf, who often is his own mirror image, something that should be said, despite its antifeminist rhetoric, of the atmosphere of his own accomplishment: "It is one of the few books of this type which are filled with good and genuine love but also, in its feminine way, with irony, amorphous sadness, and doubt of life" (*M*, 552). Auerbach's own involvement in such "feminine" traits appears at the end of *Mimesis:*

It is still a long way to a common life of mankind on earth, but the goal begins to be visible . . . . Perhaps it will be too simple to please those who, despite all its dangers and catastrophes, admire and love our epoch for the sake of its abundance of life and the incomparable historical vantage point which it affords. But they are few in number, and probably they will not live to see much more than the first forewarnings of the approaching unification and simplification. (*M*, 553)

As one of the last members of this dying elite who lives long enough to see the humanistic dream of Dante perverted into a mass collectivism, a noble but nonetheless sad pessimism is a quite unavoidable stance for one whose humanism admits no more radical possibility. Not surprisingly, Auerbach contends that the liberty of the everyday sphere of common humanity outside states and ideologies cannot resist the more powerful underlying forces of leveling and collective life. Finally, *Mimesis* arrives at a sense of hopelessness like the conclusion of certain contemporary critical theorists such as Horkheimer and Adorno.[9] The authority of Auerbach's method, its apparent victory over willfulness or relativism, results from the evident congruence of its position with the reality of the present historical moment. Freed seemingly from ideological commitments and subjectivism, Auerbach, having intuited motifs important to the present moment's self-understanding, takes them as his point of departure not only to reconstruct their genesis but also to make them yield up whatever it is that they, as concrete particulars, can tell us about the universally valid inner forces of our own moment. Indeed, Auerbach succeeds better than most critics in providing insight into his own period through his own reflections. His pessimism, his concern for synthesis, his hope to avoid willfulness, his nostalgia for high culture and fear of massification, and, finally, his endless revisionary searching into modernism's roots are some of the necessary concerns of our own historical investigation. Unfortunately, as Auerbach admits, his project can neither reverse the forces it battles nor escape abetting their ends. History's trick has been to turn humanism against itself.

III

Perhaps not surprisingly early responses to his work show some difficulty among his contemporaries in grasping the scale and nature of Auerbach's project. In *Mimesis* he is not only proposing new methods for writing and research that might be hard to recognize but also is offering a history of the present to which some of his readers seem resistant. We have Auerbach's own expression of distaste for his European reviewers. He wrote to Harry Levin that "though they were friendly, [they] looked upon *Mimesis* as no more than 'an amusing series of analyses [in?] of style.'" Levin comments that "Having hoped that his integrating ideas would be noticed and discussed, he transferred his hopes to the English edition."[10] Unfortunately, Auerbach's hopes were not to be completely fulfilled.

The first serious American reviews of *Mimesis* do not appear until mid-1949 and 1950; the German text appears in 1946. Two reviews in *Romance Philology* and *MLN* written respectively by Helmut A. Hatzfield, a former student of Karl Vossler, Auerbach's admired master, and by Ludwig Edelstein, a distinguished classical scholar, can be taken as representative.[11] *Mimesis* evokes interest only slowly among native-born American critics or among those internationally minded scholars, like René Wellek, whose own work is not primarily philological. Only very slowly does it attract notice from critics whose interest exceeds a specialist's concern with whatever Auerbach has to say about the critic's particular field or figure. The editors of *MLN* and *Romance Philology* apparently feel that *Mimesis* can best be judged, summarized, and explained to an American audience by other German-born and trained philological scholars. Not only is *Mimesis* untranslated at the time of the first reviews, but Auerbach's earlier work on Dante and "figura" seems not to have attracted a wide-ranging audience. The German reviewers do mediate between Auerbach and the American establishment, but they do not make the peculiarities of his work fully apparent to a broad range of humanists. On the contrary, their specialized interest is a sign that Auerbach does not yet have the general authority in American criticism he would soon acquire.

Both reviewers, although acknowledging the book's many beauties, judge it to be merely a collection of essays, more interesting in its early chapters, and rather confused in style and method. Hatzfield accuses Auerbach of jumbling stylistic analysis with the history of ideas and producing, as a result, "a kind of half-stylistic, half-philosophic history of literary realism."[12] Edelstein makes a similar charge. The study of Homer and the classics, he finds, is generally ahistorical, too unnuanced, and too homogenizing. More detailed and scholarly historical research would reveal to Auerbach that the classical period is much more varied than he suggests. While Edelstein praises the book for transgressing "the boundaries of departmental research,"[13] Hatzfield accuses it of being idiosyncratically eclectic.

Both reviews treat *Mimesis* as a collection of essays, not as a unified genetic history of the present. For Edelstein, *Mimesis* is so evidently a collection that matters of unity and history never come up. Hatzfield, following in Vossler's tradition of professional specialization, finds Auerbach's treatment disunified and his "history" fragmented: "The book was doomed to remain eclectic because of the working conditions of the author in Istanbul. It was not intended to be a standard history of realistic style; therefore Auerbach could afford selecting stylistic devices at random, following some of them throughout, and dropping others; consequently, the book should be considered as a collection of stimulating scholarly essays."[14] For Hatzfield, the rising and falling motifs of *Mimesis* do not unify its structure. Either he does not see the pointed analogy to modern realism or cannot accept it as an efficacious procedure for producing authoritative scholarly work. Since *Mimesis* is not "a standard history," it is no history at all. For Hatzfield, Auerbach simply has not attempted a "synthesis," namely, a complete, linked, and consistent ordering of *all* realistic literature. Hatzfield defends the traditional criteria of the philological profession for which a "synthesis" would be precisely what Auerbach claims modernity makes impossible: a mastered absorption and presentation of all the scholarship, that is, an adherence to criteria that would make the desired, idealized synthesis valueless. Edelstein takes the same position in claiming that Auerbach's reading of the ancients is uninformed. It is not surprising that a certain important part of the critical profession in the United States defends its own specializing criteria, its own commitment to scientistic thoroughness, and resists Auerbach's conscious adoption of techniques of imaginative literature to scholarly writing. These moves on Auerbach's part are challenges to the status quo of even the more eclectic American humanists.

The difficulty American critics have in grasping the unity of *Mimesis* persists for several years. For example, in 1956, reviewing the English translation of *Mimesis*, Charles Muscatine, the distinguished Berkeley medievalist, writes that the book is a "series of essays."[15] René Wellek is almost unique in sensing the unity and ambition of Auerbach's project: "The book," he writes, "is unified by several themes and theses which are pursued and expounded throughout, even though, on occasion, they seem almost lost sight of." Wellek's review is also distinguished by his understanding that Auerbach's "awareness of our own age" is central to *Mimesis*.[16] Of course, as is well known, Wellek has strong reservations about historicism; for him, with his pessimistic misperception of modernism's perspectivism, Auerbach falls into "an ultimately profound scepticism and denial of values, even artistic values."

If we put Wellek only partially aside, a survey of Auerbach's early reviewers shows that, for the most part, they fail to consider or they understate the centrality of Auerbach's interests in the modern period; they seem to miss that Auerbach is, in part, writing a genetic history of modernism and of the peculiar (and perhaps last) opportunity it affords to synthesize Western literature. There is, in other words, a strange failure among the early commentators, again with the only partial exception of Wellek, to see the drama of Auerbach's effort or to evaluate the nature and success of the modern methods he deploys. Even Muscatine's comparatively late review (1956) treats *Mimesis*, professionally, or "positivistically," as Auerbach himself might say; that is, Muscatine is primarily interested in "correcting" errors, filling in gaps, and showing the problems "of maintaining the rigors of good literary judgement."[17]

American reviewers routinely object to Auerbach's specifics, find fault with his plan, and criticize his values. Of course, they admire various brilliant insights and enjoy the pleasures of reading such artful prose; they recognize the value of Auerbach's theory of the "figura" and of the power of the vulgate. In light of these and other critical complexities, Muscatine understandably finds the book "strikingly ambivalent" while an admiring Wellek declares it is basically self-contradictory. Yet despite the breadth of what appears to be mixed and somewhat unperceptive critical response, Wellek could approve the "general sense" that *Mimesis* "has been hailed as 'the most important and brilliant book in the field of aesthetics and literary history that has been published in the last fifty years.'"[18] Both

Muscatine and Wellek could admire Auerbach and his work as exemplars—just as in *The Gates of Horn*, Harry Levin could refer to *Mimesis* as "magistral"[19]—most valuable for their effect on other scholars. Muscatine could write that *Mimesis* "is *par excellence* the book of a teacher. It is likely to have its deepest influence among that middle group of serious, younger students who are most receptive to literary criticism as an activity, and who will welcome this fresh evidence that philology can be at once important, exciting, and humane."[20] Indeed, as late as 1969, Harry Levin could directly assert that Auerbach's true achievement was "to play an exemplary role before an ever widening audience."[21] It is not until quite a few more years pass that Auerbach's project receives wider consideration and critics offer stronger theoretical explanations of his importance.

The general unextended response continues for some time and is worth considering as a window onto the ideology of literary study and its mechanisms for establishing authority. For example, as late as 1966, Frank Kermode writes in the *New Statesman* to dismiss the dramatic, performative aspects of Auerbach's work while hoping dispassionately to judge his work's value as a contribution to literary history. In a tone that catches precisely the professional dilettantism of a certain Anglo-American belletristic tradition that has little sympathy for criticism "burdened" with cultural weight, Kermode tells us to admire Auerbach's "immense synoptic inquiry" but to suspend all consideration of and concern for his "eschatological [self-] justification" in order simply to balance his arguments about Dante and what Kermode wittily calls the "imperious vulgar."[22]

The purpose of this look into early critical responses to Auerbach is not to criticize the early readers, most of whom are very accomplished scholars, but to begin to place the figure of Auerbach within the American institution of literary studies. Because of his own aspiring achievements and, more important, because of the needs, desires, and structures of the American critical institution—and despite his early commentators' reservations—Auerbach rapidly becomes a sign of critical authority and, as such, legitimates the institution's goals and methods of reproduction. In hopes of understanding the nature of power in the professional study of literature, it is essential to recognize that Auerbach's *magisterium* is in some substantial part a result of the lines of power and authority that constitute the academy and that "took Auerbach up" in their channels of distribution both to profit from the discourse he puts at their disposal and to make him a key figure in their own defense.

Once some of the effects of the operations become clear, one may judge if their contact with Auerbach is beneficial: perhaps Auerbach is other than the profession makes him seem. The academy may, in fact, distort his achievement while establishing his authority. (Of course, it is unlikely that achievement can ever be seen "outside" the profession.) Auerbach "himself" cannot be studied; he comes already mediated by the profession. The profession, however, can be studied, along with Auerbach, in these mediations. This relationship is a specific instance of the operations of power, need, interest, and desire in both the profession and strong humanistic intellectuals. Idealist, abstract notions that assert that critical authority is the result of "quality," "tact," "erudition," "style," or "perception" cannot describe or adequately account for the processes by which Auerbach becomes a "master" for American critics. Rather, as the history of Auerbach's authorization suggests, all these abstractions merely aid in creating authority to the extent that they enter, semiotically and politically, into the enabling but always mystified and mystifying system of needs, interests, and power. To the great credit of the profession, it banks on Auerbach to fill those needs and defend its ideals and interests.

Given the range of questions regarding *Mimesis*, one can see that it is not on purely rational grounds that the institution assigns Auerbach such a privileged place in the critical firmament. How this comes about is a very complicated question whose answer would require, among much else, a complete genealogy of American literary study to show both its affiliations with other discourses and cultural practices and its place in the growing postwar American hegemony. Yet, certain ideas do suggest themselves as explanations of how, despite the cultural pessimism of *Mimesis'* final chapters and despite the frequent misperception of the self-admitted goals of Auerbach's project, both he and his text became exemplars. A descriptive answer to a beginning question would be helpful: in which of Auerbach's many qualities does the American academy invest, and with which values, energies, and hopes does it carry out that investment?

Wellek, for example, admires Auerbach's "tact" and his "sense of balance and order."[23] Muscatine feels he can pay no greater compliment than to call Auerbach "humane."[24] Charles Breslin offers perhaps the most extreme compliment: "At the turn of the XIXth Century Friedrich Schlegel prophesied that the study of literature in the modern world would demand a scholar, a free and educated man, who had the power 'to attune himself at will to philosophy or philology, to criticism or poetry, to history or rhetoric, to the ancient or modern.' Surely Erich Auerbach possessed this very power."[25]

This comparatively late image of Auerbach is merely a developed version of what one might consider an initial authorizing image found in Ulrich Leo's review of *Mimesis*. Leo writes of *Mimesis* that it may be seen "not only as a seal on a philological past, but also a beacon to a philological future."[26] Leo begins a minor tradition of Auerbach commentary that reaches only one of its many occasional crescendoes in Breslin's heroic image of Auerbach's sublimity. Leo evinces and Breslin trumpets the academy's desire to assure its continuity, survival, and social effectivity. Leo's image of *Mimesis* as a "seal" evokes legal and ritual associations: *Mimesis* "seals" the past; that is, it is a mark or trace closing its tradition and assuring its authenticity, but as a "seal" it also designates or assigns that enclosed tradition as an estate to be passed on, genealogically, to those who follow and who can look after the well-tended, entailed property. In this way, *Mimesis* is also a beacon both showing the way and, as it were, summoning or guiding home. It is in this last sense that *Mimesis* frequently appears as an exemplar in the writing of Auerbach's commentators. It assures the persistence, continuity, and authority of this sacred and preserved past of culture and humanistic scholarship by calling all the best to itself, and so, to the traditions it guards and embodies. Breslin's more hyperbolic figure simply personalizes the sublimity Leo's trope implicitly assigns to the luminous, enticing father whose work enacts tradition, a literal carrying over of skills, knowledge, and values that work, that is, that make others in their own image, training them, "allowing" the heirs to acquire and value knowledge of the tradition. While the pathos, power, and desire of this set of figures is clear, it is difficult to reconcile them with Auerbach's own sense of things. As he sees *Mimesis*, it portends nothing for philology's future.

Mimesis shows that the conditions for preserving those cultural and scholarly traditions are gone. Consequently, this means that Auerbach's work *cannot be imitated;* no one has the requisite knowledge or motive. The American profession especially is ill equipped, dominated at that time particularly by New Critical "readings" produced rapidly and with little concern for historical or linguistic research. The proof of Auerbach's sense of the diminishing number of those capable of such monumental synthetic efforts as *Mimesis* can be found in the fact that the American academy does not provide its students with the skills or knowledge it claims so to admire. On the contrary (with, of course, notable but only partial exceptions), it encourages "readings" as the standard practice of critical publication and pedagogy. Language skills, historical study, to say nothing of the close study of nonliterary cultural disciplines, are all neglected. The effect of Auerbach's authority, the legitimacy of the space he signed, cannot be found in such practical matters as educational and institutional reform.

The authority invested in him can, however, be found in other areas: his authorized and authoritative status legitimates humanistic scholarship by providing an acceptable image (and substantive achievement) to attract "the best," those who will form the elite heirs to his seal; in turn, this image legitimates the profession to itself and others; and, perhaps most important, it provides an ideological justification for conceiving of the individual critic or scholar in sublime or heroic terms. To put the last point more crudely, institutional admiration of Auerbach feeds, in part, on critics' desires to be able to represent themselves as capable of making such grand gestures as *Mimesis*, of producing such monumental and "magistral" work, for such gestures give value to the profession and rewards to those capable of producing them.

Evidence of how Auerbach functions as an ideological justification of a necessary and profitable critical sublimity can be found in the constant praise of his personal, individualistic values and accomplishment. Auerbach's commentators produce a contradiction in the process: on the one hand, they value and defend the communal project of cultural preservation as a civilizing force (ideally represented by Dante's era), while, on the other hand, they locate the very essence or idea of that project in a unique individual model of an elite caste of humanists. Either literature and culture are social processes that democratize and are democratically available, or, they are a function of specialists whose privilege results from their unique, private, and thus nonsocial endowments.

From Hatzfield's piece on, all of Auerbach's reviewers directly or implicitly comment on *Mimesis* as an individual, sometimes heroic accomplishment. Hatzfield generates the image and critiques it: Auerbach's motifs are too much a private function of his perception and so the text lacks unity and real comprehensive synthesis. Hatzfield misunderstands the historical reasons for this, blaming Auerbach's exile in Turkey for the incompletion. He does not, however, find the image inappropriate, simply unfulfilled.

Wellek, however, judges *Mimesis* differently on these facts and in the process opens up a tradition of Auerbach criticism that is still with us. *Mimesis*, he tells us, "must be judged as something of a work of art, as a personal commonplace or rather uncommonplace book."[27] Wellek has, I suspect, more in mind than just acknowledging Auerbach's aesthetic graces. His later, more reserved remarks suggest that he finds *Mimesis* to be relativistic and pessimistic because, like all historism, its values can be grounded only in the individual historicist's perception. Reminding us of Auerbach's dislike for agreed upon "conceptual terms," he rather distastefully remarks that Auerbach would willingly "discard the whole conceptual structure of

modern scholarship in favor of what he calls 'philology,' textual interpretation, close reading, combined with something
which can be best described as personal insight, artistic imagination."[28] We have already seen how Auerbach attempts to
defend against this charge that historicism is not only relativis-
ing but also personalizing.

If we put aside the substance and accuracy of Wellek's charge
for a moment, we can see that he is responding, in part, to an
image of individualistic authority in *Mimesis* that provides the
ground for how Auerbach comes to function in the academy:
namely, as a legitimation of an ideology of individualistic critical scholarship that makes some almost unteachable categories
of perception and judgment the sine qua non of professional
accomplishment and authority. It seems not to matter that
Auerbach himself argues that the modern postulation of the
ontological value of the discrete individual consciousness is
simultaneously accompanied by its "de-individualization" in a
collective leveling.

Charles Muscatine, quite typically, valorizes *Mimesis* for being the representative product of the incarnate humanistic
ideal—the sensitive, learned, committed, percipient, almost
mystic, integrated self: "Few of [*Mimesis*'] conceptions are
really compatible, yet one feels that in Auerbach's hands their
contradictions have rather been embraced than resolved. The
book contains a wealth of historical data, and repeated recommendations of historicism, yet it is itself only semi-history. At
its center is something intuitive and creative, aesthetic, even
moral." Muscatine's variations of this image become com-
monplaces about Auerbach, obstructing until recently, what
might be theorized from his situation: "The book . . . was written in exile. . . . To have produced such a book under these
uncompromising circumstances is to have been both beset by
history and fortified by something personal, internal, un-
historical, but equally real."[29]

In his recollections of Auerbach and Spitzer, Harry Levin also
takes some consolation from Auerbach's presence, for he, too,
feels besieged by history and its contradictions. But interestingly, as Levin recalls it, the history besetting him in the

1950s is not the "world history" to which Muscatine refers but the more local history of critical upheaval in the profession: the battles between literary historians and New Critics produce "an assumption that the critic's and the scholar's interests were mutually exclusive." Auerbach's presence, Levin tells us, "was a reasurrance, for some of us caught in the cross fire, that our discipline embraced both erudition and esthetics."[30] Indeed, both Muscatine and Levin make strong cases for their different senses of Auerbach as a figure capable of containing contradictory strains of history. Auerbach's historicization of stylistics, of *explication de texte* is formidable and important. The Americans' appeal to this power as a value is tactically correct since in their own professional and historical situations any strong appeal to communally valued ideals of the past in hope of redeploying them in the present is a powerful way to authorize those whose privilege it might be to carry out such a task.

Yet, as understandable as this process of authorizing Auerbach is, it seems irrational. Given the serious initial and persisting doubts about Auerbach's work, the miscomprehension of his methods—which until Said's *Beginnings* goes largely undiscussed[31]—the evident distaste for his judgments on what modern realism reveals about modernity, and above all, his recognition of the limits of the humanities, the American investment in Auerbach must be understood, at least in significant part, as a result of irrational operations of will, desire, and ideology.

While the victorious postwar United States feels little of Auerbach's European pessimism and Jewish despair, the American academy finds itself undergoing enormous internal strife as the profession becomes larger, less restricted, more New Critical, less erudite, and less homogeneous in its values and sense of self-purpose. One needs only to consider how R. P. Blackmur's essays from the late 1940s challenge New Critical orthodoxy from cultural and political positions (following his earlier New Critical challenges to humanism) to picture the growing internal divisions within the profession with which we are now all too familiar.[32] The investment in Auerbach is at least in part, for critics like Muscatine, an attempt to maintain a continuity with a cultural and academic humanistic ideal that surely never has in the United States, as it did for a time in Germany, anything like the political force and cultural value American critics assign to it. Leo's sense that *Mimesis* seals the past and endows the future—when all of the conditions for Auerbach's work are gone, as he himself makes clear—most directly reveals this ideological, irrational desire for a fictive continuity and cultural legitimacy.

Also, given the New Critics' hostility to social modernism, their various assaults on leveling and mass culture, it is surprising that Auerbach's commentators do not stress this theme. Yet, it remains implicitly very much present; the reviewers constructed an image of Auerbach (and those he would call) as an ideal critic who transcends all of the forces of history, all of the destructive and simplifying collective tendencies of modernity, by virtue, not of his professional training or knowledge, but of some private, individual, intuitive humanistic core unaffected by history and able, literally, to contain and restrict conflict and contradiction. It is, I suggest, this ideological investment in Auerbach's redemptive qualities that escapes the sphere of a rational discipline. He incarnates the wished-for ideal for many of the contradictory elements of the profession, e.g., those interested in close reading who stress his similarity to Spitzer's stylistic analysis—a stress against which Auerbach reacts by asserting his own greater sense of the drama of the present—as well as those who claim him as a model for historical scholarship. And, of course, there are others, like Levin, from whom he provides a synthesis, while for Hatzfield he provides an occasion for a reactionary lecture.

Auerbach is a creation of a profession that unconsciously generates a contradictory image of him as a flawed ideal. One must put aside, I think, many of the revealing and important specific objections to *Mimesis* to see this process, even in part. The specific criticisms, while they reveal versions of the ideal held by different factions of the profession, never call into question the overriding authorized image created by and from Auerbach's work. The composite trope of Auerbach authorizes and legitimates what at first seems an unintelligible contradic-

tion, namely, the nonreproducible, ahistorical talent and mysterious intuition of the synthetic critic and the profession
whose charge it is to reduplicate its own skills, knowledge, and
values. Certain critical theorists feel that mass professionalization leads unavoidably to the cretinization of the academy. In
writing to Harry Levin, Spitzer, for example, makes a similar
but specifically German point: "'Choosing from your own
words, I would say that the "new frontiers of knowledge" con-
sist in the gigantically increasing *information* we get in our
times while a unified *Weltanschauung* or wisdom, is disappearing. Just open any of our journals and you witness the anarchy
of values while the learning displayed is (sometimes) stupen-
dous.'"[33] Spitzer's comments are not atypical; they certainly
are like Auerbach's own. How then can the profession legitimate itself in the face of its own and the public's increasing
sense of anomie?

The composite figure of Auerbach that emerges from the intersection of his work and the American critical institution
partially answers this question. His work—often criticized
and misunderstood—comes to represent a wished-for possibility, a wish that massive learning stoked by a desire to produce a synthesis crucial to and revealing of the present can be
achieved, can overcome the built-in leveling of the profession
itself and so can continually validate scholarly and pedagogical practices about which there is little reason to feel confidence. But perhaps the case is overstated. Levin's remarks
suggest the conflicts in the profession are disturbing, not critical; yet it may be that the representation of Auerbach as a
figure to relegitimate the profession loses none of its force for
that. Indeed, such an idea suggests that there is something
quotidian about the way Auerbach becomes an exemplar, a
celebrity. His story might be the ordinary and anonymous procedure of the profession in one dimension of its continuing task
of self-legitimation.

More specifically, the reception of Auerbach suggests something about the hierarchical nature of the profession. Whereas
Auerbach may seal the profession's past and future, he cannot
in real terms be an exemplar for all individual members of the

academy. He becomes an exemplar for the profession in the abstract, an internal and external sign of its legitimacy. Above all, however, in real terms, he becomes the model for those likely to become or designated to become the "leaders" in the profession. Muscatine tells us that Auerbach's authority has the most influence "among that middle group of serious, younger students," and Levin goes a bit further to say specifically that, after Auerbach, we should have hopes for "a younger generation of scholars . . . such as Paul de Man, Peter Demetz, Victor Erlich, W. B. Fleischmann, Claudio Guillen, Juan Marichal, Georges May, Alain Renoir, and Walter Strauss."[34]

These are all powerful and productive critical figures whose works and reputations give weight to the claim of both Muscatine and Levin that Auerbach's example is so strong and so magistral that it can affect only those capable of becoming masters, of having names. Not only does this sort of relationship allow for advanced scholarship to continue as a tradition within the profession, but it also suggests that movement into the hierarchy of the profession depends, not on "excellent work," but on following, with great strength, upon the traditions of authorized figures. The institutional drive to reproduce itself, not the anxiety of influence, regulates these inheritances, just as it does all bureaucratic and paradigmatic structures. The reproductive urge continually to legitimate itself underlies the internal logic of the profession and suggests why Auerbach becomes the exemplar *with these specific characteristics.* The assignment of the gentlemanly and belletristic qualities of "tact" and "balance"[35] reflects an apparently decayed and nostalgic ideology of an older disciplinary formation, and the stress on his individual achievement within a collective profession parallels corporate ideology. But for purposes of a history of literary intellectuals and their disciplinary images, one should place greatest stress on certain other specific aspects of Auerbach's image, namely, the private, irrational, almost mystical qualities of his individuality, those connections he has with the ahistorical that allow him to master history. When Breslin assigns Auerbach to the Schlegelian ideal, he is simply further disseminating and enforcing the already in place image of the critical intellectual as a representative sublime hero who, by his example, that is to say, as the expressed essence of the willed desires of the profession and its leaders, legitimates the role of "serious younger scholars" who accept as their burden trying to occupy the pinnacle, the place of authority and achievement that Auerbach opens for them and keeps open, with their aspirations, for the institution itself.

This structure produces enormous amounts of knowledge and quite wonderful critical studies. In fact, as Muscatine and Levin suggest, it encourages the development of scholars without whose work much of what critics do today might not take place. Above all, it helps to preserve the profession by allowing the leading figures to do influential work that represents and, in part, legitimates the profession in the eyes of the state and the public. In the process, it also preserves some aesthetic and ethical communal values and both stabilizes a canon and produces healthy debates about it. Moreover, it initiates literally millions of readers in the techniques of reading and writing and, to some extent, legitimates the study of literature as a way of recalling a more nearly full range of cultural and human experience than mass existence would allow. Despite all the ideology critiques that could be made of the profession, this is not a bad record.

Yet implicit in this image ideal of the sublime critical synthesizer are the roots, as Auerbach might have pointed out, of its own destruction. For one thing, it is a highly anomic ideal, promoting the individual pursuit of sublime representative status through attempts at individual magistral achievements, attempts that, in turn, leave only the achievement of the magistral as an unquestioned value for the various potential heirs to the throne as they struggle to authorize their own positions and claims to legitimacy. In the process, an enterprise that legitimates itself by appealing to its ability to preserve communal values and humane traditions produces a professional structure that too often functions like the sphere of civil society: a war of all against all, with the necessary alliances essential to preserving the hierarchical system. In short, the critical

"magisterium," whose achievement supposedly confers authority, comes to appear as an existing spiritual ideal, the "essence"
of humanistic institutions and work. Yet, like all such apparent
essences, this one reveals itself to be a man-made (or, should
one say, profession-made) measure whose existence as a predi-
cate, a function of the material structures of power, desire, and
interest, is masked by a critical institution that assigns to it the
status of an apparently independent subject, whether it is
called "tact," "transcendence," "intuition," or "creativity."
One result of masking the produced nature of these individualistic standards with an aura of privacy and mystery is that
communal values weaken; even many commonsensical criteria
for agreement collapse, and reason, itself, falls victim to soph-
istry[36] as criticism becomes "critique" and its techniques become weapons, not just to preserve and liberate the moral,
aesthetic, and pedagogical values of tradition, but also to battle against other aspiring magistral projects.

For Auerbach, the potential anomie and chaos that might
result from historicism could be controlled as long as Goethian
beliefs in the inherent meaningfulness of history and the reality of transcendental truths and values persisted; even though
the broadly based belief in such values declines in modernity,
Auerbach contends that anomie might still be prevented as
long as an elite can both remember the cultural and spiritual
benefits sustained by an order of traditional values and recognize the necessity of such an order for the prevention of leveling, the maintenance of difference, and so the survival of human
culture. The elite's memory of the desirable effects of such an
order is one condition for the role it then assigns itself: despite
the fact that modernity makes impossible the beliefs and social
conditions upon which traditional order rests, the elite, often
itself no longer able to sustain these beliefs, sets out to defend
traditional order because the consequences of its survival are
seen as socially desirable while those of its failure might be
devastating.

At times, such an attempt to defend tradition in almost functional terms results in the unquestioned priority of the will in
projects hoping to satisfy the needs, desires, and interests of the

high culture of the humanistic elite. The problematic nature of the process appears not just in its mandarin elitism but in its fantasy nature. In such projects and such roles, intellectuals assert the largely forgotten ideological ideal of other historical moments in the face of an acknowledged material and social reality that makes impossible the actualization of this ideal. Of course, such intellectual work is the expression of "real" interests and needs, that is, of the pain of apparent anomie for those raised in high culture and, as such, is a "real" expression of utopian possibility. Yet, its fantasy nature means that such a project is a distorted expression of utopian desire. The unreality of such visions results from a basic confusion, from a failure to understand that threatening modernity is a condition for, if not a cause of, the very value-laden projects these intellectuals carry out. In other words, their projects are "real" only insofar as they are responses to anomic modernity and so, to carry the argument a bit further, it is fantastical on their part to see their desired and desirable visions as having a reality over and above or against modernity.

Because Auerbach senses that modernity implicates his own techniques in the process of leveling, he does not, I think, articulate how willful and fantastical such idealistic projects are. Had he done so, the reasons why his own work contributes to anomie would be clearer. As it is, we can only catch glimpses of how the memory desire of an idealistic elite, not quite clear on its own relation to the social reality it battles, furthers anomie by fragmenting value in an elitist structure that privileges the will and judgment of a social group and of its individual members. Furthermore, we can begin to see how, as I have already suggested, this structure results in both the preservation of a hierarchical elitism and the use of critical weaponry as a means for advancement within that structure.

In the American response to Auerbach, we can see a special version of this process, especially in the way his commentators shift the center of "value" and "order" from object to subject. In *Mimesis*, Auerbach tries to demonstrate that only the memory of Goethian beliefs and tactics for revealing eternal truths in history can inhibit the willful subjectivism of humanists and give them and their works some real social authority. But the American comments on Auerbach move the source of "truth" from an "object" that presents motifs to an intuitive, but prepared, that is, educated and motivated, modern historian, to the individual soul, talent, or power of a particular would-be sublime critic. This shift makes authority a function of individualistic achievement within an institutionalized, hierarchical profession. Not only does this result in anomie—hypothetically, the current proliferation of critical theories might be one of its consequences—but also it undermines communal life and makes ego-anxiety a fact of life as momentary "sublimity" fades away with shifts in critical standards and demands of the critics greater and greater self-revision to maintain one's own "sublime" position and to fulfill the standards of critical achievement.[37] As critical and scholarly work tends more and more to be the named possession of this or that "leading figure," this (imposed, but embraced) excessively personalized aspiration levels critical and humanistic studies. Anomie grows to be such that success in this aspiration, to become like Auerbach, a magistral figure, is the expressed, replicated, and (perhaps) only common goal of powerful scholars. It is fitting that Auerbach should come to occupy this place given the political and cultural conditions that made possible his own achievement and his own revisions of individualistic standards of authority within his own tradition and immediate intellectual context.

IV

In his classic study of German academic politics and intellectual life, Fritz Ringer charges that university professors, especially in the Geisteswissenschaften, prepare the ground for Nazism by refusing to support the Weimar republic, by generating ambiguous and clichéd rhetorics that, for example, legitimate extreme nationalism as "spiritual revival," and generally degrade the standards of reason, debate, and scholarship.[38] Although Ringer's view is controversial in its particulars, its credibility is such that Gordon Craig can write: "As for the university professors and those aspiring to academic chairs, they were, with few exceptions, solidly arrayed against a regime that periodically, if ineffectually, sought to limit their privileges and whose economic policies had, in their view, been responsible for the drastic reduction of their financial emoluments that resulted from the inflation."[39] All historians of the period identify the important exceptions to this general rule: figures such as Max Weber, Karl Vossler, and Karl Mannheim resist the opportunism of orthodox right-wing extremism. Yet, as Peter Gay points out, even these exceptions do not enthusiastically defend the republic; on the contrary, they try to control what, for them, is the demagogic chaos of socialism. Gay reminds us that these men call themselves "*Vernunftrepublikaner*," that is "republicans from intellectual choice rather than passionate conviction."[40] Convinced from the beginning that the German people were not "ready" for democracy, their half-hearted defenses of the republic destabilize it. Ringer calls the academic segment of this political intellectual fraction the "accommodationists" or "modernists." Since they recognize that modernity cannot simply be renounced or overthrown, they advocate developing new methods and tactics effective in the modern world for preserving and carrying over whatever is valuable and useful from the past, but unlike the extremists, while always trying to defend their own very high standards of rational inquiry and debate. As E. R. Curtius puts it, "We Germans seek recourse too easily in destiny and tragedy."[41]

Auerbach's work intertwines with the complex intellectual and cultural politics of Weimar and of the German humanistic culture as this climaxes in the Republic. The specific and difficult issue of "the Jewish question" forms part of the context in any consideration of Auerbach, especially the issue of cultural assimilation as Hannah Arendt and others give it weight and complexity. But these questions are not only too large to deal with here; considering them might also deflect us from our main line of inquiry, the Americanization of Auerbach and what this might suggest about both the power structure of the literary academy and what there is in Auerbach's academic genealogy that either facilitates or impedes his American adoption.

Both before and especially during the Weimar period, German humanists, not only philologists and philosophers but also historians and most social scientists, that is, almost all practitioners of the *Geisteswissenschaften*, rebel against what they see as excessive "positivistic," "analytic," "Western" research and education. All seem in agreement—left and right—that matters are out of hand and that there is a pressing need for "syntheses," for "wholeness," that might be provided only by a new unifying *Weltanschauung*. This consensus emerges out of a crisis for the material interests of the professoriat. Fritz Ringer points out that from the end of the eighteenth through the nineteenth century, German intellectuals have a contract with the state, first with Prussia and then with imperial Germany:

The terms of the settlement were that the bureaucratic monarchy would give unstinting support to learning, without demanding immediately practical returns, and without exercising too strict a control over the world of learning and geist. In other respects also, the state would acknowledge and serve the demands of culture. It would become a vehicle, a worldly agent or form for the preservation and dissemination of spiritual values. Indeed, it would seek its legitimacy in this function, and it would be rewarded by finding it there.[42] (GM, 116)

Within this *Kulturstaat*, the academic elite accumulates prestige and power. Of course, the state circumscribes their power by regulating funding and key appointments, but the academics accept these restrictions, only rarely, it would seem, objecting, even as a small minority, to the exclusion of Jews or other "radicals." The state seems, for the most part, simply to reflect the academics' own values and desires. The mandarins extend their authority through the agency of the state, the control of schools, degrees, and examinations, so that, as Ringer puts it, until 1890 "academic values bore the stamp of public and official recognition. The non-entrepreneurial upper middle-class, the mandarin aristocracy of cultivation, had become the functional ruling class of the nation. University professors, the mandarin intellectuals spoke for this distinctive elite and represented its values" (GM, 38).

From 1890 to 1933, the rise of alternate power centers in industry, natural science, and the proletariat represented by the socialists continually subverts the mandarins' authority. After the collapse of the state whose very existence provides their privilege—despite their support in 1914 for its "purifying" war aims—the mandarins feel an absolute break with the past and, in their defensiveness, attack and help destroy the republic and thus blindly complete the erosion of their own power in a frantic attempt to reestablish it.

In this developing academic, social crisis, "synthesis" becomes a crucial idea, value, and rhetorical trope for these beseiged intellectuals; it is a response to their loss of authority and power, a loss for which they generally blame "positivism" and "social democracy," both forces, as they see it, of a paradoxically linked duo, "fragmentation" and "levelling." In this period "synthesis" loses any precise or exclusive definition and becomes a loosely defined, contradictory term of ordinary intellectual discourse. At times, it expresses a wish for a new social contract; often it reflects secularized religious desires for a unifying *Weltanschauung*; most dangerously, it represents the imperialistic urges of extreme nationalists hoping to unite Europe under German tutelage. During this period, "synthesis" becomes one of many unquestioned nodes around and through which the mandarins attempt to regain their lost authority.

This extreme claim for the political and ideological investment of irrational desire and will in a figure like "synthesis" seems justified when one recalls how the German academics experience their loss of authority. "The German university professors," Ringer reminds us, "felt themselves involved in a genuine tragedy. They were oppressed by the sense that their own ideals were threatened with extinction, along with their whole manner of life" (*GM*, 244). No longer the ruling class, they experience this change as a societal loss of organic cohesion and as a disastrous, anomic break with tradition. Reflecting both their earlier hegemonic position and their roots in the German romantic period, "synthesis," a reordering of society, of past with present, would, they hope, restore their own cultural leadership, sociopolitical authority, and class privilege.

There are essentially two strategies for bringing about this restoration, one represented by Max Weber's commitment to reason and social reform, the other, antiintellectual and irrational, intent on a return to past social forms. In the first case, "synthesis" requires a new social contract in which workers switch their support to an intellectually controlled state and its mandarin directors in exchange for reform. Cultural and spiritual leadership would avoid class domination in exchange for avoiding class conflict. Power and prestige would belong again to the mandarins in the form of the "representative" or "leading" intellectual. Friedrich Meinecke puts the *Vernunftrepublikaners'* hopes this way: "'We became Democrats, because we made clear to ourselves that there was no other way to preserve the popular unity and at the same time those aristocratic values of our history that were capable of living on'" (*GM*, 203). Even though these reasonable republicans want to protect Germany against those with less humane values, we cannot miss the leadership role they assign themselves in this scheme of things. Meinecke speaks clearly of an "ancient, original culture-bearing segment of the nation, which must not die, because it is indispensable for the maintenance of the first prerequisite of culture, namely tradition'" (*GM*, 211).

The antirepublican majority of professors are also complete antimodernists. They hope to aid in the overthrow of the republic and argue constantly against it. For them, a synthesis between traditional values and new realities is not possible; the new must be destroyed by a spiritual revolution in order to restore the status quo ante. The sadness of Weimar academic life consists of the victory of the reactionary and "orthodox" over the modernists and "reformers." To put the matter simply, for the most part and progressively, Weimar academics reject Weber's contention that the reason of arguments and disciplines can be judged independently of what motivates them. The political force of Weber's argument, if accepted, would result in debate, contention, and difference. But the mandarins reject this as "pluralism," or fragmentation, in the name of "wholeness," "synthesis," and "*Weltanschauung*." As Ringer puts it, Weber "was tired of hearing that the scholar had to be a personality" (*GM*, 352). But, in Weimar, Weber's position only evokes further claims that culture needs a new "human being," as Erich von Kahler put it in 1920, "in whom the teacher and the leader have not become separated" (*GM*, 360). Such statements evince the mandarins' desire to retrieve their old hegemonic position by producing "new men" who can "overcome" the contradictions of the present, embody a kind of orchestral harmony (in the age of atonal music!), and regain social authority for the pedagogue.

This social, academic process is an example of how revisionism operates in the service of humanistic intellectuals' attempts to maintain their own spiritual authority and, hence, cultural legitimacy and institutionalized material privilege. Moreover, it is a concrete illustration of the fantastical nature of idealizing, nostalgic, antimodernist projects as they further the very fragmentation that their own avowed (but mystified) projects hope to prevent.

Among Weimar's admirable exceptions to this process is Karl Vossler, Auerbach's great predecessor, who resists the orthodox attempt to restructure education and reposition the mandarins. Unfortunately, Vossler's own agitated, satirical rhetoric shows little attempt to grasp the social processes at work:

> The character and will are only indirectly trained at the university, only through the exercise of the mind, of judgement, of the critical faculties, and of comprehending reason. The independence and responsibility of thought remains our . . . most important goal. Moral sermons, moral indignations, exhortations, enthusiasms from the lectern or in the seminars therefore have the air of little powder or rouge-pots in an army barrack. . . . With us, one works with one's head; one does not sing and one does not pray. (*GM*, 390–91)

Yet, even the most "modern" intellectuals, like Vossler, Jaspers, and Spitzer, also feel that a lack of "synthesis" is to blame for their cultural and political crisis. *Wissenschaften*, with their "positivistic" divisions, even the modernists feel must be supplemented, or more radically, be replaced, by *Weltanschauung*. (The absurdity of this desire appears in the mandarins' plan to form a special college of "synthesizers" capable of world picture thinking.)

The effects of this ideology of "synthesis" converge on Auerbach from many directions; two of the most important are historism and the orthodox image of the teacher. These are crucial influences on Auerbach: historism, as we have already seen, constitutes Auerbach's method and tradition; the Weimar debate over the nature and role of the teacher is the context of Auerbach's attempt to present and enact modes of intellectual behavior and intellectual values appropriate to the modern period's need to overcome anomie. American literary critics treat historism all too abstractly; they seem to feel that its logical contradictions lead to relativism and scepticism. As Auerbach's own work suggests, however, these "dangers" result from real social and cultural change, namely, the breakdown, as he sees it, of the hegemonic consensus regarding the universal values of history that accompany the loss of stable values and mandarin authority.

The actual synthesis of history and reason the mandarins embody in their own position within the *Kulturstaat* grounds and expresses itself ideologically in historism. The frenzied attempts of Ernst Troeltsch, for example, to adopt and modify Dilthey and Richter to reground historism in substantive values, not just neo-Kantian formalism, could not but fail in its attempt to achieve legitimacy through argument when the particular distribution of state and social power necessary to such legitimacy is impossible.[43] Troeltsch's aim is to synthesize facts and ideas and to reestablish the metaphysical ground essential to his project. George Iggers traces in detail Troeltsch's inability to support this position, as well as, following German defeat, his growing doubts about its desirability.[44] Troeltsch tries initially to ground historicism theologically, a position he modifies in a more secular direction—as the influence of the Church declines; he hopes, secondly, to find reason in history and adopts other "solutions" as necessary. Troeltsch engages in an endless process of self-revision on this matter until in *Historicism and Its Problems*, as Carlo Antoni suggests, Troeltsch objectifies all history, casts it, against his own intentions, in a developmental model, and claims it as the only source of norms.[45] In his last works, Troeltsch attempts to ground values in a synthesis immune to historical relativizing. History, he asserts, in a way that prefigures Auerbach, can provide this synthesis if we select a unified and important system of "cultural interaction" for our study. On this view, the reason of history appears in the unity of the object under investigation and thus precludes subjective relativism by inscribing the historian within a rational spiritual order. The historian absorbs the "objects" and intuits the presented "unity." As Iggers puts it in summarizing Troeltsch's position: "The great syntheses of values can be neither constructed along *a priori* ground nor can they be reduced to rational formulas. They 'break forth with a feeling of pressing necessity and clarity' on the great creative individuals, the prophets, the political leaders, philosophers, artists, and historians or even in the consciousness of the masses."[46]

Auerbach does not ground his synthetic project precisely in this way. His procedure is not so idealistic and is much more perspectival. Yet Troeltsch is clearly an important figure in his genealogy. While Troeltsch asserts that intuition is divinely sanctioned, we see in his own work that it is tentative and fragile. Indeed, having studied Troeltsch's career, Auerbach sees intuition as, at best, momentary and fragile. Placing Troeltsch's attempts back into the context of the orthodox mandarins' project reveals something of the social roots of his ambitions. Historicism, once, as Auerbach himself asserts in *Mimesis*, the highest expression of German cultural achievement, becomes, for Troeltsch, one cause of modern fragmentation by genetically undermining value. The literally conservative nature of his project appears in his attempts to reground historicism, value, and so historicist culture and thinkers. Iggers' summary of Troeltsch's late work catches the problem nicely:

History has destroyed the traditional values of the West by showing their genetic character. Historical study of the West can now uncover the real essence of "Europeanism," study its course of development, and establish the values which are proper to it. Values cannot be invented; they have to be organic parts of a cultural tradition. But out of the rich tradition of the West, the historian can create a cultural synthesis of that which is best in Western development and remains worthy of aspiration and capable of realization. This "cultural synthesis" can then serve as a guide for action toward the future of the European world.[47]

Each past period is a "whole," or "synthesis," whose "tendencies" must be grasped, through the idealistic hermeneutic categories of empathy and understanding. Following Herder and Dilthey, Troeltsch believes that historians study not only themselves and their cultures but also universal aspects of human being as these are presented in the works of thinkers and makers. For Troeltsch, historiography is purely idealistic. Consciousness alone is the object of historical study, especially as it manifests itself in the structural wholeness of high cultural achievement. By predicating consciousness in this way, as both the object and means of history and historicism, as the condition of value revealed in high culture, Troeltsch tries to reauthorize the mandarins' place as regulators of value and meaning, and so, as a consequence, their leading social role. What Troeltsch fails to recognize is that changed social reality denies any chance of fulfilling his ideological desire.

Despite serious differences between Troeltsch and Meinecke, the latter comes close to Troeltsch on this matter. Meinecke concludes *Historism* with a chapter on Goethe and a supplement on Leopold von Ranke. His final remarks suggest not only his idealism but also his hope that a renewed historism would relegitimate the mandarin tradition. Defending the value of "synthesis," Meinecke writes of Goethe, "here we touch again upon the great mysterious fact underlying all history, that one and the same phenomenon can be altogether individual and inimitable, and yet part and parcel of a universal context" (*H*, 509). Even though Meinecke's areas of historical research are more material and concrete than Troeltsch's, and more clearly an influence on Auerbach, he is always an idealist when speaking of the achievements of historism: the very "principles" that make historicism "so lively and fruitful were won by the efforts of the German spirit of the eighteenth century" (*H*, 510). In a way that interestingly converges with Auerbach's sense of a neo-platonic Vico,[48] Meinecke writes that "We may legitimately speak of historism as born from the continuous working of the Platonic spirit" (*H*, 510). Prefiguring Leo's comments on Auerbach, Meinecke concludes this monumental study of historicism with praise for its past and for its future promise:

Fertilised by the interiorising principles of German Protestantism, it gave new meaning to the individual and its development, and laid a foundation on which all our work today is based. This was the highest stage so far reached in the fusing of the ideal with the real.

This lofty link, this golden chain, is both universal and yet at every moment individual. And there are yet more links in it to be forged in this our day and age. (H, 510)

Meinecke closes the text with a gloss on Leibnitz's Greek-inspired: "'*Tout est conspirant*'": "'In one cosmic, animated breath harmony is given to all'" (H, 511). Surely, when Wellek speaks of historicism's skepticism, he cannot have Meinecke in mind.

Despite their differences, Troeltsch and Meinecke are both visionaries whose works depend on and generate images of historians and of other "historicist figures" who are not only capable of sublime perception, but are also themselves sublime individuals. In their writings, the figure of the historian incarnates the Platonic spirit as it manifests itself as reason and value. Historians not only perceive the individual syntheses of periods, objects, and tendencies; they not only intuit the wholeness of history, immersed in its objects as they are; but they are themselves, in their individuality, world historical syntheses of change and fixity, timeless ground and unique event. Historians, in other words, become art works.

The figures historists use to describe their ideals echo both Aristotle and Hegel. They recall Aristotle's claim that "Poetry . . . is a more philosophical and a higher thing than history: for poetry tends to express the universal, history the particular."[49] Butcher's gloss on this passage reads: "The aim of poetry is to represent the universal through the particular, to give a concrete and living embodiment of a universal truth."[50] Aristotle positions poetry between history and truth by stressing its unique ability to embody the timeless universality of philosophical truth toward which it "tends" and the changing specificity of historical writing. Hegel and his followers take up a variation of this Aristotelian idea in their history and aesthetics and generalize it in the figure of the "concrete universal."[51] The individualizing and elitist tendencies in historism look to sublime aesthetic categories for legitimation.

The mandarins ground their claims to privilege in what they see (perhaps wrongly) as powerful and authorized traditional discourses. Since they make claims for their own value, they are consistent in employing whatever rhetorics they can to legitimate themselves as a group and as individualities. By claiming that they are "works of art," capable (as Muscatine suggests of Auerbach) of bridging and containing fundamental contradictions between the painful nature of modernity as change and the "timeless" universality of tradition, they reveal both their hope to recover their lost authority and the futility of their project. Butcher's gloss on Aristotle lets us see some of the goals the mandarins hope to achieve by their self-aestheticization: "fine art eliminates what is transient and particular and reveals the permanent and essential features of the original. It discovers the 'form' ($\epsilon\lambda\tilde{\iota}o\varsigma$) towards which an object tends, the result which nature strives to attain, but rarely or never can attain. Beneath the individual it finds the universal."[52]

In their post-Hegelian manner, these mandarin historists believe ideologically in the end of history, specifically in the fulfillment of reason in the *Kulturstaat* in which they play a literally "essential" role, in which their works and practice legitimate the state (and their own resulting privilege) by articulating its rational nature. In this social moment, they appear to be and live as if they are, indeed, the universal form toward which nature (reason) tends. A rigorous demonstration of this implication would require a detailed history of the relationships between politics and aesthetic discourse in nineteenth-century Germany. Suffice it to say here that the mandarin historists describe themselves in aesthetic categories of synthetic universals in order to present their own self-understanding and to attempt to relegitimate their claims to privilege and a leadership role. This attempt is consistent with their tradition and is explicable in terms of its crisis, but as a strategy for the recuperation of power, it seems inappropriate given the modernist forces that make such elitist aesthetic categories not only ineffective tools for social reform but also damaging weapons in the hands of other, more dangerous irrationalisms.[53]

Both Troeltsch and Meinecke hope to relegitimate historism in order to assign historians to the task of creating syntheses to guide European culture in the future. Meinecke and Troeltsch realize how difficult it would be to carry out this project given the intellectual and social challenges to any convincing historism. Their response to the problem is revisionism, that is, a willingness to modify continually their claims for and their analyses of historism. Yet they never doubt the legitimacy of the notion of the historian as a sublime figure, despite the difficulty they have grounding historism itself. Their certainty about the cultural value of the historian can be accounted for in terms of the general mandarin project of regaining authority. Historism, a traditional source of intellectual and political legitimacy, implicates a certain image of the historicist intellectual that perfectly elides with the mandarins' aims. The chief characteristics of this image limn a complex figure: as leading intellectuals the historians are sublimely capable not only of preserving the value of the tradition (and without the ironic defenses of a Thomas Mann) but also of doing so in a way that makes them the transcendence of conflict. That is, in their own sublime being, their own uniquely and fully cultured individualities, they can contain and transcend all historical contradictions, and by means of aesthetic categories of representation, transcend all contradictions between history and metaphysics so as to guarantee a mandarin future by assuring social harmony guided from their own superior positions of fulfillment.[54]

The orthodox mandarin polemics on pedagogy also produced and depended on images of sublime humanist teachers. The mandarins' victory over the modernists in the great debates on education result in the inscription of a degraded notion of the Romantic ideal of *Bildung* into the center of their educational model. Eduard Spranger, hoping to retrieve pre-1914 conditions, for example, describes the cultural role of *Bildung* in this way:

If only in order to understand the true meaning of cultivation, we must re-establish connections with those minds and those souls with whom the separation between the world of things and the world of the soul, between doing and being, between the material and the form of life, was not as yet as drastic as it is in our case. That applies to the poets and thinkers whom—probably instinctively for that reason—we call our German classical writers. They had cultivation in the full . . . sense of the word. Therefore they were still masters of life, not its wage laborers. (*GM*, 413–14)

Spranger's recuperative project for education quite typically lacks any concrete analysis of the social realities against which he is reacting. "Cultivation" functions, for him, as a panacea because, since it is an abstraction, he need not be bothered with the materialities of its implementation or of social resistances to it. This passage illustrates the usual mandarin concern with wholeness or synthesis, the usual mythic obscurantism about a past golden age, and the central role that "intuition" plays in establishing contact across or despite the ages between those sublime souls whose synthesized being let them be "masters of life." Spranger's text hopes to reactivate not only an ideal he feels is threatened (that is to say, he feels defenseless) but also the authority of the university professor as its embodiment and preserver. Like many other academics in the 1920s, Spranger knows that many youth movements are competing with the mandarins for authority and reproductive control over young people. Indeed, in this competition with often highly irrational social groups, Spranger is a comparatively enlightened figure on the mandarin side of the debate about professorial authority.

In contrast, George Kerschensteiner and Theodor Litt are very extreme mandarin polemicists, whose aim is, as Ringer points out, "to re-establish the students' respect for the sublime and its representatives." From Kerschensteiner's point of view pedagogical and cultural, social problems are the same, and as Ringer puts it, he thinks that, "Once the proper sort of cultural reverence was established, it could serve as the fundamental source of authority in society as a whole" (*GM*, 409). The specific goal of this pedagogical polemic is to generate an authorized ideal sublime figure of the great teacher, in whose name all teachers are authorized to discourse and guide, so that the youth and population generally would once more come under mandarin authority (cf. *GM*, 414).

Combined, these calls for a renewal of historicism and of

sublime pedagogical authority had residual power in Weimar, although they do not address the social forces gathering to produce Hitler. So strong are they among academics that together they constitute not only part of a self-interested ideology but also almost the sole and absolute condition for intellectual discourse and critique. How these issues constrain and direct orthodox mandarin historicist thinking is quite simple. But that these issues also constrain the work of modernist, reformist, and even oppositional critical intellectuals is perhaps not so clear but can be seen not only from Auerbach's work but also from the contradictions they induce in Karl Mannheim's efforts as well.[55] While a number of critiques of Mannheim reveal his general conservatism, his misreading of Marx, and several of his internal contradictions, Fritz Ringer's recontextualization of his work lets us see the influence of the mandarins' social crisis on this apparently anti-mandarin reformer.

Mannheim argues that all ideas are rooted in and so are understandable only as a part of specific social conditions. Further, he believes that a certain relational model could construct a synthesis of perspectives capable of achieving "truth," that is, a nonperspectival picture. Most important for our purposes, however, is not the way the circularity of this argument might subvert it, but rather Mannheim's contention that *only intellectuals* are capable of transcending their restrictive situated perspectives, of producing syntheses, and so of leading culture and society.[56] Mannheim argues that intellectual training and social mobility or "classlessness" make possible this broader, superior "intellectual view." As has often been noted, it is ironic that Mannheim, advocate of the sociology of knowledge, fails to consider the social origins of his own "science," or more important in this case, of his contention that, unlike all other social fractions, the intellectuals alone can gain nearly transcendent views of social organization. Ringer's summary of Mannheim's position suggests how, in part, the pervasive, self-legitimating mandarin ideology makes possible and circumscribes Mannheim's "oppositional" project:

Mannheim was undoubtedly one of the most distinguished rebels against mandarin orthodoxy, and yet he ended by dreaming of synthesis, and by elevating the intellectuals above the mundane realm of ideology in which the rest of humanity was presumably immersed. He forgot what he had begun by affirming: that the explanatory techniques of the sociology of knowledge can be applied to all types of groups with equal justification. Subtly and unconsciously, he shifted his ground, assuming that entrepreneurs and workers are somehow more irrevocably and narrowly "interested" than men of mind. He forgot that the very idea of "interested" thought is no more than a typological device of understanding. He was a rebel, even a self-consciously revolutionary thinker. But he was also a mandarin. (*GM*, 434)

What is most important about Mannheim's quandary, as Ringer reads it, is that it evinces how completely the mandarins deny the political nature of their own discourse, practice, and self-image. At no time, as far as I can tell, do they call into question the necessity for their own social existence as guides for the state and society, as guardians of value and cultural meaning, or as preservers of memory and tradition to ensure a continuous transition from past to future—which, needless to say, would more or less assure their own recovered authority. The failure to consider the question of their own legitimacy is not for want of knowledge. Indeed, the destruction of the *Kulturstaat* and the loss of their privileged role prompt numerous serious investigations into the intellectual and social traditions of the mandarins.[57] It seems not unfair to say that even the best of these, those not hopelessly distorted by nationalism or class bias, never take on a demystifying edge but remain no more than reformist in their revisionary attempts to recuperate authority or isolate the "errors" that cause the current crisis in order to "correct" them. Ringer's larger thesis, that these projects affiliate the mandarins with racist, nationalist, and other irrational movements to subvert the republic and prepare for Hitler, is supported by others.[58] For our purposes, his thesis suggests both some of the immediate origins of Auerbach's use and evaluation of certain terms and the cultural-political charge they carry, perhaps without his full knowledge. Auerbach's repetitive use of key figures like "synthesis" should be read as in part variations on the mandarin position.

One other consequence follows from an even incomplete evocation of Auerbach's context. Given the mandarins' use of certain notions of sublimity, tradition, and synthesis as weapons in a (failed) battle to regain power and authority, and given, as a result of his partial inscription in that battle, Auerbach's function as a link between German and American humanistic intellectuals, American critics' own needs, interests, and powers come into sharper focus when their responses to Auerbach are themselves reconsidered in light of these German aspects of Auerbach's genealogy. In other words, American critics' admiration for Auerbach's "syntheses" must be seen in light of the historical burden carried by this term "synthesis" and the type of project it designates. Otherwise understanding why the American professoriat can so easily invest in this German term is likely to be more abstract and theoretical than it should be.

Another way of saying this is that Auerbach is what Foucault might call "a relay of power"; taken up by the American professoriat his work completes a circuitry that makes available for American appropriation intellectual discourses, practices, and images that empower the academy's elitism, satisfy its needs and interests in reproduction, and legitimate its existence in its own eyes and, given the eccentric role of humanistic education in the United States, that of the state and other powerful institutions.[59] To put it simply, Auerbach's German origins charge his work with power and authority that are resources for an American professoriat always open to energies and values deployable in its own interest; make easier and more rewarding the massive American investment in his work; and, in very concrete ways, support a hierarchical professional structure that assigns the authority and privilege of the figure of the "leading intellectual" to those certified by the profession as "masters," that is, those whose success leads to the pinnacle of the hierarchy. Because of the mandarins' insistence on the sublimity of the heroic, aesthetic individual capable of containing and resolving contradictions in leading the social and cultural worlds, that figure, appropriated in the United States where the role of the "leading intellectual" never approximates the German one in the *Kulturstaat*, becomes professionalized and is adopted as a defense of the competitive "star-system" of the American professioriat. The significance of Auerbach's embattled project and the burden of his past are diminished when he becomes a way of legitimating the American hierarchical institution, which is of little weight or ambition in the American social order. Levin's unavoidably reductive praise for Auerbach as a master who helps overcome the troubling battles between literary historians and New Critics is a symptom of how the American academy, despite its claims, trivializes Auerbach by making him one of its stars. Auerbach is undone by the system that makes him; the humanities turn against the archhumanist.

4

The Last of the Latecomers (Part II): Humanist in Conflict

In his postwar essays on Vico, Pascal, and philological method, Auerbach carries out a critique of the political and intellectual consequences of some of the mandarins' traditional values and positions, but it is carried out, in large part, in the rhetoric and categories of mandarin humanism. When seen from this perspective, his postwar writings appear as a series of often contradictory and revisionary struggles to find a method and position to reground historistic humanism following the modern degradation of its tradition. In all of these essays, Auerbach's goal is to overcome the nihilistic consequences for humanists of the pessimistic vision of modernity that ends *Mimesis*. In essence, his project involves a partial revision of the historicist perspective in *Mimesis* and a movement away from its persistent idealism toward a greater insistence on the political and institutional nature of language. As a result of moving along this line of thought it becomes unavoidable that he give up both the synthetic ideal and the figure of the leading intellectual as presumed necessary ends of humanistic scholarship.

Auerbach's reconsideration of Vico begins the dramatic struggles of the postwar period. For example, in "Vico and Aesthetic Historism,"[1] Auerbach develops a new and more acceptable genealogy for historicist research than the orthodox one of the mandarins. By arguing that Vico's work provides a method and program more appropriate to the special conditions of modernity he tries to displace the nationalistic tradition of the mandarins, which they root in Herder.

*and what
of Bové's
work?*

Auerbach's dissatisfaction with Herder's tradition stems not only from the way it authorizes an extreme nationalism, or the way it claims it "is not political," but also from the way in which it makes "individuality" the subject of history. Furthermore, unlike Vico, Herder's tradition, as Auerbach sees it, irresponsibly refuses to concern itself with the interactions of power and language, an omission that Nazism shows to have been a fatal flaw to its ethical and political integrity. As Auerbach sees it, the German romantic reaction against "Western" theories of Natural Law—which the mandarins feel "fragment" the German *Geist*—leads to "an evolutionary conservatism" or "an organic conservatism" that functions both as an ideological defense against "rationalistic tendencies toward revolutionary progress" (VAH, 187) and as a defense of the social privileges of the professors. This political conservatism is part of an intellectual complex that identifies nations as "individual subjects," that is, as discrete embodiments of spirit that ideally develop according to the laws of reason cultured under the "self-conscious" guidance of the universal mandarin intellectual. As Auerbach recreates the mandarins' version of their genealogy he shows that German historists belong to and sustain this conservative tradition because they trace their origins back to and emerge from the German romantics' "interest in the individual roots and forms of the folk genius. . . . [this tradition] led many of them," he goes on, "to an extremely nationalistic attitude toward their own fatherland, which they considered as the synthesis and supreme realization of folk genius" (VAH, 187). In other words, the modern mandarins attempt to realign themselves with this origin in order to reauthorize themselves, but in the process, they also reauthorize some dangerous values and powers.

Auerbach tells us that, like Rousseau, Herder believes in an original state of nature, free of law and institutions, in which the ultimate values are those "of feeling, of instinct, of inspiration." The accuracy of Auerbach's assertions is less important for our purposes than to see that the way he characterizes Herder reflects the unsatisfactory values and attitudes of the modern nationalist mandarins and the cultural and intellectual disaster that, as Auerbach has it, their discourse helps bring about. Similarly, it would be most useful to see the important differences Auerbach finds between Herder and Vico as a sign of Auerbach's own attempts to dramatize the postwar struggle for intellectual legitimacy. In other words, one must recognize that Auerbach's essay is one step in his ongoing postwar project to replace the degraded and illegitimate discourse of the mandarins with a more politically aware tradition that he thinks can emerge from Vico. For Auerbach, this replacement is necessary to restore some legitimate social and cultural authority to historist, humanist research at a time when its traditional legitimating discourse, methods, and values have been completely discredited. For all these reasons, Auerbach counterposes Vico's severity to Herder's Rousseauism; for Vico, primitive men "created institutions more severe and ferocious, boundaries more narrow and unsurmountable than any civilized society can possibly do" (VAH, 194).

Auerbach's choice of Herder as the figure of twentieth-century mandarin political and intellectual responsibility follows, I think, from Friedrich Meinecke's studies of Herder in which Meinecke tries once more to justify the mandarins' claims to the political "disinterestedness" of their leadership by showing them to be the heirs of Herder. Meinecke writes that Herder "escaped from a disgust with his own times and the excesses of contemporary culture into the world of primitive humanity" (H, 368). (We shall see later in this chapter that Auerbach powerfully criticizes both Pascal and Goethe for just such escapes.)

Auerbach and Meinecke agree that, following Herder, the romantics and their heirs also withdraw from history and the present into a search for "identity" at the heart of origins, an "identity" they hope to find in primitive poetry. Auerbach's position is that the search for "identity" at the origins of history and culture authorizes a nationalist ideology that ranks individual nations: that is, this ideology allows the mandarins, in their role as cultural leaders, to classify and rank the various national "souls" or "spirits" of other peoples on the basis of their conformity to some preestablished idea of the "folk."

"The romantics," Auerbach writes, "were chiefly interested in the individual forms of the historical phenomena; they tried to understand the particular spirit. . . . They studied. . . . the 'folk genius'" (VAH, 196). As we shall see, Auerbach argues explicitly in "Philology and *Weltliteratur*," that despite the apparent commitment to national diversity implicit in this theory of identity, as it works itself out historically, it contributes to the leveling of diversity and so is a threat to "humanity."

In the period after World War I and the revolutions that follow, Meinecke and some few others come to see that the romantic theory of the original identity of the nation in its folk *Geist* cannot be sustained. The theory of national identity fails for these modern mandarins because during and after the war they can no longer believe that the nation is a unit, that the state and the people are one, or, to put it differently, that power and reason or power and justice combine in one entity, the nation, and come to expression in the state.

The German political crisis that undermines the ideology of "identity" creates a crisis of value and social position among the mandarins. Meinecke attempts two apparently different solutions to this crisis; the first, as *Historism* suggests, is an effort to reground the mandarins' authority in an apolitical tradition of concern with "spiritual" matters more "originary" than institutions; the second, carried out primarily in *Machiavellism* (which I shall discuss in the context of Auerbach's essay on Pascal), tries to revise the theory of identity to claim that the state can be seen as and can actually become "just." In both cases, Meinecke hopes to establish new versions of the leading intellectuals' old privileged roles, and in both cases, he tries to extend revised forms of the theory of identity to cover historically new situations (or old situations newly seen), so that the reestablished validity of this theory can reauthorize the mandarins, whose leadership position depends on it.

The principle of identity supports the mandarins' claims to privilege and leadership in a very clear way. Essentially, their authority rests on their ability to cultivate individual members of the ruling elite and to function as ideological spokesmen for that elite; this is an ability that, in terms of Herder's tradition, requires, in turn, general acceptance of the idealist claim that reason, morality, will, and power exist in a harmonious balance within the subject "cultivated" by the mandarins and that, as a result, there is no conflict either between the will of the state and the people or between an individual and others.

Meinecke points out that this theory, given its classic formulation in Hegel's *Philosophy of Right* (1821), and supported by the abstract, formalist arguments of the late nineteenth-century neo-Kantians, needs further revision. His tactics involve conceding that the identity of reason and power is not established a priori either "at the origins," in primitive folk culture, or at the end, so to speak, in the Hegelian vision of the Prussian State and, by extension, the Hohenzollern Empire. Rather, Meinecke contends, the subject must be seen as having only the *potential* for embodying such a synthetic identity.

The romantic, mandarin concept of *"Bildung"* involves cultivating an individual to become wise and sensitive. Meinecke proposes extending the concept to include the "development" of the state. Fritz Ringer provides a useful summary of the idea of *Bildung* in Meinecke's tradition:

Cultivation reflects and originates in religious and neohumanist conceptions of "inner growth" and integral self-development. The starting point is a unique individual. The materials which are "experienced" in the cause of learning are "objective cultural values." . . . the moral and aesthetic examples contained in the classical sources affect him deeply and totally. The whole personality is involved in the act of cognition. If the materials to be learned are properly selected, their contemplation can lead to virtue and wisdom. (*GM*, 87)

Meinecke proposes that since the state is a subject, if it is put under the guidance of the mandarins, it should undergo the same process of *Bildung* and achieve the same sort of "organic" wholeness as the cultivated elite. Following in what he sees as Herder's tradition, Meinecke concludes that the mandarins can regain a leading position vis-à-vis the state and culture if they take up the role of educating the state, of making it more wise and virtuous. But paradoxically, Meinecke contends, if the mandarins hope to effect this most political of institutions, they must give up any concern with politics and power and

turn more toward the "higher, spiritual" realms. (This is a position that he, in turn, shortly revises.) As Iggers puts it,
Meinecke "sought the roots of modern historicism 'in the
wholly unpolitical realm' of changes in thought and values."[2]

Meinecke is himself quite clear about the fact that the theoretical revision he is attempting aims at reestablishing the
authority of the mandarins' position. He hopes that a relegiti-
mated historicism can contain the increasingly severe postwar
social contradictions: "we escape the 'anarchy of values,'
Meinecke continues, "when we realize that every individuality
contains within it its own ideal. . . . The realization that all
values are relative to an individual is not identical with ethical relativism, particularly *if we can maintain our belief 'in a
common, divine, original cause from which all individualities
emerge.'*"[3]

In "Vico and Aesthetic Historism," Auerbach portrays the
mandarin position in essentially the terms Meinecke uses; he
writes, for example, of their "impulse focused at individual
forms of life and art" (VAH, 196). But in this essay, Auerbach
engages in a sometimes indirect critique of three aspects of the
mandarin stance: the theory of identity, nationalism, and the
separation of language and scholarship from politics. In place
of these three dubious concepts, he proposes certain Vichian
possibilities that provide, above all, the opportunity to let the
humanistic scholar get beyond the dead end of this discredited
chauvinist and "apolitical" tradition. Yet, as we shall see,
Auerbach cannot move completely beyond the mandarin impulses of his own values and training. For example, despite
Auerbach's anti-mandarin intent, his characterization of Vico
in terms of "individual genius" and "heroic sublimity" reveals
not only how Auerbach cannot "escape" that tradition but also
how it makes possible his understanding of Vico, and, hence,
his opposition to it. Another way to put this would be to say
that Auerbach's image of the Vichian intellectual is contradictory and that those contradictions reflect Auerbach's own ambiguous political and intellectual position vis-à-vis the
tradition in which he works. In fact, the contradictory use of
Vico in Auerbach's essay allows us to see some of the almost

unvarying features of the composite trope of the leading humanistic intellectual as it appears in the work of the mandarin
tradition and the American professional appropriation of it.

Auerbach feels that Vico provides an alternate focus for research to the priority that mandarin theories of identity place
on the individual subject. Vichian scholarship, Auerbach contends, concerns itself instead with the *entire* spectrum of cultural processes peculiar not to a nation or "folk" but to a
period:

The entire development of human history, as made by men, is potentially contained in the human mind, and may therefore, by a process of
research and reevocation, be understood by men. The re-evocation is
not only analytic, it has to be synthetic, as an understanding of every
historical stage as an integral whole, of its genius . . . a genius pervading all human activities and expressions of the period concerned.
(VAH, 197)

The inclusiveness of Auerbach's Vichian vision differs from
the mandarin insistence on studying only "higher" values; it
also differs in trying to show that "unity" is epochal, not national, and that it is man-made or cultural, that is, constituted
by the totality of all "human" actions. That is to say, this
understanding of historical culture is nonnationalistic; the material and "unity" under study are not defined by their identity
as part of the national *Geist*. Furthermore, since Vichian philology is a general science of culture, it is also, not incidentally, an alternative to modern professional, specialized study,
which divides its materials by traditions (French, English,
etc.) or disciplines (literary studies, philosophy, history).

As a general science of culture, it cannot be consistent and
turn away from matters of politics and institutions or the interrelationship between language and power. For Auerbach, mandarin humanism simply cannot come to grips with one of the
defining characteristics of modernity—the political use of language or the politicization of discourse—because it insists on
the apolitical nature of cultural and linguistic values in order
to justify the ideology of "disinterest" essential to its own privileged claims. Vichian hermeneutics, on the other hand, sup-
plies the basic intellectual framework for a study of this aspect

of modernity because Vico's theoretical history insists that we see that discourse and politics are always intertwined. Auerbach stresses Vico's

discovery of the magic formalism of primitive man, with its power to create and to maintain institutions symbolized by myth; it includes our conception of poetry which has, undoubtedly, some relationship to modern forms of artistic expression. The complete unit of magic "poetry" or myth with political structure in primitive society, the interpretation of myths as symbols of political and economic struggles and developments, the concept of concrete realism in primitive language and myth are extremely suggestive of certain modern tendencies. By the word "tendencies," I do not allude to certain parties or countries, but to trends of thought and feeling spread all over our world. (VAH, 197)

Vico's perception not only counters the mandarin distaste for politics and its contamination of language but also aids the engaged scholar in showing that this "distaste" furthered the establishment of Nazism by promoting irrational, irresponsible discourses which prohibited the engaged application of critical intelligence and scholarly method to the "sign-systems" that furthered Hitler's own coming to power. Had Vico rather than Herder been the "father" of mandarin historism, the theory of identity's assumptions about stability and simple, peaceful, recoverable origins would have been untenable, and intellectuals would have been more easily engaged by Vico's display of a human world always in conflict, in which "poetry" is inseparable from the maintenance of political institutions, and in which battles over the legitimacy of various discourses are, consequently, of great social importance.

It is crucial not only for Auerbach's own oppositional position vis-à-vis the dehumanized mandarin tradition and the anomic scholarly professions but also for his attempts to work out a way to carry on historicist, humanist research that Vico provides strong arguments that culture is in part constituted by the reciprocal power relationship between "poetry" and institutions and that he also suggests powerful ways of decoding these relations to disclose the political struggle they contain and carry out. Simply put, this dimension of Vico's work allows Auerbach to reject the apolitical, disinterested stance of the mandarin humanists' nostalgia for folk origins as reactionary, premodern, and self-deluded. It also allows Auerbach to argue, in a correctly Vichian manner, that this mandarin discourse in itself serves and maintains the institutional forms of the *Geisteswissenschaften* and the sociopolitical interests of their practitioners.

Auerbach finds in Vico's work reasons for moving toward a research method better able to deal with modernity's characteristic political appropriation of discourse by various states, parties, and ideologies. Vico's work shows how the scholar may study the effectivity of power deployed in and by linguistic structures in their relation to cultural institutions.

To put it simply once more, Auerbach can argue through Vico not only that discourse can be weaponry but also that even those discourses claiming to be apolitical are always implicated in power relations. Vico allows Auerbach to go even further and assert (as he does repeatedly in his essay on Pascal) that willfully "apolitical" discourses help to bring about the "levelling" and anomie characteristic of modernity precisely because of their failure to reflect upon the effects of the very institutions and social relations they help to constitute. In other words, from Auerbach's Vichian perspective, mandarin historism and demagogic propaganda exist on a continuum of political interest, stretching, for example, from Max Weber's claims for disinterested rational judgment to Kerschensteiner's boldest claims for elitist rule. The Vichian model both allows such insights and, in itself, provides Auerbach with a theoretical justification for deploying his own skills and knowledge as a weapon in a battle against such positions. It provides an alternative for the intellectul trying to move beyond the false idealistic model of political "disinterest" and an opportunity actually to do so by critiquing such "poems" or "myths" as those of mandarin "identity" in order to expose and subvert their historical and political relations.

Despite Auerbach's opposition to and his attempts to produce various alternatives to mandarin humanism and its authorized and authorizing sign, the figure of the leading intellectual (or class), many of his own claims and much of his own rhetoric nonetheless draw upon and emerge out of the discourse and values of that tradition. For example, while Vico provides Auerbach with a way to move beyond the apolitical theory of national identities, the language Auerbach uses to describe Vico's "theory of cognition" and his empathetic reevocation of culture itself rests on Diltheyan notions of understanding that are a key element of the mandarins' revisionist, idealistic heritage. Furthermore, as Auerbach develops the Vichian notion of epochal unity, it acquires some of the "unifying" characteristics of the mandarin "individual" but now transferred to the ideal of a "period." So clear, at times, is Auerbach's residual temptation to try to reground the mandarin ethos that he occasionally presents Vico merely as its justification. Vico's notion of "synthesis," Auerbach tells us, is simply a better grounded version of the mandarins' project: "the romantics knew and practiced this principle [of human understanding], but they never found such a powerful and suggestive epistemological base for it" (VAH, 197).

Most revealing of all, however, is Auerbach's use of mandarin metaphors of "sublime heroism" to describe Vico and his achievement. So extreme is Auerbach's characterization of Vico that it can be seen not only as a paradigm of the Vichian, and hence of the Auerbachian, ideal at that time but also as the fulfillment of the mandarins' fantasy of their own potency and importance. Auerbach argues, for example, that Vico's "theory of cognition" is not the result of simple "intuition" but is made possible "by his own historical discoveries," an achievement all the more remarkable given the limited historical knowledge available to Vico and his own isolated and intellectually marginal position. Vico, Auerbach recalls, "was supported only by his scholarship in classical philology and Roman law." It follows from this that Auerbach feels that he cannot adequately account for Vico in historico-genetic terms. For Auerbach to take such a position is rather anomalous since it violates the basic principles of his historicist commitment, as well as the Vichian insight into the linkage between "poetry" and institutions. Yet this contradiction is the result of Auerbach's continuing indebtedness to a humanism that resists precisely such insights, that is, to a humanism that while calling itself historical is not quite ready to historicize language and "humanity" thoroughly—a move that Auerbach argues in "Philology and *Weltliteratur*" must be made to preserve "humanity" and that, in turn, he feels by the late 1950s must still be made but at the *cost* of "humanity," itself.

This mandarin tradition persists by finding examples of ahistorical, individual, transcendent "human" accomplishment at the base of cultural achievement as a way of assuring the continuing efficacy of *Bildung* carried out by a "community of great souls" in the canon. In his image of Vico, Auerbach employs the rhetoric of this theory of the "sublime individual" in what is, by contrast to his image of Dante in *Mimesis*, a very ahistorical manner:

It is almost a *miracle* that a man, at the beginning of the eighteenth century in Naples, with such material for his research, could *create a vision* of world history based on the discovery of the magic character of primitive civilization . . . . there are few similar examples in the history of human thought of *isolated creation* due to such an extent to the *particular quality of the author's mind.* He combined an almost *mystical faith in the external order* of human history with a *tremendous power of productive imagination* in the interpretation of myth, ancient poetry, and law. (VAH, 190; my emphases)

Auerbach's text presents us with a strange dichotomy: Vico makes possible and would seem to require a method of historical research into the historicized culture of human production as the only strategy for understanding the social world; yet, at least as Auerbach images him, the author of this theory is not only himself inexplicable in its own terms but does not derive his theory by practicing his advocated method. Nor are we presented with some metatheory of theory production. Auerbach simply appeals to Vico's power as a great originator as a way to explain the grounding of a procedure and politics inimicable to theories of such original authority.

Auerbach falls back upon these mandarin humanistic irrationalisms not simply because of some unshakeable, unacknowledged pernicious influence; rather, this rhetoric is readily at hand for Auerbach to accomplish his goal of authorizing Vico as an alternate "source" for humanistic research and, by extension, himself and his own projects against the nihilism and despair evoked by his study of Pascal. (That Vico's marginal, "exiled" position reminds us of Auerbach's position is clear, as it is that the position of both scholars reminds us of Said.)[4] So Auerbach's use of these metaphors is a tactic to gain authority and influence for a position seemingly opposed to the tradition from which he derives these metaphors. Even so, such a move on Auerbach's part contradicts his project and, on a higher level, replicates those of both the mandarins and the American professionals. In the process of tactically authorizing Vico, he submerges the research project he hopes to authorize in a pool of irrationalism and perpetuates the basic authority of the opportunistic and naive traditions against which he is struggling.

Granted that Auerbach employs the rhetoric of the sublime genius to describe Vico as a tactic against Herder et al. and that he is not simply caught in an unconscious struggle for influence—nonetheless, his tactic misfires. Not only does he authorize Vico, but in so doing he reforms, extends, and redeploys the ideological commitment to the figure of the ahistorical leading intellectual so essential to the mandarins and the professionals. Auerbach's text becomes just the opposite of what he wants it to be, namely, a relay through which crucial elements of the ahistorical, apolitical legitimation of the mandarin ideology are reactivated and transmitted. Auerbach's essay does not modify the basic features of the figure of the leading intellectual in any way. The characteristics of Vico's method are subsumed in the visionary qualities of Auerbach's own revisionary move.

Acting more like Herder that Vico, Auerbach writes an essay in which the measures of intellectual greatness and cultural significance would not have disturbed his intellectual predecessors. "Vico and Aesthetic Historism" is not a Vichian essay, not if Auerbach's description of Vico's commitment to the politics of language and historical specificity are the standards—despite Auerbach's announced deployment of Vico *against* the mandarins. But the essay is Vichian if the image of the visionary Vico is the standard, for then Auerbach appears to have produced an equally re-visionary assertion of priority based on the irrational powers of sublime will and imagination. Auerbach will not, however, remain caught in this particular set of contradictions. As we shall see, in "Philology and *Weltliteratur*" he moves strongly *against* the priority of critical or revisionary will toward a more consistent commitment to historicist research. Rather than submerge "history" in some form of "originary" human potential, as he does in his essay on Vico, in "Philology and *Weltliteratur*," he produces his most sophisticated attempt to sustain both "history" and "humanity" by specifically theorizing the latter as a historical product, but, nonetheless, it soon becomes evident that even this monumental effort cannot maintain itself, and Auerbach's compulsory abandonment of synthetic projects attests his inability to sustain the humanists' vision in modernity.

In "Vico and Aesthetic Historism," his use of the sublime trope of the originary intellectual puts Auerbach in an untenable position contradicting the Vichian stress on the importance of historical specificity in cultural research. Trying to be true to that Vichian emphasis, we might say that Auerbach's critical and scholarly failure is one of method: committed to both the defense of any still valuable remnants of humanistic discourses and to the analysis of "poetry's" political relation to institutions, he resists turning his analytic, scholarly, genetic tools upon the still powerful enabling elements of intellectual sublimity. Of course, he could not easily stand "inside" humanism and do this; had he been more consistent, however, Vico might have provided him with some way to carry out part of such a reflexive investigation. Instead, true to his mandarin tradition, Auerbach deploys Vico in a familiar revisionist manner and rather than take up the opportunity to carry out perspectival research into the "affiliations," as Said might say, of discourses legitimating humanism with other discourses and practices, he regresses in some ways from the methodological cautions of *Mimesis* and restores the radical subjectivism at the heart of the mandarin conception of history. Specifically, the priority Auerbach assigns to Vico's originary powers unsatisfactorily restores the individual subject to priority in history not just by making all historical process a function of consciousness but also by reasserting the power of the isolated visionary to produce syntheses by immediately intuiting and representing the *integrity* of historical periods and the order of history itself.

Such a reassertion betrays the progressive aspects of Vico's historicism to the mandarins' conservatism by reassigning "sublimity," not just to Auerbach's "Vico," but in turn to the Vichian researcher, that is, to the scholar whose work is authorized either by sharing in the legitimacy flowing from the source or by aspiringly hoping to imitate and so perhaps displace the origin. Of course, to accomplish such a goal, to follow this Vichian model, the ephebe must, like Auerbach's Vico, be specially cultured and almost mystically endowed.

Several consequences follow from this genealogical pattern. It covertly restores the principle of individualism—against which Auerbach again later takes up the fight—by assigning its virtues to the "researcher." It turns the scholar into a visionary synthesizer who must be "mystically" sympathetic to the wholeness of history. And, to complete the relay from the mandarins to the American profession, it authorizes a model of scholarly research not unlike the hierarchical competitive structure that reveals itself in its appropriation of Auerbach. In other words, Auerbach's comments on Vico and few other heroes capable of "isolated creation" not only parallel the similar remarks about Auerbach made by Leo, Muscatine, and Said but also suggest that there is a similar discursive structure of intellectual authority and legitimacy in two historically different institutions. Since Auerbach is one of the most important links between these two institutions, it is possible to derive from his own work and part of the discursive tradition in which it is inscribed some insight into at least one of its major facets, that is, the enduring figure of the authorized and authorizing "sublime" or "leading intellectual."

First of all, within the tradition in which Auerbach is inscribed, such powerful figures must be visionaries, capable of producing imaginative images of the whole of "world history," often taking a very limited amount of knowledge and a quite specific, often narrow, point of departure. Secondly, while not without "context" or "influence," these visionary figures are often in opposition to the orthodoxy of the day: they are not merely heterodox but also, as in Vico's case vis-à-vis Cartesianism, both marginal and actively in opposition. Hence, those figures are marginalized, oppositional visionaries. Thirdly, the source of their power to produce totalizing visions and to stand (often alone) in opposition, at least in intellectual opposition, is some frequently private, perhaps intangible, certainly abstract quality of internal personal being. In Vico's case, it is "productive imagination," an unaccountable phenomenon, source, or name for a power that makes possible visionary work otherwise equally unaccountable, that is, transcendent and ahistorical (as in Muscatine's vision of Auerbach) or miraculous and mysterious (as in Auerbach's image of Vico—or as in Vico's view of poets). Fourthly, these figures are always *re*visionists; that is, they are interpreters whose vision compels and enables the making over of all "myth, . . . poetry, and law," namely, past and present culture, in an act of interpretation that, by its very visionary nature, totalizes what it treats according to the dictates of the particular visionary's historical needs to remake the past. Fifthly, the revisionary successors of these figures hail them as great originary sources and exemplars. Their visions and the image of the intellectual they represent enable and authorize "new directions," "new projects," and "new lines of thought." Of course, there is a strange and, for our post-Nietzschean age, familiar mechanism at work here: the great originary figure's authority is often a function of the successor's own revisionary pursuit of legitimation in the rereading of the past. Primitive fathers, that is, are often the children of their heirs. Sixthly, such figures legitimate their own power and desires by identifying themselves, directly or not, with some version of this composite trope. The particular variations matter, but in modernity, as least, seemingly not so much as the ability to deploy a recognizable version of this figure as not just a textual ideal but as an authorizing self-image.

In modernity, as least among humanists and in their institutions, this trope is so powerful, unrecognized (even when acknowledged), and essential as a keystone of discourse legitimating intellectual life and individual intellectuals that its success in containing, expressing, and satisfying intellectuals' needs for authority, influence, and ability forms a repetitive pattern whose variations seem less significant than at first sight. Moreover, the efficacy and importance of this trope for intellectuals is repressed; while literary intellectuals may acknowledge its existence, they do not investigate its origins or consequences. Its ubiquity facilitates its repression under the sign of the "obvious" and "necessary." But what it means—that this is the general pattern and specific sign of the elitist group of powerful literary intellectuals—does not get probed. It may be an "obvious" pattern as humanists claim, but it does not follow that it is "natural" as, for example, is heat's relation to fire.

Some, like Foucault and Gramsci, suggest other images for the intellectual and social roles other than those of the leading and representative intellectual or of the critic as star or celebrity. Alternatives to this authorizing figure of intellectual action and status require not just taking up an "oppositional" or "marginal" position or ideology vis-à-vis the hegemonic order; many such moves can be accommodated under the sign of Vico. Rather, and we can see the necessity for this in the work of both Foucault and Gramsci, any serious alternative must involve a historical critique of the power structure and social role of the intellectual and intellectual discourses and institutions in order to understand what the authority and power of this magisterial composite trope both allows intellectual practice to be and what it prevents it from becoming.[5]

Such a structure does not prevent the production of knowledge, nor does it inhibit humanistic defenses of the cultural utility and desirability of the traditions it defends and makes possible. Indeed, as Auerbach's use of Vico makes clear, certain intellectual revisionary productions can have politically and culturally "progressive" results and can emerge from equally admirable intentions. But from the fact that strong, disinterested, humanistic critics can develop arguments to defend the utility of the trope as the course of authority justifying certain ways of seeing canons and traditions as culturally needed bulwarks against modernity, it does not follow that such arguments do not repress the role individual and human interests play in the sustaining and utilization of this trope. Even the most sophisticated and disinterested heirs of this tradition censor the effects of interest in literary intellectual discourse, and they often do so by making it appear as a "given" not to be excessively examined without, from the point of view of this tradition, undue consequences, that is to say, without shaking the foundations of the entire edifice of a hierarchically structured and individualized institution of intellectual rewards and frustrations.[6]

II

Auerbach's highly complex attitude toward the consequences of his own pessimism are perhaps most fully worked out in "On the Political Theory of Pascal." In that essay, Auerbach struggles against the same nihilistic temptation to close off the future in despair and resignation as critics must resist when they are tempted to see Auerbach's appropriation by the structure of power/interest as a sign of that structure's total power.

A full consideration of "On the Political Theory of Pascal" would require a detailed study of the modern German debate over the strengths and weaknesses of natural law theorists, theorists of the *raison d'etat* (such as Machiavelli and Hobbes), and of the German thinking on the questions basic to all of these: are there norms in history, or can the state be expected to be rational and ethical?[7]

The German mandarins do not begin to question the state's identity with ethical norms until the disastrous growth of military influence on the home front during World War I makes the question unavoidable. Before that time, Meinecke, for example, argues that the state cannot but be a norm. In the postwar years, however, he turns his efforts to trying to show that while the state is irresistably driven to unethical, irrational, excessive, and self-glorifying acts of violence, it is restrained by a parallel "logic" of self-preservation and culminates, at best, as we have seen, in a harmonious balance (or *Bildung*):

It has been justly pointed out . . . that, although it is in the essence of power to rule blindly, yet nevertheless the blind and unregulated rule of power in real life is a very exceptional occurrence. Power which gushes out blindly will end by destroying itself; it must follow certain purposive rules and standards, in order to preserve itself and grow. Cunning and force must therefore unite in the exercise of power. . . . In such a way there comes into existence a supra-personal entelechy, which leads the ruler beyond himself, but which at the same time is always nourished and approved by the personal impulse and interests of the ruler himself. . . . *Raison d'etat* forces the power-impulse to satisfy more general needs, but the power-impulse forces this satisfaction back again within definite frontiers.[8]

Although Meinecke no longer holds the earlier mandarin position that, in a Hegelian fashion, identifies reason and the state in a philosophy of right, his theory (and the interests it defends, do not permit him to consider either that their relationship might be random or that the state and power should be considered in other terms. So strong is his resistance to these options that he postulates a historical model in which developing theories of the *raison d'état* are held, contrary to tradition, to act as a form of *Bildung* and progressively to point out and reenforce the rational and ethical restrictions on power. In order to support this thesis Meinecke argues, for example, that Hobbes is only tactically an absolutist for the "higher" goals absolutism can bring to a people. "Hobbes' doctrine of the State," Meinecke concludes, "is one of the most remarkable examples of the dialectic of development, of the transitions possible from one idea to another, and of the way in which the very culminating point of the older idea can lead over into the more recent and modern idea."[9] Meinecke claims to be optimistic about the relationship between power and justice because, as he sees it, dialectics can ensure not only that the self-interested, personal, and, therefore, despotic exercise of power can be contained but also that its "progressive" or "developing" transformation and transcendence will lead society to higher states; culture is a rational product of the ethicization of power:

Once it has come into existence, this supra-personal entelechy is of extraordinary significance, leading on further and further towards higher values. Now one is serving some higher entity which rises far above individual life, one is no longer serving oneself—that is the decisive point, where the crystallization into nobler forms begins, where what was formerly no more than necessary and useful now begins to be felt also as beautiful and good. Until finally the State stands out as a moral institution for the provision of the highest qualities of life—until finally the impulsive will-to-power and to-life on the part of a nation is transformed into that morally conscious national mode of thought, which sees in the nation a symbol of an eternal value.[10]

Yet Meinecke is not convinced by his own vision. The transcendence of the state's self-interest into a national morality is put off, in his theory—as it was in Kant's, which drew Hegel's critique—till some final time, perhaps when history ends. He seems only able to believe, at best, in the fact that history is the striving toward the coincidence of power and virtue. But in the passing epochs of life itself, as even Meinecke admits, reality is much more mixed. Meinecke's sense of this mixture seems to be the nightmare side to his vision of a finally moral power:

But it is always toward this belief in some higher power, which demands both human service and sacrifice, that the intellectual and moral elements in Man are constantly straining forward. The history of the idea of *raison d'etat* will make this clear. But such a history will have to do more—it will at the same time have to show the eternal bondage of Man to physical nature, the ever-recurring lapse of *raison d'etat* back into the basic elemental powers.[11]

As a practical historian, in the face of this inevitable ambiguity, Meinecke finds that all he can do is study specific instances of the state's transgression of morality, as well as specific theories of *raison d'etat*, while hoping to understand how and why the state always, inevitably, exceeds the moral limits it should come to embody and while trying to judge how near a particular state comes to the harmonious ideal. As he points out at the close of his "Introduction," the "collapse" of Germany in the social upheavals of 1918 have driven him to this tortuous project of telling the tragic history of *raison d'etat's* murderous conflict with truth and beauty.

While it would be reductive to argue that Meinecke's pro-
digious effort begins as merely a defense of mandarin intent,
one can point out, after Ringer, that Meinecke's sense of the
crises of 1918 involves an immense anxiety over the loss of mandarin authority. Meinecke continually worries that 1918 marks
an irreparable break in German traditions and feels "the need,"
as Ringer quotes him, "to 'bridge the huge split which has appeared in our nation as a result of the World War and the Revolution'" (GM, 211). Like the other mandarins, Meinecke not
only is suspicious of the Social Democrats but also fears their
denial of the mandarins' cultural authority. For him, the most
important postwar division is that between the cultured and
uncultured classes. Ringer argues that "The Revolution had
revealed a deep popular resentment of mandarin traditions."
Since Meinecke is one of the most progressive leading intellectuals of postwar Germany, Ringer is correct to emphasize the
importance of understanding his political position and his
efforts at cultural renewal in any history of German intellectual politics:

There was a real danger that the new society would totally reject the
values of the German past and those who had "hitherto guarded" them.
Meinecke addressed one of his passionate speeches in behalf of national
reconciliation to the "ancient, original culture-bearing segment
[Kulturschicht] of the nation, which must not die [untergehen], because it is indispensable for the maintenance of the first prerequisite of
culture, namely tradition." Unless the "tear" in the nation, the "rent"
in history, could yet be mended, the future would indeed be an age of
reckless levelling and cultural shallowness. The mandarins' whole
value system was at stake. (GM, 211)

Meinecke finds himself in a contradictory situation: given
the horrors of the war, he can no longer accept the idea of the
state as the guardian and embodiment of ethical and cultural
norms. Yet given the crises he experiences after the war,
Meinecke feels that reasserting the traditional cultural authority of the mandarins is necessary. Yet how can this be done
when the state structure and power in cooperation with which
the mandarins built their privilege and authority, which allowed them to sustain and enforce their own values—when this
state suddenly appears irrational and murderous and the na-

tional moral unity it supposedly structured fragments in revolution and multiparty parliamentary chaos?

In *Machiavellism*, Meinecke tries to deal with this problem
in two ways: one result of the scholarship developed in such
works should be to establish or give arguments to establish that
the state is moving in an essentially evolutionary direction
while simultaneously acknowledging and being on guard
against its naturalistic tendencies of *raison d'état*; also, the
mandarins should, as another result of this scholarship, regain
a legitimate, authorized cultural role that only they can perform; namely, bringing informed, cultivated judgment to bear
on history's examples of statist irrationalism and immorality.
That is, humanists can now, in specific cases, *judge* why and to
what end a state exceeds morality, and whether such moves
threaten the civilizing march toward the regained (but seemingly infinitely postponed) identification of state with national morality. But there are severe limits to Meinecke's
solution. He not only gives us no idea of how mandarin research and publication might *effect* the state's actions—indeed, it is not clear that for him it can or should try to do so—
but his position has very conservative consequences: since the
state will always and inevitably go beyond the limits of reason
and morality, revolutionary action aimed at correcting the
state's abuses is quite pointless, especially when such action
intends to impose a culture and leadership inimical to the
mandarins.

No matter which of Meinecke's two contradictory hypothe-
ses is uppermost in his theory and research at any given moment, the consequences are the same. Resignation, acceptance, and passivity result both from his optimistic sense of the
inevitable but always postponed victory of morality over power
and from his nihilistic sense that the state cannot be ra-
tionalized. Both positions serve the same interests; they are, in
fact, the same position in different guises: both justify the reactionary interests of the mandarins and others hoping to recap-
ture past privileges, and both subvert the revolutionary forces
of 1919, which hope to alter the distribution of power by seizing
the state. Effectively, this position is reactionary for more than
one reason: in contrast to Vico, for example, it implicitly de-

nies that man makes history and it explicitly denies Marx's variant that men can change it; also Meinecke's pessimistic and optimistic positions are nihilistic; that is, they both support models of history as a closed system, immune to struggle, and coopting all opposition. To revert to Pound's metaphor, Meinecke is a historian who leaves no gaps.

Meinecke's importance for Auerbach cannot be overstated. As we have already seen, his *Historism* is an important influence on and provides a context for Auerbach's own methods and sense of tradition. In a similar way, Meinecke's *Die Idee der Statsräson* (*Machiavellism, The Doctrine of Raison d'État*) (1924) is an important part of the context for Auerbach's postwar considerations of the relationship between power, the state, ethics, and language, especially in his essay on Pascal. Just as Meinecke responds to the dreadful slaughter and murderous revolution of 1918–1919 with his book, which tries to judge the role of humanists and their discourse in a society confronted by the new conditions of culture and mind, so too Auerbach, in the years after his exile and World War II, returns to just these questions. He discusses the same issues of justice, ethics, and *raison d'état* as Meinecke does in *Machiavellism* but aims to arrive at different conclusions appropriate to a different moment.

To put the matter most simply, "On the Political Theory of Pascal" is concerned with the legitimacy of national inquiry and critique in the face of the complete breakdown of state morality and nationality before, during, and after the Nazi period. As such, it is a partial revision of Meinecke's book. Meinecke had tried (under neo-Kantian influence) to exorcise from mandarin ideology the nostalgic desire for Hegelian synthesis in the face of contradictory reality, but given the contradictions of his own position and the inadequacy of his self-critique, it is not surprising that he lapses into a rather silly, but expected, cautionary solution to the problem of the relationship between power and justice: Contemplation, he writes, "can only appeal to the executive statesman that he should always carry State and God together in his heart, if he is not to let himself be overpowered by the daemon (which he is still not quite capable of shaking off completely)."[12]

In "On the Political Theory of Pascal," Auerbach attempts three revisionary responses to the total alienation of morality from the state and the potentially nihilistic response of Western humanists in the face of the cultural and political disaster of World War II. First, he tries to establish the grounds for an individual ethics. Second, he hopes to legitimate the activity of scholarly reason. Third, he retrieves, perhaps unavoidably, a version of Meinecke's idea that, under certain circumstances, the state not only can be ethical but also can actually cultivate civilization. As is the case with *Mimesis* and the essay on Vico, Auerbach's essay on Pascal should be read as an intervention into the intellectual crisis provoked by the war and the holocaust. Auerbach's enormous humanistic courage consists precisely in his assuming the full burden of the immediate historical situation as it confronts him and other humanists after the war—not in his "heroic" exile or his "transcendental" concern with matters of a timeless "canon."

Meinecke's argument does not solve the crucial problem his own work poses: how to know when the state's actions taken in its own interest are, in fact, moral—or, if immoral from a certain perspective, nonetheless necessary and unavoidable. Surely Auerbach's memory of the ethical humanists not just employing rhetoric appropriated by the Nazis but also actually for varying lengths of time supporting the regime that its own traditions had prepared for renders Meinecke's "solution" to the problem of evil and the state transparently ineffective and naive. The state cannot be counted on to preserve itself, nor the statesman to think of God and power. Since in many ways, Meinecke's work is the high point of the mandarin's response to the political crisis, it would not seem unjust to conclude from it that the tradition of historical idealism worsens the problem and provides no solution. Despair would then seem to be the unavoidable consequence for the high humanistic intellectual since his political and cultural tradition is hopelessly compromised and he would seem to be unable to do anything except perhaps turn from this world altogether.

Pascal has two functions in the drama of Auerbach's essay that is his response to this situation. Pascal is the sign of those whose despair makes high intellectual activity impossible, and he is also the sign of the dangers of Meinecke's approach. Meinecke's "solution" founders because the conditions of its possibility no longer exist—indeed, their nonexistence is the reason for the problem he tries to solve. Social and economic contradictions had fragmented the consensus on which the *Kulturstaat* had operated. Without that consensus or some god miraculously justifying the possibility of making certain and clear judgments about the morality of state action, errors like those that lead to the professors' cultural support of the Nazis could always be made. In the seventeenth century, in absolutist, Catholic France, Meinecke's solutions might have been accepted. After Hitler, they could have no force.

Under the influence of St. Augustine and Port-Royal, Pascal argues that resistance to injustice is legitimate only when God requires that resistance. When personal desires are successfully repressed—even those desires for the truth or justice rooted in our human needs—we are capable of legitimately struggling against injustice only as part of God's will: "But if it is really God who is acting through us," Auerbach paraphrases Pascal as saying, "we experience no feelings that do not spring from the principles of our actions. . . . Awareness of this gives peace of soul, and such inner peace is the best sign that it is really God who is acting through us" (*SD*, 119). But Pascal distrusts inner beliefs as a test of God's will, recommending instead that an examination of our behavior is a better measure of divine presence. Specifically, as Auerbach sees it, Pascal insists that the Christian must passively bear *all* injustice as the will of God: "The patient endurance of outward obstacles indicates a harmony in our soul between Him who inspires our will to fight and Him who permits opposition to our struggle, and since there can be no doubt that it is God who permits the opposition, we may be justified in humbly hoping that it is He who inspires our will to fight" (*SD*, 120). Yet Pascal's suspicions cast doubt even on his strategy since a fighter might still be deluded about his motives in fighting. Auerbach skillfully extracts the only notion on which Pascal could ground this theory of judging the injustice of power: "For provided we desire nothing but God's will, we must be just as content if the truth succumbs and remains hidden as if it conquers and is made manifest, for in the latter case it is God's mercy that triumphs and in the former his justice" (*SD*, 120).

Taken theoretically, Meinecke's claim that all that the intellectual can do is judge individual instances of state power to see if they conform to some ideal (but with no possible way to ground that judgment) makes sense only if the judge is radically indifferent to whether justice or injustice eventuates. For example, the judgment of the mandarins against Weimar and for the nationalists is a judgment authorized by Meinecke's position; that is, the mandarins aspire to authority under the flag of a higher "indifference," which is, in fact, a mask for their own values and authority. Of course, their vaunted "disinterest" makes them impotent to oppose the warmongers and racists (whose hatreds they often shared) and, by setting up the history of state power as a closed system immune to resistance, discourages such resistance, inhibits the development of scholarly methods to deal with the material relationships of power and struggle, and so strengthens the rising authority of various irrationalisms (by denying reason's efficacy) in the Weimar period.

For Pascal, the Christian misanthrope, the resulting horror of failed struggle against injustice is inconsequential. For Auerbach, not only are the consequences intolerable, but also Meinecke's and Pascal's positions are implicated in the horror; they are both failures of critical intelligence and scholarly method:

Although this doctrine, to which Port-Royal adhered in theory and still more in practice, relates to injustice in the world, it did not lead to political criticism: it taught men to endure whatever happens in the world, whether it be right or wrong. The question of whether what happens is sometimes or always wrong, or wrong only in particular cases, was not taken into consideration. To be sure Port-Royal followed St. Augustine in regarding the world in general as evil; but it did not ask, and certainly it did not apply the methods and standards of human reason to ascertaining, whether individual legislators and governments might not be moved by God's grace and mercy, so causing a certain amount of justice to prevail frequently or occasionally, or whether this was never the case. (*SD*, 116–17)

Just as Port-Royal prevents the application of politically informed reason and research to particular cases, so too does Meinecke's commitment to the late neo-Kantian and neo-Hegelian idea that, despite the conflict with nature (which is bestial), the state will become a moral ideal also preempt political considerations. His position substitutes for such considerations "judgments" about how "closely" a particular state, given its power nature, comes to approximating the ideal—an achievement, Meinecke's conclusion suggests, that depends solely on the almost superhuman skills and knowledge of the statesmen or leader.

Paradoxically, as Auerbach points out, Pascal goes beyond Port-Royal and studies the political realities of his time, that is, the absolutist state, in some detail. Auerbach tells us that the result of this study is "a tragic paradox, both powerful and dangerous" (SD, 117), that is, a rigorous demonstration that the state is completely unjust and the radical Augustinian conclusion that it is justly so; it is the will of God for Pascal and cannot be changed and should not be struggled against. "These same ideas recur in the Pensées," writes Auerbach, "where the absurdity and fortuitousness of human institutions are described in such a way that would be highly revolutionary if not for the Augustinian setting" (SD, 113). Instead, the consequence of the nonpolitical manner of dealing with power is to suspend "the methods and standards of human reason," to put God in place of man, fate in place of culture, and to produce a closed system of injustice in which struggle is inconsequential.

In the late 1940's, given not only the horror of the war, but also, for the "culturally enlightened" intellectual, the illegitimacy of the traditional high cultural discourses for dealing with power, reason, justice, and desire, given, in other words, the apparently final failure of the intellectual class to understand and account for history ("Past and Present," as Meinecke entitles his last chapter), even for those intellectuals who see that much of humanist discourse at least indirectly aided the Nazi horror, no possibility for making sense of a world where power and reason are permanently fragmented seems to exist. Intellectuals should, then, despair. They seem to be dealing with a closed system of power and irrationality unanswerable to morality or reason. Pascal's world without his God is what is left; perhaps the accurate contemporary image is Sartre's *Huis Clos (No Exit)*.

Auerbach's response is to suggest that despair (or religion) amounts to a politically impossible abandonment of reason that is not just a response to injustice but one of its causes. The central issues can be posed in the form of two questions: can the weak be legitimate, that is, do they have the right to struggle against injustice (Pascal would say "no," because might defines right, and injustice is God's will); can humanistic intellectuals be legitimate in a period that sees their frequent complicity with power and the universal servility of their discourse to power?

For Pascal power is everywhere and all is subservient to it—except the realm of the mind. Auerbach points out this inconsistency in Pascal: "Either the human mind can triumph over might or might can repress it" (*SD*, 115). The second alternative is consistent with Pascal's politics, but holding the position means that "he would have had to abase science and thought to the same level as all other aspects of man" (*SD*, 115). Auerbach stresses that Pascal's separation of power and intellect is so total that where he speaks of might he never speaks of mind. As Auerbach shows, Pascal cannot in theory maintain this separation. (It is one of Auerbach's lapses not to ask how and why Pascal might do so nonetheless.) If mind is independent of power, power cannot repress the truth and "this would justify revolution in the name of the mind." At the same time, Pascal cannot admit, despite his own writings on Galileo, that politics can interfere with "such relatively unpolitical forms of human thought as mathematics and physics" (*SD*, 115). What Auerbach leaves unsaid is that Pascal's aim is to prevent the contact of reason with power in any "impure," that is, political value where the criteria of reason and scholarly inquiry might be brought to bear on ethical and political questions. The theoretical reasons for this are clear in Pascal: pure reason is a gift of God, found in mathematics; the injustice of the world is a divine mystery closed to human comprehension. The effect is to foreclose the possibility of a "science" of society, power, or public ethics. Without Pascal's God, this would be called despair or nihilism. That is to say, to conclude that human reason is useless in the face of an apparently mysterious and incomprehensible and absolutely resistant (or random) reality has nihilistic political and cultural consequences against which Auerbach is warning his contemporaries. Such apolitical, nihilistic responses are exactly like those that help bring about the crises out of which they supposedly emerge.[13]

Auerbach's essay, however, is not restricted simply to warning against the consequences of such intellectual despair, against the cultural and human irresponsibility of intellectuals who like Pascal feel "the political order of this world is madness and violence . . . the triumph of madness and violence, the triumph of evil on earth" (SD, 119), and so retreat into the equally irrational worlds of private experience or religious values of contemptu mundi.[14] In a dialectical move like that with which he ends many of the chapters of Mimesis, Auerbach turns to the highly inadequate position of despair he locates in Pascal and discovers there positive possibilities for moving beyond it. The difference between Pascal's avowed aims and the conclusions to be drawn from his critique of existing social institutions is precisely the space Auerbach needs not only to retrieve some of the insights of Pascal's work but also, more generally, to find evidence (against Pascal's own claims) of the efficacy of the rational critique of existing power structures:

In Trois Discours sur la condition des grands, he proves to a grand seigneur that his prestige and power are not based on any national and authentic right, but solely on the will of the legislators—a different whim, a different tour d'imagination on their part, and he would be poor and powerless. (SD, 112)

Auerbach proposes psychological, political, social, and intellectual reasons why Pascal cannot pursue his own insights but arrives, instead, at an absolute quietism and apoliticism. In so doing, especially in the form of an indirect intervention in his own contemporary scene, Auerbach is giving an example of the critical reason Pascal sometimes practices, but in

Auerbach's case, the horrors of genocide and his historicist consciousness do not allow him to lapse into the temptations of contemplation.

In addition, Auerbach finds, once more in the space between Pascal's intent and his disclosures, an attractive possibility for ethics. In a fragmentary digression, and against the force of Pascal's misanthropy, he announces that he finds in Pascal's argument that justice can be done even if truth is hidden (SD, 122) the point of departure for a modern ethics:

The proposition that in the sense described a man can commit injustice but not suffer it, seems to me valuable as an ethical working hypothesis. At least in the initial phase, ethics can only be individual, that is, a question between me and my conscience. Anyone who succeeds in recognizing that whatever happens to him is just, regardless of how wrong others may have been in doing it, has, it seems to me, not only acquired a foundation for ethical thinking and his own ethical attitude, but also has found a new way of looking at everything that happens in the world. But it is no easy matter to make this insight a lasting basis for one's practical behavior. (SD, 123)

Fascinatingly, however, Auerbach does not comment on the political implications of what is for him an apparently Archimedian point for renewing the humanistic ethos. While making clear that this ethical position seems inconsistent with Pascal's misanthropic reversal of the command "love thy neighbor"—"without it," Auerbach writes of the logic of Pascal's position, "one would hate one's neighbor as oneself" (SD, 111)—he fails to consider its consistency with Pascal's political position, which, as Auerbach acknowledged, aligns him, not just with Machiavelli, but with Hobbes and other seventeenth-century theorists of raison d'ètat.

Indeed, Pascal goes beyond even their pessimistic position:

Like Hobbes he stresses the necessity and legitimacy of a powerful state, but he is much more profoundly aware that this "legitimacy" is evil. . . . In Pascal, too, the purpose or rather the natural function of power is to create and preserve peace . . . but even if the individual gains nothing by this, even if he suffers perpetual repression and never gains peace, he must obey. (SD 127)

This theory brings Pascal to the position of believing in a closed system: "power as an institution is an evil . . . whence it follows that no exercise of it can be anything but injustice and folly" (SD, 128).

The ethical position that interests Auerbach also allows a version of Meinecke's "solution" to reappear. In both Meinecke's and Pascal's stances, an ultimate indifference to the link between justice and power can alone ground the position. Both fail to provide conditions for even intellectual struggle against unjust power. Meinecke's neo-Kantian failure results from his commitment to the evolutionary link of the state and reason as this appears in the also evolving political understanding of German idealists. Humanists measuring the state's conformity to an ideal are not necessarily applying the standards of human reason and scholarship; they are, in short, in contrast to Auerbach's efforts, "apolitical" and so irresponsible and reactionary. But Auerbach's ethic, difficult and undeveloped as it is, runs the risk of reestablishing the intent or goal of Meinecke's solution, not in its dialectical echoes of Meinecke's comparative evolutionary optimism—although Auerbach does speak as if Voltaire's use of Pascal's arguments against the latter's intent is a sort of progress—but rather in its suggestion of a certain indifference to the matter of *political* injustice. The point here is not that Auerbach's position looks individualistic; he is simply saying ethics should begin by striving to overcome the "divided self;" nor is it that it might well require intellectuals to lead a population to accept such an ethics. On the contrary, it is that this ethics, too, fails to justify struggle. In a sense that is the issue of the entire essay: how to ground and legitimate both struggle against injustice and the intellectual's role in the process.

If Auerbach seems strangely silent on this issue in his digression on a personal ethic, one should consider that the affinity of Pascal's position with Hobbes' and other theorists of *raison d'état* might suggest the difficulty Auerbach would have in grounding an ethically and intellectually legitimate form of humanistic struggle on Pascal's misanthropy. The space Pascal leaves Auerbach to attempt his project is not large, and given that Pascal is, as I have already suggested, the name for the real pessimistic conclusion of the postwar moment, Auerbach's way could not have been simple. Pascal's ethics could end injustice only if everyone agreed to see himself as justly transgressed; short of that, it not only cannot "end" injustice, but it apparently cannot authorize struggle against unjust powers. But in making this attempt to struggle, to relegitimate intellectual discourse as both an element in political, cultural life and a method for finding in the spaces texts leave open future possibilities for social and intellectual life, Auerbach not only resists the terror of nihilism, of despair over the seemingly closed system of power, but also gives new sense to one of Pascal's most quietistic ideas and so succeeds, despite his "ethics," in his project as well: he finds the opportunity for turning Pascal against himself and so authorizing our own future. Escaping Meinecke's foolishly Hegelian nostalgia to provide a totalizing solution to the problem of power and justice, Auerbach, through the entire struggle of which this essay is a part, gains a victory over timeless, ahistorical, Pascalian misanthropy and despair.

Auerbach's essay overturns Pascal's claim that it is illegitimate to struggle, while giving new meaning to Pascal's own warning against struggle: "Some men, however, act as though their mission were to bring about the triumph of truth, while in reality our mission is only to fight for it" (SD, 120). Without either the shaken faith of Meinecke or the skeptical, severe belief of Pascal, Auerbach's own effort, which is a victorious sign that struggle can go on, neutralizes the relativizing, daemonic strength of Pascal's question, a question that, in its implicit call for an impossible certainty, reflects a habit of mind and set of cultural values that during the modern period authorizes some forms of totalitarianism, as well as the figure of the leading intellectual as the power supposedly able, as professional, expert, and sublime hero, to provide answers to these questions:

Yes, but is there a justice independent of might? Can we recongnize it? No, we cannot. Are those who are oppressed by might without justice justified in complaining? Certainly not, for how do we know that they are in the right? Are the transgressors who challenge a justice without

might objectively evil? Who can decide. *La justice est sujette à dispute.*
(*SD*, 124)

Meinecke's pathetic oscillation between positive and negative
answers to these questions is a result of his wanting to avoid
conceding the truth of Pascal's statement that *"La justice est
sujette à dispute."* Auerbach concedes its truth, but unlike Pascal does not want to withdraw from the interminable battle it
tells us must go on. On the contrary, Auerbach sets out to find a
way humanists and literary critics can engage in the struggle
and help set the sense of "justice," itself. "Justice" is not an
abstract a priori, easily applicable in social situations as some
might suggest[15]; rather the meaning of "justice" must itself be
struggled over by the forces in play at any given time. In "On
the Political Theory of Pascal," Auerbach begins to do a genealogy of certain modern notions of justice and its affiliated terms
and outlines some of the political and intellectual consequences that flow from the empowering of various of these notions and intellectuals' commitments to or struggles against
them. Justice requires that humanistic intellectuals find a way
to join in the debate over justice, itself.

III

"Philology and *Weltliteratur*" is Auerbach's most important
and complex essay of the 1950s. In it he expresses what he sees
as the need for the reestablishment of philological research; he
analyses the obstacles to it that result from modern conditions
of massification and obliteration of cultural diversity; and he
also outlines the set of scholarly procedures he feels can overcome these obstacles and make philological research an important means of modern cultural study. "Philology and *Weltliteratur*" is Auerbach's most programmatic essay and, at the
same time, the most nearly complete statement of his own
goals for culturally engaged philologists like himself struggling
against forces that make the achievement of those goals far
from certain. In the procedural sections of this essay, the idea
of "synthesis" reappears as a sort of intermediate goal: philologists must adjust their techniques to produce "syntheses" under

modern conditions, but these "syntheses" are important only insofar as they serve the larger end of preserving the memory of cultural diversity as the very ground for humanity.

The less procedural, opening section of this essay begins with a reflection on the history and continued meaning of *Welt-literatur*, and it moves slowly toward the pronouncement that the engaged philologist's goal is to produce "myth."[16] In fact, in a few pages, Auerbach explains why changed historical events make the traditional vision underlying philological, humanistic research untenable, and, then, after daring to prophesy the continuing need to preserve at least the memory of the humanizing impulse, he suggests it is the modern humanists' moral obligation to transform memory into myth through skill, research, and knowledge—and, most important, he argues the modern philologist must do this despite an awareness that the project may well be doomed to fail from the start.

Part I of "Philology and *Weltliteratur*" is a visionary meditation on the history and present and future role of the humanistic tradition, which Auerbach feels is in danger of no longer working, that is, of no longer *being* tradition. In a more direct way than in *Mimesis* or the other essays from the late 1940s or early 1950s, in this essay Auerbach makes absolutely clear that it is the possibility of humanistic historism that is crucially at stake in modernity. Given the seemingly irreversible massification and cultural amnesia of modernity, given that is, the destruction of the possibility of the further development of "humanity," philological historism assumes both a new burden and opportunity: it alone, if it can find the will and the procedures, can for a time escape modernity's forgetting, and it alone, for both that reason and its deeper connection with "humanity," can generate, preserve, and hand on the recorded totality of human unity in diversity that will become the new myth of a leveled people.

"Humanity" is not a timeless essence or natural concept for Auerbach; rather it is a product of cultural and historical action. True to his Vichian heritage, Auerbach insists that man *makes* "humanity," the conditions for it, and, at least since the eleventh century, records and publicly interprets the process. Because Auerbach's humanism has this precise sense, one must take literally his claim that modernity might make humanity impossible: "*Weltliteratur* does not merely refer to what is generically common and human; rather it considers humanity to be the product of fruitful intercourse between its members. The presupposition of *Weltlituratur* is a *felix culpa*: mankind's division into many cultures. Today, however, human life is becoming standardized" (PW, 2).

To understand the central role assigned to historism in Auerbach's work it is necessary to understand that he sees philological historicism, which first appears in different forms in the works of Vico, Herder, and Goethe, not only as the means by which "humanity" becomes aware of its own spectacle of "humanisation," but also, in traditional idealistic fashion, as the highest point or culmination of that spectacle, the drama of history come to self-consciousness, as it were. In these pages, Auerbach recreates a history of "humanity" and historism's place in it. "The inner history of the last thousand years," he tells us, "is the history of mankind achieving self-expression: this is what philology, a historicist discipline treats" (PW, 5). "It is approximately five hundred years since the national European literatures won their self-consciousness from and their superiority over Latin civilization; scarcely two hundred years have passed since the awakening of our sense of historicism, and a sense that permitted the formation of the concept of *Weltliteratur*. . . . And already in our own time a world is emerging for which this sense no longer has much practical significance" (PW, 3).

"Historism" is an awakening created by and reflecting the process of humanization, that is, of the unfolding of human development resulting from social intercourse among different figures. As humanity comes to self-consciousness, historism makes possible the discovery of a new reality and the writing of its history; that is, it makes possible the writing of a new kind of history that is itself in turn enabled by the humanizing process resulting from the "common humanity," the "unity" achieved in diversity, which it records and dramatizes. Auerbach believes that reality can be found in the sense of history that "guides" the humanizing process over the course of its development. He speaks of "the *inner bases* of national experience" and "an *inner history* of mankind" (PW, 2, 4; my emphasis). Historism is not just a product of the process of this "inner history"; rather, once it emerges as its fulfillment, it is an agent, too, in the humanizing process. So much is humanity dependent on historism that its threatened end in modernity's amnesia also threatens the long-term process of mankind humanizing itself.

Since modernity destroys the conditions for the continuing development of "humanity," the destruction of historism means the loss of the *memory* of humanity, the loss of example, and the possibly final loss of the potential and energy for renewing the process of "humanity" in any further society. Auerbach's logic is quite consistent on this point. If modernity destroys the social conditions for the further unfolding of humanity, specifically if it levels all diversity, then the memory, the history of such diversity will be the only space in which difference exists, in which a leveled society will be able to experience or know about the fruitful humanizing possibilities of the social interaction of various peoples. In such a vision of modernity, the destruction of history would be a monumental and, perhaps, irrecoverable loss; such a loss would close down the very cultural space in which "humanity" has come to be and so might foreclose the chance that it might reopen in the future. The preservation of history so that it in turn may be our preserver is essential. When Auerbach tells us historism must create a myth of diversity, he is not only saying, as some of his heirs might, that we must preserve a canon as a reservoir of educative examples for future behavior; more important, he is also saying that the preservation of historicist texts, historicist gestures, historicist examples, that is, of historical humanity come to historicist self-consciousness, is the only reason there might be some way to avoid the total dehumanization that massification threatens.

In simple terms, modernity poses two dangers, as Auerbach sees it: the reduction of national differences and the failure of education. Auerbach's experiences with German nationalism no doubt combine with the increasing number of postwar na-

tionalist conflicts to move him toward a cautious and dialectical sense of the essential importance of national cultural
difference to the formation of "humanity." Unlike Meinecke
and other mandarin historists who for class interests announce their belief in the absolute uniqueness and hierarchy of
national spirits as a political counterbalance to Western
"positivistic," "liberal" believers in a "universal human nature," Auerbach insists that national differences are important, not for their (hierarchized) uniquenesses, but for their
interactive contribution to the formation of "humanity," that
is, for their individual roles in the general drama of the transnational process of humanization. Indeed, one reason why
Dante is so important for Auerbach is that his work is the first
textual evidence of and gives the first voice to the transnational character of humanization. Of course, throughout his
discussions of the mixture of styles in earlier literatures, Auerbach points out how "humanity" struggles to be itself and how,
at times, it progresses and partially succeeds. Dante's importance, however, lies in his use of the vernacular to register the
weight of everyday experience. More precisely, Dante's contribution consists in making the various national languages fit
instruments for the expression of "humanity" and so in making
possible the interchange among different cultures that is dialectically necessary to the increasingly rapid development
and articulation of "humanity." "Dante" becomes a sign for
humanity in history in Auerbach, and modernity might be said
to be a battle for Dante's survival.

Postwar nationalist conflicts associated not only with the
breakup of Western empires but also with American and Soviet
chauvinism suggest to Auerbach that, despite appearances, national diversity is not enduring: "To be sure, national wills are
stronger and louder than ever, yet in every case they promote
the same standards and forms for modern life; and it is clear to
the impartial observer that the inner bases of national existence are decaying" (PW, 2). Indeed, for Auerbach, the world is
dividing itself into two undifferentiated camps centering on
the superpowers. The truly different cultures of India, Islam,
and China are being appropriated. (What Auerbach would

make of the Iranian revolution is not clear.) Paradoxically, even as this great leveling is going on, national conflicts become more acute: "But for those cultures not bound together thus [i.e., in "a rapport based on political developments" (PW, 6)] there has been a disturbing (to a humanist with Goethean ideals) general rapport in which the antitheses that persist nonetheless . . . are not being resolved except, paradoxically, through ordeals of sheer strength" (PW, 7). One of the basic historical changes threatening "humanity," then, is the displacement of the discrete "inner natures" of various local customs and traditions by the "will to power" taking the form of a "will to modernity," whose own "inner logic" drives the various weaker nations not just into opposing political camps but into the worldwide process of modernization. German nationalism leads to war for racist motives; as Auerbach sees it, postwar nationalist conflicts reflect the absence of any humane possibility of incorporating difference in a "higher" unity. In the language of "On the Political Theory of Pascal," it reflects the degenerations of state policy to *raison d'état*, that is, a degeneration of order into chaos, war, and anomie before the final mass leveling in superpower spheres of interest.

Auerbach's comments on the importance of national traditions, of national literary languages and cultural lives, should not be read as a continuation of German nationalist ways of conceiving such ideas. Indeed, like other romance philologists, Auerbach is much less a "nationalist" than either the classicists or Germanists. Nor would Auerbach like his position to be seen as necessarily giving support to nationalist struggles in the postwar years. His support would, I suppose, depend on the direction of those struggles. Rather, his theory of national difference is a requirement of his dialectical manner of thinking: how to resolve many into one, how to describe the changes of history as a sensible, unified pattern or process. Moreover, in Auerbach's thinking, the "many" cannot be subsumed into the "one," because the "many" is the origin of Auerbach's humanism.

It would perhaps be an error to rush to condemn Auerbach for conceiving the problems of modernity in such idealistic, abstract, and personalized terms. While they are undoubtedly not the terms best suited to achieve an understanding of the operations of power and interest in class-based societies, when Auerbach deploys them he not only shows how far such terms can be carried to provide a sense of the cultural changes in modernity but also presents us with a very important example of a historicially engaged critical intelligence deploying all the scholarly tools at his disposal in the struggle against what he perceives to be the greatest dangers of modernity. To dismiss such a project out of hand, as it were, on the basis of an ideology critique without first attempting a historicized, contextualized description of his project would be to abdicate critical intelligence for sloganeering and hopelessly to prejudice the case. From Auerbach's point of view, such a rush to judgment would be not only a failure of intelligence but also a sign of the educational problems of modernity. More important, it might cause us to miss Auerbach's own tragic sense that the threat to "humanity" is a consequence of some of its own impulses.

Postwar German and American education fail for Auerbach precisely because they are ahistorical and so inhibit, if they do not actively destroy, our sense of how a common "humanity" comes to be formed through the detailed and precise struggles of everyday life that take place *inside* and *out of* the diversified many. The importance of history as a discipline is that it brings us to consciousness of ourselves as struggling beings:

History is the science of reality that affects us most immediately, stirs us most deeply and compels us most forcibly to a consciousness of ourselves. It is the only science in which human beings step before us in their totality. Under the rubric of history one is to understand not only the past, but the progression of events in general; history therefore includes the present. (PW, 4–5)

Throughout his work, Auerbach stresses what he sees as history's unique ability to modify and enrich human reality by making dramatically present the complex purpose, meaning, and reality that form the totality of "humanity."[17] Indeed, it is the possibility that history can be effective even in modernity that underlies Auerbach's slim hopes for humanism and grounds his more daring Vichian idea that humanists can become the mythographers for both the present and the future.

Auerbach is quite explicit about what it is that history represents and how, as a result, it has effects:

The inner history of the last thousand years is the history of mankind achieving self-expression: this is what philology, a historicist discipline treats. This history contains the records of man's mighty, adventurous advance to a consciousness of his human condition and to the realization of his given potential; and this advance, whose final goal (even in its wholly fragmentary present form) was barely imaginable for a long time, still seems to have proceeded as if according to a plan, in spite of its twisted course. All the rich tensions of which our being is capable are contained within this course. An inner dream unfolds whose scope and depth entirely animate the spectator, enabling him at the same time to find peace in his given potential by the enrichment he gains from having witnessed the drama. (PW, 5)

But how does Auerbach intend this myth of the mythographer's power to be empowered? Surely it would be an error to read this passage as if Auerbach were simply a Hegelian. History is not the progressive revelation of the *Geist;* it merely "*seems* to have proceeded as if according to a plan." Modern humanism cannot stand on a naive Hegelianism. Yet, modern humanism can hope to achieve results similar to those Hegel might empower.[18]

Without Hegel, there are two sources of textual authority empowering this Auerbachian vision: one is the philological historist's ability to shape the "records" of history into a unified pattern; the other, also a visionary scheme, is the humanistic reversal of man's relation to God. In other words, following Vico, Nietzsche, and Freud, Auerbach understands God to be a projection of human power, desire, and fear. Completing this reversal, however, means seeing not only God but "man" as a product or projection of human history. That is to say, the "inner dream" presented to all observers as the origin or guide of history has its source in the same energies that, in a religious age, project god figures. In a secular age, gods become inner dreams that are represented, and so are always mediated, by the work of historians. It would not be un-Vichian or out of keeping with Auerbach's position in this essay to say that the same energies that invent God to account for and mask the cultural origins of human activities also empower the historists who alone are able and obligated (grounding themselves in the need to cultivate, humanize, and authorize) to present the drama of history to enrich and give pleasure to humanity. The dream of the humanistic historist is the self-consciousness of the "inner dream." It involves recalling tradition and defending it (and so its defenders) as the only way an elite can educate, form, and lead a larger public. Yet, unlike many other humanists, Auerbach senses that this tradition is, in modernity, a function of the historian, that it is a ward of and has its sole reality in his self-consciousness. Not only Auerbach's consistent and stressed use of "writing" and "aesthetic" metaphors to describe history suggests this interpretation but also his repeated and clear insistence that the social, cultural, and economic conditions for the continuation of *Weltliteratur* and so of humanity no longer exist. Humanism turns against itself, or, as Auerbach puts it in this essay, in modernity "the notion of *Weltliteratur* would be at once realized and destroyed" (PW, 3).

Through a series of not very subtle mediations historicists come to occupy a place of responsibility and power in Auerbach's scheme, not unlike other earlier and more transcendent figures of origin and myth. The residue of power and authority accrued to historists culminates in an ethical responsibility to humanity to create myths telling not just of past diversity but also of its loss in "mass movements" (PW, 3) and of its "coalescence" (PW, 7). While insisting on these responsibilities, Auerbach suggests, in terms echoing his essay on Pascal, that accepting these duties can provide historically aware intellectuals with an ethics that will allow them to escape in part the degrading effects of the ubiquitous conflicts for power throughout modernity while, at the same time, carrying on their project despite antagonists whose victory seems assured: "we will not hate whoever opposes us" (PW, 7).

Only very few are capable of being mythographers, and their success depends on two sides of the same coin: memory and loss. Out of the insight, pain, and energy resulting from the tortuous exchange between these two, a privileged, but burdened, dying caste persists whose self-envisioned, as well as self-assigned, task is to recall, to mark loss, and to preserve for future generations, to function, in other words, in Auerbach's scheme, as the main link between one thousand years of human self-expression and some unknown future. Auerbach's hope is that, no matter how "dark" the future, at least some elite will survive who will take these myths as their scripture and will some day be made fruitful by them. If only that small hope were fulfilled, then humanity will not die and another renascence will set history unfolding once again.

Auerbach's moral charge to these few humanists to accept their task is quite clear:

The loss of such a spectacle—whose appearance is thoroughly dependent on presentation and interpretation—would be an impoverishment for which there can be no possible compensation. To be sure, only those who have not totally sustained this loss would be aware of privation. Even so, we must do everything within our power to prevent so grievous a loss. If my reflections on the future . . . have any validity, then the duty of collecting material and forming it into a whole that will continue to have effect is an urgent one. For we are still basically capable of fulfilling this duty, not only because we have a great deal of material at our disposal, but above all because we also have inherited the sense of historic perspectivism which is so necessary for the job. (PW, 5)

The most important aspect of this complex of ideas is Auerbach's insistence on the moral obligation of historists of "middle-age." Unlike the old or young they have the existential and scholarly knowledge, as well as skills and energy, to register and organize the records of "humanity's" unfolding. They have an obligation to structure them in such a way that they may have an effect on any public that might encounter them in the dehumanized present or unknown future. In other words, far from suggesting that scholarship should be "disinterested," Auerbach insists that it must emerge from the most profound political sense of crisis, loss, and desire that can be evoked by those whose memory is still active and who can, therefore, respond to the spectacle of humanity's seemingly lost struggle for self-expression and self-responsibility. Humanistic scholarship must be passionately engaged; if not, it despairs without knowing it, no matter what professional or careerist legitimations it offers for itself. One necessary condition for carrying out this project is, as we have already seen in

Mimesis, the power provided by historic perspectivism to organize the multiplicity of humanity's records. But this, in turn, is grounded in an even more necessary historical condition of existence for those scholars of the middle-age: "The reason we still possess this sense [of historic perspectivism] is that we live the experience of historical multiplicity, and without this experience, I fear, the sense would quickly lose its living concreteness" (PW, 5). Auerbach is less than optimistic that other generations will share this experience, but "Philology and *Weltliteratur*" is his most profound attempt to provide for them.

One reason why future generations may not share this experience has to do with the dehistoricization of postwar education in an era of growing obsession with the "present" image or spectacle. Although Nietzsche feels in "The Use and Abuse of History" that education is excessively, parlyzingly historical, Auerbach believes that the lack of historical education in the postwar period is both a characteristic of modernity's amnesia and an element in its dehumanization:

We are already threatened with the impoverishment that results from an ahistorical system of education; not only does that threat exist but it also lays claim to dominating us. Whatever we are, we became in history, and only in history can we remain the way we are and develop therefrom: it is the task of philologists, whose province is the world of human history, to demonstrate this so that it penetrates our lives unforgettably. (PW, 6)

This passage reasserts Auerbach's sense that his is quite likely to be the last generation of scholars capable of the only sort of historically motivated research that can preserve a continuity with both our traditions of self-formation and the limited self-consciousness achieved in the process. Given the refusal, for the most part, of the American academy to provide the skills or to support the work essential to such historical writing, Auerbach's foreboding seems to have been fulfilled. Indeed, his warnings on the potential dangers to historical knowledge contained in literary criticism—and we must remember he is writing in the "good-old days" of 1952, the age of "literary history," of Northrop Frye, and of the New Criticism—seem to have been uncannily prescient:[19]

The problematics and the ordering categories of contemporary literary criticism are always significant, not only because they often are ingenious and illuminating in themselves, but also because they express the inner will of their period. . . . Most of them are too abstract and ambiguous, and frequently they have too private a slant. They confirm a temptation to which neophytes (and acolytes) are frequently inclined to submit: the desire to master a great mass of material through the introduction of hypostatized, abstract concepts of order; this leads to the effacement of what is being studied, to the discussion of illusory problems and finally to a bare nothing. (PW, 10)

The crisis in education, then, quite specifically involves the usurpation of historical research by hypostatized critical concepts that function as machines to "read" or "interpret" whole "bodies" of texts, but it also involves the more material role literary criticism plays in reproducing a structure of professional education that rears "acolytes" who, Auerbach implies, succeed, given they are of the right race and sex, simply by applying the already powerful and authorized concepts of a sponsor or patron to different areas or materials. In other words, the crisis in education, which is an aspect of the crisis of modernity, is, in part, the result of a professional structure that grants authority to those able to invent or apply "new concepts" or "new categories" in a revision of previous interpretations. Once the academy establishes "reading" (of individual texts, authors, genres, or periods) as the sole and adequate criterion for success (which respected editors, historians, or bibliographers are among the leaders of our profession?), the appropriate educational goal is for a student to acquire skill in "reading" according to the dictates of some more or less powerful model of explication. The crisis in education, then, is the result not simply of promulgating the ahistorical ideas of the New Criticism, for example, but of the founding and persistence, especially in the United States, of an institution more interested in reproducing itself and gaining its own rewards than in preserving the skills, values, and knowledge of historical research. From this point of view, the New Criticism, instead of being the "cause" of the dehistoricization of literary study, is an apology for an academy unwilling and unable to sustain the traditions of historical knowledge and humanity.[20]

The decline in historical education means that there is a serious professional and, given Auerbach's sense of the leading role intellectuals play, a cultural loss in the species' memory. That is, the pool of examples illustrative of the range of human action and feeling that is so important to human development suffers an irrevisible decline, and, more important, the intellectuals and the culture forget the historical, interactive nature of humanity, itself.

These problems are the primary obstacles against which the visionary, recollective philologist, pained by loss, yet pleased to accept the responsibility of opportunity, must struggle. Yet, the important aims of this struggle are modestly circumscribed:

The conception of *Weltliteratur* advocated in this essay—a conception of the diverse background of a common fate—does not seek to affect or alter that which has already begun to occur, albeit contrary to expectation; the present conception accepts as an inevitable fact that world-culture is being standardized. (PW, 7)

The modesty of Auerbach's position should not, however, be confused with a now-fashionable impotence.[21] Philological research, cannot, after all, immediately alter world history. One might, however, justifiably question Auerbach's sense that there is such a thing as "world-culture." His belief that "world-culture," some sort of transnational monolith, does exist can be explained on several grounds: his idealist tradition often mistakenly assigns ontological reality to the predicates of a concept; the rise of "democracy" and mass markets in the West do, indeed, eliminate local markets and culture differences[22]; the postwar American international hegemony and the Soviet "challenge" do divide the world into two indistinguishable "materialist" and "levelling" camps; and the Eurocentrism of "high culture" not only projects European phenomena on the "world" as a whole but also rarely examines the various popular forms of culture in "advanced" or "developing" societies. This is to say no more than that Auerbach may be unjustified in asserting not only the "levelling of world culture," but its very existence. At the very least one can say Auerbach does not make his point convincingly; he simply announces it from the vantage point of an "impartial observer" (PW, 2).

But Auerbach's reasons for so hastily taking this unjustified position are clear; he is responding to a Western European cultural crisis that involves not only a challenge to the authority of the cultured classes but also a series of challenges to European suzerainty. At the same time, given the spread of modernity throughout the world, Auerbach's engaged response, although cast in purely Eurocentric terms, does address itself to a worldwide phenomenon rooted in Western Europe and the United States. In other words, Auerbach takes up a position meant to respond to the worldwide phenomena of modernity that he has encountered very brutally in his personal experience.

Indeed, this experience leads Auerbach to adapt a traditional Idealist claim to argue that *alienation* is the necessary condition for a rational, scholarly confrontation with the leveling forces and resultant anomie of modernity.[23] As part of his project of moving the intellectual away from nationalist commitments and in helping with his dialectical sense of the unavoidable interpenetration of part and whole, Auerbach concludes that the humanist who hopes to be effective in preserving or renewing humanity *must* experience exile and alienation (as he and Dante both did), in order to be able to transcend the traps of nationalism that threaten humanity's very existence. In other words, out of his considered response to his own historical experience, Auerbach tries to generate a new, transnational, ethical ground for critical intervention into culture in the postwar era. The global nature of modernity gives Auerbach's project its particular shape:

In any event, our philological home is the earth [this had been Goethe's original insight in "Weltliteratur"]: it can no longer be the nation. The most priceless and indispensable part of a philologist's heritage is still his own nation's culture and language. Only when he is first separated from this heritage, however, and then transcends it does it become truly effective. We must return, in admittedly altered circumstances to the knowledge that prenational medieval culture already possessed: the knowledge that the spirit [*Geist*] is not national. (PW, 17)

Is literal geographical and cultural exile the only way such knowledge can be acquired? Certainly, such exiles have made and continue to make important contributions to knowledge and perhaps even to the transnational development of "humanity." But not even all such literal exiles form part of Auerbach's historicist community. His sense that the narrowness of Spitzer's stylistic preoccupations keeps him from engaging with the pressing historical questions of modernity illustrates how literal exile is not a sufficient condition for the transcendence of alienation he has in mind. Alienation is a required first step in the process of recognizing the necessarily transnational character of humanity. Exile, utter detachment from the given assumptions and effects of one's own culture, forces confrontation with difference; it allows for a recognition of the possible contributions to the development of "humanity" made by often conflicting, diversified peoples struggling for self-expression. It also provides an opportunity not only to demystify chauvinst notions about one's own culture, which is a useful idea in a fascist or postfascist era, but also to perceive the way in which one's own culture, in fact, has been, at least since the eleventh century, only one element among many in an international concert of human evolution. To be a humanist in exile is to be the self-conscious product of the transnational development of humanity in and out of diversity. It is to be beyond even the realm of *Bildung*, which conceptualizes a process of acquiring wisdom (and social position) by internalizing a narrowly defined and stable canon of ancient and German classics. It becomes, as well, the necessary condition for a certain very advanced form of "comparative literature." But in all cases it requires that the "humanist" be, not just a student, but, at least in knowledge and morality, an exemplar of "humanity."

But humanistic work can succeed only if it draws on its own national resources, as Auerbach draws on German historism, that is, in a way effected by and directed toward transnational priorities. By implication, then, the exiled humanist can legitimately support only those elements of his own training, profession, and culture that, after close examination, appear able to make useful and effective contributions to the unfolding of humanity. As Auerbach's own rather arch comments on "literary criticism" suggest, such a position would require a politically informed debate over the nature and efficacy of literary and historical education. But given Auerbach's sense of the unlikelihood of any alteration in modernism's basic tendencies, reform in higher education, even to strengthen its historicist elements, seems impossible. Effectively, the unlikeliness of reform forces the intellectual to acquire knowledge and resources wherever possible, to scavenge in those areas modernity has not leveled, and to struggle against not only the cultural and institutional forces likely to inhibit such directed and engaged research but also the cynical forces of nihilism and despair that Auerbach paradigmatically tries to exorcise from his own being in his essay on Pascal.

But how does one become an "exile," free to return to and exploit the resources afforded by one's own tradition and circumstances? Auerbach's theory of modernity explains how intellectuals become unknowingly alienated from their own traditions and situations. It is an unavoidable feature of leveling and amnesia, but Auerbach offers no clear guide to how individuals gain this necessary victory over alienation, without which no meaningful work can be done. What he does offer as guidance is an insight from Hugo of St. Victor, namely, that loving the world means not only transcending one's heritage and one's alienation from it; it means especially being an exile throughout the world: " *'Delicatus ille est adhuc cui patria dulcis est, fortis autem cui omne solum patria est, perfectus vero cui mundus totus exilium est'* " (PW, 17). By virtue of this total and loving exile, the philologist becomes a universal intellectual whose very "marginality" to the forces or powers of modernity, as well as to the orthodox effects of a national or institutional tradition, empowers him to do work basic to the humanist enterprise. That is, he can both create syntheses relating diversity in unity and he can judge to what ends history demands that he direct his efforts.

The first of these two tasks is clearest in "Philology and *Weltliteratur*" because Auerbach spends a great deal of time formalizing and revising the synthetic method of *Mimesis*. Although the second is not explicitly thematized, it nevertheless forms the basis of the entire essay. Auerbach creates the image of the exiled historicist struggling to preserve the memory of humanity's historical being and development because he judges that now (1952) is the time for such an intellectual who, as he sees it, is alone capable of carrying out the task history seems to evoke. To see that Auerbach understands history requires his project, the following quotation must be read with his identification of "history," "humanity," and "*Weltliteratur*" in mind:

Yet this conception [of *Weltliteratur* advocated in this essay] wishes to render precisely and, so that it may be retained, consciously to articulate the fateful coalescence of cultures for those who are in the midst of the terminal phase of fruitful multiplicity: thus this coalescence, so rendered and articulated, will become their myth. In this manner, the full range of the spiritual movements of the last thousand years will not atrophy within them. One cannot speculate with much result about the future effects of such an effort. It is our task to create the possibility for such an effect; and only this much *can* be said, that for an age of transition such as ours the effect *could* be very significant. . . . By token of this, our conception of *Weltliteratur* is no less human, no less humanistic, than its antecedent; the implicit comprehension of history—whch underlies this conception of *Weltliteratur* —is not the same as the former one, yet it is a development of it and unthinkable without it. (PW, 7)

Auerbach's entire project emerges from and rests upon the presumed-to-be legitimate judgment of the historically trained universal intellectual that history, come again to self-consciousness in the modern, developed concept of *Weltliteratur*, demands that the philologist become a mythmaker. That history itself assigns this "task" to the scholar-as-mythmaker follows from Auerbach's claim that the conception of *Weltliteratur* he proposes is a genealogical development of the traditional, Goethean notion of the concept. As such a continuation, Auerbach's modern version is also an unfolding of humanity's historical self-consciousness, which had initially come about with the origins of historicist thought.

The rigorous development of these relationships establishes, for Auerbach, not only that history, through its historicist self-consciousness, directs the form of humanity's self-expression, but also that in the modern world it leaves the self-conscious elite only one task: mythographical preservation in hope of having "an effect." Put simply, the transnational humanity that has been unfolding in culture and consciousness for more than one thousand years, commands and needs its own conservation, but the end of that conservation is the future possibility of "humanity": "the full range of the spiritual movements of the last thousand years will not atrophy within . . . those people who are in the midst of the terminal phase of fruitful multiplicity."

Despite echoing the self-interested claims of both the mandarins and the American professionals, Auerbach's vision rests its authority upon its *transcendence* of all but the most "humane" interest in human and intellectual identity. Humanism, for Auerbach, is precisely this self-transcending "dis-interested" interest in engaging the intellectual in the universal project of summing up, preserving, and transmitting effectively all the "spiritual" developments that a philologist can find recorded in the material and cultural history of "humanity's" unfolding. Of course, one consequence of this vision is the need to establish or re-enforce the authority of an ethically minded, engaged, humanistic elite capable, by necessity, of toting up and judging almost any aspects of cultural history and practice. By the same token, these universal figures who become leading intellectuals do not engage, in any precise way, with the specific historical or material conditions of their own institutional and discursive situation. On the contrary, since their role requires often direct battle with or against the forms that inhibit or appropriate their work, despite isolated, but illuminating instances of incipient struggle such as Auerbach's comments on the demerits of "literary criticism," his project would essentially disengage these mythmakers from the struggle. While the mythographer's work is an engaged, world-historical act in the dramatic spectacle of "humanity's" existence, while, furthermore, it is a very powerful defense of the priorities of historical reality, and, especially, while all of these historical projects result from the desire to effect the destructive consequences of modernity's political processes, Auerbach's primary aim is to find a way to transcend modernity, to

escape its degradations, to allow the last generation of philologists to go about their hopeful, but gruesome, task of belatedly
summing up as unimpeded as possible by the fact that social,
political, and cultural conditions have changed so much that
the very possibility of humanity and history is greatly in doubt.

Auerbach's engaged and committed response to the ethical
and historical demands of an evolving (but perhaps ending)
humanity is to try to enable a form of scholarship that, while
aiming at goals and values often precisely the opposite of those
in modernity, will be free to develop those antagonistic goals
without any immediate contact with or critique of the modern
forces making their mythographical enterprise necessary. To be
in exile from all the world in order to love humanity and not to
hate one's antagonists often also seems to mean avoiding conflict with those very forces, powers, or structures that make the
the development of the grand strategy of exile so necessary.
Auerbach's critique of ahistorical investigation does not, for example, eventuate in an analysis of how history transmutes its
own obsessive cultural fascination with historical knowledge
(witness Nietzsche) into its exact opposite; nor does it suggest
that a detailed critique of the interests involved in perpetuating this ahistorical education would be useful or effective.

Another way of saying this is that the universal humanistic
intellectual, no matter how historically engaged, rarely, if
ever, carries out the sort of detailed investigation into the material, institutional, and discursive origins of or conditions for
his being. As a result, as we have seen in the case of the American appropriation of Auerbach, the most powerful heroism of
the humanistic ethos cannot resist its own abuse, its own mis-
firing. As we have also seen, Auerbach sometimes intuits that
the end of humanism, that is, its real, historical goals, so contradictory to its announced Goethean intents, are always present, implicit in its vision. At the end of *Mimesis* and again in
"Philology and *Weltliteratur*," Auerbach intimates that humanism culminates in its own destruction. *Weltliteratur*, for
example, as the literary concept of humanism, expressed its
desire for one people, for one humanity, the fulfillment of the
fertile interaction of different cultures. In *Mimesis*, and in this

Goethean spirit, Auerbach evokes the desirability of recognizing what "men in general have in common" and of achieving "a
common life of mankind on earth" (M, 552). But with very
gentle understatement, he tells us that this Goethean vision
has been fulfilled in a quite unexpected way: "If I assess it
correctly, in its compulsion and in its dependence on mass
movements, this contemporary situation is not what Goethe
had in mind" (PW, 3).

Auerbach's reservations about Goethe are important to any
clear sense of what he expects of the historically engaged humanist. At times Goethe appears merely irresponsible: "For he
gladly avoided thoughts about what later history has made
inevitable" (PW, 3). In contrast, at other times, his irresponsibility appears to account for the catastrophes of the twentieth century:

Goethe's views prevented him from grasping revolutionary occurrences
with the genetico-realistic-sensory method peculiar to him on other
occasions. He disliked them. He tried harder to get rid of them than to
understand them . . . . We are left with the conclusion that Goethe
never represented the reality of contemporary social life dynamically,
as the germ of developments in process and in the future. Where he
deals with the trends of the nineteenth century, he does so in general
reflections, and these are almost always value judgements: they are
predominantly mistrustful and disapproving. The technical developments of machinery, the progressively conscious participation of the
masses in public life, were distasteful to him. He foresaw a shallowing
of intellectual life; he saw nothing to make up for such a loss. He also,
as we know, remained aloof from the political patriotism which, if
conditions had been more favorable at the time, might well have led to
a unification of the social situation in Germany. If that had happened
then, perhaps too the integration of Germany into the emerging new
reality of Europe and the world might have been prepared more calmly,
have been accomplished with fewer uncertainties and less violence. He
deplored the political conditions of Germany, but he did so dispassionately and accepted it as a fact. (M, 448, 451–52)

These comments on Goethe reflect Auerbach's own historical, political, intellectual, and moral situation. On the one
hand, Auerbach considers reprehensible Goethe's magisterial
aloofness from the politics of his time; on the other hand, at
least in 1952, he doubts if Goethe or any one "could then sus-

pect how radically, how unexpectedly, an unpleasant potential could be realized" (PW, 3). In other words, the universal intellectual cannot be expected to foresee all of the undesirable consequences of the historical unfolding of even the most noble humanistic vision; yet, nothing would seem to justify either the intellectual's aloofness from the pressing political and cultural issues of his own period or his moralization of those same issues. If we put aside the accuracy of Auerbach's remarks on Goethe, what is most interesting is precisely the terms of his criticism. Implicitly, Auerbach proposes that the moral and cultural obligation of the universal intellectual is to be engaged in the political life of the day, no matter how distasteful, precisely because that engagement may, in fact, make a difference in nothing less than world history. In other words, in *Mimesis* unqualifiedly and in "Philology and *Weltliteratur*" more hesitantly, Auerbach's dissatisfaction with Goethe arises from a moral and historical sense of the power, necessity, and efficacy of the leading intellectual, a notion partially grounded in the historically conditioned assumption of those intellectuals' own responsibility for the politics and culture of a nation.

In "Philology and *Weltliteratur*," Auerbach seems more doubtful about the power and responsibility of the universal intellectual. He has grown either more pessimistic or more realistic about the role of the humanist. Perhaps there has simply been a transference of responsibility from the sociopolitical role that Goethe had a chance to play to the less immediately effective role of the belated mythographer who, in what is for Auerbach the much less revolutionary and diverse world of postwar modernity and superpower hegemony, simply has much less opportunity to take effective action in any realm of public power. But if Auerbach sees effective action as impossible or its possibility as at best uncertain, then does he not begin to take on some of the very characteristics he attributes to Goethe? Surely Auerbach is never dispassionate and surely he thinks much about matters he finds distasteful, but his project of finding ways to insulate mythographers from the effects of modernity and to direct their work toward the preservation of the past as a hedge against an all-too-likely future—surely such a project does not encourage direct political engagement with those forces he has decided it would be pointless to attempt to "affect or to alter" (PW, 7). And, like Goethe, he has become pessimistic and sees nothing to replace the "humanity" produced by the historical concept of *Weltliteratur:* "he saw nothing to make up for such a loss." Indeed, one consequence of the humanistic tradition is that its adherents can find no other way to imagine or talk about value, meaning, culture, or politics. Most important, however, is humanism's difficulty in engaging with the specific institutional and discursive conditions that not only have disrupted the social consensus or political domination upon which humanism rested but also have made possible the humanists' own passionate sense that the restoration, in some revised form, of their values and visions alone will defend "humanity." But what Auerbach's own work illustrates and what he himself acknowledges is that humanism turns against itself in modernity and serves the class interests of the mandarins, the professional interests of academics, the mad and barbaric purposes of fascism and, in fact, facilitates the modern leveling that is its own daemonic fulfillment.

But it would be unwise to offer a blanket condemnation of humanism for its inability to resist appropriation or escape contradiction. Such an opinion would uncritically reinstate the nihilistic daemon Auerbach labored so hard to exorcise in "On the Political Theory of Pascal." Indeed, it would be best to avoid such a judgment since it would too closely parallel Auerbach's own sense that it is inappropriate to attempt to "affect or alter" the tendencies of modernity. Rather the most fruitful procedure might be to judge which aspects of Auerbach's humanistic project might be efficacious in any scholarly attempt to understand or modify the modern intellectual's situation.

One particular dimension of Auerbach's project and of his own understanding of humanism's contradictory development seems particularly problematic, namely, the assumption that the scholar should or can legitimately be a universal intellectual whose leading role might be modified—from politician to mythographer—but can never be suspended without cataclysmic cultural consequences. The result of this belief is, as Auerbach notes, that humanists would be foolish to attempt to alter the modern tendencies that force them into the conservative role of mythographers.[24] In other words, there is a tendency toward political quietism that we have already seen in Auerbach's essay on Pascal.

What must be preserved from Auerbach's project, though, is not just his passionate commitment to the historical sense or his equally passionate belief that intellectuals should be engaged in the cultural struggles of their period—no matter how abstractly he conceives these. Rather what is perhaps most important is his ceaseless attempt to find ways to enable scholarship of any "human" sort to be carried out in the face of statism, subjectivisim, professionalism, and the myriad other forces that either trivialize or dehumanize scholarship by making it a part and parcel of the dominant powers of a largely valueless culture.

In "Philology and *Weltliteratur*," Auerbach makes two distinct contributions to this struggle. The first is his concept of the "*Ansatzpunkt*"; the second is his insistence that scholarship must be presented in forms able to give it some effect. He proposes both of these ideas in response to the degraded nature of the academic profession and to the complexity of experience the engaged scholar must confront. Auerbach begins by suggesting that professional academic specialization is inadequate to the struggle against dehumanization and by identifying the intellectual disorder and conceptual chaos with which the engaged scholar *must* contend:

The scholar who does not consistently limit himself to a narrow field of specialization and to a world of concepts held in common with a small circle of likeminded colleagues lives in the midst of a tumult of impressions and claims on him: for the scholar to do justice to these is almost impossible. Still, it is becoming increasingly unsatisfactory to limit oneself to only one field of specialization. (PW, 9)

The humanistic scholar has a twofold responsibility to history and humanity, namely, to study the full range of new knowledge that modern disciplines provide and, where possible, to learn from it and account for it; and also to attempt to comprehend the complexity of modern experience to understand the significant contemporary changes in human history. For Auerbach these are two integrated processes that combine to form the subject matter, as well as the training, of a humanist.

Auerbach argues that neither postwar education nor the German and American traditions of research cultivate this scholarly model or provide the training needed to embody it. The mandarins' tradition is inadequate because it attempts to minimize the disruptive effects of new knowledge and changed social conditions on their traditional beliefs and privileges in two essentially repressive ways. On the one hand, in association with the government's department of higher education, they conspire to prevent the creation of new professorships; in other words, they defend their own disciplines from contamination by surpressing whole bodies of knowledge. On the other hand, they try to achieve the same conservative effect by producing a new *Weltanschauung* that would contain (or exclude) the unruly *Geisteswissenschaften* in a visionary order unlikely to alter their dominant position. And, of course, they insist on maintaining the rigid *Gymnasium* system of university qualification to ensure the continuation of class-distinct educational opportunities.

The American university system may be less rigidly class restricted, but it is not for the most part organized to produce scholars sensitive to the problems concerning Auerbach. American style professionalization is inadequate because its structural values are those of career advancement while its disciplinary organization encourages the fragmentation of knowledge into "fields." In effect, the American academy relieves scholars of their humanistic obligation in two ways: having become "professionals," humanistic scholars accept the values and rewards of career advancement (leading to "celebrity" status) that comes from success in practicing many social and disciplinary skills; one among many of these is the professional scholar's pursuit of "recognition" in a specialized field, which requires that the scholar recognize and remain within the protocols of that specialization and of the ethos of specialization itself.

Since postwar education is increasingly specialized, it is increasingly unlikely that scholars can be trained to deal, as they must, with the intellectual and experiential complexity of modernity: "Formerly, what could be taken for granted in the university (and, in the English-speaking countries, at the postgraduate level) must now be acquired there; most often such acquirements are either made too late or they are inadequate" (PW, 9). Auerbach's intellectual response to these situations is based on his own philological practice and on the stylistics of Leo Spitzer. He tries to build a modern scholarly method around the term *Ansatzpunkt* that can overcome the obstacles to the perpetuation of humanistic scholarship by enabling another generation to be trained to carry on the mythographical work of effective preservation.

In "Philology and *Weltliteratur*" Auerbach feels that mythography can be effective only if it is synthetic; his idea is to retain as much of "humanity" as can possibly be formally structured. His first task is clear; Auerbach needs a programmatic answer to the question: "how is the problem of synthesis to be solved?" (PW, 11); he must find some procedure that is *teachable*, consistent with humanistic historism, and so able to guarantee the reproduction of modern historicist scholars and the traditional values and knowledge they embody:[25]

The historical synthesis of which I am speaking, although it has significance only when it is based on a scholarly penetration of the material, is a product of personal intuition and hence can only be expected from an individual. Should it succeed perfectly we would be given a scholarly achievement and a work of art at the same time. Even the discovery of a point of departure [*Ansatzpunkt*]—of which I shall speak later—is a matter of intuition: the performance of a synthesis is a form which must be unified and suggestive if it is to fulfill its potential. Surely the really noteworthy achievement of such a work is due to a coadunatory intuition; in order to achieve its effect historical synthesis must in addition appear to be a work of art. (PW, 11)

In this method there is no "objectivity"; the scholar is unavoidably present in the work from the moment of its inception to its completion. Derived from both German idealism and modern hermenuetics, "intuition" signifies the scholar's intent to proceed in a certain direction through a mass of mastered material. At their best, as in the case of *Mimesis'* "motifs," such "intuitions" are dialogic and not willful, but they are always circular, for they lead to their own testing, expansion, or denial. Said rightly suggests that scholarship that proceeds from intuition becomes a formal project: "In both senses of formal [differentiated coherently and integrally. . . . differentiated by virtue of constitutive function], therefore, the beginning of an enterprise is a hypothesis projected; it is subsequently to be tested and confirmed."[26]

Said does not, however, capture all of Auerbach's thinking about intuition. Auerbach rules out not just those intuitions that can be falsified by testing but entire types of "knowledge-producing," visionary intuitions, as well. Auerbach is not simply a hermeneutic positivist. Most important is the fact that he is not satisfied with fortuitous or visionary intuitions dependent for their "authority" either on the instantaneous glimmer of imaginative apprehension or the willful desires of a critic. The "truth" of such apprehensions is not the issue for Auerbach; rather, their "significance," which I think can best be measured in terms of their "effect" alone, determines the value of a synthetic intuition. Effect can best be acheived by a total mastery (or "penetration") of the materials that makes possible not just the *apprehension* of an order (as an unschooled intuition might),[27] but the actual textual enactment of the unifying, formal movement of rhetoric and argument from intuition to final ordered synthesis. "Synthesis," then is an active process, a "performance," in Auerbach's view, which, to be effective must be put on publicly in the achievement of a "form."

In his attempt to produce a general theory of critical work, Said's gloss on this idea in Auerbach suggests that synthesis must be a performance recorded in form: "In the critic's work, therefore, a vigilant method and a record of that method's accomplishments are produced together." Said explains the need to draw attention to the *performance* of work as a function of beginnings: "A beginning is a formal appetite imposing a severe discipline on the mind that wants to think every turn of its thoughts from the start. Thoughts then appear related to one another in a meaningful series of constantly experienced moments."28

While Auerbach certainly acknowledges that synthesis is a "product of personal intuition," his theory does not seem to give so much authority to the relationship among the critic's "thoughts" as they are recorded in the "performance," or to his willful intention to announce his own "difference" from other critics within the conventions of his profession. Rather, Auerbach stresses the scholar's immersion in the material; Auerbach's project is not to allow the critic to find a means of articulating the individualities of his own mind, but a way to do research that will come as near as possible to recording the truth as his post-Nietzschean perspectivism permits. Indeed, at times Auerbach seems to be warning against the consequences that might flow from such "critic centered" or willful positions as Said seems to be advocating. Saying that scholarship must approach the condition of art neither denies art's autonomy nor permits the scholar the artist's "freedom":

The traditional protestation, that literary art must possess the freedom to be itself—which means that it must not be bound to scientific truth—can scarcely be voiced: for as they present themselves today historical subjects offer the imagination quite enough freedom in the questions of choice, of the problems they seem to generate, of their combination with each other, and of their formulation. One can say in fact that scientific truth is a good restriction on the philologist; scientific truth preserves and guarantees the probable in the "real," so that the great temptation to withdraw from reality (be it by trivial glossing or by shadowy distortion) is thereby foiled, for reality is the criterion of the probable. (PW, 11–12)

The "movements of the critical mind" should be severly restricted by the scholarly research program Auerbach's project requires. Indeed, criticism, he sometimes suggests, is one form of trivializing and distorting withdrawal from the obligatory scholarly examination of an ever-more complex experience. The difference between Auerbach and Said on this matter can be specified through the latter's statement on the *necessity* of beginning: "we find [the *Ansatzpunkt*] for a purpose and at a time that is crucial to us; but the act of finding it ought never to be all interrogation, examination, and reflection unless we are willing to forego work for preliminaries."[29] I suspect that Said underestimates the role of research in Auerbach's project because he feels that the *critical* project must place primary emphasis on the individual critic's ability to generate concepts; as a result, Said may exaggerate the values of a performance meant to show the relations between a critic's "thoughts," rather than the relations among historical materials. Said's opposition between "work" (that is, "writing," or publication) and the "preliminaries" of "interrogation, examination, and reflection" suggests Said sees the basic problem of scholarship in modernity differently from Auerbach. For Auerbach, the problem is not that a scholar might be tempted by too many preliminaries and so never write; the problem is to produce procedures for dealing with the complex and often new demands on attention so they do not turn a scholar into merely a "critic":

The difficulty is not only in the copiousness of the material that is scarcely within the grasp of a single individual (so much that a group project seems to be required), but also in the structure of the material itself. The traditional division of the material, chronological, geographical or typological are no longer suitable and cannot guarantee any sort of energetic, unified advance. (PW, 12)

For Auerbach, the point is to establish a research project that can deal with those problems and to produce effective, written performances that will function as myths. Auerbach argues that the personal or perspectival point of departure or intuition cannot be avoided in modernity, but we have seen in *Mimesis* that the problem for Auerbach is how to use this unavoidable presence of the subject without having it seem that he is trying futilely to legitimate a research project on the basis of the subject conceived as a unifying and unified will.

Commentators have at times noticed that in the 1950s Auerbach grows uncertain about the value of author-centered studies. Unfortunately, he died before elaborating fully the reasons for his doubts. I would hypothesize, however, that they had to do, in part, with his long-held belief that, in modernity, it is illegitimate to rest claims to authority on the subject. *Mimesis* shows that historism leads to perspectivism and that the inviolability of the metaphysical subject on which Herder and Hegel depended can no longer ground value, research, or writing. Indeed, Auerbach claims, whenever the attempt is made to base authority on the subject, it quickly betrays itself as some form of "will to power." In history, the subject is irrecuperable:

It has even become a matter of some doubt to me whether monographs—and there are many excellent ones—on single, significant authors are suited to be points of departure for the kind of synthesis that I have been speaking about. Certainly a single author embodies as complete and concrete a unity of life as any, and this is always better than an invented unity; but at the same time such a unity is finally ungraspable because it has passed into the ahistorical inviolability into which individuality always flows. (PW, 12–13)

How to resist the transformation of individuality—upon which all *Ansatzpunkt*, synthesis, and so humanity depend— into the mystified notion of an ahistorical subject—this becomes Auerbach's question. Part of his answer involves seeing not only that the individual is an agent capable of choice but also that he must be subservient to a historically necessary cultural research project; without such subjection, knowledge and will do not produce humanistic works. For example, Auerbach argues that Ernst Robert Curtius' unconscious partial discovery of the goals and methods of a necessary research project alone allowed his work to have meaning and shape:

Only by the discovery of a phenomenon at once firmly circumscribed, comprehensible and central enough to be a point of departure . . . was the execution of Curtius' plan made possible. Whether Curtius' choice for a point of departure was satisfactory . . . is not being debated. . . . For Curtius' achievement is obligated to the following methodological principle: in order to accomplish a major work of synthesis it is imperative to locate a point of departure [*Ansatzpunkt*], a handle, as it were, by which the subject can be seized. The point of departure must be the election of a firmly circumscribed, easily comprehensible set of phenomena whose interpretation is a radiation out from them and which orders and interprets a greater region than they themselves occupy. (PW, 14)

In comparison to Auerbach's emphasis, Said's interpretation of the *Ansatzpunkt* assigns too much priority to the critic's will as the source of a meaningful project: "There must of course be an act of endowment or assertion on the critic's part before an innocuous verbal 'point' can turn into the privileged beginning of a critic's journey. The critic's belief, as well as his reflective examination of the point, together germinate into a criticism that is aware of what it is doing."[30] But Auerbach's mythographer is not primarily recording his own quest or *Wanderjahre.* Insofar as he searches at all it is to find a tool that makes the preservation of the material records of humanity possible. Also, Auerbach suggests criteria to identify an appropriate *Ansatzpunkt* precisely to guarantee that the point of departure is not random or willful: "A good point of departure must be exact and objective" (*PW*, 15). The *Ansatzpunkt* does not have self-awareness or reflexivity as its goal. Alway suspicious of the relativistic consequences of subjective performances, Auerbach proposes the *Ansatzpunkt*, not to authorize work recording the enactment of a critic's thoughts, but to establish a model of scholarly research and training in which a humanistically impersonal research project subsumes the individual will.

The method Auerbach proposes has specific aims. First of all, the *Ansatzpunkt* is a response to the seemingly endless proliferation of fragmented knowledge that is a consequence of the degraded fulfillment of historism:

it seems to me to be necessary to emphasize the method's general significance, which is that it is the only method that makes it possible for us now to write a history-from-within against a broader background, to write synthetically and suggestively. The method also makes it possible for a younger scholar, even a beginner, to accomplish that end; and a comparatively modest general knowledge buttressed by advice can suffice once intuition has found an auspicious point of departure.

In effect, this method reestablishes a master-apprentice model of scholarly work in which the close, personal transmission and preservation of knowledge, skills, and values is meant to act as a brake on the temptation to make academic writing into the recorded expression of a critic's mind or students into acolytes. Auerbach also intends the procedure both to set in motion the continuing education of all who practice and to record the expanding results of the developing knowledge and insight:

In the elaboration of this point of departure, the intellectual perspective enlarges itself both sufficiently and naturally since the choice of
material to be drawn is determined by the point of departure. Elaboration therefore is so concrete, its component parts hang together with
such necessity, that what is thereby gained cannot easily be lost:
the result, in its ordered exposition, possesses unity and universality.
(PW, 14)

Not satisfied by stressing the concrete, necessary, and almost
corporate nature of the method's intended results, Auerbach
adds the explicit caution that the point of departure and the
ordered result should not be a function of a "critical" will or
subsumed in any way to the "critic's" interests:

a point of departure should not be a generality imposed on a theme
from the outside, but ought rather to be an organic inner part of the
theme itself. What is being studied should speak to itself, but that can
never happen if the point of departure is neither concrete nor clearly
defined. In any event, a great deal of skill is necessary—even if one has
the best point of departure possible—in order to keep oneself focused
on the object of study. (PW, 16)

The difficulty in maintaining the focus stems not just from the
plethora of data that might (and should) force a change in
direction but also from the unwillingness or inability of the
scholar to work hard enough—often against the constraints of
discipline—to discover the "essence" of the movement under
study (PW, 16).

As Auerbach elaborates the method of the *Ansatzpunkt*, it
seems to be a historically motivated demonstration that the
synthetic work required to create myths, to save "humanity," is
a valid intellectual possibility despite the modern degradation
of scholarly education. Auerbach's proposal should be seen as,
in part, an attempt to displace literary criticism and "critical
subjectivism" in the academy; at the same time, it is also an
attempt to alter the excessive and ineffective forms or categories of all professional specialization (PW, 15).

In effect, then, "Philology and *Weltliteratur*" is an example
of the Vichian use of rhetoric Auerbach discusses in "Vico and
Aesthetic Historism." It is an attempt to deauthorize specific
modes of intellectual, critical discourse, practices, and institutions by implying their connection with the dehumanizing

forces of modernity and by proposing as a substitute the configuration of method, knowledge, education, and purpose associated with the term *Ansatzpunkt*. One might say that Auerbach enacts his method in reverse; rather than pursue the significance of a term and its radiations, he interweaves many disparate notions—such as intuition, specialization, and postgraduate education—by gathering them around *Ansatzpunkt*. Auerbach shapes "Philology and *Weltliteratur*" in such a way that it unmistakably is meant to affect the cultural world and the intellectual institutions with which it engages.

Yet, this attempt has not succeeded. The reduction in historical knowledge and research skills continues unabated. (Said reminds us that the recollections of Auerbach and some others "tell a rather humbling story about the researcher today, who can barely read another language."[31]) The academy seems still too much to reward the successful application (or summary)[32] of "critical concepts" to texts and to support the patronage system that makes acolytes rather than apprentices of young scholars (who hope to succeed). Most important, however, has been the failure of even an engaged humanism to subsume the will and interests of individual critics within a larger, impersonal institutional and cultural project. Even Auerbach's struggle could not inhibit the development of an academic star system within the institution of literary study.

But could it have done so? Humanism, especially its historicist or revisionary forms, always argues for and depends on the authority of the universal intellectual as a leading figure in culture and the universities. As I have suggested, humanism regularly produces images of and arguments for the leading intellectual as a necessary figure of sublime power, insight, and influence. As Auerbach shows (he blames Goethe for running from the insight), the unfolding of humanity in itself leads to the possibility of a purely subject-centered, willful criticism that, for success in moving upward from the position of acolyte within a hierarchical profession, would sacrifice humanity, the presumed object of study, by reducing it "to a bare nothing."

For Auerbach, all this matters. He comes close at times to dismissing all hope for preserving significant literary or cultural study and the tradition he feels depends on them. While his Hegelian or mandarin nostalgia makes alluring the image of synthetic myths to prevent modernity from destroying humanity, this same nostalgia for or memory of the belief in the possibility of a progressively humanized world leads him to struggle to invent ways of carrying on this development while giving memorable form to what had gone on before.

I have already suggested that one reason why such humanistic visions must fail is because they do not research the institutional and discursive conditions of their own work, conditions that seem, as in the case of Auerbach's project, to assure their ultimate disappointment. Speculation about what other direction Auerbach's work might have taken had he done such research is fruitless. As a humanist in his moment he could not have carried it out. Different modes of analysis than mine would suggest other explanations of the failure of Auerbach's intervention into postwar institutions for literary and cultural study. Class-based analyses in particular might follow Lukacs' comments on the critical ideological contradictions of German humanism resulting from conflicting modes of economic organization. But I hope that treating Auerbach within the categories of his own humanism and, in turn, trying to locate them in part within the power of interest structures of both the prewar German mandarin reaction and the postwar American professionalization of literary criticism might supplement those other forms by suggesting some of the disciplinary restrictions on Auerbach's project, that is, the way in which discursive and intellectual practices both enable and restrain his efforts. In the process, such an analysis should illuminate, not just these practices, but also Auerbach's tactics for developing or revising them. Rather than take him as a heroic figure or an embodiment of sublime transcendence, I have tried to see Auerbach as a specific historical figure dealing with problems that are still too much our own and his work as an exemplar of how humanistic research should try to get beyond professional specialization and engage with the full range of intellectual and cultural problems it is obligated to confront. The way I have gone about discussing Auerbach has also made it possible to describe and evaluate for our own use some of his attempts to reform the institutions around him and to fend off the most deleterious effects of modernity on scholarship. Such a view as I propose lets us see that Auerbach has a historical and ethical sense of responsibility that commentators forget whenever then insist on describing him as a sublime figure whose efforts authorize "critical work" of a subjective, willful, or transcendental kind. Such a characterization betrays his own deepest values.

IV

At the end of his career Auerbach recognizes that neither he nor any one else in the United States could carry out the project of a historically synthetic humanism.[33] The method formulated in "Philology and *Weltliteratur*" does not produce the sort of mythographically effective synthetic work he had hoped for, and its failure leads him to accept nonsynthetic fragmentary forms of history as the only possible and appropriate goal of humanistic research. Furthermore, the image of the humanist as perpetual student recording the process of his education that appears in "Philology and *Weltliteratur*" effectively displaces the last vestiges of the humanist as a leading or universal intellectual from Auerbach's work. In its place there emerges a much different intellectual figure whose work involves following wherever the radiants of the successive *Ansatzpunkt* lead with no thought to achieving synthetic myths. Auerbach completes the project of subsuming the critic's will in the scholar's work of pursuing unsuspected and difficult connections and relations in his historical records. In the process of this final version of his humanistic engagement, Auerbach recognizes, I think with growing satisfaction, that the sketch is a more possible and appropriate mode of historical writing than the achieved form he had recommended in his earlier work.

This final series of changes in Auerbach's position can be seen in *Literary Language and Its Public in Late Latin Antiquity and in the Middle Ages*, a text itself based on the method of the *Ansatzpunkt*. For example, Auerbach takes the "*sermo humilis*" as the point of departure of the opening essay and proceeds from it to study the entire range of Christian writing; in addition, by pursuing some of its radiants he can also explore the emergence of vernacular literature in Dante and his period: "We have taken a sermon as the basis of our investigation. But the domain of *sermo humilis* in late antiquity includes all the forms of Christian literature. It pervades philosophical disquisitions as well as realistic records of events." It involves "theoretical literature" and also solves "new problems . . . in the realm of narrative" (*LL*, 53).

In *Literary Language* Auerbach tells the story of how, proceeding from such forms as the *sermo humilis* and combined with certain educational and demographic changes (especially in Northern Italy), a literary public came into being that could consume and inspire a sizable corpus of vernacular literatures. The sad lesson of *Literary Language* is that such publics are not only necessary but also fragile and disappearing. That Auerbach writes the book out of and with an eye toward the situation of the cultivated classes in (especially American) modernity is clear from such comments as the following on the failure of an earlier, Roman public:

Gradually literature lost its function. Ultimately social satire, with its direct grip on life, was abandoned, and the other forms of literature became pompously rhetorical. The literary public lost its contact with the lower classes, ceased to be embedded in the greater community of the people, *from which it is always distinct*, but with which it must maintain constant communication if it is to survive. (*LL*, 247; my emphasis)

The situation in the United States (and some of Western Europe) brings about the same result, only from the opposite direction. After Dante, the public grows more and more progressively bourgeois and "the proletariat, whose leadership it has provided, are beginning, both in their private and public lives, to resemble it like two peas in a pod. . . . Today the existence of this elite minority, the 'public,' is threatened by expansion; then [in antiquity] it shrank into nothingness" (*LL*, 334).

True to the impulse of "Philology and *Weltliteratur*," Auerbach concludes his record of part of the development of humanity with an assertion that justifies his Vichian attempt at preservation and (it is hoped) transforms his scholarship into a mythical resource for the future:

When once again [after the Dark Ages] a society came into being that possessed cultural self-awareness and a *will to cultivate its humanity*, it was not one but many, each possessing its forms and its language. Nevertheless we may venture to speak of *a* European society and even of a European *Hochsprache*. What unites them is their common root in antiquity and Christianity. For this combination contains the dialectical force which—even if Europe, like Rome before it, should now lose its power and even cease to exist as such—has prefigured the forms of a common social and cultural life on our planet. (*LL*, 338)

Acknowledging the ethnocentrism of European utopianism means admitting that this post-Hegelian vision of unity preserving diversity is not acceptable in its particular formulation. But insofar as it records humanism's memory of and desire for a model of peaceful, mutual coexistence, it is not only admirable but also an important sign that no matter how closed the world-system may appear to such a humanist, it does not extinguish either all desire for a more humane culture or the ability to imagine (even partially unacceptable) alternatives.

It is inescapable that Auerbach's humanism entangles him in unavoidable contradictions he neither resolves nor contains. At the end of his career these contradictions are nowhere more evident than in his image of himself as an intellectual. Perhaps the key element here, as throughout his career, is his relation to and understanding of Dante. Throughout his work, Auerbach studies and admires Dante more than any other writer, and he tries very often to transfer Dante's authority and legitimacy as a humanist to himself and his projects.

A book-length study would be needed to trace the origins, influences, variations, and purposes in Auerbach's relation to Dante. For example, in *Dante: Poet of the Secular World*, Auerbach bases his reading upon the classical notion that each human being is a capable individual, a metaphysical subject that, when taken as a totality, is inseparable from his fate:

Homer's inventive gift carries within it a conviction that neither observation nor reason can wholly justify, although everything in his work supports it; the conviction that every character is at the root of his own particular fate and that he will inevitably incur the fate that is appropriate to him. But this means appropriate to him as a whole, not to any one of his attributes; for his attributes, taken in the abstract, never coincide with the figure as a whole. What can be represented in poetic terms and what demands belief on the part of the reader, is not that good things happen to a good man and brave things to a brave man, but that the fate of Achilles is Achillean. (D, 2)

Auerbach maintains this line of reasoning when he argues in *Mimesis* that Dante's achievement is to make the entire personality of the individual character, fixed forever in death, come alive as the totality of a human subject whose "fate" is inextricably a reflection of what he or she is.

In *Mimesis*, Auerbach adds a new element to his discussion of the *Commoedia*, that is, a new interpretation of the figure of the poet Dante as this is represented in and constituted by the poem itself. In effect, Dante becomes through his work a unified subject essentially like Homer's Achilles. There is, however, a difference; Auerbach claims (perhaps under Hegel's influence) that Dante embodies characteristics and a fate that make him a figure of universal not just personal significance; he becomes a transhistorical subject; literally nothing that is part of the tradition of European culture finds no place in him. Indeed, the fate or destiny of European culture climaxes in Dante:

compared with [his predecessors'], his style is immeasurably richer in directness, vigor, and subtlety, he knows and uses such an immeasurably greater stock of forms, he expresses the most varied phenomena and subjects with such immeasurably superior assurance and firmness, that we come to the conclusion that this man used his language to discover the world anew. Very often it is possible to demonstrate or to conjecture where he acquired this or that device of expression; but his sources are so numerous, his ear hears them, his intellect uses them, so accurately, so simply, and yet so originally, that demonstrations of the sort can only serve to increase our admiration for the power of his linguistic genius. (M, 182–83)

The poet reveals such a depth and breadth of emotions in such an awesome and apparently unmediated way precisely because he internalizes and transforms all of the human attitudes, stances, and values fixed within the entire range of previous literary production. He makes them totally his own, and in the cauldron of his own genius and in the new world of his time, he redeploys them so successfully that his work seems to be completely original. Tracing the endlessly complex genealogies of all that makes up Dante only enhances the awe in which Auerbach holds the poet. Moreover, in Auerbach's scheme of things Dante is capable of such originary power because he *can* understand, contain, and represent—out of his own capacity for experience, out of his own humanity, so to speak—the entire range of human experience as it has existed and been recorded in literature throughout history. This is an important point because it aligns Dante, as Auerbach represents him, quite specifically with Auerbach's own position, project, and values in *Mimesis*.

Dante appears as the paradigm of humanity developing its own diversified self-expression and so, by sharing and containing its differences, forming a community. Auerbach's description of Dante's effect is in turn the paradigm of all humanistic considerations of literature: "we experience an emotion which is concerned with human beings. . . . The result is a direct experience of life which overwhelms everything else, a comprehension of human realities which spreads as widely and variously as it goes profoundly to the very roots of our emotions, an illumination of man's impulses and passions which leads us to share in them without restraint and indeed to admire this variety and their greatness" (*M*, 202).

Auerbach reminds us that the changing social order of the Italian Renaissance, particularly the rise of largely independent cities, produces an educated class of politically active public figures all of whom have their primary professional training in rhetoric. Out of this class, Dante and the poets of the *dolce stil nuovo* set out to attract an elite interested in and capable of producing a literature that is not only modeled on antiquity but that also takes current forms of life seriously. Auerbach postulates not only that the "universal human impulse to expression" found a mature subject at this time but also that, in the figure of Dante, it found a genius capable of shaping both the means of expression and the public to be the audience for this expression as well.

In other words, Auerbach figures Dante as an expression of the humanistic ideal: consciousness, talent, and knowledge combined with great expressive energies to reshape the material cultural order itself. When Auerbach insists that Dante imposes order upon the world, he does not mean this only in the weak formalistic sense of giving an aesthetic order in his poem to the density of the complex experience he knew. Rather Auerbach makes a stronger social and cultural claim for Dante: by creating the public sphere through the agency of his powerful vernacular poem, Dante concretely and materially makes possible a cultural order, dependent on an elite's self-consciousness and self-culturation, which not only assures the production of literature but also "prefigured the forms of a common social and cultural life on our planet" (LL, 338). In Auerbach's analysis, Dante himself assumes the characteristics of this sublime vision.

Dante's privileged position results, so to speak, from his making Auerbach and all humanism possible. In other words, Dante's achievement consists of having so empowered the humanistic ideal and having so made possible "humanity" itself in *Weltliteratur* that its very tradition, perhaps culminating in Auerbach, must regard him as its origin. Auerbach's strongest claims for Dante do not rest upon his forming a historically specific audience in the Renaissance; nor is Auerbach claiming Dante's privilege solely on the basis of his powerful expression of the humanistic vision: "His theme is the quintessence of the concrete, earthly here and now, as it appears to the eye of God. It concerns every single man just as it concerns Dante" (LL, 311). Auerbach is making a much stronger claim for Dante as the great original of the now-endangered cultural process of Western Europe:

Dante imposed order upon the world but at the same time breathed life into it. In so doing, he made Italian (not as such but as one of the vernacular languages) into the language of the European spirit. And by letting earthly passions, with all their tragic contents, live within the divine order, he focused attention on man in a new way. Thus he inaugurated modern European literature (or perhaps it would be more accurate to say the modern self-portrayal of man) and began to build up a public that would be receptive to this literature. (LL, 314)

Just as Dante originates this self-portrayal of man by taking seriously, in the sublime work, the drama of ordinary life on a cosmic scale, so too Auerbach takes very seriously the representation and creation of human reality in and by *Weltliteratur*.

But by the late 1950s Auerbach cannot take too seriously the
possibility of any humanistic renewal of the world Dante created. As a result, *Literary Language* presents a contradictory
image of what Auerbach as the type of the universal humanistic intellectual should be doing. On the one hand, *Literary
Language* invokes echoes of Dante's achievement to describe
Auerbach's own: Dante's knowledge of and ear for the tradition
are not unlike those of a critic who asks his audience to realize
that his "task calls for an unconscionable amount of reading"
(*LL*, 23) and also asks it "not to assume that anything I fail to
mention is unknown to me" (*LL*, 24). Dante and Auerbach
completely internalize the tradition, but despite his earlier
hope that his work will gain mythical status, for Auerbach the
internalized tradition can become simply monumental history.
It is actively defensive. This internalization is not only, as he
represents it, a necessary act of memory but also a necessary
feature of his retelling the story of the West's decline in such a
way that the pathos of his dramatic representation of lost humanistic values will have an effect on some present or future
audience. The power of the pathos depends on the greatness of
the fall, which, in turn, depends on the sublimity of the
heights, that is, of Dante, from which the fall begins. Moreover, that power to move a modern audience must emerge from
Auerbach himself whose memory and humanity register and
reproduce our loss, shaping it so that its glow reflects us. It
becomes our myth. In short, in these terms, Auerbach assumes
Dante's sublimity.

But on the other hand, Auerbach knows he cannot function
like Dante, but at best as his shadow. He cannot create a world,
as Dante could: "He molded, as potential readers of his poem, a
community which was scarcely in existence at the time when
he wrote and which was gradually built up by his poem and by
the poets who came after him" (*LL*, 312). On the contrary, all
he can do is record fragments of the tradition and beg the for-
giveness of his disappearing audience for being incapable of

"synthesis." So while Dante improves Auerbach's vision, he also marks its limits and sadly mocks its belated ambitions.

Consequently, Auerbach finds that his strategy of resisting modernity's degradation by producing syntheses based on points of departure cannot succeed. He comes up against the "inexplicable" phenomena of history that his demands for synthesis compel him to explain. For example, summarizing the rise of the Renaissance and dismissing all Marxist models of explanation, he finds himself at a loss and retreats to an idealistic discourse that flies in the face of all his injunctions in "Philology and *Weltliteratur*" and echoes his own earlier inability to account for Vico: "But all in all, the spontaneous force which at a given moment gives rise to such movements and enables them to unfold is no more subject to analysis than the force which gives rise to individual talents" (*LL*, 277). Auerbach does not simply object to naive causal explanations or continuous models of history in this passage; rather he evinces an instance of the failure of rational and scholarly inquiry and substitutes instead the irrational "explanations" he judged so severely earlier in his career.

Such gestures of futility are entirely unlike the more informed and carefully presented arguments so typical of Auerbach. They are a sign, I think, of the frustration and despair confronting Auerbach as he finds his categories less and less able to account for the knowledge and experience relevant to his project. At his best, Auerbach is so much the master of his materials that when he dares suggest a notion he cannot demonstrate for want of documents, he offers careful reasons for his hypothesis. At such times, he is successful because, unlike in a complex historical moment such as the Renaissance when the method of the textual *Ansatzpunkt* will not extend adequately to circumscribe the matter at hand, in these instances his discourse is not overwhelmed by what is known or frustrated by what is not. Discussing the origins of the *chansons de geste*, for example, Auerbach suggests that even though he lacks "compelling proofs," he can legitimately contend that his "feeling for what is natural and plausible" is enough to assert that there must have been a great literary culture that preexisted and made possible the *chansons de geste* (*LL*, 202).

Such speculation on Auerbach's part is one of the more modest results of the programmatic subjection of the scholar to study at the heart of the *Ansatzpunkt* method. Such moments shrug off the synthetic ambitions of the same method; in them, we see Auerbach willing to propose and present a more fragmented, nonexplanatory but nonetheless scholarly research attitude. That is, it is an example of the historist who not only rests in an incomplete knowledge of cause or origin but is willing, without synthetic ambitions or intuitions, to pursue a specific piece of historical research and to leave the results open ended. Concluding his "Introduction," Auerbach announces that his hoped-for unity could not be achieved; the point of departure he followed has proved to be important not only for what connections it suggests and what unity it intimates but also for how much more it leaves to be done:

> Despite its singleness of purpose, this book is a fragment or rather a series of fragments. It lacks even the loose but always perceptible unity of *Mimesis*. It is not brought to a conclusion, but broken off; it achieves no proper integration of its subject matter. Nevertheless, some readers may sense the unity behind it. In his preface to the *Quaestiones in Heptateuchum*, Augustine wrote: *nonnulla enim pars inventionis est nosse quid quaeras* (a considerable part of discovery is to know what you are looking for). What is being looked for in the following pages has, I hope, been made plain enough. But I should have liked to make more evident the connecting thread that unites the whole. In this light the book is still in search of its theme. Perhaps its readers will help in the search; perhaps one of them, by giving more precise and effective expression to what I have tried to say, will find the theme. (*LL*, 24)

Auerbach does not disown his humanistic and synthetic ideals; he has simply no way to combine them. True to his early position in *Mimesis*, he will impose no order where he finds none. Although he seems hopeful that there is a unity to the history he treats, he fails to find a "theme" or "handle," as he puts it in "Philology and *Weltliteratur*," to foreground that unity. In his postwar essays Auerbach constantly revises and extends the synthetic strategy of *Mimesis*, but in *Literary Language*, that strategy is inadequate; he cannot, for example, create a historical narrative focused on one theme such as "The Representation of Reality in Western Literature." In some ways, his renunciation of, or inability to find, such a unifying and radiating theme is closer to the historical commitments of the recommended method in "Philology and *Weltliteratur*": "concepts like 'the Baroque,' or 'the Romantic,' 'the dramatic' or 'the idea of fate,' 'intensity' or 'myth' or 'the concept of time' and 'perspectivism' are dangerous. . . . For a point of departure should not be a generality imposed on a theme from the outside, but ought rather to be an organic inner part of the theme itself" (PW, 16).

Singleness of purpose does not provide the theme needed to demonstrate the unity he feels is there in history, and consequently, Auerbach fears, this text may not be as "effective" as it otherwise would have been. Of course, Auerbach already cautioned that the philologist must get beyond singleness of purpose, beyond the will: "It is essential to remark that a general synthetic intention or problem does not suffice in and of itself" (PW, 14). The figure of the *sermo humilis* alone or taken with other tropes investigated in this text does not allow Auerbach to demonstrate the unity he feels and hopes underlies the development and decline of the literary public.

In effect, Auerbach acknowledges in this passage his inability to sustain the synthetic mode of humanistic scholarship that he had earlier felt to be not only essential to the preservation of culture but also the proof, as it were, of the absolute importance of the unfolding of "humanity" and its coming to self-consciousness in historicism. Auerbach tries, as I have hoped to show, many powerful inventions, strategies, and tactics to adapt and preserve humanistic historicist values and work in modernity. He continually struggles with himself, his own earlier positions, the ideas of his predecessors, and the almost inevitable despair of the postwar, postholocaust period. Even though his battle produces new methods and techniques, his career primarily demonstrates how unlikely it is that in modernity (or postmodernity) an adequate historical humanistic scholarship engaged in conflict over the pressing issues of "humanity" can ever be achieved. Indeed, Auerbach's heroic effort to invent, adjust, and adapt, before finally abandoning the struggle to produce "effective" and "synthetic" myths, seems to have exhausted all readily available resources for legitimating such work. This is not to say, of course, that with Auerbach's publication of a fragmented, "failed" attempt all synthetic humanistic work ceases. On the contrary, a great deal goes on; on the one hand, some scholars attempt to find other strategies to ground such work;[34] on the other hand, and for the most, academic specialists go on about their business under the shield of humanistic rhetorics, supported by an ever-decreasing financial base, teaching fewer and fewer students, and remain for the most part, unaffected by the immense scholarly, political, and ethical struggles of an Auerbach. Indeed, when these academically specialized professors invoke Auerbach, it is more often than not in defense of the status quo and to attack "deconstructors" and their "threats" to civilization (all the while, of course, reading if anything, "guides" and "introductions" produced by already powerful critics).

But Auerbach's unhappiness with the failure of his synthetic project, and so of his hope for preserving "humanity" as the unity of difference, should not be discouraging. Auerbach's struggle has always been to combine "synthesis" and "history" to preserve "humanity." In his final book, although not abandoning such a combination as his goal, he does record, with some "effectiveness," a certain sort of fragmentary history that not only leaves "gaps," as it were, but suggests another ethos.

In "Philology and *Weltliteratur*," Auerbach repeatedly insists that historicist projects can be carried out only by individuals. Yet, in *Literary Language*, in a more than formulaic manner, he acknowledges that the limits on any individual scholar's time and talent mean that the recording and production of history cannot be the product of one person: "Perhaps its readers will help in the search." In addition, it is most important that he implicitly acknowledges the contribution that nonsynthetic, "fragmentary" historical investigation can make in an attempt to describe in specific detail how we have come to be who we are. Auerbach objects to Curtius' *European Literature and the Latin Middle Ages* (is one wrong to hear an echo of that title in Auerbach's own?) not only because it was "planned and executed in Germany, roughly between 1932 and 1947,"[35] but also because of "the monstrosity of the materials it mobilizes" (PW, 13). Of course, we have seen Auerbach's objections to totalizing academic syntheses. Yet his objection to Curtius is not that he tries to deal with everything and fails but that Curtius' book is fragmentary, elliptical, and disorganized: "if one collected the scattered observations on individual phenomena . . . it would be sufficient for several studies."[36] Whatever value and order Curtius' text has results from his employing something like Auerbach's own method of the *Ansatzpunkt*.

While in order to avoid producing a monstrosity, Auerbach may not have presented all his material in *Literary Language*— after all, he could not organize it—this book does come closer to Curtius' text, as Auerbach describes it, than any other of his works. It is elliptical, full of gaps, fragmentary, and excessive. It is also meant, like Curtius' book (and, of course, *Mimesis*), to take "'European Literature as the intellectual field of study'" and to show that European literature is a reality, but of even greater complexity than Curtius supposed (*LL*, 23).[37]

Of course, it is precisely that unity Auerbach cannot show as he moves his research into ever finer points of historical analysis, following his *Ansatzpunkt* method, into areas where the documents and records for which the method is intended are not available. Indeed, Auerbach's project works out its own contradictions between synthesis and history to the point where he gives us an example of how to write discontinuous history—even with the (impossible) hope of going beyond it: "The general conception that can be set forth is, I believe, that of an historical process, a kind of drama, which advances no theory but only sketches a certain pattern of human destiny" (*LL*, 21). It is this general intention, echoing his own earlier Homeric reading of Dante's achievement, that he cannot accomplish. This synthetic notion of "humanity" cannot survive the driving historicist impulse, and Auerbach is left a historian first and a "humanist" second—a split that, as we have seen, he dislikes and struggles to avoid:

My purpose is always to write history. Consequently I never approach a text as an isolated phenomenon; I address a question to it, and my question, not the text, is my primary point of departure. . . . These themes [of sublimity, the influence of Christianity, etc.] are of the utmost importance for us, but far too vast and varied to be treated as a whole; one can hope to throw light on them only by tracing them back to specialized points of departure. Of course a single starting point cannot suffice for such enormous subjects; at most it can perform a function of guidance and integration; each part of the investigation raises problems of its own and demands its own points of departure. (*LL*, 20)

In other words, the new kind of specialization Auerbach recommends in "Philology and *Weltliteratur*"—"constant rediscovery" (PW, 15)—which is essentially a revisionist tactic, gives way in *Literary Language* to a mode of specialization that requires the scholar to follow the lines "radiating" from the starting *Ansatzpunkt* wherever they may lead. The synthetic vision so essential to Auerbach's sense of "humanity" cannot survive a commitment to research that obliges the scholar so totally to follow his or her material. Nor does Auerbach substitute for the impossibility of synthesis the will of the critic as a regulative ideal.

Furthermore, and most important, the scholar's commitment does not prevent writing and publication: the scholar produces "sketches." It would, after all, be unacceptable to feel that since getting beyond sketching is impossible, knowledgeable silence is somehow better. As a practicing historian, Auerbach is not paralyzed by his failure to be synthetic or even adequate. Rather, his commitment to the priority of life in history sustains his writing and research; he can only be a sketcher:

What can thus be achieved under the most favorable circumstances is an insight into the diverse implications of a process from which we stem and in which we participate, a definition of our present situation and also perhaps of the possibilities for the immediate future. In any event, such a method compels us to look within ourselves and to set forth our consciousness of ourselves here and now, in all its wealth and limitations. (*LL*, 21)

Like Foucault not long after him, Auerbach values history writing as an activity essential to the present moment and the historian as a scholar willing to work unsupported by any totalizing historical model. For this reason, also like Foucault, Auerbach suggests that this fragmentary history sketched by

pursuing the process of life wherever it leads, even into our own consciousness and conditions, is a necessary alternative to the totalization of "historical materialism" (*LL*, 21). Not only is his objection to Marxism part of his mandarin heritage, but also it is consistent with his own persistent sense that the destructive conditions of modernity are not easily ideologically differentiated. No form of synthetic totalization (neither Frye nor Lukacs) aids the scholar in carrying out the sort of research Auerbach feels alone is possible in late modernity. In fact, it may contribute to cultural leveling.

Indeed, even though his project is somewhat too pessimistic and abstract in its objects and methods, Auerbach does point to at least two necessities for contemporary scholarship: to write a discontinuous history as engaged history of the present and to bring the skills of rational, scholarly inquiry to bear on the present social and political conditions out of which all cultural and intellectual discourse emerges. While Auerbach's career exhausts so many humanistic possibilities, his work points beyond that humanism in a direction taken up more recently by Said and Foucault.

5

Intellectuals at War: Michel Foucault and the Analytics of Power

> In a general way, I think that intellectuals—if this category exists, which is not certain nor perhaps even desirable—are abandoning their old prophetic function.
> —Michel Foucault "Power and Sex"

Michel Foucault seems to be involved in so many areas and issues in criticism, history, politics, and the social sciences that honest men and women find it hard to study or work in any of these fields without stumbling across him—if only to kick him aside. Foucault is immensely plastic. Scholars seem to make whatever they want of him, which is a risk attendant on his unusual style and interests. He is at once celebrated, castigated, and caricatured—and sometimes even critically examined. But despite the relative ease with which the distribution network has circulated images of Foucault and his work, there always seems to be something at stake for intellectuals who write on and after Foucault. At issue, even though it is rarely, if ever, acknowledged, is the investment intellectuals have made in certain discourses, institutions, and practices. Above all what seems to be at risk is the image that intellectuals (and others) have of themselves as intellectuals, and the very means by which they sustain their role in society as representatives of perspicacious intelligence and as producers of symbols and values for society, the state, the party, and the "disciplines."

Foucault actually offers very little support to those who want to preserve or defend this leading intellectual role. In fact, I would suggest, Foucault's thinking about and analysis of power is fully intelligible only when seen as a challenge to the legitimacy of the leading intellectual as a social subject. Taken in this context, many important critical discussions of Foucault can be seen, above all, as *defenses* of the discourses and practices that always and variously validate and extend the privileged social, political, and psychological positions of both hegemonic and oppositional intellectuals.

Many radical intellectuals with differing attitudes toward Foucault warn that his work should not become celebrated dogma endlessly explicated in pursuit of the "final word." Rather, they argue, Foucault's work should be judged on the basis of its efficacy. What types of analysis and action does it empower and restrict?[1] What possible methods and positions does Foucault offer intellectuals attempting to act as intellectuals in the world? Are his theories and practices adequate to the conceptions of effective intellectual work that radicals hold or into which, as Foucault might say, discourse and discipline inscribe them? Is Foucault a historian, they ask?[2] Should he be taken seriously as a historian, a philosopher, a genealogist, a theoretician of power? Often the question of Foucault's intellectual identity is asked by a practitioner of a specific discipline who tries to answer the question: do we need attend to Foucault and, if so, what effect might such attention have on our discipline? Other intellectuals, less defined by and worried over the shape of their disciplines, take a more global view and wonder if Foucault can join in the fight to alleviate human suffering. But both groups of Foucault commentators share a certain uneasiness about his intellectual practice because his genealogical research often subverts the social and cultural authority of traditional disciplines and discourses—the very means by which intellectuals (no matter what their "politics" or "intent") normally acquire power and identity.

To take a specific instance of the problems Foucault can cause, one might ask what would be the fate of the historian who accepted not only the idea that history writing is fiction—

certainly this is by now a cliché—but also that history has no reality in and of itself, that its "reality" is a function of textual practices inscribed within discourse and ideology. I cannot take up the question of whether or not such radical perspectivism is correct. It would, I think, be futile to do so. Rather, I want to recall, after Nietzsche, that one reason why this question of radical perspectivism is always contested—or simply ignored by most academic historians—is that, as Wellek and Meinecke believe, radical perspectivism can destroy "history" as a discipline.[3] It depends for its very existence on the legitimacy of its claim that there is some sort of "reality" not completely dependent on the historian's position and textual practice. To take a more general case, one can point out that since Foucault's genealogies represent much of psychoanalysis and Marxism as themselves part of the tactics and strategies of power, radical or oppositional intellectuals who identify themselves with and use these discourses find Foucault challenging their very power and identity as oppositional intellectuals. Foucault's genealogies often show these discourses and practices to be inscribed into filial relations with undesirable ancestors and so provoke debates with those heavily invested in the "revolutionary potential" of those discourses over charges of who is more radical, concrete, humanistic, metaphysical, or effective. Since one of Foucault's aims is to defeat many of these other discourses by pointing out their unsavory complicities wherever he sees them, he cannot and should not remain above these debates.

Dismissive critiques of Foucault by intellectuals closed to any practice different from those of their own disciplines can tell us much about those disciplines but little about Foucault.[4] Adulations of Foucault are even less interesting. Attempts on the part of critics, film scholars, historians, philosophers, and others to come to terms with Foucault as a new figure to be considered in their respective fields tell us much about the possibility that even the most radical theories can be academicized with complex political and scholarly results. But there is no space to go into any of these readings of Foucault here, and above all, the most interesting and revealing insights into what is at stake for critical intellectuals in Foucault are clearest in those very critiques that take him most seriously as an intellectual and theorist of power.

II

Along with Hayden White, Edward W. Said has been consistently the most influential English-language commentator on Foucault, and critics frequently identify his *Orientalism* as the only American example of critical scholarship to rival Foucault's own analyses of power and discourse. So when Said warns critics against accepting Foucault's work on power because it is a "theoretical overtotalization" that attempts to account for all aspects of society in terms of one unquestionable concept, the status of Foucault in the academy should be reexamined.

Said's recently expressed reservations about Foucault appear in "Traveling Theory," an essay that carries forward his long-anticipated study of criticism and theory "between system and culture."[5] Said's essay is a cautionary analysis which reminds us that theories appear in and as responses to certain specific historical and cultural situations and cannot be transported with impunity, for their effects vary in different contexts. In this essay Said argues, against the claims of the Bloomians and the deconstructors, that responsible methods can be developed to judge the efficacy of the various "misreadings" or "misinterpretations" that occur whenever a theory is recast by a successor in a different cultural-historical context. For Said, critics can be better served by developing these more concrete and specific criteria for judgment than by invoking the unnecessary and restrictive rhetoric of "creative misreadings" and universal "complex intertextuality."

In the past, of course, Said has argued for the relative importance of Foucault's procedures as opposed to Derrida's precisely because the former allows for openings toward the specific historical, discursive, and institutional practices that embody power and because he is not, like Derrida, circumscribed by his own angelic ironies.[6] But, for Said, Foucault's writing on power, especially in *La Volonté de savoir*, reflect how easily even such theoretically "open" constructs can become abstract and rarefied when left "unexposed to the complex unfolding of the social world" (TT, 60). As Said points out, Frank Lentricchia had previously made precisely this point in his judgment of the current state of literary criticism.[7] Said adds his own claim that "social reality" is susceptible to what he calls "theoretical overtotalization," and so the theorist and his or her followers must always be aware of and resist the implicit dangers that weaken oppositional theories whenever they reduce social complexity to a study of one variable. Said's argument is that Foucault's theory of power is abstract, totalizing, closed (yet incomplete), omnivorous, and simplifying. In sum it is politically inadequate and easily academicized, assuring its believers of their own political commitment because of its apparent seductive opening to the world, while immuring them within comfortable and authorized dogmas. Said's critique, only partially outlined here, is important and compelling. His attempt to shape a method to study the translation of theories between cultural moments is itself an instance of critical history, reminding us not just of the contextual nature of theoretical production but also of the intellectual responsibility to measure theory against social reality so that it does not totalize its object at the expense of its practical and scholarly efficacy.

Said's comments provide a privileged opening into a discussion of Foucault's conception of power and a special instance of intellectual conflict prompted by what we can discover about intellectual functions in "Foucault's" texts. Said clearly understands that the issue at stake is which discourses will guide, constitute, and represent intellectuals and how these discourses will escape academic neutering by undergoing continuing trials in the political world of concrete social reality. That is to say, Said's text enacts the struggle to establish the political efficacy of one conception of intellectual discourse and practice in the *very process* of establishing criteria by which the efficacy and history of theories can be judged. In other words, while "Travelling Theory" argues that the test of a critical theory is its efficacy, it enacts a *textual* or *rhetorical* battle against, in the case of Foucault, an empowered antagonistic representation of intellectual practice, one that perhaps invalidates the immensely attractive image Said generates. Said's text happens to illustrate in an especially pure and complex way the unavoidable struggle over the self-conception of the intellectual that appears in all advanced speculation and scholarship among radical intellectuals now that many Marxist and humanistic images of intellectual practice and purpose have been destabilized.

I hope it is clear that it is not a question of whether or not Said is "right" about Foucault. Any success Said might have in cautioning us against Foucault depends entirely on his tactical ability, in this essay, to intertwine Foucault into a complex system of images, values, and reactions. Said is not rejecting or discrediting Foucault, as some seem to have imagined. In Said's later work, Foucault is a necessary adversary, a crucial element in the tactics he deploys to empower his own position. If even Foucault falls prey to a "theoretical overtotalization" uncritically accepted by his ephebes, where else, Said asks, can one turn to legitimate models for authorized images of intellectual behavior and self-regard?

Said's essay begins by announcing that it is concerned with judging the power of theories and formulating a scheme for understanding their transmission. Acknowledging that the circulation of ideas nourishes and sustains civilization, Said sketches his own project: "one ought to go on to specify the kinds of movements that are possible, in order to ask whether by virtue of having moved from one place and time to another an idea or a theory gains or loses in strength" (TT, 41). As a general matter regarding all theories, mapping this process of transmission is immensely complicated and must take account—and this is crucial to Said's position—of the resistances to any transplanted theory (TT, 41). Said elaborates his ideas on the transmission of theories in the context of and as an intervention into the labyrinthine world of contemporary "literary" criticism and theory. Old unities of criticism and even older humanistic ideologies that assured a "Goethian sense of a concert of all literatures and ideas" (TT, 43) have been fragmented under the pressure of historical events, and none of the new, highly technical theoretical imports—semiotics, deconstruction, French psychoanalysis, and so on—have the power to impose order on the field or the right to universal assent from critics. The essential element, for Said, in this new critical scene is the fundamental inability of critics to define the constitution of the literary field or the literary object. No critical operation is, a priori, illegitimate. Said rightly and importantly insists that in this situation, the persistant invocation of older humanistic, literary shibboleths merely repeats residual terms whose authority continues to decline: "Convention, historical custom, appeals to the protocols of humanism and traditional scholarship are of course regularly introduced as evidence of the field's enduring integrity, but more and more these seem to be rhetorical strategies in a debate about what literature and literary criticism ought to be rather than convincing definitions of what they are" (TT, 43).

The Nietzschean element of Said's thought surfaces here. Behind that stylistically decorous, gentle "more and more," Said insists that we recognize in the most humanistic assertions of "Goethian" values and beliefs the agon waged by individual critics and groups of critics for the right to define both the limits of literary study and the legitimate stance of the critic in our culture. In other words, Said suggests that the very discourse that most hopes to separate literature and criticism from the chaos of competition has revealed itself to be, as in the instance of Pound's "Kung" or Richards' "Practical Criticism," only a strategy in a power game. Some critics are exuberant over the free play of language this situation provides; others darkly remind us of the real economic interests behind this competition of ideas. Said correctly sees that "In the absence of an enclosing domain called literature with very clear outer boundaries, there is no longer an authorized or official position for the literary critic." Without a commanding method, or "synoptic view," or "synthetic vision" "there is a babel of arguments for the limitlessness of all interpretation." Said concedes that others see this situation as "pluralistic or desperate." "For my part," he writes, "I prefer to see it as an opportunity for remaining skeptical and critical, succumbing neither to dogmatism nor to sulky gloom" (TT, 45).

To this point in his essay, Said has argued that the circulation of ideas and theories is everywhere and always a test of strengths and that this is especially true in criticism where the boundaries of the field and its traditional unifying ideologies and practices have been irretrievably broken. What he offers is, first, a way to study and learn how to judge these contests by schematizing the "three or four stages common to the way any theory or idea travels" (TT, 41) and, second, a way to examine the babel of competing critical "systems that in asserting their capacity to perform essentially self-confirming tasks allow for no counter-factual evidence" (TT, 45). In other words, Said quite specifically refuses to follow Richards' example in a similar situation and try to impose unity through a monolithic practice that reduces criticism to "training" in hegemonic values. Some might wish to disagree with Said's description of contemporary criticism; I certainly do not, nor would I do so here if I did. The real interest in Said, in this essay as in his books, lies in the absolute clarity with which he dramatizes the unavoidably agonistic nature of high intellectual production. His comments on criticism and literature in "Travelling Theory" are a miniature display of his talent—shown to its greatest advantage in *Orientalism*—to characterize an entire discourse or discipline while positioning himself and his practice somewhere above or to the side.

Effectively, his texts produce two images of intellectual practice—one that, in its very variety, represents the intellectual discipline he is studying and the other, himself. Of course, in the complexity of *Orientalism* there are multifaceted relationships established between the politically directed genealogist that is the image of Said and the various images of orientalists as different as Massignon, Gibb, and Bernard Lewis. Much of the hostility directed at *Orientalism* results not just from Said's indictments of orientalists' too frequent complicity with repression but also from the success his project enjoys in delegitimating entire ranges of intellectual practice and discourse

upon the power of which intellectuals have come to rely for
their identity, position, and influence.[8] In showing the complicity of humanistic scholars with the hegemonic forms of
repression, Said attempts to give new legitimacy to the humanist by advocating a commitment of critical intelligence to the
genealogical battle against the use of power knowledge by the
forces of oppression. But Said has written too often, too fully,
and too self-consciously of the agonistic nature of scholarship
as a struggle to establish certain representations for us to believe that he does not know that his strategy in "Travelling
Theory" is to generate and make available an image of intellectual practice and position superior to and more attractive than
those others his texts represent. That Said sees this as an admirable project is clear from his comments on Raymond Williams'
revisions of Lukacs and Goldman (TT, 57).

Indeed, we can learn from Said—and because of this he is
infinitely preferable to most of his critics and disciples—that
something like a pattern of critical decomposition, recomposi-
tion, and self-projection is the inescapable situation of modern
humanistic intellectuals. It is an unavoidable feature not only
of the lack of firm boundaries in contemporary criticism but
also of the intellectual ideal Said cautions must be defended:
"Theoretical closure, like social convention or cultural dogma,
is anathema to critical consciousness, which loses its profession when it loses its active sense of the open world in which its
faculties must be exercised" (TT, 60). This warning against
closure is theoretically, imagistically, and ideologically consistent with the earlier statement of Said's skeptical openness.
Said's arguments bring his readers to a recognition of the following position: to oppose theoretical openness is to deny critical consciousness, but the latter is always in major part a
conflict for authority between competing representations of
intellectual practice. Said would have us conclude that critical consciousness is always the battle between instrumental
discourses.

It would, of course, be difficult, as Said clearly knows, to
argue against or to deny the value of "theoretical openness"
especially when judging matters of closure and efficacy means

avoiding "impoverishment and rarefaction" by testing theory against the "social world" (TT, 60). Yet Said's position should itself be skeptically examined: despite its power we should see nonetheless that there is a peculiar circularity and closure to Said's own argument, for he begins from the position that the circulation of theories and ideas depends on strength—struggle and resistance—and brings us to the conclusion that it is necessary to resist "theoretical closure" or to defend "openness" as the sine qua non of critical consciousness. In other words, the "openness" which must be preserved is that inscribed by a theory of critical consciousness which depends for its very survival on the endless agon(y) of theoretical amd intellectual warfare. At this point, we have not just a description of the state of affairs but an attempt to give a legitimate place to a theory of the endless conflict of theories both as a way to master that agon—which is real—and, more importantly, as a condition for the very existence of the kind of intellectual Said images in this text.

III

Said's remarks on Foucault seem to be a coda to the body of his essay, which is taken up with detailed discussions of the transmission of theories in Lukacs, Goldmann, and Williams. Said does not discuss Foucault's work as a transplanted version of another's theory nor does he analyze in any detail the writings of those whom Said calls Foucault's "disciples." Surprisingly, he does not sketch the mechanisms by which the institutional network distributes Foucault, how this circulation affects his theory, or why the American academy has, to even a limited degree, admitted Foucault within its walls. On the last point, though, Said does remind us that Foucault provides critics "with a conceptual apparatus" for studying effective institutions and discourses that is far superior to the "arid metaphysics produced habitually by the students of his major philosophical *competitors*" (TT, 61; my emphasis). Said develops the implicit but ruling metaphor of power and struggle when he offers a less flattering and somewhat more general explanation of Foucault's attraction:

In fact, I think, Foucault's theory of power is a Spinozist conception, which has *captivated* not only Foucault himself but many of his readers who wish to go beyond Left optimism and Right pessimism so as to justify political quietism with sophisticated intellectualism, at the same time that they wish to appear to be realistic, in touch with the world of power and reality, as well as historical and antiformalistic in their bias. (TT, 64)

Foucault, or at least his theory of power, has no charm for Said, no irresistible appeal. Surely, the theory of power does not dominate or influence him as he slides from his previous defense of Foucault to a warning: since Foucault has not always understood what he has been about (which is true if his work is viewed retrospectively, that is, with the theory of power seen as the end of its development), his new position on power, as Said sees it, imprisons Foucault so he cannot take seriously oppositions to power.

Given Said's concerns in "Travelling Theory," his criticism can, of course, be taken as a caution against the wholesale importation of Foucault into the academy and as a warning against the quietistic temptations of Foucault's textual practice. Yet it still seems somewhat out of place, for it is not, I repeat, a discussion on the same order as those of Lukacs, Goldmann, and Williams. But there is another reason for it to be here. Although it was never possible to identify the Said of *Orientalism* with Foucault because of their essential differences over the role of the individual subject vis-à-vis discourse, it does seem fair to point out that in this passage Said is revising his own previous authorization of Foucault as an alternative to "metaphysical aridity" and in so doing is projecting a seemingly different image of himself as intellectual.

This revision becomes apparent in Said's comments on Frank Lentricchia. In *After the New Criticism*, Lentricchia develops an argument, emerging, in part, out of Foucault and Said, which describes the paralyzed state of contemporary criticism. Said represents Lentricchia's achievement this way: "In instance after instance he demonstrates the impoverishment and the rarefaction that overtake any theory relatively untested and unexposed to the complex unfolding of the social world, which is never a merely complaisant context to be used for the

enactment of theoretical situations" (TT, 60). This characterization echoes Said's own earlier comments on contemporary
criticism and so whether it is entirely accurate or not should be
seen as one version of Said himself.[9] When he quickly moves
away from this position by cautioning that it is inadequate
because social reality is "susceptible to theoretical overtotalization," he is revising not only Lentricchia's position—as he
sees it—but himself. He delegitimates Foucault, as he had earlier authorized him, and detaches himself, not just from
Foucault, but also from his own earlier images of him(self).
Foucault has simply become the latest example of the fate
awaiting many critics whose successful articulation of a theory
betrays his own earlier brilliant "theoretical and practical performances." Foucault, Said writes, "falls victim to the systematic degradation of theory in ways that his newest disciples—
with few exceptions—consider to be evidence that he has not
succumbed to hermeticism" (TT, 60). As Said would have it,
Foucault *has* "succumbed to hermeticism." This is a strange
phrase. It continues the metaphor of violence and competition
that permeates the essay, but it leaves ambiguous whether
Foucault has been overpowered and defeated by superior
strength or yielded in the throes of desire to an irresistibly
succulent fate. In either event, as Said sees it, Foucault seems
to have died, to have given in, to have been brought to an end
in the process.

It is quite uncertain just what this "hermeticism" is. Does it
mean that Foucault is recondite? Indeed, yes. Does it mean he
is occult? Abstruse? To the former, no; to the latter, perhaps for
some. Does it mean Foucault has built a system itself sealed
tight, closed off to external influences? This is what Said seemingly intends, namely, that Foucault's thinking about power
has become a self-confirming system not open to "counter-
factual" evidence. No matter how crucial these comments on
Foucault might be to understanding Said's considerable project
or the patterns of intellectual self-creation, they do take the
form of a coda, and so Said cannot be expected to do the detailed reading of Foucault needed for him to demonstrate con-
clusively Foucault's new hermeticism. Nonetheless, through

paraphrase, summary, and brief citation he points to the "disturbing circularity of Foucault's theory of power" and can "note that Foucault's history is ultimately textual" (TT, 66). Perhaps in an attempt to link Foucault and his disciples further to quietism, Said suggests he has an affinity with Borges. In keeping with his persistent strategy of counterpointing two images of intellectual practice, Said contrasts Foucault with Chomsky and Gramsci. This is an absolutely crucial point in Said's text and returns us directly to Foucault (whose analytics of power, I hope it is clear, we have never left).

Under the sign of "Chomsky/Gramsci," Said projects an image of the acceptable and adequate intellectual. Space no doubt constrains him to paint the image in broad strokes. What are the highlights of this image? Intellectuals should oppose repression, imagine alternative societies, and recognize that there are always actual concrete forces of resistance to power that must be described, especially as part of the intellectual's responsibility to engage sensitive issues and to try to improve the human lot. Let us be absolutely clear that these are politically and morally attractive ideals that have a very long history. The ends they pursue are essential to human life and hope. No merely formalist argument should be brought against them. In Said's staging of the scene, Foucault, having "succumbed" to "hermeticism," ranges himself and his "theory of power" against the responsibility of the intellectual in all these areas. Most especially, Said stresses that Foucault has not written a history of "resistances" but only of universally dominant micropowers. Said's statements seem to simplify Foucault somewhat; his summary description is not complete, but it is polemically effective.

"Succumbed" suggests not only defeat but guilt, an unnecessary giving in, a yielding to pleasure, desire, or temptation. There is a moral tinge to Said's critique of Foucault's "theory of power." Unfortunately, he does not develop a rigorous political critique, accepting rather Poulantzas' critique and referring to Ian Hacking as a representative of the irresponsible Foucault discipleship. What have Foucault's and his disciples' succumbings cost the intellectual? What are the immoral consequences of Foucault's speaking, as Said sees it, in such general terms about power? Said hopes to convince us that such theoretical generalizations prevent Foucault from recognizing resistances to power and that they deny him the ability to imagine alternative social orders. As he sees it, Foucault's thinking about power reduces all social phenomena to power and makes resistance a dependency of an inescapable network that inhibits reconceptualizing the social order.

I have already suggested that some criticism of Foucault stems from a felt need for intellectuals to delegitimate his work in the name of various ideologies and practices that define the identity of the leading intellectuals. I am also suggesting that Said's essay is crucial because it both thematizes the issue of intellectual conflict and, by engaging Foucault antagonistically, is the paradigm of all defenses of the leading intellectual imaged as a competitor for social power and authority. This defense becomes clear not just in the "content" of Said's critique but in the image of the intellectual he projects as an alternative to the hermetic theorist and in the process by which his essay builds that image: Said continually argues for the social responsibility of the intellectual and cautions against the dogmatic potential of all theorizing, yet, at the same time, his metaphors reveal that continual contest and violence are the actual nature of the intellectual "openness" he counterpoints to theoretical "closure."

Whatever success his essay achieves depends on its ability to legitimate this image of the agonistic intellectual within the visions and values of humane and often nonviolent social goals. This pattern is very clear in the final paragraph of "Travelling Theory," where Said cautions once more that theories can become "cultural dogma" (but, "they are to be distinguished from grosser forms of cultural dogma like racism") and can dull "critical consciousness" into believing "that a once insurgent theory is still insurgent" (TT, 66–67). Summarizing his essay, Said writes that theories are always engaged in conflict, that they can lose their strength in transmission, and that critical consciousness, to preserve its integrity, must judge the efficacy of competing theories. It can do this only if it moves out from behind theoretical walls, immersing itself "skeptically yet investigatively in the broader political world." And, Said tells us, while "these are not imperatives, they do at least seem attractive alternatives" to theoretical closure.

Having made of Foucault the exemplary case of the intellectual who has succumbed to hermeticism, Said ends up on another counterpointed rhetorical question: "And what is critical consciousness at bottom if not an unstoppable predilection for alternatives?" (TT, 67). Said, in other words, offers a set of alternatives and at the same time legitimates the most attractive alternative of all—for intellectuals: the image of the non-dogmatic critic, who has not succumbed to hermeticism, unstoppably generating alternative images of intellectuals, intellectual practice, and the social order—images whose value is determined competively in a battle for authority. And it is indeed a battle for authority that Said enacts in this essay between his own "unstoppable predilection" and Foucault and between this self-image and his other, "earlier" "Foucauldian" "self." I am suggesting, in other words, that whatever authority "Travelling Theory" acquires will be to a substantial extent the result of its defense of the traditional role of the leading intellectual to envisage and legislate alternative societies while, more importantly, by so doing, it legitimates the intellectual's "individual" right to reimagine himself or herself as such reimagining becomes necessary to establish or preserve authority and identity.

Said is admired by much of the contemporary academy because the incredible purity of his talent is always at work legitimating the critical need for self-definition through conflict that defines our humanistic political intellectual milieu. His work suggests not only its unavoidable necessity in the present moment but also its propriety, by insisting that such constant redefinition and repositioning is the socially responsible *mode* of intellectual behavior. At the risk of being reductive, let me be as clear as possible: despite its oppositional commitments, Said's image of critical consciousness is essentially a legitimation of the status quo of intellectual life; imagining alternatives means competing against other intellectuals and their work; being "unstoppable" means being free to reposition oneself whenever the felt need to preserve authority or identity requires it; and judging theories on the basis of their "insurgent" power means granting the intellectual and self-interested judge an unfortunate amount of authority. And in all, this adds up to a model of intellectual life, more revealing of the current state of intellectual life than any *specific* image of the intellectual offered as legitimate by any critic at any given time. Said's essay is brilliant and troubling at the same time—brilliant because of the clarity with which it presents the unavoidably agonistic nature of contemporary intellectual life and practice—troubling because it offers, as no other American critic has been able, a legitimation of that practice as the proper critical role of leading intellectuals. Indeed, in practice and theory, Said legitimates the endless repositioning of intellectuals vis-à-vis other intellectuals in their battle for social awards.[10] The "unstoppable" imagination of alternatives is precisely the form this repositioning takes. The identity of the intellectual is inseparably bound up in and made possible by the way his or her work represents a position and so a self-image. Thus when a "position" gains authority by gaining an audience or influence and so becomes efficacious—at least in the eyes of many—the intellectual is also legitimated, given an identity and authority, whose preservation within our consumeristic society depends on the "unstoppable" repositioning by which Said defines "critical consciousness."

Why then Said's coda on Foucault? It is not, I believe, just to detach himself from a commonly perceived (false) identification of their works. Rather, Foucault's work, as some of his "disciples" recognize, poses a direct challenge to the legitimacy of both traditional and oppositional intellectuals. It makes it difficult for them (us) to authorize the competition for power, authority, and identity. Foucault argues that many of the "oppositional" rhetorics are in complicity with the hegemony of power. He, therefore, not only refuses to assume the role of the leading intellectual whose traditional job is to imagine alternatives but also destabilizes the inherited rhetorics authorizing that image of the intellectual. I shall return to this idea, but it is necessary first to reconsider Said's two major criticisms of Foucault to suggest that Said knows what is implied for intellectuals by Foucault's analytics of power—Said misleadingly calls it quietism—and that Said is specifically defending the traditional and privileged role of the leading intellectual by making Foucault, a critic of that role, seem morally culpable for abandoning it.[11]

Given the tradition in which he is working, one should perhaps not be surprised by the rather moral, almost Arnoldian tones, of Said's final comment on Foucault: "One could not imagine Foucault undertaking a sustained analysis of powerfully contested political issues, nor like Chomsky himself and writers like John Berger, would Foucault commit himself to descriptions of power and oppression with some (perhaps misguided) intention of alleviating human suffering, pain, or betrayed hope" (TT, 66). These are fine and attractive sentiments, but one must notice that they *assume* that the role of the intellectual is to exercise critical consciousness *for* the oppressed to alleviate their oppression. It is precisely this assumption of intellectual authority that Foucault has attacked as arrogant and historically unnecessary.[12] More important, Foucault has tried to show—successfully or not is open to debate—that the leading oppositional discourses, Marxism and psychoanalysis, do not constitute breaks within the history of power but, as in the case of Freud, completions of impulses—in this case, to speak of sexuality—already pervading culture.[13] Oppositional critics are, therefore, already inscribed within a genealogy of power knowledge to which their practice makes further (sometimes modifying) contributions. The genealogy of these defining intellectual discourses—humanisms, Marxisms, psychoanalyses—circumscribes the positions and "alternatives" intellectuals envision and attempt to "legislate" or "disseminate." In his genealogies Foucault is actually attacking both the belief in the revolutionary potential of these empowering discourses and the intellectual type they empower. His aims are political. Throughout many of the documents collected in *Power/Knowledge* for example, Foucault clearly intends to deny economistic Marxists or Maoists the right to use what they think are "self-evident" concepts like "popular justice" without recognizing the complicity between intellectuals' interests in their own power and identity and their deployment of such figures in (perhaps misguided) efforts to better society.

Only one specific and limited example of Foucault's critique of the leading intellectual can be treated here. In "Our Popular Justice,"[14] Foucault argues mockingly, yet seriously, that the very form of the court preempts acts of popular justice by re-inscribing them into a penal model genealogically identical with the history of the bourgeoisie and, implicitly, the intellectual group. Courts, he argues, reflect and extend the division of labor, and he asserts, at the expense of his Maoist interlocutors, that those who believe in their revolutionary potential are not materialists, because they do not understand the actual organization of a court or how it operates when under the control of a "revolutionary" cadre:

There are those who judge—or who pretend to judge—with total tranquility, without being in any way involved. This re-inforces the idea that for judicial proceedings to be just they must be conducted by someone who can remain quite detached, by an intellectual, an expert in the realm of ideas. When, into the bargain, the people's court is organized or presided over by intellectuals, who come along to hear what on the one hand the workers and on the other hand the bosses have got to say, and to pronounce: "This one is innocent, that one guilty," then the whole thing is infused with idealism. (PJ, 30)

This passage is part of a more sustained debate over the question of the revolutionary potential of seizing state apparatuses in which Foucault clearly suggests a connection between, on the one hand, the forces of oppression embodied in the state and/or the vanguard party and, on the other hand, the leading intellectual. Foucault specifically rejects one version of the most attractive role a leading intellectual might play. He does not accept the necessity for even organic intellectuals to provide political direction to the masses: "I would prefer to say that an act of popular justice cannot achieve its full significance unless it is clarified politically, under the supervision of the masses themselves" (PJ, 3). Throughout this exchange

Foucault has two goals: the first is to discredit the authority of this revolutionary rhetoric by revealing its historical and political naivete regarding courts and justice; the second is to force out into the open the authority this rhetoric provides to those who wield it in the present world and who will wield it in the alternative society they envision and hope to bring about through a revolution they will lead.

On this second point it is essential to see why Foucault links his assertion that the people do not need—even revolutionary—state apparatuses with his critique of leading intellectuals. It is not simply that, as we shall see in chapter 6, since Kant, the state depends on intellectuals in any one of the number of ways such a relation can be theorized. Nor is it that intellectuals cannot in specific cases act against oppression. Rather the state and leading intellectuals try to deny to the people the power of self-regulation and self-imagination, either individually or in groups, and try to prevent or at least to inhibit others from coming to political clarity. Leading intellectuals tend to assume responsibility for imagining alternatives and do so *within* a set of discourses and institutions burdened genealogically by multifaceted complicities with power that make them dangerous to people. As agencies of these discourses that greatly affect the present lives of people one might say leading intellectuals are a tool of oppression and most so precisely when they arrogate the right and power to judge and imagine efficacious alternatives—a process that we might suspect, sustains leading intellectuals at the expense of others.

In the context of this type of argument in Foucault's work, one of Said's criticisms becomes more doubtful. Said refers to Foucault's exchange with Chomsky on Dutch television in which Foucault refuses to accept Chomsky's assertion that one of the two tasks of any intellectual engaged in "the sociopolitical battle" is ' "to imagine a future society that conforms to the exigencies of human nature' . . . 'as best we understand them' " (TT, 65). According to Said, Foucault rejects the idea because such imaginings are a product of *our* civilization and because such a project would be "too utopian" "for anyone like Foucault." Said's text is worth examining in detail on this point: "anyone like Foucault," he writes believes that "the idea of justice in itself is an idea which in effect has been invented and put to work in different societies as an instrument of a certain political and economic power or as a weapon against that power." This is a perfect instance of Foucault's unwillingness to take seriously his own ideas about "resistances" to power. If power oppresses and controls and manipulates, then everything that resists it is not morally equal to power, is not neutrally and simply "a weapon against that power." Resistance cannot equally be an adversarial alternative to power, and also a dependent function of it, except in some metaphysical, ultimately trivial sense. Even if the distinction is hard to draw, there is a distinction to be made—as, for example, Chomsky does, when he says that he would give his support to an oppressed proletariat if as a class it made an ideal of justice the goal of its struggle. (TT, 65–66)

One should notice that Said does not directly address Foucault's point that present imaginings of alternative futures are products of the present social order. This is because Said believes that it is not the truth or falsity of Foucault's claim but its effects that are at issue. If one holds Foucault's position, as Said sees it, the ability to imagine alternative societies as a guide to action and an expression of hope and desire in the present must be lost. To Said, such a position is also morally weak because it prevents intellectuals from making difficult judgments over the efficacy and desirability of ideals. In keeping with the thesis of "Travelling Theory," this inability on Foucault's part to take resistance seriously is a consequence of his entrapment within a self-confirming system not tested by external evidence: resistances are trivialized by a theory that makes them dependent on the power they oppose.

Said presents here a complex and highly respectable position that gets at the heart of what Foucault seems unable to do, but an alternative reading can be presented that is a bit more sympathetic to Foucault. It is worth taking Foucault's reasons for not agreeing with Chomsky more seriously. Foucault is not saying that action is impossible because all judgments proceed from our own limited point of view. Rather, Foucault is saying that the grounds for our points of view must be critically and genealogically examined. They are not "ideals," in any absolute sense; they are always "ideology" and, at best effective inventions. Said has chosen to ignore Foucault's figure of a "regime of truth.["15] Whatever Chomsky, Said, or any other intellectual judges to be one of "the exigencies of human nature" or an "ideal" imagining to "conform" to these exigencies; whatever is seen to be desirable, acceptable, efficacious, or even "truth" is so judged largely because the regime of truth of a particular social order makes that judgment possible. What is this regime? Can one be liberated from it? And how do intellectuals stand in relation to it? Foucault writes:

Truth is a thing of this world: it is produced only by virtue of multiple forms of constraint. And it induces regular effects of power. Each society has its regime of truth, its "general politics" of truth: that is, the types of discourse which it accepts and makes function as true; the mechanisms and instances which enable one to distinguish true and false statements, the means by which each is sanctioned; the techniques and procedures accorded value in the acquisition of truth; the status of those who are charged with saying what counts as true. (TP, 13)

No doubt one can argue that the consequence of this view of things is political paralysis, but such an argument can be made only if one conceives "politics" in terms that quite precisely and in advance refuse or severely restrict this Foucauldian insight. That is, to give just one example, if politics is taken to be a class battle for control of the means of production, then the intellectual defending that position and hoping to define political-intellectual practice by it cannot accept a position that argues that his or her own discourse is part of a larger regime of truth without diminishing the truth claims and legitimacy of that discourse and its discipline. Above all, accepting such an insight would lead one in the direction of seeing both the intellectual and his or her practice as functions of their positions within a massive material network of political discourses and institutions. In this view, intellectuals are "relays" and not originary or privileged subjects so that their visions, judgments, and practices serve interests and structures only very little like those they profess to defend.

To criticize Foucault's position for blurring or ignoring the real and significant differences resulting from which discourse is in the ascendancy is unjust. *Discipline and Punish* shows clearly and specifically how societies differ, for example, when carceral power displaces sovereign power. To say that Foucault's position on power knowledge is too "textual" or too "abstract" when compared, for example, to the more "humanistic," empirical concerns of an E. P. Thompson for the details of everyday life also misses the mark. Such a criticism is equivalent to killing the messenger who brings bad news, for it assumes in advance that such humanistic discourses and practices like Thompson's, which are devoted to "liberation," should not be significantly affected by Foucault's critique.[16] "So be it" is the response of at least one critic of Foucault who realizes that Foucault's position indicts in part the ideology and method of such powerful oppositional humanists as Thompson or Raymond Williams. Taking seriously Foucault's investigation into such postulates as the "regime of truth" does not eventuate in close-minded adoration of his work as some polemicists (not Said) suggest, but it does mean being willing to measure discourses and practices *against* Foucault's and others' genealogies to understand to what extent our ruling figures are indeed implicated in the "regime of truth" and how this recognition might affect our conception of the power and utility of key terms and discourses, as well as our very models of leading intellectual practice. Anything less is dishonest and a sign of closure dictated by blind adherence to a line.

It is not surprising, therefore, that Said cannot risk taking Foucault's response to Chomsky seriously, for it would mean at least examining open-mindedly the idea that the "alternatives" "imagined" by intellectuals *are* products of a "regime of truth" helping define the present or it would mean demonstrating that they were not, that they were really part of tommorow, not today. Moreover, taking Foucault seriously might involve explaining how imaginings produced by our "regime of truth"—acknowledged as such even as "desires"—could be expected to guide society toward greater freedom in the future. It is not enough to say that there are many local freedoms and resistances to the supposed monolith of power and that these traces of the possibility of human community ground and authenticate such imaginings. Such imaginings *may*, in fact, be traces of freedom and they *may* be the local sources of tomorrow's greater liberation. But the burden is on the imaginer to show this, not to risk futile repetitions of past oppressions and disappointments by heroically but naively acting upon ("perhaps misguided") good intentions. Such rigorous demonstration would necessarily involve a critical reexamination of basic and supposedly self-evident ideals and values. It would involve taking seriously the idea that "justice" is a representation generated by power (in the practices of oppression and resistance) whose function in a given society depends on its place in a network of political relations. It would not be difficult to do a modern genealogy of "justice," but such a genealogy might make it difficult for intellectuals to employ such a term because it would suggest the burden of self-interest and complicity with power (as oppression and resistance) that could minimize its value as an "ideal." But in place of Foucault's caution—perhaps misguided in this case?—Said advocates Chomsky who, we are told, makes difficult discriminations and supports the struggle of an oppressed proletariat when he is certain that "an ideal of justice" is its goal. Yet who measures the *truth* of this idea? Who determines that the justice pursued is an "ideal" and not "false consciousness"? Who understands how it has come to be an "ideal," in whose interest, and with what effects? By what criteria? How is it established that these criteria are not themselves part of the "regime of truth" whose function in our society leads not only to what one of Foucault's critics calls "unmitigated malignity" but also to regulative authority for intellectuals who continually reestablish their identity by exercising the discourses of this regime to reposition themselves in their own interest—namely, to achieve influence and an audience?

Foucault raises uncomfortable questions among intellectuals, and he is not well served by those who have become his ephebes. But too much of the assault on Foucault from oppositional intellectuals, especially in the United States, does not address Foucault seriously. It settles for summary dismissals based on incomplete, unsympathetic caricatures of his work often, I think, precisely because detailed responses to his work on a theoretical level would require calling into question some of the global rhetorics and research practices—as well as automatic political reflexes—of his critics. Charging that Foucault's analytics of power denies the possibility of any revolutionary practice is not critique. It is the assertion of a set of assumptions unexamined by those who hope to lead that revolution—or at least its imaginings. Our ruling oppositional discourses not only tell us that such a revolution is desirable— even though they can no longer guarantee its inevitability— but also suggest, in broad outlines, what its goals should be and what can be learned from past revolutions. How disabling, then, to see these discourses as rooted in another time, as part of a history in which there is no necessity and as part of a regime of truth in which intellectuals have a profound stake! Critical consciousness, when not reduced to imagining "alternatives" within the current politics of truth, is not afraid to question even such notions as the value of revolution. A worldly skepticism must question such self-evident assumptions. But to do so it must suspend its arrogant imaginings and affirmations of other peoples' struggles. "I believe," says Foucault in "Power and Sex," "that to engage in politics . . . is to try to know with the greatest possible honesty whether the revolution is desirable."[17] For a displaced and homeless people assaulted militarily and culturally such a question is a foolish luxury of Western wealth. But for that reason it must be answered by those critical intellectuals whose dangerous imaginings often lead the people to shed blood: "the question can be answered only by those who are willing to risk their lives to bring it about" (PS, 161). (This is a thought that some of those who carelessly rely on their own simplified sense of Said's position should meditate in advance of their overzealous use of revolutionary rhetoric.)

Intellectuals cannot separate themselves from the regime of truth so long as they refuse either to employ the critical skills needed to examine genealogically the discourses they employ or to suspend the short-sighted test of efficacy. Judging efficacy always involves anticipating results that confirm the desires of the judge and his or her discourse. Sometimes, as in the case of Said's report of Chomsky's attitude to the oppressed proletariat, such judgments lead intellectuals to rather arrogant decisions regarding others' struggles. Not only is "efficacy" not an obvious criterion for judgment (any particular tactic or statement is judged efficacious because it seems to promise to produce or describe results in conformity with a predictive discourse) but, moreover, "efficacity" as such, independently of any or all individual discourses, always functions as a device in a particular but larger or more encompassing regime of truth. It is, of course, a modern moral notion that the good is efficacious. "And moral ideology," writes Foucault, after Nietzsche, "must be submitted to the scrutiny of the most rigorous criticism" (PJ, 36). At the end of his discussion with Maoists over popular justice, Foucault analyzes how a particular example of judging efficacy can have unanticipated and undesired contradictory results whenever intellectuals do not critically question a ruling discourse in the process of employing it. A "peoples court" might in a specific instance usefully bring out the truth suppressed in a parallel bourgeois trial and expose its judgments as lies. But the genealogy of the court suggests two self-contradictory results whenever it is employed: first, its symbolic function is to create contradictions and divisions among the masses whom the Maoists claim they want to unify under their own leadership; and second its ideological function is to confirm bourgeois "moral ideology." The Maoists do not simply make a mistake in accepting courts for their efficacy. Rather they fall victim to the weakness of all such tactics by unwittingly producing a situation that replicates the people's secondary status: all that has changed is that they are now themselves the new directors. Such traps always lie in judgments of this sort and should be acknowledged even by those who claim to have scientific or dialectical knowledge.

Since intellectuals cannot, even in their ideological practicality, step outside the limits of a regime of truth and so are always a threat to struggling peoples when they attempt to lead or legitimate them, what then is left for the intellectual to do? Not to correct untruth or to produce more truth but, for Foucault, to alter, if possible, the regime of truth:

The essential political problem for the intellectual is not to criticize the ideological contents supposedly linked to science, or to ensure that his own scientific practice is accompanied by a correct ideology, but that of ascertaining the possibility of constituting a new politics of truth. The problem is not changing people's consciousnesses—or what's in their heads—but the political, economic, institutional regime of the production of truth.

It's not a matter of emancipating truth from every system of power (which would be a chimera, for truth is already power) but of detaching the power of truth from the forms of hegemony, social, economic and cultural, within which it operates at the present time.

The political question, to sum up, is not error, illusion, alienated consciousness or ideology; it is truth itself. Hence the importance of Nietzsche. (TP, 133)

My objection, therefore, to Said's position is that it leaves this regime unchanged insofar as it validates the traditional role played by the leading intellectual who, above all, will not call into question his or her own interests in exploiting the ability to imagine and promote "alternatives" continually in order to maintain or achieve authority and identity in society. While *Orientalism* teaches us about the degrees of voluntary and involuntary complicity of orientalists in the oppression of the Arabs, Nietzsche and Foucault more generally tell us that it is the linkage of the very power of truth (including that produced by "oppositional intellectuals") with the network of oppression and resistance that forms the hegemony of the present that must be struggled against.[18] Not to struggle against this regime and its affiliations is inevitably to reproduce and extend it and the misery it causes. To imagine alternatives within it without at the same time struggling against it—by, for example, calling into question the seemingly highest ideals we have and desire—is not critical at all. Critique is practiced only when the appropriation of truth itself is at stake, not simply morals or attitudes.

In his fine essay, "Power, Repression, Progress," David Couzens Hoy carefully and precisely demonstrates that "power/knowledge" "should be regarded as a heuristic device, a pragmatic construction to be tested in terms of its value in reconstructing the history of the sciences and man."[19] For Hoy, this is a political act since the very battle over the concept "power" in a society is a political struggle. Therefore, Foucault's concept is politically intended although it has no prophetic, predictive, or prescriptive powers: "his project is historical, and his construction of the concept power/knowledge is a device for studying the social and scientific practices that underlie and condition the formation of belief."[20] One might add to this that the genealogical studies Foucault conducts into sex and prisons are intended to dissolve the legitimacy and limit the authority of politically powerful discourses like Marxism and psychoanalysis.

"Power/knowledge," then, is a tactic in Foucault's struggle against the regime of truth, and with it he *intentionally* limits himself to a concern with the present. Foucault ironically asceticizes the role of the intellectual by lopping off its visionary powers and apocalyptic tendencies, which, all too often, not only aggrandize the intellectual at the expense of the people but also sustain the intellectuals' institutions. In a passage that reminds us of Said's comments on Chomsky and the proletariat, Foucault notes that the leading "intellectual, through his moral, theoretical and political choice, aspires to be the bearer of this universality in its conscious elaborated form. . . . Some years have now passed since the intellectual was called upon to play this role" (PK, 126). The new role of the intellectual requires an unceasing critical concern with the present to detach "truth" from its monopoly by the current forms of hegemony. This detachment does not, of course, assure that the future will be any better. The negative function of the intellectual in the present moment is to locate and exploit breaks in the very linkage he or she opposes. Foucault anticipates an "intellectual who destroys evidence and generalities, the one who, in the inertias and constraints of the present time, locates and marks the weak points, the openings, the lines of force. . . ." With the passing of the universal intellectual, "the rhapsodist of the eternal," the "specific intellectuals" arise defined by expertise in their own fields and engaged, like the proletariat, in local struggles against power and oppression "within specific sectors, at the precise points where their own conditions of life or work situate them" (TP, 126). Without assuming a leading role in cultural imagining, specific intellectuals can effect the regime of truth because their expertise makes them important in a scientific-technological society:

This new configuration has a further political significance. It makes it possible, if not to integrate, at least to rearticulate categories which were previously kept separate. . . . And it has become possible to develop lateral connections across different forms of knowledge and from one focus of politicisation to another . . . . in a global process of politicisation of intellectuals. (TP, 127)

People who take Foucault seriously do so, not because they believe he has said the final word on social reality, but because he has said a few words on the relationship between truth, intellectuals, and human misery. In opposition to the agon of intellectuals—which Said rehearses—whose imaginings, even in the service of "liberation," sustain dominant humanistic institutions and the hegemony they serve, Foucault, in perhaps his only utopian moment, dreams of an intellectual who will attend to the present, who "doesn't know exactly where he is heading nor what he will think tomorrow" (PS, 161). He realizes a specific intellectual can have life-and-death power and that "a polymorphous ensemble of intellectuals" acquires more importance with more responsibility. But these politicized, assembled, specific intellectuals can wage an important part of the battle over how "truth" is produced, about its status, and the political role it plays (TP, 132). As critical intellectuals they can test their own discourses against their awareness of the regime of truth to understand their involvement in that regime and by so doing help to find some weak spot in it. As specific intellectuals they can try their weapons against the forms power/knowledge takes in their own situations. In so doing they can join with others in their own local struggles. Having given up their arrogant pretensions, intellectuals can care for their own part in the struggle, carry out the critical version of the tasks they are trained to do, and try to detach the role of truth, discourse, and imagining from the forms of the present hegemony. It is not irresponsible, detached bemusement for the critical mind to renounce its most foolish and dangerous charades. They have abetted intellectuals' interests only in the short run, in any case. Intellectuals must theorize their own past and present roles in modern and postmodern society in more restrictive, local, and less aggrandizing ways. It is not certain that society can survive our old bad habits.[21]

6

Critical Negation: The Function of Criticism at the Present Time

Everything I have said in this book up to this point has been meant to recall that critical practice is always situated and occasional, that is, positioned within sets of discursive and institutional formations that are parts of larger constellations of cultural and political power. In other words, following, for example, Nietzsche in *The Genealogy of Morals*, Foucault in *Discipline and Punish*, and Said in *Orientalism*, I have described, in one of any number of possible ways, some of the important elements of interest and desire in the recent history of literary criticism precisely as they, in part, enable and delimit such practices and their related institutions. Following in their tradition, I have sketched this genealogy of interest, desire, and power with an eye toward the present moment. That is, I have focused on the figure of the leading or representative intellectual as a way of linking apparently disparate texts and authors in a genealogy of this constitutive interaction of discourse, power, and desire. My goal has been to suggest that some of the most important aspects of both traditional and oppositional critical claims and methods have a family likeness within a larger set of extended relations that can be sketched by outlining the key role played in critical discourse by the self-legitimating figure of the "masterful" or "sublime" critical intellectual. I hope to be able to judge the relative importance of some of the various procedures within this larger

set and, by limning its genealogy, to draw attention to some of
the less sensible and progressive consequences of criticism's
common inscription within what I call the discursive and institutional domain of anthropological, liberal humanism.

In this chapter, by focusing on some of the general tendencies
and structures of what Kant calls the "anthropological attitude," I extend the analysis and generalize it from the specific
cases of the preceding chapters. I illustrate both the defining
aspects of intellectual, critical practice within that "attitude"
and suggest where, as in Auerbach, its often destructive or
contradictory limits can be seen. Since Foucault has done most
to sketch the genealogy of the human sciences, I begin with a
discussion of the most important topic in his critique—the
humanistic necessity of constituting "man" as finite origin
and limit in and through death itself. In this context, Kant's
Anthropology is a pivotal text. It reveals what is politically
and discursively at stake in humanistic attitudes and procedures, not just in traditional literary study, but in such
equally critical and yet different positions as those of Marshall
Hodgson and Edward W. Said.

In fully elaborating this set of anthropological practices,
such critics illustrate its limits and futility. In fact, in such
authors, anthropological intellectual work points beyond itself
not only to revisions and reforms that radicalize this attitude
but, what is more important, to both a critique of its own
essential structure and to other kinds of intellectual practice.
As with Foucault, such critics sometimes put the figure of the
leading intellectual and his privileged claims to "truth" out of
play, although only momentarily and not in any "final" or
liberating way.

II

In *The Birth of the Clinic*, Foucault hopes "to make a structural
analysis of discourses that would evade the fate of commentary
by supposing no remainder, nothing in excess of what has been
said, but only the fact of its historical appearance."[1] Foucault
proceeds on the basis of a certain reading of Nietzsche, whom
he sees as having problematized the Kantian possibility of a

critique "linked, through certain scientific contents, to the fact that there is such a thing as knowledge" (BC, xv). Nietzsche more severely links critique "to the fact that language exists and that, in the innumerable words spoken by men . . . a meaning has taken shape that hangs over us, leading us forward in our blindness, but waiting in the darkness for us to attain awareness before emerging into the light of day and speaking" (BC, xvi). The human sciences, or what we might better call in the context of literary studies, the "interpretative sciences," operate in this closed field. Read through Beckett, Nietzsche leads Foucault to write: "We are doomed historically to history, to the patient construction of discourses about discourses, and to the task of hearing what has already been said" (BC, xvi).

Foucault's critique of humanism is, then, not an anxious effort to avoid replicating the discursive practice of the present and recent past; it is rather a representation of and movement away from the "event," which can be said to mark the opening of the Beckettian universe of doubled discourse. The essential features of Foucault's archeological purposes and methods are well known and easily represented:

> The research that I am undertaking here therefore involves a project that is deliberately both historical and critical, in that it is concerned—outside all prescriptive intent—with determining the conditions of possibility of medical experience in modern times. . . . It is a structural study that sets out to disentangle the conditions of [medicine's] history from the density of discourse. . . .
> What counts in the things said by men is not so much what they may have thought or the extent to which these things represent their thoughts, as that which systematizes them from the outset, thus making them thereafter endlessly accessible to new discourses and open to the task of transforming them. (BC, xix)

Following Nietzsche, Foucault reverses Kant's postulation of the transcendental grounds of knowledge and claims that the "conditions for the possibility of" knowledge are instead contingent discursive systems. Because these conditions are historical and manifestly tied to power they require a genealogical critique, that is, a demonstration of their (metaphysical) randomness, a reconstruction of their political determinants, an outline of how they become "accessible" to other discourses and how, since these conditions are "events" at the "founding" of the present, they constitute "man's" discursive apprehensions of not only his works but also, "reflexively," of himself and his discourses. In other words, Foucault's decision to study the origins of modern medicine is not simply based on a desire to demystify the ideology of medical practice any more than it is on merely antiquarian or "scholarly" disinterest. Rather his aim seems to be to make available instruments for getting a grip on the discourses and practices which have constituted and continue to constitute not just "Western Man" and his representations but the institutions in which those discourses and constitutive practices persist and through which they are dispersed. Furthermore, his work makes it possible to trace the relationships between and among institutions and discourses without invoking such difficult postenlightenment notions as the "totality" and "mediation." As we shall see when we look at the work of Marshall Hodgson, Foucault's Nietzschean challenge to the "rationality" of knowledge and culture strikes at the center of humanists' claims for man's pragmatic reason. Indeed, so essential is it that the contingent operations of power and "unreason" in history not be directly acknowledged that when Hodgson's severe self-criticisms and methodological reflections lead him seemingly unavoidably to Foucault's conclusion he loses his rigor and falls back on a metaphysical notion of "great men" to explain change and rationally assured progress.

So, from a metaphysical and perhaps even a historicist point of view, Foucault's focus on the origins of medicine is random, just as the "history" of medicine he writes appears to historians to be eccentric and misdirected. But these perceptions, while correct in their own ways, misperceive the important function of Foucault's texts. He has frequently referred to his work as "fiction," attempting by so doing, as I see it, to free it from the constraints of "truth" and "knowledge"—something about which I will say more—and also to announce its availability for political struggle against the subjugating practices of the human sciences.[2] Indeed a corollary of Foucault's project is that it helps us understand one more reason why even those most aware practitioners of the human sciences insist their work, like the canon of spiritual achievements they supposedly preserve and study, is benign, nonviolent, and generous. Humanistic discourse is a self-sustaining practice that remarkably finds ways to observe the omnipresence of power and unreason—as we shall see in Kant's legend of "ill-natured men"—as the condition for perpetuating its own often totalizing and always normalizing and exclusionary subjugating violence. What we can see after Foucault and Nietzsche, after reading a century or more of critical, textual, and political struggles, is that these humanistic discourses are gambits for maintaining the power of leadership and sublimity, while fulfilling other desirable and possible professional and cultural interests. Auerbach deplored this pattern, yet he could not escape it. Now we can see it is a broader problem by far than he imagined.

So, when Foucault writes about the clinic, he is not only writing "the history of the present" but also writing at, against, and for it, especially the politics of its knowledge and truth-producing apparatus: "The clinic . . . owes its real importance to the fact that it is a reorganization in depth, not only of medical discourse, but of the very possibility of a discourse about disease" (*BC*, xix). Such specifically focused statements become important when seen as gestures sketching the limits and undermining the apparently "self-evident," "natural" legitimacy of the interpretative human sciences. Foucault writes, in preparation for his critical genealogy, that "The clinic is both a new carving up [!] of things and the principle of their verbalization in a form which we have been accustomed to recognizing as the language of a 'positive science'" (*BC*, xviii).

The complex relations between words and things undergo an equally complex set of transformations as clinical medicine becomes dominant and as the autopsy makes death the condition of medicine: "It will, no doubt, remain a decisive fact about our culture that its first scientific discourse concerning the individual had to pass through the stage of death" (*BC*, 197). Only death constitutes a science in which man is subject and object. "Western man could constitute himself in his own eyes as an object of science, he grasped himself within his language, and gave himself in himself and by himself, a discursive existence, only in the opening created by his own elimination. . . ." (*BC*, 197). Such a move negates the classical concept of finitude, itself merely the negation of infinitude. As such a double negation, the inscription of death into medicine, gives a positive value to finitude and to the anthropological representation of man that appears paradigmatically in Kant:

> A pragmatic anthropology which has been systematically devised and which can be understood by the general reading public (because of reference to examples which can be checked by every reader), has the advantage that the completeness of headings, under which observed human characteristics of practical consequence have been subsumed, offers many occasions and challenges to the reading public to study each particular characteristic in order to classify it accordingly. Any study of a certain characteristic will attract the attention of specialists in the same area and, because of the unity of the design, they will be integrated into a comprehensive whole. Thus the development of a science which is beneficial to the human community will be furthered.[3]

Human finitude, "human characteristics of practical consequence," becomes the object of specialized disciplinary study, carried out under the synthesizing sign of "anthropos." We can see that Foucault's specific concern with clinical medicine helps shade in the critical genealogy of humanism when it leads him to spell out what is at stake: "the anthropological structure that then appeared played both the critical role of limit and the founding role of origin" (*BC*, 197). Death is everywhere in humanism and appears especially at the moments of greatest strength, throughout the self-confident, technical, and combative forms of the finite and future-directed life humanism promises individuals and the species in a secular world.

Among those life-forms will be, Kant insists, certain intellectual disciplines studying "human characteristics of practical consequence." These humanistic disciplines, emerging from the double negation of finitude, depend, we might say, on what is symbolized by Hölderlin's Empedocles: the flight of the gods, "the end of the infinite on earth" (*BC*, 198). Concretely, the

power of secular finitude, having driven out the gods, positions
these humanistic disciplines, and especially their leading practitioners, in a guiding role, directing the species toward its
future and, in the process, themselves through their own careers. Indeed, to occupy persistently authoritative positions,
such careers require continued intellectual and political self-
revision. Without such revision—based on and leading to new
knowledge and "higher consciousness"—intellectuals cannot,
as individuals, fulfill the function that modern humanism assigns them. If the humanistic disciplines are to play the leading
role we see assigned them in Kant's text, then they can assure
their own survival only by filling their leading positions with
sublimely masterful figures. As we have already seen in chapter 3, one task of these figures is to fulfill the systemic demand
for structural stability by replicating themselves and thereby
sustaining the legitimacy of the institutions whose hierarchical "slots" they occupy as "life-peers," as it were.

What Said says of Renan is an excellent illustration of this
structure's existence in the nineteenth century and of current
critics' awareness of it. Said reminds us that Renan, who abandoned an ecclesiastical vocation to study semitic languages
and the origins of religion, premised all his work, and the material satisfaction of his interests, on the scientific study of
language. In other words, Renan's work represents how this
anthropological attitude takes "man" not just as "all there is,"
but as secular limit and origin: Said writes of Renan that he
thought

it was necessary to invest in disciplines like philology that moved history away from the existential problems of revealed religion and toward what it was possible to study, toward those real things that
mankind still had to worry about long after primitive excitement (or
revelation for that matter) was definitely over. One's career took shape
inside this accessible reality, which is modern culture of course as
Renan defined it. . . . The philologist's job must be to connect that
postlapsarian moment just after language's birth with the present,
then to show how that dense web of relationships between language
users is a secular reality from which the future will emerge.[4]

Said's strong reading would have it that "this accessible reality" means that Renan's interests in certain types of work

must be seen as having been made possible and rewarding by "the authority of massive centralized institutions" that support them. I add that they must also be seen, perhaps more "originally," as depending on the highly eventful inscription of human practice within finitude. Such work as Renan's or Hodgson's rests on the unavoidable disciplinary and discursive compulsion to speak of human practice and to take "the dense web of relationships between language users" as an "object" in which these language users become knowable subjects at the origin of the species' future. "It is understandable, then," writes Foucault, "that medicine should have had such importance in the constitution of the sciences of man—an importance that is not only methodological, but ontological, in that it concerns man's being as object of positive knowledge" (BC, 197).

In *The Order of Things*, Foucault argues that the act of representation could not itself be represented on the table of representations:

> In classical thought, the personage for whom the representation exists, and who represents himself within it, recognizing himself therein as an image or reflection, he who ties together all the interlacing threads of "the representation in the form of a picture or table"—he is never to be found in the table himself. . . . the essential consequence is that classical language, as the *common discourse* of representation and things, as the place within which nature and human nature intersect, absolutely excludes anything that could be a "science of man." As long as that language was spoken in Western culture it was not possible for human existence to be called into question on its own account, since it contained the nexus of representation and being.[5]

Yet, by the time of Kant's *Anthropology*, the human sciences displace the table of representations with the double negation of finitude: "The possibility for the individual of being both subject and object of his own knowledge implies an inversion in the structure of finitude" (BC, 197).

In the classical age, the clarity of representation not only prevented the formation of the "sciences of man" but also excluded the possibility of problematizing the discourses of representation and their practitioners. The double negation of finitude, epitomized by the inscription of death into pathological medicine, created a cultural possibility in which the human production of knowledge and art could itself become the object of discourse and, having displaced its predecessor, become, as such, the only possible ground for human existence and the only means presumably to guarantee its future. In other words, with what Foucault might call "the birth of man," the function of discourse changed. It not only constituted "man" as the object and subject of knowledge but also, more specifically, ascribed to what had been traditionally known as "secondary" discourses, such as literary criticism or philology, the task of working out what is inscribed within the double movement of finitude, namely, the fulfillment of human moral and cultural potential in the face of death, a potential that often takes ideological form in Utopian imaginings or, conversely, when confronted by the limits of finitude, death, takes the form of cultural despair. These alternative possibilities, and a host of others on the spectrum, are all played out within the human sciences—and, traditionally, especially the "humanities." We must recognize the inscription of the humanities within this space of finitude and death in order to understand their particular genealogy and, given their evident crises, to see, in part, where they have left us.

I suggest that, after Marx, Nietzsche, and Freud, not only have the human sciences been called into question, but the very grounds for their legitimation have also been historically undermined, leaving us, as with Auerbach and Said, experiences of despair and attempts to overcome this groundlessness to move the human sciences into "different" roles. I also suggest, though, that these "different" roles are essentially reactions to the slow disintegration of the anthropological attitude and that they, unavoidably, remain within it. Furthermore, I stress, since Said and Auerbach are among our finest critical humanists, that their work both marks the limit of what is now possible, even in a revision of that attitude, and also reveals some elements of a new attitude different from that defined, for our purposes, by Kant's *Anthropology* and Foucault's discussion of the clinic.

One can see, I think, from a close reading of Auerbach and Said, that in their work the critic often appears as an originating subject but only to disappear as such in order to reappear quickly as a subject who is an inscribed function of discursive and institutional structures. One can also see that these structures are more constitutive of critical practice than Said's stress on the independence of critical consciousness might suggest. Indeed, it seems to me that the inscription of their work within the genealogy of the "leading intellectual" and the hierarchical disciplinary structure of desire and interest characteristic of the professional organization of literary study is a practical concretization of the humanistic attitude, of the role Kant's text assigns to knowledge-producing discourses, and a sign of its own transformation in the recent past and present.

I show that this figure of the leading intellectual takes on its peculiar functions within the anthropological attitude and suggest some of the political difficulties with its operation and the institutions that sanction it and, in turn, depend on it. Further, I elaborate on how, along the lines of Auerbach and Said, it becomes possible to move a bit away from that attitude in a direction that Foucault has recently taken, a direction that involves his own increasing turn toward not just the problem of power but the relation between power/knowledge and the dominant forces of our culture. In the process, I argue that while no one provides "a way out" of our historical moment, Foucault's work suggests some useful tactics for confronting the hegemonic deployment of this still-powerful anthropological attitude, which allows others to take up elements of what seems different from it in the work of critics like Auerbach, Said, and Hodgson.

III

In keeping with the double movement of finitude that constitutes "man" as origin and limit, Kant gives definitive form to the idea of secular humanism: "he has a character which he himself creates, because he is capable of perfecting himself according to purposes which he himself adopts" (A, 238). Kant goes on to insist that "man" differs from all other species in that "individuals" are not naturally fitted to reach perfection independently. Rather "man" can become perfect as a species and only by virtue of two "higher" species-gifts, which are "pragmatic" and "moral." Kant's text argues the necessity for the seemingly endless task of cultural discourse to fulfill the possibilities of the origin and defer the experience of the limit by setting up the leading role of humanistic discourses and their sublime practitioners to guide and preserve the species. When seen from the other side, however, such discourse appears, not only as the mark of finitude as limit—for all there is is endless waiting while discoursing—but also as the strategy for keeping open the space of "man" for as long as possible despite the always present assault on its "identity" by "death," which tragically and paradoxically, lies at the heart of its self-constitution—as Auerbach painfully discovered. When displaced into the discourse of humanistic anthropology, this constitutive conflict between death and the "full-life" promised by secular science appears in the figures of "culture" and "morality." Although Kant does not obscure their necessary interrelationship, it is only Nietzsche who, as I have already argued in chapter 1, problematizes their relationship as one of power.

Kant tells us that the *pragmatic gift . . . .* refers to becoming civilized through culture. It particularly has to do with the cultivation of social qualities and the natural tendency of this species to advance in social matters from the crudity of mere self-reliance to a well-mannered (but not yet moral) being bent on concord" (A, 240). Kant concedes "man" is, in part, "innately evil," but he is, overall, as a species, by nature, "rational." In addition, "Providence" assures that, in nature, species always fulfill their destiny. In effect, such claims allow Kant to solve the problem of social evil, as it were, by locating in providential nature a guarantee that in culture "man" can and will make himself by "reason": "the species' natural destiny consists in continued progress toward the better" (A, 241). It is not Kant's bourgeois utopionism that is of primary interest here. Rather, it is how in his work "culture," as the product of "reason," is constituted as the "site" of humanistic finitude's double identity.

Kant would have it that "man"—and it is the "species" he is discussing—is always marked by limits, not only moral evil, but death: "What a mass of knowledge, what discourses of new methods would now be on hand if an Archimedes, a Newton, or a Lavoisier with their industry and talent would have been favored by Nature with hundreds of years of continuous life without the loss of vital power!" (*A*, 243). Kant argues that the unique aspect of the "pragmatic gift" assures that "culture" is not only the space in which the species advances in its education but also the means by which this "education" "perpetuates itself once it has come into existence." Indeed, this perpetuation in turn assures us "that we should not despair about our species' progress toward the better" (*A*, 246). Of course, as we have seen, it is just such an assurance Auerbach could not sustain, although, as we shall see later, equally powerful humanists like Hodgson struggle to maintain it.

Kant's texts present a version of "culture" as a scene in which the social, political, and moral education of "man" is carried out. But in this scene only great men, "scholars," who have "advanced in culture," invent, lead, and make possible further progress; but the progressively civilized species-being, through the devices of its cultural memory—one of which is interpretative, canon-making scholarship—preserves in turn those "discourses" by which it is educated. As to the possibility of cultural amnesia or reversion, history and experience join providential nature, Kant claims, to give us confidence that nothing of significance will be lost. Only "interfering revolutionary barbarism" threatens "regression" (*A*, 243). (One must keep in mind how, from the beginning, a great deal of liberal humanist discourse has been antirevolutionary in its politics, if only to understand revolutionaries' attempts to appropriate humanism.)

It is this massive cultural optimism that Auerbach discovered, in part, at the origins of fascism. Foucault's representation of the constitution of "man" in finitude lets us see fascism as the darkest side of humanistic practice, the most direct encounter between origin and limit. While Kant denies any real potential for the destruction of civilization to those "limits" against which the "origin" of the anthropological attitude must play—enfiguring all challenges to humanism's vision as "other" and "barbarous"—Adorno, adapting Freud's *Civilization and Its Discontents* to his analysis of fascist culture, insists that the "category of destructiveness" must be stressed in any analysis of how fascism emerged from within liberal humanism. Foucault points out that the anthropological attitude is contemporary with Hölderlin's lyricism in "which death is no doubt the most menacing, but also the fullest" form of finitude. For Foucault, it is not surprising that the same law of finitude "should dominate . . . this relation of man to death" both creating the rational forms of discourse and opening up "the source of a language that unfolds endlessly in the void left by the absence of the gods" (*BC*, 198).

The ease of Kant's assurance is clearest in a passage that *must* underlie Nietzsche's demonic account of the origin of morality in asceticism. For Kant, as we shall see for Hodgson as well, the essence of the "pragmatic gift" is that human rationality assures that "sometime in the future the development of the good out of the evil [will occur] through its own efforts." Only "natural upheavals," no longer even "barbaric revolutions"—so secure is Kant's faith in human reason—can prevent this "moral certainty." Evil and death serve culture conceived as the space of human priority and fulfillment. It is Kant's submergence of limits in culture that is truly dangerous, for it not only obscures the dark side of finitude but also empowers culture as a regulative concept, along with a subsidiary set of concepts and practices—will to knowledge, science, instrumental reason, the leading intellectual—that, among others, delimit humanistic and critical discourse up to the present time. One must add that this Kantian optimism, this brilliant concept of the "pragmatic gift," effectively nullifies critical practice, submerging it, in turn, in the role of "policeman" guarding against barbarism and other threats to the preserved rational order. Critique becomes quietistic. It cannot be either active negation or the positive projection of alternatives. It merely discriminates and externalizes while serving what it and its masters take to be the "rational order." As we have seen earlier and will see again, "criticism" in this tradition subjugates, totalizes, and excludes (often by including):

Then there are men, truly ill-natured men, who nevertheless are gifted, rational beings endowed with an inventive and a moral capacity as well. As their culture grows, they become more and more aware of the wrongs which they themselves selfishly inflict upon each other. And since they see no other remedy for them than subordinating the private interest (of the individual) to the public interest (encompassing all), they subject themselves, reluctantly though, to the discipline (of civil restraint) which they only obey, however, by following the laws which they themselves have given. They feel themselves ennobled by the knowledge that they belong to a species which fits the calling of man as reason represents it to him in the ideal. (A, 247)

Modern humanism, as we find it in Kant, bases itself and its claims for civilization's survival on the necessity of repressing conflicts resulting from a clash of interests, of sublimating narcissistic and egoistic energies in a "naturally" progressive group conception. I do not cast this discussion in terms of Kant's relation to the bourgeoisie, but it is impossible not to at least mention Adorno's discussion of group psychology in fascism: "As a rebellion against civilization, fascism is not simply the reoccurrence of the archaic but its reproduction in and by civilization itself."[6]

I suggest that Kant's text typifies modern humanism: by claiming that its vision of human perfection is based on providential nature and reason, it legitimates the disciplinary production of subjugatory knowledge. Humanistic discipline individually and collectively acquires a regulative cultural role. Yet, in fact, Kant's claims rest upon the rhetorical power of his text to obscure its own irrational suppressions, ideological distortions, and its situation within an entire constellation of events constituting the anthropological attitude. I am not saying the text could or should be more than this—even though it does claim to be much more, that is, to be "meaningful truth." Rather, I stress that this is all humanistic discourse can be and that some of its consequences need to be considered.

Most of the best humanistic criticism and scholarship is a consequence of Kant's concept of the "pragmatic gift," which assures that "culture" and "acculturation" occupy regulative roles in secular societies. The essential requirement of "culture" is that it parallel, reinforce, and embody the political regula-

isn't fou. just such a clinzy man for Bové ?

tions of civil society and the state. Cultural and political control have the same origin and goal for Kant. In both cases, an
elite group of powerful and outstanding men establish the ideals and laws of society. In the cultural sphere, these men are
geniuses like Archimedes; in the political world, they are the
"law-givers." Kant's text presents both groups in the same figure: the "ill-natured" men. Kant's liberal humanism insists
that society functions freely and harmoniously; he argues that
all human beings voluntarily submit to "civil restraint" out of
a rational and moral recognition of the species' good. Yet, the
functions of producing, disseminating, and policing the political and cultural forms of social order fall to elite groups.

Of course, as we have seen, this argument creates a political
problem for later humanists: why do those powerful, ill-
natured men not simply themselves rule society? how can elitism of this sort assure reason and power will be one? Kant's
answer is to postulate a "moral gift" more fundamental than
the "pragmatic." Tactically, it seems clear that the concept of
the "moral gift" is defensive and less important than that of the
"pragmatic." Kant invents the "moral gift" simply to make a
case that the "ill-natured" geniuses must expend their talents
for the species' good. Liberal humanism is certainly not popu-
list and usually not socialist; faith in the people's power to
make their own judgments is not typical of its disciplining
structure. The "moral gift" is Kant's proleptic answer to the
socially destabilizing existence of those Nietzsche calls "blond-
beasts." Its effect is to insist that civil and human progress
depend on the top-down imposition of cultural and political
order whose human value is assured by their sublimation. The
"moral gift" means that the exercise of power and talent for
anything other than the common good of the species is un-
fulfilling and that those "ill-natured" men are, like all others,
reasonable enough to understand that social unity and progress
alone will provide the happiness they desire. Their violence,
aggression, and power will, thus, be turned to inventing and
establishing political laws and cultural institutions to lead the
race to perfection.

Humanistic culture, so justified, is a political reality that

generally mistakes bourgeois interests for "human" ones and
that essentially reduces the sphere of cultural values, as we
see in Kant, to a subset of conservative and aesthetic values
typified by Kant's stress on antirevolutionary progress, order,
and private individual imagining. In other words, within this
humanistic conception of "culture," intellectual production
has a special role: this group of culture-producers supports the
political-legal structure of a given society by acting as agents
for the material distribution of the hegemonic culture throughout society. Scholarly, critical, and literary texts are always
positioned in relation to this social and discursive cultural apparatus and so are material and political acts whether consciously thought of as such or not. Generally, the distributive
role of such "traditional" intellectuals, as Gramsci might call
them, can be summarized as educating the population in the
invaluable experiences of the past as they are preserved in a
canon whose "meaning" is tended by these mandarin humanists: "The wisdom is to affect the perfection of man through
cultural progress, even if this should mean some sacrifice of the
pleasures of his life" (A, 238).

Given that the species is perfectible and not the individual,
guidance is necessary for the latter to participate in and contribute to the human drama. The individual (and his irrationality) is a limit of humanism that requires a political
solution in the cultural realm. Kant's solution tellingly prefigures Foucault's critique of disciplines and foreshadows Richards' aim in practical criticism. "Man," Kant writes, "can be
and must be educated through instruction as well as correction
(discipline)" (A, 240).

Some may choose to see as "progressive" Kant's reliance on
reason, culture, and normalizing education as regulative structures. Indeed, Kant does, at one point, specifically argue that
such values can be found only in a "republic." The perfection
of the species involves finding a "higher" form of government,
one which is "higher" precisely because it would create and
sustain the conditions for the species' perfection. Kant claims
that there can be "Authority, with freedom and law" only in a
republic and that only this "last combination deserves to be

called a true civil form of government." But Kant's political sympathies are not as direct as they seem here. Following these seemingly progressive claims Kant makes a conservative move that I think typifies humanistic attempts to unify society by the actions and authority of a culture produced and imposed by a leading elite. Kant empties "republic" of any specific progressive meaning when he goes on to explain that by the term he means "only a state as such" (A, 248).[7] Kant's commitments to stability and order effectively stop history; the species will come to perfection without changing the state. Such a move aims to sever culture's connection to politics and to fix intellectuals in the service of the state. Historically Kant's statement justifies the political status quo in Germany; genealogically it legitimates the cultural role of all humanistic intellectuals.

Culture and the state support each other in this hegemonic project, and the intellectuals are one of the central relays of power between the two. The "civil constitution of the state" is the essential mechanism for this education and correction in "concord" and "invention"—essential conditions for the perfection of humanity: the state "represents the highest degree of artificial enhancement of the good characteristics in the human species toward the final purpose of its destiny" (A, 244). It is crucial to understand what it is at stake in Kant's refusal to discriminate among political forms:

The old proverbial rule, *salus civitatis* (not *civium*) *suprema lex esto*, does not mean that the psychological welfare of the common citizen (the happiness of the citizens) should serve as the highest principle of the political constitution. Such well-being, which each individual envisions for himself according to his own personal inclination in this way or that, is worthless for any objective principle such as universality requires. That proverb says only, the rational welfare, expressing itself in the maintenance of the political constitution that was once established, is the highest law of civil society as such; after all, society lasts only because of that constitution. (A, 249)

These lines are understandable in terms of the immediate politics of the French revolution and the attempt to impose some constitutional restraint upon the absolutism of the German princes.[8] They are also remarkable as a revision of Cicero's *"Salus populi suprema lex esto."* But they are most remarkable for how they outline a liberal humanistic constellation in which the leading intellectual is bound to what is essentially an antidemocratic, conservative, sometimes bureaucratic, and often authoritarian set of positions and practices.

The leading intellectuals' practical, material alliances to state institutions result in the rather common postenlightenment production of an ideologically useful sense of the "tradition." The specific "content," the values and discoveries contained within individual versions of this liberally constructed tradition, matters less to this argument than I would like it to. Of course, it is important how a particular cultural or national memory is constructed. Milan Kundera, for example, from his own despairing position, repeatedly stresses the horror of state-organized suppression of memory. Said and others have pointed out how difficult it is for the historical narrative of an oppressed group to appear in history or memory. And Walter Benjamin has foretold the dire consequences of its complete loss in a presentifying culture of the spectacle. Nonetheless, I stress it is crucial to see that within humanism, the production of an image of "tradition," no matter its content, is always a necessary tool for the elite to go on "guiding" the species (or nation or race or class) toward perfection by stabilizing and preserving the unity and uniformity of the state and its institutions as an essential means for achieving this perfection. In other words, just as Kant empties the idea of "State" of any historically specific sense to ground its ordering function, so too "tradition" and "canon" become empty functions, operative tropes essential to the humanistic project and essential "objects" of intellectuals' productive and educative roles. The result is that functionally such tropes as "canon" exist to serve the interests of the class of leading intellectuals. Hence intellectuals have a stake in sustaining individual canons and in perpetuating the struggle over them. Since humanism defines so much of our knowledge and action, a great deal of critical and intellectual political activity unavoidably takes the form of continuing this struggle. How to avoid canonicity, whether such a thing is entirely desirable—this is a crucial question that must be treated elsewhere. The point is simply that revisionism is carried out within the structure I am describing.

As I have suggested throughout, this revisionist pattern involves right and left. Lukacs' *History and Class Consciousness* can be read, for example, as an appropriation of this humanistic practice for the vanguard party and the Soviet revolution. Historical and political differences should not be too quickly elided here. That way lies a barren formalism. Literary critics are trained to deal so exclusively with texts that in their rhetorical obsessions, they often miss the real-life consequences of texts as events. Yet the fact remains that in *History and Class Consciousness*, Lukacs substitutes the vanguard party and its revolutionary institutions for those of the liberal authoritarian state and, defending Lenin, reinscribes the representative, guiding intellectual role essential to anthropological humanism within the party, and he ascribes to its tacticians and theoreticians an understanding of "imputed class consciousness" that assures the species' progress and their own authority. The form of intellectual practice is of concern here. The problem is always how to function as an intellectual without arrogating the leading role—in its conservative or revolutionary mode—and its seemingly universal potential for antidemocratic, self-interested replication of politically undesirable practices.

I am suggesting that the anthropological attitude, first of all, constituted "man" as finite origin and limit; second, that, in turn, it makes cultural production and discourse about the production key to "man's" progressive history; third, that to carry out its project it generated the figure of the representative intellectual so powerfully that it enables and restrains the practice of both hegemonic and oppositional humanist intellectuals as well; and, fourth, it made "culture" and the humanistic, intellectual, political realities largely responsible for organizing society in the interests of an "elite" arrogating to itself the production of knowledge to bring the species to perfection. The left must be careful not to be caught up by the seductive role Kant's text offers the intellectual and must not make the mistake of thinking that substituting one set of "leaders" for another will escape the structure or effect a social change in the direction of autonomy and self-determination. As early as 1765, Kant wrote: "If there is any science which man really needs, it is the one I teach of how to fulfill properly that position in creation which is assigned to man, and from which he is able to learn what one must be in order to be a man."[9] This sentence clearly takes "man" as the object of human study and marks his destiny of "self-making." "All of Kant's philosophy is ordered to a single purpose: By means of an analysis of the essential principles of human nature, it discloses his proper destiny, and indicates how he must work toward its fulfillment."[10]

Of course, Kant is the most canonical of figures, and his claims about "man" and the "intellectual" have power within the human sciences and the critical tradition especially. Indeed, since his *Anthopology* is one of the "original" texts of that tradition, querying it is a way of coming to an understanding of the entire tradition's practices and positions. Specifically, we can see theorized and defended in Kant how the coming-into-being of anthropological humanism requires the construction of interlocking discoveries and institutions for the production and distribution of knowledge to carry out the role assigned to "culture" in humanism.

Kant's *Anthropology* comes near to embodying that double movement of finitude that Foucault's archeologies foreground so sharply. Furthermore, his text is a metadiscourse; that is, it not only functions as a "leading" text, making certain practices and values available for the ephebes it helps make possible, but also comments on the practices it encourages both to defend them "rationally," as it were and, more important, to articulate, in the process, some of the key practices and figures that will become "normal" and so occupy the cultural, social, and political space opened by finitude's double negation. I have already commented on how this anthropological humanism genealogically inscribes leading intellectuals; in addition, as we can see from Kant, it requires and produces generalized modes of secular intellectual disciplinary practice that appear in the concerns, work structures, and cultural positions of all disciplinary practitioners. The primary role of the leading intellectual in anthropological humanism requires, as we have seen in the case of Auerbach's reception, an institutionalized discipline—this might be provided by the party or the university—producing knowledge and knowledge-producing methods as the ground for the representative intellectuals' claims to authority. Not just leading intellectuals but an extensive apparatus, basing its own authority on the "truth" of its "discoveries," is necessary to fulfill the humanist project. To "interpret" the "meanings" seemingly everywhere in "man" and his "nature" requires effective institutions in which the material and discursive structures become the literal embodiment of finitude's double negation, of man as origin and limit.

Said helps us to understand this with his perceptive comments on Renan while letting us see how tentatively aware contemporary intellectuals are of their genealogy: for Renan, "the past has been superseded entirely, transvaluated into what only a rationalistically investigative and daring mind can exploit, revel in, feel creative about" (WTC, 279). Said rightly points out that Renan's identity "is in fact supported by all sorts of institutions and figures giving it authority and gravity."[11] Such important and exiciting intellectual practice within such powerful and supportive institutions—an experience some of us still can know—becomes the "true plentitude of postlapsarian existence" (WTC, 280). Said's metaphor must be taken literally and not subjectively: following Kant we can see that in a culture produced and made politically effective for the most part by the secular drive to knowledge and truth defining anthropological humanism the ubiquitous intellectual practices, discourses, and institutions that support, and depend on, the leading intellectual, the master scholar—these are meant to be the only space and means for producing a plenitudinous present and future. In other words, our own intellectual institutions, which aim to fulfill anthropologism's visionary projects and promises, reflect, constitute, and sustain the cultural politics of Kant's humanistic attitude. My concern is that humanism too often fulfills its dreams of cultural rule only in nightmares.

Auerbach's work, for example, is a variation of the Kantian

version of the leading intellectual figure, whereas the humanistic discourse and practices that supported Hitler had their "origins" in Kant's hoped-for sublimination of death. Auerbach's project, especially *Mimesis*, is a variation on that side of the "humanistic" discourse that takes, as in the case of Renan, "the dense web of relationships between language users" as the only possible object of and space for European cultural affirmation. Whereas Hölderlin and Shelley mark the withdrawal of the gods and the resulting ambiguous position of "humanity," fascism marks the demise or paradoxical fulfillment of the dream of anthropological or historicist humanism. Auerbach's failed struggle to retrieve it makes this clear. Indeed, such struggles should perhaps be read, even in Auerbach, as the residual persistence of powerful discursive functions, with all their consequent values and desires, rather than as the self-directed actions of a critical consciousness or subject. Certainly, the repeated resurfacing of the defining and limiting figures of historicist humanism in each and every one of Auerbach's gambits shows how, even in such a transitional critic, the discourses and practices of the highly problematic humanistic formation constitutively determine "his" consciousness and writing.

I have shown how a reading of what we might call Auerbach's "career" raises the curtain on the structure of humanistic discursive practices in our recent past. On the one hand, its "contradictory" play between "limit" and "origin" sustains this discourse, compels its multiplication as a fulfillment of its own "purpose." On the other hand, what I am calling the Kantian repression of the socially devastating consequences of the humanistic dependency on the demonic in culture—and the antithetical need to sublimate it—works itself out in fascism, as one reading of Nietzsche suggests it must and, in the process, delegitimates itself. Yet, despite this tragic delegitimation, despite humanism's failed attempt at self-resuscitation in Auerbach, the concrete and material apparatus, the discursive and nondiscursive practices of finitude's double negation, continue to grind on. The persistence of the failed structure and discourse is like the persistence of a neurosis; reflection cannot change it; only action can. This humanism has become the commonsense, the ideology, of knowledge production and so tries to define the range of possible intellectual work within its own terms—on the left and right. I take Foucault's and Said's work, among others', to be attempts to challenge this common sense and to deal with the now apparent consequences of this grinding-on. I say more about their tactics a bit further.

I repeat my claim that despite the real historical changes that have shifted the relationships between the state and party, on the one hand, and the leading intellectual, on the other, from what Kant and Lukacs described and represented, the figure of the leading intellectual still legitimates the discursive project of anthropological humanism, especially within the profession of literary studies. A detailed material institutional history of the relationship between "lit. crit." and the state in England and the United States cannot be done here. Nonetheless, one can say that anthropological humanism always validates and insists upon the need for leading intellectuals on both national and cultural and disciplinary levels. In turn, these elite intellectuals always assume the role of guidance, of "representativeness." No matter whether they be "organic" to the ruling or subordinate classes, to the capitalist state or vanguard party, to the ideologically leading fraction of the upper classes (as with Irving Babbitt or Walter Jackson Bate), or to a highly professionalized and seemingly apolitical academic institution, these intellectuals are necessary within anthropological humanism. In Kant's text, all this surfaces explicitly at the end in language that traces an almost unchanged outline from Goethe to Auerbach:

Thus we tend to present the human species not as evil, but as a species of rational beings, striving among obstacles to advance constantly from the evil to the good. In this respect our intention in general is good, but achievement is difficult because we cannot expect to reach our goal by the free consent of individuals, but only through progressive organization of the citizens of the earth within and toward the species as a system which is united by cosmopolitical bonds. (A, 251)

It is the dark side of these "cosmopolitical bonds" that Auerbach tries to deal with in his stress on "alienation" and his version of "*Weltliteratur.*" It is the same potential for the abuse of power that others like Habermas theorize and hope to avoid. Yet, paradoxically, even such attempts as Auerbach's to "reform" the attitude or to reinscribe its beneficent side, to see it again as assuring the "true plenitude" of secular society—these attempts not only fail—witness Auerbach's final admissions—but, most importantly, can be carried out only within and by virtue of this anthropological humanism.

It is extremely difficult, perhaps impossible, for intellectual discourse to function (entirely) anywhere else. Often when it tries to, it is accused of anarchism, irrationalism, amoralism, or threatening civilization. The point is, however, that what look like examples of nonanthropological humanism are appearing in what are still called "the human sciences," although, where they do appear, the traditional institutional and discursive structures seem under strain. I examine some of these examples. I make no claim to being inclusive.

IV

The three figures I consider in this context are Marshall Hodgson, Edward W. Said, and Michel Foucault. I choose them because they are all powerful revisionists of humanistic disciplinary discourse and because they represent differing positions in relation to humanism, the critique of representation, the materiality of discourse, and the figure of the intellectual. My primary focus is on Hodgson's *The Venture of Islam: Conscience and History in a World Civilization*,[12] Said's *The World, the Text and the Critic*, and Foucault's *Discipline and Punish*.[13] I include Hodgson's work here because it fits a broad definition of critical paractice; that is, it engages in "reading," comments on the canonicity of texts, and studies the way literature creates and preserves culture. Somewhat outside the main tradition of literary study, Hodgson is well within the genealogy of historicist, revisionist, and critical humanism. One additional reason for introducing Hodgson here is that his work is not "Orientalist" in the way in which Said has discussed much of the scholarship on the Middle East: it is a fine example of how self-critical and humanely generous an essentially humanistic scholarship can be.[14] It also seems to me that despite the enormous political urgency that always differentiates Said's work, its position is nearer Hodgson's powerful humanistic scholarship than is Foucault's antihumanism. Yet, in another way, which has to do with the politics of critical practice, Said and Foucault are similar and crucially different from Hodgson. Finally, I treat Hodgson here because he is a better representative of the anthropological humanism that constitutes (or ideologically legitimates) the profession of literary studies than any "literary" critic I know of in the recent past or present.

V

Marshall Hodgson is an extraordinarily subtle and learned scholar whose encyclopedic study of the various Islamicate cultures adheres to methodological cautions and principles explained in his astute metadisciplinary remarks. Anthropological humanism's basic charge to scholars is to study "culture" as the coming-into-being of the species' progress and the reservoir of its "meanings." In a sense, the project prescribed in Kant is still being taken up in Hodgson. He tries to think through the methodological problems facing any scholar attempting to study "culture" or cultural institutions no matter whether the scholar does or does not share that "culture's major traditions" (*VI*, 28). Hodgson and Auerbach share, in large part, the same set of discourses and values. For example, Hodgson's most important methodological section is entitled "*Historical Humanism*," and even though he has strong objections to the excessively philological bias of most Islamic studies, he defends the basic humanistic premises and desires embodied in Auerbach's concept of "*Weltliteratur*." Indeed, we can find the same respect for cultural memory, for the importance of difference within "humanity," and for the historicist humanist in *The Venture of Islam* as we can in *Mimesis*.

Yet the tone of Hodgson's historical humanism is fundamentally different than Auerbach's. While Hodgson has Auerbach's sense of the importance of the scholarly production of historical narrative and of the crucial role such narratives play in the continuing global process of civilization, his approach is more "rational" and less "severe" or "poetic." Rather than appeal to Vico's authority for scholars to become (belated) epic poets and mythmakers, Hodgson develops rigorous methodological criteria ranging from his discussion of transliteration to the problem of representation to ground his project firmly within the authority of disciplinary humanism. Yet it would be wrong to think that Hodgson simply inscribes his work within a given continuous "authoritative" and "authorizing" tradition of Islamic studies; on the contrary, he is a hostile critic of much of his own discipline, dissatisfied with its confusions, biases, and naiveté. In general terms, one could say he attempts to re-ground his discipline scientifically, in a way more consistent with his reflexive humanism. Indeed, he sometimes seems less concerned with the specific disciplinary problems of "Islamic studies" then he is with what he sees as the greatest of anthropological or humanist historicist projects: producing an interrogative discourse about the (presumed) timeless realities of humanity in history, a discourse of such scope and mastery that it not only can engage with the other (comparatively few) comparable projects in history but also can become an effective cultural monument and force—not just a "record" of "history," but a contribution to sustaining it, to keeping its potential global civilizing project alive.

Hodgson clearly understands that scholarship plays a material and political role in culture. In fact, when one reads him carefully it is clear that his actual methodological and disciplinary remarks grow out of that awareness and reflect his attempt to produce institutions and practices that will redirect the humanistic disciplines within the politically operative culture they administer and sustain. In other words, as we shall see, Hodgson appears in and through his texts as a nodal figure recuperating humanism's vision and revising its institutions in the ongoing cultural process of interpretation, commentary, and canon construction. Let me concede once more that I do not intend to suggest there are no consequent differences among practices and canons. Yet I want to draw continual attention to the persistence of a certain type of intellectual practice that genealogically burdens even the most progressive aims with seemingly, at the present, unavoidable and undesirable political consequences.

Kant's *Anthropology* is an early modern expression of how the humanistic intellectual's work is inscribed in a complex figure of responsibility and self-love. As I suggested in chapter 4, this figure, whose most common variation is the "sublime master," persists even in the professionalized academy, although, as I also showed, when professionalized, the figure tends to serve the institutionalized interests of those at the pinnacle of the academic hierarchy. This is, in part, what I mean when I say anthropological humanism requires leading figures within disciplines, as well as on a national or cultural level. Horkheimer takes a rather totalizing and hypostatizing attitude to the value of all work done in this tradition and in the process gets at a central support of its system and proposes an alternative—to which I shall return. In "On the Problem of Truth," he writes that the bourgeoisie and their intellectuals falsely assume their own domination over nature, culture, and history:

the beavers of this spirit, with their critical capacity and their developed thinking, do not really become masters but are driven by the changing constellations of the general struggle which, even though summed up by men themselves, face them as incalculable forces of destiny.

Horkheimer's severe and accurate critique accounts for and goes beyond my more limited attempt to describe the circumscription of these figures of the "master." Yet the breadth of Horkheimer's statement may make it somewhat reductive:

This is why the intellectual situation has for decades been dominated by the craving to bring an eternal meaning into a life which offers no way out, by philosophical practices such as the direct intellectual or intuitive apprehension of truth and finally by blind submission to a personality, be it an anthroposophic prophet, a poet or a politician.[15]

While what I have been trying to suggest about the intellectual in anthropological humanism finds support in Horkheimer, his position precludes differentiating and specifying the various practices within this cultural situation. We need to be able to discriminate and judge politically among the intellectual products of the "era of finitude."

Politically and intellectually important work can be carried out under this figure of the "master," and it must be recognized and defended. The point is not to hypostatize the professional structure or the discourses of humanism and so lose sight of the relative strengths of different configurations of discourse and practice. Yet I also want to argue that the criteria for these judgments must themselves be complex. As I see it, they must operate on at least two levels: first, what claims can be made for particular work representing elements of a nonhumanistic discourse and practice; second, "within" this still dominant discourse of "man," which tactics for producing knowledge, for positioning the intellectual, and for defining the disciplines are most efficacious for furthering the political goal of challenging the hegemonic order's exploitation of intellectual work.

Although a great deal can be learned from Auerbach's struggle to redeem historicism and through it humanistic intellectual life and the order of Western culture it served, studied, and loved, Auerbach is finally too morally attached to that tradition to see the necessary consequence of his own struggle, namely, to abandon the nostalgic, proprietorial, bourgeois attachment to the task of repeating the precious "meaning," the "truth" of the tradition, and to turn critical practice boldly against the discourses, practices, and institutions that embodied the "modernity" he so much despised. But as we have seen, Auerbach's work precludes this very sort of institutional and discursive local engagement. Hodgson's work is of great interest, then, if only because, sharing so many of Auerbach's attitudes and values, he actively tries to grasp the material dimensions of cultural constitution and distribution; he directly engages with the material aspects of "Islamic studies" in a real but limited way. In other words, if Auerbach ultimately experiences the dire and dark consequences of the loss of the gods—Hölderlin's despair simultaneous with but marked by the power, promises, and success of the human sciences—Hodgson remains firmly in the affirmative tradition and so, as an heir of Renan, revels in the cultural plenitude of secular study and discourse.

I suggest, then, that we cannot judge the value of work carried out in humanism simply by valorizing Hölderlin over Renan, or vice versa. Each makes its own progressive contribution: the former critically reminds us of what anthropologism gives up. For example, opening *Nature*, Emerson writes:

Our age is retrospective. It builds the sepulchres of the fathers. It writes biographies, histories, and criticism. The foregoing generations beheld God and nature face to face; we, through their eyes. Why should we not also enjoy an original relation to the universe?[16]

But the latter reminds us of how much has been purchased at that price.

As I have already suggested, we must judge the importance of critical practice by the degree to which and the ways in which it turns against the hegemonic institutions so intertwined with anthropological humanism. The more effectively antihumanistic these variations "within" humanism, the more important and democratic they can be. An essential element of humanism's success in masking the politics of culture is the idea that the production of knowledge is devoted to "truth." As Foucault would have it, anthropologism's form of the will to power is the will to truth, whose value and desirability cannot be questioned within the commonsensical realm of positive scientistic affirmation. The political nature of this "truth" needs to be sketched in so that, "truth" can be freed into politics, into the service of whoever can produce and deploy it for their own determination. In discussing the "problem of truth," Horkheimer dialecticizes the concept. I would like to reread his text to suggest "truth" can be effective even in nondialectical local struggles against power. But first, it is necessary to suggest briefly how essential "truth" is to anthropological humanism.

Auerbach, and other serious humanists, put criticism in the service of the Western tradition's "truth." To oppose hegemonic institutions effectively, critics must abandon that project and see "truth" as the figure empowering the compulsive, discursive production of culture's regulative goal. It should be seen in other words, as political on the largest scale, as constituting and sustaining the dominant structure of finitude and all the consequent cultural institutions now largely sustaining the hegemonic forces of society. Of course, there are many who are already doing such things. The "truth" of humanism's "tradition" has been problematized over and again, and this has taught us that criticism requires two things of "truth": on the one hand, its political appropriation, where necessary, for anti-hegemonic purposes; on the other, its delegitimation as an essential function within humanistic or anthropological culture in order to weaken that culture and prepare for whatever might follow.

Horkheimer develops a very strong theory of "truth" that frees it from any nostalgia for unearthing or preserving deep "meanings" (PT, 415). Horkheimer repositions "truth" as a tactical weapon in political struggles. He makes his claim for the politics of truth by critiquing Hegel, and implicitly, all systematic philosophers and critics who feel "truth" resides in the store of experience available to its heirs in their community:

The belief that this system is the completion of truth hides from him the significance of the temporally conditioned interest which plays a role in the details of the dialectical presentation through the direction of thought, the choice of material content, and the use of names and words, and diverts attention away from the fact that his conscious and unconscious partnership in regard to the problems of life must necessarily have its effect on a constituent element of his philosophy. (PT, 416)

Horkheimer is not simply accusing Hegel of false consciousness, of not realizing the priority of material life to thought. Nor is he simply avoiding relativism, the dark side of historicism against which Auerbach struggled. Rather Horkheimer suggests a rethinking of "truth" that would put notions like false consciousness and relativism largely out of play. "Truth," he asserts, is a *function of political struggle*. Even though Horkheimer follows Marx and Lukacs in insisting on a dialectical "theory of society as a whole" (PT, 430), the concept of the totality produces no "truth" for Horkheimer in that the "image" it produces cannot be "proven" or "verified," and, in fact, "is never identical with reality" (PT, 432). The truth of this totality "is itself only to be thought of in terms of particular interests and tasks with one's own point of view and activity" (PT, 430). "Truth" is not just historical and so changing; it is a function of human desire to modify reality for one's own and one's own class or group interests. This is, of course, precisely what it is in humanism as well. The difference is humanism's attempt to mask the politics of truth in the claims of pragmatic reason:

the truth is advanced because the human beings who possess it stood by it unbendingly, apply it and carry it through, act according to it, and bring it to power against the resistance of reactionary, narrow, one-sided points of view. The process of cognition includes real historical will and action just as much as it does learning from experience and intellectual comprehension. (PT, 422)

Above all though, if it is to be critical, such a use of "truth" cannot be "pragmatic."[17] Kant's sense of the "pragmatic gift" has become, in relation to truth, a "limitless trust in the existing world" and its progressive future and a refusal to believe another "explosive truth" might disrupt the anthropological vision of unlimited human development (PT, 425). Once established, humanistic "truth" is antirevolutionary and unitary and insists on continuity. As we shall see, Said tries to change this tendency through his concept of "critical consciousness," whereas Hodgson powerfully reasserts its necessity.

Although he is an anthropological humanist, Hodgson is no easy pragmatist. Intellectual disciplines, for Hodgson, neither reveal a priori truths nor unearth the hidden meaning of humanity in culture. Nor is he confident of any assured "progress" within or between cultures to ever "higher" states, although he does feel sure that cultures reinforce their discovered rationalities. Even though Hodgson's work is important for its critique of disciplinary structure, for its analysis of disciplines' relation to their objects, and, like Auerbach's, for its stress on cultural diversity, it does nonetheless rest on a very sophisticated version of the "pragmatism" we have seen in Kant and with some contradictory, often undesirable consequences.

Hodgson is a complex case. Although he was objectively a faculty member at an elite university training scholars and bureaucrats essential to the functioning of government, as well as the academy, he surely represents no dogmatic politics or disciplinary method. On the contrary, Hodgson's most important contribution within humanistic discourse is to call on scholars to provide their own self-justification and not simply to operate professionally and uncritically within given and dogmatic categories. But even in his call for self-criticism, one can hear the disciplinary operations of the trope of the sublime master and recognize Hodgson's problematic genealogy:

Unless a scholar is content to accept his categories (and hence the questions he can ask and hence the answers he can arrive at) as given by the accidents of current predispositions, he cannot escape the obligation of justifying his selection of units for study, which means justifying his point of view. Such a justification, in turn, must imply an explicit stand on his role as a scholar. (VI, 22)

Embedded in this call for critical responsibility is an important and often ignored acknowledgment of the situated nature of scholarly production, of its "directedness," and of the reality of the scholar as a positioned subject functioning at the intersection of various and often contradictory forces. For Hodgson, the scholar is not "free floating" but is positioned within a network of knowledge-producing, self-correcting, interrelated institutions constituting a politicized culture. Nonetheless, as we shall see, Hodgson insists that, from this position, a scholar must address questions of general, almost "timeless human" concern. For example, it matters for Hodgson not only that scholarship is never transcendentally disinterested but that it be seen as emerging from and intending to sustain specific cultural biases. In fact, given the professionally, culturally, and personally situated nature of the scholar, scholarship itself is a function of converging powers located in the scholar and his or her discipline. Implicit, therefore, in this humanistic historian's discourse is a nonmetaphysical concept of the scholarly subject as cultural "function."

In fact, in Hodgson's attempt to adjust scholarship to the unavoidability of bias, scholarly production comes to serve the role, not just of "objectifying" the topic of investigation, but also, through the reflective practice of the scholar, of presenting the various forces converging on the critic. In effect, then, scholarly work always contains an element of not just "self-presentation" but of the representation of the present as an attempt to inscribe more deeply and further extend a regulative cultural apparatus. This last allows for the humanistic interaction between some facet of the present culture and some other or past cultural moment that, in turn, allows for more, newly legitimated scholarly discourse.

Auerbach argues that alienation from one's culture in order to return to it is necessary to explicate one's beloved world. Said, following Auerbach, gives a materialist turn to this notion of alienation and changes it into exile: "*Mimesis* itself is . . . a work built upon a critically important distance from [the Western cultural tradition] a work whose conditions and circumstances of existence are not immediately derived from the culture it describes . . . but build rather on an agonizing distance from it" (*WTC*, 8). For Auerbach, alienation redeems the world and the humanists' project; for Said, exile is the condition for the ironic oppositional criticism of culture and system he invokes to defend the importance of the individual critical consciousness. I will say more on how this claim can be seen as part of anthropological humanism a bit further on.

Hodgson insists differently that scholarship valuable to the extension of a regulative culture can emerge only from the deeply imbedded position of the intellectual in a culture. He feels that the condition for the possibility of a culturally productive scholarship, one that actually furthers the processes of human unity emerging from difference—which we might say is the simplest articulation of culture's regulative role—is an exceptionally aware commitment to and use of the valuable resources of one's own culture. Indeed, for Hodgson, disciplines are possible only on such a basis:

The cultural allegiance of a serious scholar is crucial in his work . . . not only the scholars' cultural environment at large but their explicit precommitments, which brought the greater of the scholars to their inquiry in the first place, have determined the categories with which they have undertaken their studies. Only by a conscious and well-examined understanding of the limits of these precommitments and of what is possible within and beyond them can we hope to take advantage of our immediate humanness to reach any direct appreciation of major cultural traditions we do not share—and perhaps even of traditions we do share. (*VI*, 28)

Auerbach's critique of Herder's tradition in "Vico and Aesthetic Historism" reminds us how difficult it has been for scholars engaged in comparative cultural studies of a philological or folkloric sort to be both in a culture and critical of it. Yet in different ways, Auerbach, Said, and Hodgson define such a complex position as the necessary condition for both comparative and rational cultural study. Hodgson's honorable contribution to Auerbach's sense of alienation is to concede the scholar's obvious predispositions within normal practice, to suggest ways to turn them to advantage, and to argue that such predispositions, taken up at a higher level of conscious critical commitment, alone make possible human unity within diversity. Scholars must be aware of their general political, cultural, and disciplinary biases; they must make critical commitments to those biases they hold toward whatever in their culture or discipline is of unquestionable value. For Hodgson, "greater" scholarship results only from such consciously made positive commitments. Furthermore, the phenomena to which the scholar is commited have three functions: they aid the scholar in recognizing phenomena of similar value in other or past cultures; they correspondingly allow the scholar to begin the important task of constructing, recovering, or preserving a canon or tradition of such phenomena; and they justify the scholar's power to judge as unimportant or not worth preserving an entire range of other phenomena perceived to be of lesser value and so not a crucial part of the canonical configuration.

Hodgson's model of valuable, situated, critical practice does not then depend on a legitimating image of the scholar as hero. Rather, committed as Hodgson is to the humanistic figure of the leading intellectual, he wants to represent scholarly skepticism—which is nothing less than striving to acknowledge and critique one's necessary precommitments—as a professional or disciplinary possibility that, while drawing on the individualized experience and practice of the scholar, does not require a highly atomistic and romantic conception of the "alienated" or "exiled" individualized intellectual for its legitimacy. Despite the many who think, after Arnold, that culture must be in the hands of "the best," Hodgson often suggests a more democratic model for serious scholarly work that, at the same time, is not depersonalized into a professional routine or dogma. The necessary balance between self-criticism and persistent commitments—this is Hodgson's important variation on anthropological humanism in contemporary critical practice. Like most liberal humanists, however, Hodgson finds it difficult to implement the democratic promises of self-determination while working with discourses and institutions that sustain themselves and elitist interests by arrogating the power and right to speak for and lead others. In Hodgson's case, the contradiction between forming an exclusionary canon with claims to universal value and stressing the individual scholar's skeptical self-critique results in his reinvoking a theory of elite achievement and of a unitary culture to regulate scholars' "critical" judgments. As we shall see, Said's insistence on endless critique to prevent such hypostatization is an important corrective but one purchased at the cost of what Hodgson can contribute: a positive content to critical work.

In "Secular Criticism," Said warns that critics do not realize how deeply inscribed they are within the cognitive and value structures of their culture or how much they depend on them for their work and comfortable, "nonaliented" lives. "Culture" is more a Gramscian than Arnoldian concept in Said:

I shall use the word *culture* to suggest an environment, process, and hegemony in which individuals (in their private circumstances) and their works are embedded, as well as overseen at the top by a superstructure and at the base by a whole series of methodological attitudes. It is in culture that we can seek out the range of meanings and ideas conveyed by the phrases *belonging to* or *in a* place, being *at home in a place*. (*WTC*, 8)

Such "culture" and its dogmatic effects must be resisted; it is a "possessing possession," which Said, following Foucault's conception of the dual nature of power, finds can both repress and produce: "to authorize, to dominate, to legitimate, demote, interdict, and validate." In other words, "culture" operates within humanistic scholarship and especially contemporary literary criticism in much the same way I suggest "practical criticism" operates within the academy, no doubt as a specific agency of that "culture": "the power of culture [is] to be an agent of. . . . powerful differentiation within its domain" (WTC 9).

Said's contribution here is twofold: to take seriously the conservative nature of culture, even in its productivity as, for example, canonicity; and to point to the powerfully ambiguous nature of culture: it is both an "environment, process, and hegemony" and, at the same time, a weapon for the preservation of the hegemony. It is the latter, not simply as an ideological set of values, but as an operative tool of the hegemony, an empowered (as well as empowering) form of (and weapon for) closure that—and this is Said's crucial insight—negates the negative or critical function of scholarship, of what can only be called "criticism, itself." In other words, I am suggesting that even though it is not directly thematized, in "Secular Criticism," Said attempts to return to criticism the power of the negative as more than "exclusion," a power and value lost in the double negation of finitude that is (or was) anthropological humanism's founding act. "Culture," as Said represents it, has the double function of limit and origin that, following Foucault, I have been calling "finitude."

But it is absolutely crucial to see that Said's strongest move is not simply to appropriate "culture" for progressive purposes, as, for example, one might give new meaning and force to "democracy" in a struggle against imperialist republics who also use the term. Rather, Said's text negates "culture," empties it out, delegitimates it as a conceptual shibboleth within the canonical practice of humanistic criticism by revealing its function in the oppression of those who are excluded from its "benefits," of those who are "other" to it. Paradoxically Said empties the term by showing how full it is of power, interest, and injustice—how it operates materially in society—full of precisely all of those dangerous and killing tendencies of modernity that Kant feels are successfully sublimated in humanism. But while Said marks the failure of this sublimation and the return of the repressed, he remains a humanist. The point I want to make is simply this: when Auerbach insists on alienation, Hodgson on committed self-scrutiny, and Said on critical negation of culture, what we are seeing are momentary movements away from anthropological humanism that suggest that some nonhumanistic possibility is emerging. Such moments should be identified and pursued.

In "Secular Criticism," Said advocates a modification of institutions and practices of criticism so that alienation from "culture" is recognized as the necessary condition for critical practice. One could say that by making such an effort, Said is trying to "normalize" alienation or criticism, that is, make it a defining element of professional training and practice. In this, he is closer to Hodgson than Auerbach; that is, he recognizes the political materiality of culture and wants to modify or contest its relation to the hegemony. But there are some important differences between them nonetheless that are worth identifying to specify the range of possibility for enfiguring and institutionalizing such skeptical criticism.

Said sounds most like Hodgson in remarks like this:

On the one hand, the individual mind registers and is very much aware of the collective whole, context, or situation in which it finds itself. On the other hand, precisely because of this awareness—a worldly self-situating, a sensitive response to the dominant culture—that the individual consciousness is not naturally and easily a mere child of the culture, but a historical and social actor in it. (WTC, 15)

Yet even at such moments in Said there is a little of the sense one has in reading Hodgson, or even Auerbach, that there *are* elements of one's present culture to be committed to. (We know, however, from his other work that Said values such figures as Swift and Conrad.) Auerbach's exile leads him to love the world; it also allows him to return to and exploit what is valuable in his own tradition, its language and cultural resources. Exile is a condition for *Mimesis*, but a love for and commitment to all in Europe that is not institutionalized murder is what drives him to write it. Said, however, at times comes near to voiding all such commitments in his valuable attempt to restore effective negation to criticism.

I will suggest a bit further on that Said has no choice but to take this radical position in putting forward criticism as the negation of dogma and culture. Operating within humanism as he is, but powerfully aware of its oppressive role, he tries to make liberal humanism responsive to its own avowed ideals of bettering the life of the species. But humanism offers only one primary means for its own critique, namely, the subtradition from Hölderlin to Auerbach that comes to know the failed promises of anthropologism's positivity and responds with some charge of betrayal, loss, or impoverishment.

Another way of saying this would be to point out that while Said frequently praises Raymond Williams for his materially and politically complex critical stance, he effectively reverses the value assigned "culture" in *Culture and Society*: it is not an appropriate sign but a social structure and concept that must be negated. Williams tries to take the term from the romantic reactionaries, who made of it a mode of critique and value; Said restores its inevitable dark side to put it out of play, substituting notions like "irony" and "oppositional" for it.

Above all Said's Palestinian experience accounts for his negative attitude toward what he sees as a fairly monolithic "culture". He has perhaps also been influenced by Williams and E. P. Thompson in their studies of "resistance" to hegemony. Surely, it is the combination of these two that leads Said to reject Foucault's theory of power as reductive. He does, however, accept the part of Foucault's theory that stresses the productivity of power, so it is a bit surprising that he does not analogously accept the valuably productive aspects of culture, those that "authorize," as well as "molest"—to use his own terms from *Beginnings*. Indeed the paradox for all literary critics, which follows on Richards' achievement, is that we engage in whatever form of oppositional, negative, critical practice we can only by virtue of our having been trained to deal with sign systems by the very discipline we contest. Strangely, then, humanism has its way: oppositional discourses are not independent of it but, as I suggested in chapter 1, part of its genealogy.

Said cannot be serious about negating "culture" while advocating the reform and renewal of valuable oppositional critical training, yet he is and must be. He moves in the only direction now possible while illustrating, by the contradictions his work reveals, how restrictive liberal humanism really is. But he makes the most of what is possible for us.

Given Said's strong sense of culture's oppression, it is not surprising to find him advocating the critic's *alliance* with "contesting classes, movements, and values" (WTC, 15). Such an alliance would be, on one level, a serious revision of the Kantian paradigm of the role of the cultural hero: scholarship would no longer support the given state constitution. Gramsci's influence on Said is crucial here since what he seems to be advocating is a version of the organic intellectual. Said allows us to think through to the point where it appears that the critic is "organic," not just to the "class" he belongs to or the sex she is "part of," but, given the complete alienation of the critic from culture, to all forms of resistance. Said's revision of Gramsci's model is not, it seems to me, an abandonment of the value of "class," not given Said's invocation of that category against Foucault in "Travelling Theory." Rather, Said seems to be trying to adjust the figure of the "organic" to the contemporary fact that resistance is not "simply" (or perhaps primarily) class based but forms along other lines of nation, sex, and class fraction as well. Said's position is an important contribution to the metatheoretical and political discourse about the literary intellectual and his or her possible response to the political operation of culture, often in the interests of hegemony. But since my concern is with the limits we discover even in such powerful, oppositioned critical practice as Said's, I must make some further points about those limits against which Said's work brings us in his attempt to reconceive critical practice.

Above all, it seems to me that, as I have been suggesting since chapter 1, much oppositional and critical practice is inscribed within the discourse and institutions of the humanistic figures of the leading intellectual. I think this fact defines a problem for critical intellectuals who hope not to repeat the structure of anthropological humanism in which the defining reality of death is forgotten or repressed. Recalling such a definition means being excruciatingly wary of reactivating the liberal humanistic model in which discourse about and for others occupies a leading and legitimating role for state, party, profession, or caste. I should say explicitly, as I try to suggest in my earlier discussion of Pound, that "escaping" such a structure is a naive aspiration. What we must do now is sketch our anthropologism by tracing the enabling and constraining history of these leading and oppositional figures to identify some partial alternative to that structure. As I see it, this must be done so that the position of "leading" intellectual can be contested, particularly with an eye toward somehow weakening the link between the present regime of truth and the hegemonic interests of Western society as this exists in culture. For this reason, Said's contest with and against both what he calls the critics of system, such as Derrida, and the cultural critics, who could be Arnold or Renan, must be admired and supported, even if one has some impatience with Said for his refusal to acknowledge that deconstruction might be politically useful in some forms of feminist resistance.[18] That is to say, one should concede the "truth" of Said's claims regarding the problematic tendencies of contemporary criticism as an important political gesture. Above all, Said's move, and my reading of it, should not be dismissed by denigrating it as "mere tactics." For once negation is reactivated to problemetize the humanistic illusion of "truth," to minimize its terrorist effect, and to contest culture's structural aims, what is left to criticism but politics and tactics?

Following along after such figures as Auerbach, Hodgson, and Said, one must grasp how thoroughly inscribed the figure of the leading intellectual is in the work, limiting while enabling it. I shall return to Hodgson shortly. For now one must see that Said struggles to deploy the critical resources of humanism for oppositional or negative ends more powerfully than any other contemporary American critic: "criticism must think of itself as life-enhancing and constitutively opposed to every form of tyranny, domination, and abuse; its social goals are noncoercive knowledge produced in the interests of human freedom" (*WTC*, 29). This admirable sentence abstracts the best of what Kant, of what anthropological humanism, can be read to say. It would be silly to quibble with it. But along side it and elsewhere in Said's text is a transformation of another less politically and intellectually attractive image from Kant upon which this powerfully humane commitment rests and which, I fear, might undermine much oppositional criticism. I want to suggest that Said can make this powerful remark—which does not just state a goal and is not just a call to arms but is also the legitimation of all critical enterprise—only because he images the critic as one of those powerful and "ill-natured" men whose task it is to function as lawgivers out of their own privileged beings. Oppositional intellectuals do not, however, fulfill precisely the Kantian purpose. They do not aid in the pragmatic persistence of the given order.

Rather, on one level, they destabilize that order. Of course, there are important political differences between and among these oppositional figures, and those differences must not be minimized. There are even greater differences between them and those traditional humanists who dogmatically pursue the regulative role of Kantian humanism. Yet on the genealogical level I have been trying to sketch out in this book, all of these intellectuals are too much the same. That is, they are all "the same" within anthropological humanism—and it is up against this sameness that Said brings us. As I show in my discussion of Auerbach, to justify itself, oppositional intellectual practice can and almost must reinscribe the figure of the leading intellectual as representative. There are dangers to this. At its worst, such a reinscription can lead to tyranny and betrayal. In more "ordinary" circumstances, however, it perpetuates some of the essential aspects of the current regime of truth and makes more difficult the furthering of participatory democracy, the struggle against oppression, and the restructuring of culture.

More important, however, precisely because more "normal," the need for critics to ground their own revisionist practice by invoking this figure can only align the intellectual's being and practice with what *the intellectual* understands or takes to be the "positive," or "progressive," "resisting" elements in a culture. Such an alignment reinscribes and furthers the general anthropological project of giving the intellectual producers of discourse the "right" and power to comment on, explain, and (help) put in place the forms of human society most likely to "fulfill" human nature—as that is discursively produced and represented. Of course, the political differences between such forms and representations are, I must repeat, vitally important. They are tactically crucial. Nonetheless, such tactical differences do not change the fact that one of the ways anthropological humanism maintains itself and helps support the dominant interests who manipulate it is by reinscribing intellectuals—even oppositional ones—unavoidably into its movement of finitude at the very moment intellectuals seek authority.

There are at least two problems with this repetition: first, it perpetuates the authority of both general and specific intellectuals to produce discourse in which "man" is known; second, it perpetuates another kind of authority, based upon the legitimacy of the first, that is, of the nondemocratic practice of some speaking for, directing, or representing all—of some imagining for others. Such a structure also sustains the form of political leadership, which Kant first identified with the stability of state order, in which most lose the means and the right to self-determination.

In Said's theory of the critic, which is the most progressive within the American academy today, this humanistic re-inscription appears in his figure of the critic as opponent of dogma. We should not be surprised at this. The disciplinary effects of finitude's secular discourse appear precisely at the moments of greatest strength in oppositional criticism. We should accept this as a general law of critical practice today. Said concedes that Julien Benda is wrong "to ascribe so much social power to the solitary intellectual whose authority, according to Benda, comes from his individual voice and from his oppositon to organized collective passions" (*WTC* 15). Said argues the critic must be in the culture but not of it. As a result, the oppositional critic is always precariously perched. Avoid dogmatic sloganeering groups, attitudes, and ideologies yet support resisting groups. Above all, to do this, the critic must be defiantly free from the sort of persistent precommitments to elements of one's own culture that Hodgson requires:

> I take criticism so seriously as to believe that, even in the very midst of a battle in which one is unmistakably on one side against another, there should be criticism, because there must be critical consciousness if there are to be issues, problems, values, even lives to be fought for. (*WTC*, 28)

Said implicitly insists criticism is always self-criticism; indeed, this differentiates oppositional from hegemonic intellectuals. Would his advocacy were taken more seriously! His text suggests, however, that something called "critical consciousness" is responsible not only for theoretical and practical corrections but also for the issues and lives at stake in struggle itself. This seems to be going too far in taking "critical consciousness" seriously. Said's secular humanism carries him to this extreme.

I want to draw attention to the way anthropological humanism reifies the negative in Said's discourse into an abstract, individualized image that recalls Horkheimer and Adorno's critique of Kant and Hegel. Said announces that this "critical consciousness" is his real subject:

> it is probably true that an isolated individual consciousness, going against the surrounding environment as well as allied to contesting classes, movements, and values, is an isolated voice out of place but very much of that place, standing consciously against the prevailing orthodoxy and very much for a professedly universal or humane set of values, which has provided significant local resistance to the hegemony of one culture. . . . All this . . . shows us an individual consciousness placed at a sensitive nodal point, and it is this consciousness at the critical point which the book attempts to explore in the form of what I call criticism. (*WTC*, 15)

This passage reinscribes the heroic figure of the Auerbachian exile that has itself been used to legitimate the elitest structure of professional study and cultural politics. Said is contesting its professionalization here. Yet this "critical consciousness" is somehow, unaccountably, privileged to attach and detach itself from historical, material conditions that more effectively mire others. It is the "critical consciousness" that, out of its superior understanding, corrects, guides, and preserves the human project. Such critics, like Kant's ill-natured men—and these critics would look like such men to a Kant—give laws and align themselves with others when, as they see it, their own and the others' judgments and interests require and allow it. And like Kant himself as the paradigm of humanistic intellectuals, such critics would speak in the name of the universal, out of and for the local.

Said's text brilliantly illustrates the contradictions at the heart of oppositional intellectual struggle within humanism. On the one hand, like Kant, Said must repress the dark side of leading intellectual practice, of the dangers posed by such ill-natured men; on the other hand, he understands and reveals the horrors of cultural repression. Paradoxically, even his most powerful attempt to avoid this contradiction only deepens it. Said insists that the critic must always be ready to turn against dogma and institutions in his attempt to mitigate the political effects of the dark side. Yet, as I have already suggested, it is precisely the authority of the intellectual to make such moves and judgments—precisely as a defense against intellectual arrogance (among other things)—that replicates the figure of the ill-natured man. Said helps us to see this unavoidable contradiction better than most, and we must recognize that it is just this contradiction that accounts for the rather surprisingly reified and hypostatized notion of "consciousness" in Said's late work.

The limit anthropological humanism imposes even on Said's critical practice suggests we should further examine the strength and weaknesses of Hodgson's apparently different claims. His major weakness is his uncritical commitment to affirmative science, to the idea that careful method and skeptical self-criticism can make a scholar "conscious" of chosen "precommitments." Such a scientific dream obscures the need for and makes impossible a calling into question of anthropological humanism's scientific claims. Consequently, essentially cultural and political questions about disciplines' relations to power and knowledge are displaced onto the epistemological and methodological level, where they are treated abstractly, as "first principles," free of social and discursive determinants. Ultimately, such a displacement furthers the humanistic disciplines' role in extending a unitary culture in a society by regrounding a set of anthropological practices on a more persuasively justified methodological base.

Yet before Hodgson brings us up against the limit of this position, we can see that his cautious procedures and positive content make two politically valuable contributions to the progressive intellectual struggle within and against "culture": by producing, at the time of a crucial upsurge of "Western" conflict with "Islam," a generous narrative that represents Islamicate cultures in terms of their "human" achievements and by stressing that comparative cultural studies can begin to see and understand their own Western conceptual limits only by employing non-Western concepts, which are comprehended and available. But we do rather quickly come up against an unfortunate consequence of Hodgson's sense of science: it keeps him from an active political sense of "truth," such as we find implicitly in Said's turn of criticism to politics.

Historicist humanism rarely if ever acknowledges the politically regulative function of culture to normalize or exclude. Even more rarely does it concede the role of power and interest in its own vision or in the utility of its vision and its institutions to hegemonic forces. Auerbach, for example, resists such insights as perversions or demonic fulfillments of humanism distorted in modernity and he tries to correct them. Hodgson's sense of the material ways in which knowledge-producing discourses and institutions must be revised or reestablished to extend a coherent humanistic global culture is about as far as historicist humanism can go in understanding its own involvement with material operations of power and its too often repressive cultural functions.

Hodgson believes that cultural values are the result of human actions and that by virtue of their canonical preservation and pragmatic effect they regulate successive actions and our judgments of their value. Hodgson's conception therefore repeats the Kantian model of a timeless, unitary culture whose regulative, educative, and disciplinary function is not only ahistorical but also coercive. It exemplifies a basic humanistic intellectual structure: the imposition of a self-established order of things that denies its own historical complicities with power by resting its claims on "reason," persuasion, common sense, and already existing institutional and discursive authority:

> So far as there is moral or spiritual solidarity among human beings . . . the fate of each people is relevant to all human beings whether or not it had permanent external consequences otherwise. It is, then, also, and perhaps above all, as events and acts have altered the moral context of human life that they are of universal significance, for they have set irreplaceable standards and norms, and they have posed distinctive challenges and established moral claims which as human beings we dare not ignore . . . . even now we dare call no man great whose ideals cannot somehow measure up to theirs. (*VI*, 25)

The timeless order captured and preserved by scholarly reconstruction cannot be ignored. "Greater" scholars must lead disciplines and institutions in producing the knowledge and distributing its efforts throughout culture. Hodgson's project is continuous with Richards' disciplinary practice of literary study and with Auerbach's great desire. But Hodgson seems unworried by the proliferation of knowledge; "greater" scholars can systematize and use it in the monumental cultural conversations that are their *chefs d'ouevres*.

Said rightly reminds us that culture is a "possessing possession," and we can see how true that is when we recognize how Hodgson's scientism makes it impossible for him to question or identify his deepest commitments. Possessed by them, he becomes their function just as we might say historicist humanism appropriates Auerbach and tragically compels him to a futile reassertion of a traditional humanistic commitment to the existence and reproduction of a unitary history. In fact, we can see from Auerbach's work that historicist humanism can no longer legitimately sustain its proprietorial and exclusionary relation to past and to present means of producing knowledge.

If we recognize the contradictions and limits of humanistic criticism rather than accept the often persuasive affirmations of its practitioners, we can see, more or less explicitly, the necessity for two alternative responses: first, the production of a multiplicity of histories or canons, as, for example, in the women's movement; second, the questioning of the legitimacy of canonicity and historical revision itself.

One reason Hodgson is so important is that his work, like Auerbach's, brings us to the point where humanism recognizes the need to give up its unitary impulses and to represent multiplicity but inevitably finds itself reforming differences into a continuous, directed canon of human achievements. In other words, Hodgson exemplifies the problematic of genealogical struggle: his work is defined by a set of practices, discourses, and values inherited from, inscribed within, and in part determined by a powerful set of predecessors, as well as the ongoing power of the institutions that they helped establish and that the current dominant interests support.

Yet Hodgson, like Said and others, hopes to fulfill the progressive moral and political potential of that tradition, largely in response to the historical forces of his own time—specifically, in Hodgson's case, the need to represent the humanity of Islamicate cultures at a time of their increasing struggle with the imperialist West. The result is contradiction. Indeed, unfortunately as we shall see, the complicity of the humanistic discourses within which Hodgson works and which enable even his best insights—their complicity with the darker powers of repression and the current oppressive regime of truth finally moves Hodgson's work, against his will, as it were, in a direction that cancels his desire to represent diversity and difference in a generous and humane narrative. Even in Hodgson, the "Orient" becomes an "object/subject" for the extension of Western anthropological humanism's unifying obsessions. What is of most interest, however, are the details of the conflict between these contradictory movements in Hodgson. For his struggle both marks the coming into being of a move against humanism and sketches out some of the tactics to be deployed and avoided.

At times Hodgson explicitly argues that cultural history should not be written by the hegemonic elements of society. Historians must retrieve *all* examples of action that set standards of cultural and moral behavior, not simply those that

Fou doesn't describe 'low' culture except of criminals

have been successful and so become part of official history. One way to assure this attention to multiplicity, to unofficial history, is to admit the value of "low," as well as "high," culture. Scholarly procedures that do not and cannot see the true complexity of culture need to be replaced. Hodgson criticizes the philological biases of "Islamic" studies, for example, because among other things, philologists neglect or obscure the multi-layered historical and social sedimentation of culture: "Islamic studies have tended to be concerned, above all, with high culture, to the neglect of more local or lower-class social conditions; and within the high culture, to be preoccupied with religious, literary, and political themes, which are most accessible to a philological approach" (*VI*, 41).

Hodgson's commitment to recovering and preserving the moral and spiritual legacies of the past wherever one finds them could not take the form of narrowly defined professional specializations, nor could it take the equally salubrious form of some ethnocentric and self-assured commitment to "*litterae humaniores*."[19] To be authentic, for Hodgson, humanistic work must be critical, committed, first local and then international, but, above all, historically thorough. But no matter how recuperative, Hodgson's extraordinarily admirable standards in themselves express a desire for and result in work that submerges historical difference back into unitary narratives while, in addition, blocking any further insight into the productive materiality of scholarly systems of representation and their political role in culture. One of humanism's tactics for legitimating and extending itself is to acknowledge the existence of "difference" rhetorically, to study, recuperate, and produce knowledge about it, all the time "intending" as it were to attempt the incorporation of the newly produced knowledge into its own regulative and selective canon-making procedures. It is precisely this tactic that needs to be contested in two ways: by marking its irrationality and violence and by producing knowledge of a sort unassimilable to its unitary, imposing tendencies.

I have suggested that Hodgson and Said represent two different fulfillments of humanism's drives: the production on the one hand of meticulous, massive research projects and, on the

other, of the immediately occasional political essay. Two different stages of the humanistic will are operative in these projects
that qualify and complement each other. Both are critical and
oppositional practices, both are dissatisfied with the present
practice of the academy and its role in culture, and both represent simultaneously the limits of humanism and attempt to
break them.

As I argue in chapters 4 and 5, Said's sense of the critic's will
is highly individualized. Auerbach clearly hopes to contain
that will in larger humanistic research projects, in severe epic
poems. Hodgson similarly hopes to contain the individual will
by subordinating it to the discipline of humanistic research.
For Said, the critic's will is the possibility of critical action,
judgment, and consciousness. The strength of both notions is
obvious: the production of knowledge in organized, dissemina-
ble, coherent form; the unsettling of dogma, the maintenance
of debate and skepticism. The weaknesses are equally clear: the
unquestioning extension of unitary culture as political order
throughout society; the voiding of all content in critical practice, despite the apparent positivity of the critically imagined
alternatives.

Hegel gives the definitive analysis of the position Said must
take. For Said, critical consciousness can position and reposition itself within its project of negating dogma and imagining
alternatives only because, despite its historical situation,
within consciousness, "right" is determined in "mind," more
specifically in "will."

In "Secular Criticism," Said stresses that for him criticism
must be "oppositional" and "ironic." "If criticism is reducible
neither to a doctrine nor a political position on a particular
question, and if it is to be in the world and self-aware simultaneously, then its identity is its difference from other cultural
activities and from systems of thought or method" (*WTC*, 29).
The sort of irony Said intends is what Kierkegaard calls
"mastered irony" in which the critic is capable of negating
what is in the name of something "higher," but a "higher" that
is always situated in history, always confronting and emerging
from an occasion: the critic must be "against the prevailing

orthodoxy and very much for a professedly universal and humane set of values" that has been locally useful to antihegemonic forces. In the previous chapter I argued, following
Foucault, that Said and Chomsky stand in a problematic relationship to that "justice" to which they would commit themselves and other intellectuals. My objections to their position
are not merely epistemological nor the evil consequence of
yielding all to power and abandoning reason.[20] Rather, the
problem lies in the way this conception of the critic gives priority to the critic's will and its "ideal" reflections in the critic's
consciousness.

A cento from Hegel's *Philosophy of Right* describes this structure and suggests its limits within even oppositional humanism:

The basis of right is, in general, mind; its precise place and point of
origin is the will. The will is free so that freedom is both the substance
of right and its goal, while the system of right is the realm of freedom
made actual, the world of mind brought forth out of itself like a second
nature. . . . In the first place, anyone can discover in himself ability to
abstract from everything whatever, and in the same way to determine
himself, to posit any content in himself by his own effort; and similarly
the other specific characteristics of the will are exemplified for him in
his own consciousness.

   The will contains . . . the element of pure indeterminacy that pure
reflection of the ego into itself which involves the dissipation of every
restriction and every content. . . . This is the unrestructured infinity of
absolute abstraction or universality, the pure thought of oneself. . . .
This is the freedom of the void, which rises to a passion and takes shape
in the world. . . . Of course it imagines that it is willing some positive
state of affairs, such as universal equality . . . but in fact it does not
will that this shall be positively actualized, and for this reason: such
actuality leads at once to some sort of order, to a particularization of
organizations and individuals alike.[21]

We recall not only that for Said the critic is opposed to tyranny and for "noncoercive knowledge produced in the interests
of human freedom" but also that, as Hegel's analysis of this
preliminary stage of negation predicts, for Said "criticism is
most . . . unlike itself at the moment it starts turning into
organized dogma" (*WTC*, 29). Furthermore, the critic must
work "on behalf of those alternative acts and alternative intentions whose advancement is a fundamental human and intel-

lectual obligation" (*WTC*, 30). No matter how admirable this position to which Said brings us, it rests upon precisely the structure of indeterminancy Hegel describes. The critic's ability to change position, to remain free of all cultural and political commitments except to those general values of "freedom" and "resistance," to support the "alternatives" only as long as they do not become "dogma," that is, run afoul of the critical will's self-determination of what is "right," or "just," or "resistant"—all such moves testify to the "void" that is critical consciousness once it has swerved from Gramsci and lost its *organic commitment*, its cultural roots in the specific social structure whose interests it serves, to which it subordinates itself, and for which it produces a useful positivity, a truth the oppressed can use in their struggle to take power as they see fit.

As Hegel suggests, only the indetermininacy of the pure reflection of the ego loses sight of the need to aid others as they build institutions that embody forms of freedom (and unfreedom). Such productive activities require, as Hegel insists, "the transition from undifferentiated indeterminancy to the differentiation, determination, and positing of a determinacy as a concept and object."[22] In other words, it involves transforming the apparently absolute freedom of ironic negation into a freedom that is restricted to the productive negation of a higher, which it joins in trying to constitute. Critique from the point of view of endlessly revisionist imagining must become critical practice carried out in the historically specific, situated locale of the critic's work. Without such a return to history, oppositional criticism remains little more than yet another variation of the self-empowering, transcendent, ironic practice of practical and New Critics alike.[23] Said's stress on the individualized critical consciousness, empowered by an origin-less will, combined with his perhaps too unitary conception of a "dominating" culture, limits the aid such criticism can be in the production of a noncoercive society because, among other things, it essentially reinscribes the powerful role of the leading intellectual whose "representative" functions are, as Said says of "culture," useful tools "for a particular class in the State" intent on exclusion and repression (*WTC*, 11).

Hodgson's project, like Auerbach's, is the obverse of Said's on this and would require seeing critical scholarship as an attempt to furnish a positive content to the will, in other words, to produce "institutions" to fulfill the complete program of anthropological humanism's image of the pragmatic gift. But Hodgson's humanism is neither an indeterminate negation nor a positive professional discipline like Richards' "practical criticism." Hodgson can be read as a direct rebuttal of Richards and the disciplinary society he represents and furthers:

> any discipline, ideally, should not be defined exactly by the category of the objects it studies nor even by the methods it uses, and still less by the form of its results. . . . Ideally, a discipline needs to be set off just to the degree that there is a body of independent questions that can be discussed in relative autonomy from other bodies of questions, at least according to some one perspective. In a discipline so set off, it cannot necessarily be decided in advance what forms of questions will be required or what sorts of methods will prove necessary to answer them effectively. (*VI*, 23)

Not least of what Hodgson is saying here is that scholarship produces publicly needed and useful forms of questioning and telling. Scholarly disciplines are not, in advance, determined by their methods or objects; rather they are constituted in the process of recognizing and preserving what is seen in the present age to be of human value while, at the same time, in their own practice, making a contribution to what they see as the public project of building cultures and civilizations.

Hodgson rightly argues that historical, humanistic scholarship must outline what is "normal" and "recurrent" to understand and value the "non-recurrent" as the moment of a value's emergence, of a contribution to standards of human behavior and organization—no matter whether these are recognized by the hegemony. For a moment this position differentiates Hodgson from Richards' urge to normalize by training. Ultimately, however, the two come together in aiming to normalize by educating in the values of the "non-recurrent," which, paradoxically, come to be the standard "no one dare ignore." Scholars modify and produce disciplines then, not for professional goals, not for antiquarian interest, and not for generation of easy "universal" knowledge. "We study Islamdom as a whole," Hodgson writes, "as a great complex historic event, as well as the various less extensive events that compose it, not primarily as examples of something more general but as something unre-current and unrepeatable, and as having importance precisely for that reason" (VI, 24). Hodgson is neither able to offer nor interested in offering historical accounts for the emergence of the "new." Like Auerbach in his reading of Vico, Hodgson's historical humanism comes up against an insoluble problem: important "originary" events in history cannot be explained by historical genetic method, and as a result, like Auerbach, he invokes the concept of the individual creator or genius to "explain" a reality that both contradicts and supports their projects. It limits their method but validates their humanism.

Historical events and scholarship intersect, for Hodgson, in-sofar as they are both functions of individuals in a public realm. Like Auerbach, Hodgson hopes scholarship can legiti-mate itself by promoting and sustaining public values: "Such inquiry remains legitimate public inquiry, and not just private antiquarianism, to the extent that the exceptional events were in some sense or other outstanding in the context of mankind generally, and not just for private individuals or groups" (VI, 24–25). Again, like Richards, but with important tactical dif-ferences, Hodgson wants to establish humanistic work in a public sphere to discipline and train a population in the sta-bility of cultural values and habits. From Hodgson's own work on "Islamicate" cultures, we can see that he understands the productive power of scholarly work to be critical, localized, and directed, and while it begins with a negative moment, always moves to establish some "actuality" in the realm of public culture.

Hodgson's concerns with the unavoidable necessity for such production in "greater" scholarship appears in his methodologi-cal statements about what constitutes a "civilization" in his-torical study. In an extremely rich passage he succeeds in calling into question the kind of position we see in Said's support for the Chomskian critic aligning himself with the "just" and in suggesting how much more complex and material the multiplicity of historical cultural existence is than one gathers even from Auerbach's conservative, revisionist humanism. Hodgson is worth quoting at length because in passages like these he brings one politically and intellectually important dimension of anthropological humanism to its limit:

> The reason for distinguishing a "civilization" cannot be a single, universal one, however; it must almost be special to each case. For no more than language does any one criterion necessarily determine a grouping that will be worth studying as a major large-scale culture. Even a localized culture, at least on the level of citied and literate life, cannot be defined simply in terms either of component traits or of particular families. In cross-section, a culture always appears as a pattern of lifeways received among mutually recognized family groups. Over time, it may be more fully defined as a relatively autonomous complex of interdependent cumulative traditions, in which an unpredictable range of family groups may take part. It forms an overall setting within which each particular tradition develops. But even within one relatively local culture, some traditions—a given school of painting, say, or a particular cult—may come to an end, and new ones may take their place. It is not possible to distinguish, in any absolute sense, authentic or viable from inauthentic or unviable traits in a culture, authentic from inauthentic traditions. . . . Over time, then, what sets off a culture as an integral unity in some degree is whatever makes for cultural continuity in that particular culture.
>
> On the wider and more rarefied level of what may be called a "civilization," cultural identity is even more problematic and what will make for continuity is even less predictably formulable. (*VI*, 32–33)

Scholarship of this sort has a positive critical content: it produces "knowledge," as well as "images," of what a "civilization" may be and does so in response to and out of precommitments to values it intends to further. But just as Said's project abandons its positive content to criticism, Hodgson loses criticism to positive content. Specifically, he refuses to carry to its conclusion his insight that what a "civilization is" is a function of how it is studied. Such a perception would involve a negation of humanism's sense that knowledge is produced to find the "truth" and would reveal that scholarly systems of representation are rhetorical, institutional, and hence, political apparatuses for putting certain sets of representations in place. Said, of course, allows us to see all this from his critical perspective; Hodgson, writing in the positive tradition from Kant to Renan to Richards, cannot work through his insight into disciplines' power. He insists on the possibility that method can align image with object and that concept, while historical, is not dependent for its effect and existence on its place in a network of concepts. But by refusing to make this radical critique, he gets himself into a dilemma typical of scholars trying to sustain humanism's contradictions.

His specific dilemma involves wanting to do a materialist analysis of history and cultural change but being forced by the needs of liberal humanism's ideology to explain change by means of idealist "great men" theories. Hodgson wants to answer Goethean genetico-historical questions in a more materialist manner than Auerbach: "how the Arabic language and with it so much of the Arabian background managed to emerge as a cultural framework in a society when they were so greatly disadvantaged" (VI, 43). Such questions move him ever and again near recognizing the active role systems of discourse, knowledge, and economy play in such change. But since his overarching project is to establish the noncontradictory, non-revolutionary unitary progression of the species' development, he cannot admit the role conflicting interests or systems might play in historical change. Such a move would weaken the claim of leading intellectuals for their own authority by suggesting that the so-called "progress of the species" is not so crucially a necessary function of their agency—as scholars, politicians, or artists. Hodgson does not "want" to reauthorize himself by "distorting" history. Humanism can persist, however, only when it does nothing to deauthorize the role of the "leading" figure.

Like Kant, Hodgson repeatedly comes up against "limits": the distortions of scholarship, the fragility of cultural achievement, the problematic "existence" of the very large-scale realities—"culture" and "civilization"—which "greater" scholars both somehow represent and constitute; yet, like Kant, his goal is to reassure us of the programmatic rationality of culture in history by putting our fate in the hands of inventive genius and scholarship. The contradiction is simple: on the one hand, he stresses the constitutive nature of discipline (admittedly in hermeneutic dialogue with the "other"), while, on the other hand, he *assumes* and *asserts* the rationality of both cultural and scholarly processes in which will and power, particularly as they appear in those "greater" and "ill-natured" men, are shown to have priority throughout his work.

In the second of these two positions, we can see that the contradiction is unavoidable. Kant and Hodgson always directly present the power and privilege of "ill-natured" men as guarantors of culture, yet they also always deny that constitutive power, desire, and interest rather than "reason" or "the pragmatic gift" make civilization possible. As a result, they not only lose sight of the danger to life with which their "humanism" infests society but also minimize the possibility of autonomous groups' successfully determining their lives, and so they reinforce culture's political and often oppressive role by obscuring it. The claims they make for the authority and leadership of ill-natured men in history devolve into an image of humanists' responsibility for preserving the "delicate flower" of spiritual achievement from and for those not among the privileged elite (*VI*, 38). For example, in a way that explicitly echoes Auerbach's invocation of Vico to reground the role of the leading humanistic intellectual in modernity, Hodgson insists that on the "humanistic historian" falls the burden for revealing the rationality of culture, for preserving and adapting its values as "tradition," and for furthering (or reestablishing) the value and importance of such discursive practices in modernity.

In his hurry to accept this burden, this guiding and disciplining role, Hodgson seems unaware of one additional burden historical humanism places on the intellectual. Many humanists can now acknowledge what Foucault's work suggests on one level, namely, that humanism involves an endless commitment to infinitely mediated commentary and interpretation, a proliferation of discourse perpetuated by the inability to arrive at the "goal" or "origins" it promises to reach or unveil. What they resist conceding, however, is that they too must see their "object," and "see it whole," see that assuredly pragmatic and rational culture through the killing, the death, and burial of those fleeting "irrationalisms" so certainly surpassed—from their point of view—by history. Unlike Auerbach, most humanists do not have the courage to see this complicity with that killing, which appears in humanism's aggressive self-imposition on others and its compulsion to totalize and exclude.

In an extraordinary passage, all these issues come together in Hodgson:

Ultimately all historical "why's" must be driven back . . . . to circumstances of hominid material and cultural ecology—the circumstances which determine that what would otherwise be the individual random "accidents" that shape history will not simply cancel each other out but will be reinforced and cumulatively lead in a single direction. However irrational human beings may be, in the long run their irrationalities are mostly random. It is their rational calculations that can be reinforced in continuing human groups and can show persisting orientation and development—even when they are calculations on misconceived presuppositions. Hence group interests have a way of asserting themselves. . . . But such . . . circumstances merely set the limits of what is possible. Within those limits the personal vision has its opportunity. For when habitual routine thinking will no longer work, it is the man or woman with imagination who will produce the new alternatives. At this point, the concerned conscience can come into play. It may or may not prove adequate to the challenge. But in either case, it is such personal vision that is the most human part of human history.

Hence the humanistic historian must concern himself with the great commitments and loyalties that human beings have born, within which every sort of norm and ideal has been made explicit; and he must concern himself with the interactions and dialogues in which these commitments have been expressed . . . Islamdom as a morally, humanly relevant complex of traditions, unique and irreversible, that can form [such a historian's] canvas. (VI, 26)

Hodgson's theory of the individual's conscience producing "alternatives" to maintain the "persisting orientation" of humanity could be seen to authorize scholars as leading figures on a historical model while more specifically grounding Said's claim for the critic's responsibility to imagine such alternatives. But if Said were consistent in his skepticism, he must negate Hodgson's humanism, which, no matter how generously, reveals its violence when it refers to "Islamdom" as a

"canvas" on which the scholar displays the power of "his" discourse. Despite Hodgson's moral and political "intention," despite his revisionary commitment to a tradition certain of
"reason's" direction of the species and scholarship's role in sustaining the idea and accomplishment of that "reason"—despite
his "conscious" commitments and aspirations, the slips in
Hodgson's language indicate how he is a function of discourses
and practices extending their disciplinary reach through him.
His generous reason and careful science justify reifying practices that subjugate the "Other" to the superior science of Western humanism and its own purposes. Once more, I suggest,
"reason" appears as at least dependent on power and, more
realistically, as power's projection, its innocent mask and its
most effective weapon for defense and expansion. Unable to
separate "truth" from its role in humanism's power-structure,
oppositional humanists blunt their own projects and ultimately replicate the "enemies'" structure.

In real history historicist humanism is limited in carrying
out its humane "intentions" by its genetic ties with the power
of the liberal state, with political, economic, cultural, and
sexual imperialism, and by its suppression of power and death
in its understanding of the world and its own global dispersion.
Since it is only within such a genealogy that the modern intellectual has (or is) a function, the question to be answered is
how to resist or minimize (as Hodgson has tried to do) the
effects of humanism's constituting power upon the minds,
bodies, and effects of disciplined intellectuals. The first step is
to emulate Hodgson's insistence on self-criticism but to insist
that it take on a material character and be turned back, as far
as possible, on the very practices and institutions that make
even such critical work possible.

Humanism excludes "irrationalisms" as inessential to the
progress of the species. It disapproves of revolution and discontinuity. As a result, does not its will to a unitary narration
impose itself by defining the "Other" as "in" or "out" of the
canon of spiritual, cultural achievement? While it normalizes
certain practices as "rational," it defines the *history* of the
"Other" in Western-made terms and, in so doing, vitiates Hodg-

son's avowed intention to deal with a multiplicity of cultures, histories, and canons. Hodgson's humanism rhetorically reveals the pluralistic value of these differences but submerges them in a less generous project of self-perpetuation.

Of course there are valuable differences between the way this process occurs in Hodgson. and in the most racist Orientalist. Those differences must be preserved and developed, if only to move along a different line within this genealogy. Recognizing the family resemblance, though, reveals how extensively and thoroughly aligned even the most humane intellectual work is with some of the most dangerous elements of our political and cultural order. Humanistic denials of this connection hinder its transformation. Such a transformation would be an important step in furthering the democratic self-representation and self-assertion of groups oppressed by the very ways Western humanistic institutions have "produced" them to bring them into the drama of our unitary history. The familiar move of appealing to humanism's own liberal values against its real practice is important but must be supplemented by the critical negation, on every local level, of finitude's own double negation. This second move is necessary because the strongest oppositional critical positions taken within humanism often have their effects blunted even while pointing to the need to do something else.

Said's and Hodgson's positions represent the fulfillment of the two major possibilities open to scholars working within and against that tradition. Each of the two marks the limits of the other. Said's radically active skepticism can be seen as an important corrective to the fundamental unexamined presupposition of even such highly reflexive positive human science as Hodgson's. We should not conclude from Said's work, though, that more nearly complete self-criticism would allow Hodgson to escape his dilemma. Rather, it puts forward what it sees as a completely different practice that essentially tries to "solve" the intellectual and political problems of such humanism by avoiding the massive scholarly recreations historicist humanism so depends on.

Said wants to establish criticism as a safeguard against the

cultural imperialism of liberal humanism by blatantly breaking the scholar's habitual analysis of meaning and pursuit of
truth. But, as we have seen, such a move excessively valorizes
the will, results in forms of projective self-representation, and
eventually reproduces another version of the figure of the leading intellectual. Indeed, I further suggest that one reason why
Said partially approves of figures like Hodgson and Richards is
that they are simply tactical variations on both the benevolent
intents and discursive extension of humanism. In other words,
while it is clear, I think, that Said could, without difficulty
both note the difference between Richards and Hodgson and
the notoriously racist orientalists he condemns, to notice their
similarities, their common ground, would involve extending
his critique from the figure of the orientalist to that broader
one of the representative, even oppositional, leading intellectual and the humanistic discourse it reflects and sustains.

Said's project in *Orientalism* and *The World, The Text, and
The Critic* consists, in part, in an attempt to relegitimate critical practice, especially as this is based in literary study, by
providing it with greater purpose and a broader range of topics
of public relevance. Essentially such a move, while seemingly
politically radical in its attack on both narrow professionalism
(which produces much seemingly irrelevant discourse) and
right-wing canon making, is, on another level, also conservative. Like Hodgson and Auerbach, Said must be seen as regrounding humanistic critical practice in the university. This
is worrisome because, as we have seen in the case of the academy's appropriation of Auerbach as a "sublime master," and as
I suggest in the previous chapter, Said's appropriation by the
academy might actually do more to sustain the professional
institution's structure and affiliations than to subvert or challenge them. Liberal, humanistic institutions have a way of
turning marginalized opposition to their advantage. The inscription of the oppositional critic within the genealogy of
"mendacious innocents" facilitates their institutionally conservative function.

In Richards, Auerbach, Hodgson, and Said we find more and
more evidence of humanistic finitude's uncanny ability to re-

new, reposition, and sustain itself. At the same time, we see, especially with and after Auerbach, how increasingly difficult that process has become and how, in the moments of its redeployment, elements of another kind of practice are emerging. This new practice changes the intellectual's relation to "truth" and "truth's" relation to the hegemony. We can see this, for example, in Hodgson's albeit inconsistent stress on the constitutive character of scholarship and in Said's valorization of will, which makes "truth" a function of a politically committed critical consciousness. In *Discipline and Punish*, Foucault contributes two other elements of importance: first, a critique of representation and, second, a way of thinking about intellectual work not dependent on the priority of the critical subject. I have followed Foucault's lead in trying to show how the "subjects" of critics like Richards and Auerbach are functions produced at the intersection of already given and emergent discourses, desires, and political purpose. Such a claim has two goals: to make the role of the leading intellectual less legitimate and authoritative in criticism and to attack humanism at its core, its insistence that the species depends on the leadership of ill-natured men—no matter what the cost.

VI

Foucault turned away from the limited materialism of such books as *The Birth of the Clinic* following the events of May 1968. It seems clear that he needed to move toward a greater materialism if he hoped to account for the way the powerful "human sciences" are taken up and distributed throughout society. As Foucault and others often suggest, May 1968 also confirmed his already developed distrust of centralized forms of power and led him both to analyze power in its positive distributions and, I would add, to provide whoever is in a struggle for self-determination (a struggle "against power," so to speak) with a way of understanding, that is, "grasping" the actualities of dispersed power to further their own resistance. Said's charge that Foucault is not enough concerned with resistance, is true on only one level. It does not take into account how Foucault's

work has become a tool for others to use in their own "resistance," their own local struggles.[24]

What would intellectuals be if not producers and guardians
of truth? For Nietzsche, the will to power and interpretation
are synonyms; one might add, for Foucault, the will of truth.
Not to produce or guard truth; the strong reader of Nietzsche
(through Beckett) insists his works are fictions written by discourses and forces functioning through his agency. But not
"fictions" as poems of Vichian imagination (à la Auerbach)
nor "interpretations" as commentary squeezing truth from the
human organism's bodily and intellectual finitude. Fictions,
rather, as tools for others; fictions presented as anarchic tools
for others to do with as they want. Fictions that rupture the
political alignment of intellectual discourse with "truth" and
"meaning" and release it publicly into what it has always been
in modern humanism: power and politics, positive production
that extends itself even through the critiques of revisionist,
oppositional intellectuals. What can we say, in these terms, of
all humanism, no matter how suspicious: "True discourse, liberated by the nature of its form from desire and power, is incapable of recognizing the will to truth which pervades it; and
the will to truth, having imposed itself upon us for so long, is
such that the truth it seeks to reveal cannot fail to mask it."[25]

While Richards institutionalized the will to truth in the
power of practical criticism to make literary study a discipline,
Auerbach, Hodgson, and Said metadiscursively and institutionally try to reconstitute "truth" as the product of discourse
and reinscribe the central device of the masking of truth: the
intellectual as the speaker of truth, as mandarin or archon
within or "against" institutions and in the name of their goals.
No one discipline, but disciplinarity itself, depends on their
redistribution of the intellectual's authority to speak for and
represent others. Whereas one discipline may control "the production of discourse" (DL, 224), the authorized existence of
the sublime or greater scholar/intellectual/teacher is a necessary and essential condition for all disciplinarity and its political consequences. When a member of a discipline speaks, the
entirety of that discipline is actuated. Said understands this of
Renan. When Hodgson makes the "greater scholar" an inventor

of productive methods and disciplines, humanistic discursivity, and its imperialism, its ability to take "man" as the measure in "Western" humanism, as the "object" of science—all this is globally reextended. Strangely, when Said praises Hodgson for generously narrating the actuality of Islamic cultures, he is praising Hodgson for functioning as a means of extending humanism's will to truth by making "Islam" recognizable as a valuable human project—this, as I have said, despite Hodgson's remarkable openness to so-called non-Western concepts. But recall these concepts too come to function inside humanistic discourse and do so without modifying its basic tenets in any way. In its "openness," humanism is, rather, simply being true to itself.

Discourses, like professions, are exclusionary: "none may enter into discourse on a specific subject unless he has satisfied certain conditions" (DL, 224–25). Disciplines aim to fulfill the anthropological goals of future reason: the vision of Kant, saddened in Auerbach, sustained in Hodgson, and displaced in Said. This liberal anthropological humanism is sometimes arrogant. Excluding most from the power of discourse and making most the objects of exclusion, differentiation, or training, this project not only restricts democratic self-determination but depends on real political power to sustain such structures, which can be found, metonymically, in the aspirations of intellectuals to sublime, masterly authority.

We have seen this occur differently in the cases of Richards, Said, Hodgson, and Auerbach. In Said's text, the individualized critical consciousness obscures the discursive underside functioning in and through the image of an originary subject that it itself produces. "The task of the founding subject," as Foucault puts it, "is to animate the empty forms of language with his objectives; through the thickness and inertia of empty things, he grasps intuitively the meanings lying within them." Such an image of the critic as subject "permits us to elude the reality of discourse" (DL, 227).

How to proceed? Foucault's response is to subvert the continuous forms of historical narration of a sort we find in Hodgson and Auerbach. His project has two parts: first, a critical study of the processes of exclusion and appropriation going on in disciplines. Such critical projects, like *Orientalism*, recognize the violence of discourses as they sustain themselves and constitute their objects. When carried through to the "origins" of all such discourse, critiques of this sort effectively challenge the unitary and proprietary practices and concepts in Richards "practical criticism," Auerbach's *Mimesis*, and Hodgson's "persistent orientation." They recognize how elements of humanistic disciplines oppress groups, classes, and sexes and deny their right to history and self-representation. Foucault's second tactic is more global and involves writing "genealogies" as a way of suggesting how the humanism of the present solidified and distributed itself, of showing how it is "random," "specific," and an "interpretation," that is, a structure of power/knowledge with particular consequences and alignments. For Foucault, these two tactics must be practiced together: "The difference between the critical and the genealogical enterprise is not one of object or field, but of point of attack, perspective and delimitation" (*DL*, 233).

I have tried to carry out precisely such a dual attack to show some of the limits in practical and humanistic critical discourse; above all, I have tried to show how these limits are reconstituted in widely dispersed but regular ways around the figure of the leading intellectual. I have stressed the latter because it seems to me essential to call it into question both in terms of the problematic nature of scholarly hierarchy and practice and because such leading figures are politically antidemocratic and essential to the preservation not just of humanistic discourses but its political institutionalization as well— from Kant to the vanguard party to the bureaucratic expert or political, intellectual leader. I have shown how the reformation of this figure has gone on in one segment of scholarly practice.

VII

In *Discipline and Punish*, Foucault brilliantly reveals how discourses and disciplines are marked primarily not by "negation," but by what he calls a "power of affirmation." Foucault's fictions, like *Discipline and Punish*, are ways of gripping the results and existence of the "power of affirmation": "the power of constituting domains of objects, in relation to which one can affirm or deny true or false propositions" (*DL*, 234). Foucault hopes to grasp this "modern" "regime of truth" in his fiction and, in the process, make available to others some way of "grasping" and "negating" the discursive "power of affirmation." This grasping is not primarily a hermeneutic "understanding" or an ironic demystification; it is a coming to grips with a positive reality. It is not an empty negation but the production of a political-intellectual device whose mode and value have little to do with historical reconstruction. It is not historicist and so not a part of the humanistic project of uncovering and presenting a "meaning" from a past "site" for future purposes. This humanistic project is politically and intellectually inappropriate. Its political liberalism is divisive, disciplinary, often oppressive and imperialistic; intellectually, it is self-contradictory, at best tragically belated, at most comically self-betraying. What is significant about it is its *power*.

Foucault's alternative practice involves critically unmasking this power and its consequences by drawing lines between and among surface events so that the resultant emergent figure, the shape emerging from the matrix, loses much of the authority and legitimacy, in a somewhat different configuration, that matrix had held and holds for intellectuals and others. But Foucault's tactics are double edged. Genealogy sketches another figure in the "past" but aims it at the present. The aim is always to discredit and offset the operations of power in *our* time. To accomplish this, genealogy reconfigures the archive of the past to show the complicity of our contemporary discourses' ancestors with patterns of subjugation, subjection, and discrimination carried out, in large part, by the representations and institutions produced by the power of anthropological discipline. Genealogy lets us see that the history of our human sciences is itself another deployment of disciplinary power that obscures humanism's darker side and replicates its basic compulsion: discourse about discourse to gain knowledge in the name of truth, of the species' fulfillment. Foucault's fictions help prisoners, women, gays, minorities, and even intellectuals avoid this gambit in their own interests insofar as they come to know them. When intellectuals represent, know, and discipline others, that self-knowledge is at least endangered and restricted, perhaps even destroyed. It is always "marginal" in relation to hegemonic, metropolitan interests, canons, and traditions. As long as criticism, no matter its "intent," sustains the latter, the former are endangered.

Foucault's alternative to the Whiggish history of prisons in *Discipline and Punish* is an example of how critical negation can aid in that self-determination, but it is also an example of the ambiguity that results from taking such a stance.

Foucault's uneasy relation to Rusche and Kirchheimer's great Frankfurt analysis, *Punishment and Social Structures*, illustrates precisely the dilemma Foucault's work involves. His ambiguous relation to Marxism, which is apparent in his interviews, his severe criticisms of the vanguard party and economistic reductionism, and his refusal to use the major categories of historical materialism in his works, reflect the fact that his genealogical procedures allow him to sketch past resemblances in such a way that relationships between what we normally think of as progressive texts and actions appear to have a necessary and problematic family relationship to blatantly reactionary forms of practice. The virtues of this procedure are clearest in the discussion with Maoists about popular justice. Its chief vice is its tendency to hypostatize the human sciences into a monolithic unity. Such a tendency duplicates humanism's own worst totalizing impulse to be reductive and coercive. This formal echo is hardly surprising given the extent and power of the enabling effects of the institutions of anthropologism. It merely shows how Foucault's own critical work is positioned in the discursive conflicts of our age. No one escapes them. More important, however, this programmatic reduction blinds Foucault to the historical moments in which an emergent alternate practice can be seen within humanism. Such a blindness threatens despair and paralysis because it postulates only Hölderlin and Kant as possible and equally unsatisfactory possibilities.

Foucault is certain that politics has changed and groups are struggling locally against power and that his own work can help those who want to use it. Yet his reduction forecloses on the possibility that useful tools for self-determination can be found within those spheres he designates by unitary terms like "the micro-physics of power" or "bio-power." Such an unjustified restriction has one other less than desirable effect: he makes his work the one important available source of intellectual tools for self-determining, struggling groups. To prevent both these possibilities Foucault's work should be modified and his thinking about the guerilla struggles of the specific or local intellectual extended so that the negative and democratic possibilities of the sort of critical work we have examined can be recognized and used. We must never forget that even genealogical work is made possible by what is conveniently marked by Nietzsche's negation of Kant. In addition, Foucault could move a bit in this direction by giving more weight to the "critical" dimension of his "critical genealogies." At the same time, however, since Foucault's *critical* project is concerned with discourses' exclusions and violations, it provides a way for him to be open to the critically and politically progressive contributions of revisionist and often Marxist work like Rusche and Kirckheimer's, which is, of course, finally humanistic. But we must not lose sight of Foucault's major contribution: Above all, the genealogical inscription of even such progressive, revisionist work within the humanistic will to truth means that its progressive political contributions to "self-determination" will come up against the limits of its discursive unconscious and so will produce undesirable coercive political consequences.

The "analytics of power" gives Foucault and others a way to redraw the lines of force among documents and events so that we can represent "discipline" as a derivative mask, a variation of the will to truth. As a result, we can draw connecting lines between such seemingly disparate phenomena as the leading intellectual, the vanguard party, Lukacs' *History and Class Consciousness*, and the state-supported liberal professions. But the point is simply that the "analytics of power" is a useful conceptual operator within a larger intellectual and political project. It is a more concrete and effective device than the concept "will to truth." Since, as Foucault would have it, "discipline" is an effective material tactical incarnation of the "will of truth," an "analysis" of it demands in turn another conceptual apparatus better able to limn and counter its material effects. "Discipline," it is well agreed, is for Foucault a tactic for producing truth on the body by creating our souls. The operations of normalization, exclusion, preservation, and self-defense typical of the humanisms we have examined can be said to rest on this set of tactics: "Beneath an apparently determined, impatient search for truth, one finds in classical torture the regulated mechanism of an ordeal; a physical challenge that must define the truth" (DP, 41). When the human sciences come to occupy the space of torture, the production of truth on the body, because dispersed into technics, is less visible but more extensive and productive. As it is further bureaucratized and supplemented by the devices of "bio-power" ("what brought life and its mechanisms into the realm of explicit calculations and made knowledge-power an agent of transformation of human life"), it not only becomes even more dispersed but produces its own particular form of local resistance. The Foucauldian inventions are like chemical baths for materializing local instantiations of power in ways that enable decentralized struggles against such power and for greater autonomy and self-determination.

The critical intellectual, then, should function in two ways: resist being implicated in this tortuous process of writing truth across the body of the population; use Foucault's inventions and any other available and appropriate resources to develop an image, a configuration of the particular form power/knowledge takes in one's locale. Do this last for two reasons: to succeed in weakening the forms of power in one region requires sketching it clearly; outlining one's genealogy and its present variations alone allows one to know where one has come from, what one's resources are, and how even they (and, hence, oneself) are constituted by the very intersecting lines of force converging in "one's" own practice and attitude. The goal should be to challenge and change specific forms of power by encouraging and furthering local struggles.

My aim here has been to try to carry this out within my own locale of literary study in the humanities. As Hodgson suggests one must do, I have posed a general question and then tried to find, not an answer, but *ways* and *means* to answer it: how to negate the practice of representative leadership, which, at least since Kant's "ill-natured men," has defined the function of intellectual life? The question is important for those who are uncomfortable with the human sciences' general tendency to thrive in and support what is, in the United States at least, an essentially imperial culture.²⁶ (Of course, there are exceptions everywhere. How they come into being is too difficult a question to be taken up here.) Auerbach's struggles make the importance of finding ways to deal with the question immediate for whoever shares Auerbach's unimpeachable commitment to respect for human difference, peace, and the ethics of self-sacrifice and love. What Auerbach learned, revealed, regretted, and tried but failed to overcome was the unavoidable complicity of historical humanism in fascism and the other Western barbarisms of the twentieth century. Auerbach's testimony is invaluable because, unlike Adorno, for example, he did not position himself outside that tradition, and so even after its exile of him he struggled to renew it against its own history. As he recognized, humanism had become its demonic self-fulfillment. What Kant foolishly but powerfully repressed returned most vengefully. I have sketched in Auerbach's situation at such length hoping that, ironically, the statement of such a master would not be without effect on the heirs of Richards and Kant who try, sadly, to sustain Kant's repression in any number of professional and ideological ways.

Discipline and Punish is particularly useful in trying to find some ways to answer this question that do not involve taking up too dogmatic a position, which take seriously the skeptical attitude Said formulates in "Secular Criticism." Specifically, the configuration of "power/knowledge" Foucault sketches in the technics of discipline suggest genealogical relationships between anthropological humanism and forms of bureaucratic and administrative organizations that effectively call into question the "natural" value and existence of man's "pragmatic gift" on which so much humanistic scholarship still depends even in its most linguistically subtle forms. In short, *Discipline and Punish* is an effective sketch of humanists' functions within material practices that both explains and countervenes humanists' insistence, in practice if not theory, upon the originary nature of the "subject." Also, Foucault helps us see that the institution and extension of the anthropological attitude depends on graspable materialities, on those institutions that, so to speak, make Renan possible. The result of this figure is that historical humanism's self-legitimating claims to subordinate all will to reason for the species' perfection can be contested. The "origins" of the claims in specific material and discursive practices can be traced out so that the exaltation of pragmatic reason can be challenged as a form of power inscribed within a political structure of desire and interest. In short, humanism loses its benign and seductive allure.

Foucault also adds, as I suggested in the previous chapter, another operative concept useful for answering this question I pose: the "regime of truth." One of many things at stake in this question, as it is somewhat differently in Said's "Secular Criticism," is how critical intellectuals should work in relation to an essentially imperial and oppressive hegemony. A full analysis of the major interrelations between state, corporation, and ruling class, on the one hand, and university intellectuals, on the other, is beyond the scope of this project. I have shown part of the structure that sustains these interrelationships. A "regime of truth" is constituted by the operation of discursive and institutional practices for producing knowledge within the particular political structure of interests, power, and desire dominant at a given time. The representative or leading intellectual functions, in some significant way, to sustain the humanistic disciplines and so the current "regime of truth." This figure legitimates the humanistic drive to representative knowledge, which is, as we know, most often produced by the incremental contributions of anonymous laborers. The aim of such a critical genealogy is to challenge publicly the legitimacy of its self-history, to make visible its integral affiliations with the hegemonic political and cultural structure, and to carry out a different practice whose results are not in the interests of the present academic configuration. The critical effect should be to develop an image of the latent function of "representative intellectuals" and so "negate" their practice and its structures. Once this image emerges, it should be harder for these intellectuals to go about quietly functioning within and supporting the "regime of truth" without being recognized and challenged.

For Foucault, much of what I have been saying comes together in a passage from "The body of the condemned":

The overthrow of these "micro-powers" does not, then obey the law of all or nothing; it is not acquired once and for all by a new control of the apparatuses nor by a new functioning or a destruction of the institutions; on the other hand, none of its localized episodes may be inscribed in history except by the effects that it induces on the entire network in which it is caught up.

Perhaps, too, we should abandon a whole tradition that allows us to imagine that knowledge can exist only where the power relations are suspended and that knowledge can develop only outside its injunctions, its demands and its interests. . . . We shall admit rather that power produces knowledge . . . that power and knowledge directly imply one another; that there is no power relation without the correlative constitution of a field of knowledge, nor any knowledge that does not presuppose and constitute at the same time power relations. Those "power-knowledge relations" are to be analysed, therefore, not on the basis of a subject of knowledge who is or is not free in relation to the power system, but, on the contrary, the subject who knows, the objects to be known and the modalities of knowledge must be regarded as so many effects of these fundamental implications of power-knowledge and their historical transformations. In short, it is not the activity of the subject of knowledge that produces a corpus of knowledge, useful or resistant to power, but power-knowledge, the processes and struggles that traverse it and of which it is made up, that determines the forms and possible domains of knowledge. (DP, 28)

Systems and products of knowledge become representations generated by the roles of discourse serving the regime of truth. "Truth" is its humanistic cover. Attacks on the regime cannot be made in the name of this same "truth" but only in the form of knowledge asserting local "counter-truths" against the regime to modify it or resist it. Critical scholarship should seize the power function of "truth" and sophistically enlist it for political work intended not only to reveal the dark side of humanism's oppression but also to knock the underpinnings from humanism and the dominant regimes it supports. Criticism must be negative, and its negation should be of two sorts: invested with knowledge and the skills to produce more, it should destroy the local discursive and institutional formations of the "regime of truth," but this local negation will be most effective when aimed at necessary conditions for the extension of that regime, at those nodal points upon which humanism rests its own power and banks its own reserves. But this "negation" must have a "positive" content; it must carry out its destruction with newly produced knowledge directed not only against the centers of the anthropological attitude but, with an eye to its utility, to others in one's own locale and elsewhere.

The temptations to build a better world, to discover the truth about human life, to rely on genius, sublimity, mastery, and prophetic wisdom: even though all these must be put aside, they will recur for a long time. The emergent cannot be forced. Forceps in the hands of male medical experts—can this image have benign force any longer? Such an appropriation of truth to political work, such a releasing of it from the shapeless, indeterminate background of the power structure of humanistic discourse might seem amoral or immoral. But the morality of humanism and its professionalization has worn out its welcome; it has announced its own betrayal of its own highest ideals, not only, as Auerbach would have had it, by helping produce fascism, but by being structurally and institutionally allied with other "masters" whose "morality" is indefensible and, above all, by relying always and everywhere on death for its own survival.

Notes

PREFACE

1. John Fekete, *The Critical Twilight: Explorations in the Ideology of Anglo-American Literary Theory from Eliot to McLuhan* (London: Routledge and Kegan Paul, 1977).

2. Francis Mulhern, *The Moment of 'Scrutiny'* (London: New Left Books, 1979).

3. See, for example, Stephen Toulmin, *Human Understanding: The Collective Use and Evolution of Concepts* (Princeton: Princeton University Press, 1972).

4. Edward W. Said, *Covering Islam* (New York: Pantheon Books, 1982).

5. Of course a great deal of such countervailing work has been done by a number of people. Although, as will become clear in chapter 6, I have some reservations about his position, the work of Noam Chomsky is exemplary. See, for example, *American Power and the New Mandarins: Historical and Political Essays* (New York: Vintage Books, 1969); *Towards a New Cold War: Essays on the Current Crisis and How We Got There* (New York: Pantheon Books, 1982); and *The Fateful Triangle* (Boston: South End Press, 1983).

6. See Paul A. Bové, "Closing Up the Ranks: Xerxes' Hordes Are at the Pass," *Contemporary Literature* (Spring 1985), 26:91–106.

7. Walter Jackson Bate, "The Crisis in English Studies," *Harvard Magazine* (Sept.–Oct. 1982), 85:46–53.

8. The second and third volumes of *Histoire de la sexualité* appeared too late for me to incorporate their considerable achievement into this text. See Michel Foucault, *L' usage des plaisirs* and *Le souci de soi* (Paris: Edition Gallimard, 1984).

9. "Powers and Strategies: An Interview with Michel Foucault conducted by the *Révoltes Logiques* collective" (1977), reprinted in Paul Patton and Meaghan Morris, eds. and translators, *Michel Foucault: Power, Truth, Strategy* (Sydney, Australia: Feral Publication, 1979), p. 53.

1. MENDACIOUS INNOCENTS

1. *The Cantos of Ezra Pound* (New York: New Directions, 1970), 58–60, hereafter cited by page number in my text.

2. Edward W. Said, *The World, the Text, and the Critic* (Cambridge Mass.: Harvard University Press, 1983), pp. 1–30. Said's position, I will show, is a version of Kung's.

3. Harold Bloom, ed., *Selected Writings of Walter Pater* (New York: Signet Books, 1974), p. 135.

4. Friedrich Nietzsche, *On the Genealogy of Morals*, trans. Walter Kaufman (New York: Vintage Books, 1969), hereafter cited in my text as *GM*.

5. See Daniel O'Hara, *The Romance of Interpretation* (New York: Columbia University Press, 1985).

6. For some of the most important recent writing on genealogy, see Paul de Man, "Genesis and Genealogy in Nietzsche's *Birth of Tragedy*," *Allegories of Reading* (New Haven, Conn.: Yale University Press, 1979), pp. 79–102; Michel Foucault, "Nietzsche, Genealogy, History," in Donald F. Bouchard, ed., *Language, Counter-Memory, Practice* (Ithaca, N.Y.: Cornell University Press, 1977), 139–64; Edward W. Said, *Beginnings* (New York: Basic Books, 1976), pp. 158ff; Jacques Derrida, "'Genesis and Structure' and Phenomenology," *Writing and Difference*, trans. Alan Bass (Chicago: University of Chicago Press, 1978), pp. 154–68; and Gilles Deleuze, *Nietzsche*, trans. Hugh Tomlinson (New York: Columbia University Press, 1983).

7. See Alexander Nehamas, *Nietzsche: Life as Literature* (Cambridge, Mass.: Harvard University Press, 1985) and Foucault, "Nietzsche, Genealogy, History," pp. 16off.

8. Foucault, "Nietzsche, Genealogy, History," p. 161.

9. See Jacques Derrida, *Spurs, Nietzsche's Styles*, trans. Barbara Harlow (Chicago: University of Chicago Press, 1979), pp. 55–63.

10. See, e.g., Edward W. Said, *Beginnings: Intention and Method* (New York: Basic Books, 1975), where Said shows the incessant dialectical struggle to maintain unity of purpose in any authorial project.

11. See, for example, Michel Foucault, ed., *I, Pierre Riviére*, trans. Frank Jellinek (New York: Pantheon Books, 1975) and *Herculine Barbin*, introduced by Michel Foucault, trans. Richard McDougall (New York: Pantheon Books, 1980).

12. The celebrated oppositional intellectual so common in our media-based era is not explicitly present "at the origins," so to speak, of Nietzsche's work. See Regis Debray, *Teachers, Writers, Celebrities: The Intellectuals of Modern France*, trans. David Macey (London: New Left Books, 1981); Paul A. Bové, "Celebrity and Betrayal," *Minnesota Review*, (Fall 1983), NS 21:72–91; and Stanley Aronowitz, "The Critic as Star," *Minnesota Review*, NS 9 (Fall 1977), 71–111.

13. See, for example, Martin Heidegger, *Nietzsche: The Will to Power as Art*, trans. David Krell (New York: Harper and Row, 1979), esp. pp. 3–6 and 59–66.

14. Michel Foucault, *The Order of Things*, Foreword to the English Edition, trans. anón. (New York: Vintage Books, 1973), pp. xiii–xiv.

15. Foucault's project has been adequately described by any number of scholars. See, for example, Edward W. Said, "Criticism Between System and Culture," *The World, the Text, and the Critic*, pp. 178–225; Hayden White, "Michel Foucault," in John Sturrock, ed., *Structuralism and Since* (Oxford: Oxford University Press, 1979), pp. 81–115; Jonathan Arac, "The Function of Foucault at the Present Time," *Humanities in Society* (Winter 1980), 3(1):73–86; Karlis Racevkis, *Michel Foucault and the Subversion of Intellect* (Ithaca, N.Y.: Cornell University Press, 1983); Hubert L. Dreyfus and Paul Rabinow, *Michel Foucault: Beyond Structuralism and Hermeneutics*, 2nd. ed. (Chicago: University of Chicago Press, 1983); and Pamela Major-Poetzl, *Foucault* (Chapel Hill: University of North Carolina Press, 1983).

16. See Pierre Bourdieu and Jean-Claude Passeron, *La reproduction* (Paris: Les Édition de minuit, 1970), esp. pp. 85ff.

17. For a different sense of Foucault's relation to genealogy, Nietzsche, and interpretation, see Dreyfus and Rabinow, *Michel Foucault*, pp. 122–30.

18. For a sense of this *amor fati* in the best of modern criticism, see Sacvan Bercovitch, *The American Jeremiad*, (Madison: The University of Wisconsin Press, 1978), especially its final pages on Hawthorne.

19. Michel Foucault, *Discipline and Punish*, trans. Alan Sheridan (New York: Pantheon Books, 1977), p. 19; hereafter cited in my text as *DP*.

20. Edward W. Said, *Orientalism* (New York: Pantheon Books, 1978), pp. 131–32, 203–04, 337, 343; hereafter cited in my text as *O*.

21. See Edward W. Said, *The Question of Palestine* (New York: Times Books, 1979) and *Covering Islam* (New York: Pantheon Books, 1982).

22. See Daniel O'Hara, "Criticism Worldly and Otherworldly: Edward W. Said and the Cult of Theory," *boundary 2* (Spring/Fall 1984), 12(3) and 13(1) pp. 300–25.

23. *The World, the Text, and the Critic*, pp. 1–30.

24. The quotation from Gramsci is to be found in Valentine Gerratana, ed., *Quaderni del Carcere* (Turin: Einaudi Editore, 1975), 2:1363.

25. Let us not forget, that many orientalists were quite clear about their discipline's complicity with political and cultural imperialism. We are not concerned here simply with the benevolent but misguided few.

26. Edward W. Said, "Opponents, Audiences, Constituencies, and Community," *Critical Inquiry* (Sept. 1982), 9: esp. 22f.

27. Surely we are not meant to think that literally each individual

314 I. MENDACIOUS INNOCENTS

essay or book forces a realignment of the compasses; most, as we all well know, only settle into place.

28. Some reviewers of *Orientalism* have simplistically suggested that Said does with orientalism what orientalists do with the "orient," that is, produce an undifferentiated "object" about which he unjustifiably generalizes. See Daniel O'Hara, "The Romance of Interpretation," *boundary 2* (1980), 8:259–84, for a discussion of this and other questionable charges made against *Orientalism* by its initial literary reviewers. For a discussion of the continuing prejudiced attacks on Said, see Paul A. Bové, "Closing up the Ranks: Xerxes' Hordes Are at the Pass," *Contemporary Literature*, (1985), 26:91–106. For an intelligent analysis of Said, see James Clifford's review of *Orientalism* in *History and Theory* (1980), 19:204–23.

29. Said suggested as much in a response to my presentation at the University of Minnesota conference on "The Mediation of Received Values," held in October 1984.

30. For a further discussion of this counterpractice, see Paul A. Bové, "The End of Humanism: Michel Foucault and the Power of Disciplines," *Humanities in Society* (Winter 1980), 3(1):23–40. It would be a mistake, I believe, to argue that Foucault operates as a hegemonic intellectual within his texts. Above all, one should not assert that he assumes the role of the prescriptive or universal intellectual—a role he frequently eschewed. For a rather comic illustration of Foucault's reluctance to play the game of universal intellectual, see Colin Gordon, ed., "Questions on Geography," *Power/Knowledge*, trans. by Colin Gordon et al. (New York: Pantheon Books, 1980), pp. 63–77.

31. On the repressive effect of culture, see Said's "Secular Criticism," esp. pp. 9–16.

2. A FREE, VARIED, AND UNWASTEFUL LIFE

1. Stephen Potter, *The Muse in Chains: A Study in Education* (London: Jonathan Cape, 1937); E. M. W. Tillyard, *The Muse Unchained* (London: Bowes and Bowes, 1958), hereafter referred to respectively in my text as *MC* and *MU*. For two books that attempt to elucidate the ideology and practice of English criticism, see John Fekete, *The Critical Twilight* (London: Routledge and Kegan Paul, 1977), esp. pp. 25–37 on Richards; and Francis Mulhern, *The Moment of 'Scrutiny'* (London: New Left Books, 1979). For a discussion of the more recent history of the American institution, see Frank Lentricchia, *After the New Criticism* (Chicago: University of Chicago Press, 1980).

2. Evidence that such a book is seriously needed can be found in Terry Eagleton's short course in "The Rise of English," *Literary Theory: An Introduction* (Minneapolis: University of Minnesota Press, 1983), pp. 17–53.

3. Muriel Bradbrook, "I. A. Richards at Cambridge," in R. Brower et al., eds., *I. A. Richards: Essays in Honor* (New York: Oxford University Press, 1973), p. 74.

4. William Empson, "The Hammer's Ring," in Brower et al., eds., *I. A. Richards*, p. 74.

5. W. K. Wimsat, "I. A. Richards: What To Say About a Poem," in Brower et al., eds., *I. A. Richards*, p. 103.

6. Michel Foucault, *The Order of Things*, trans. anon. (New York: Random House, 1970), hereafter cited in my text as *OT*.

7. I. A. Richards and C. K. Ogden, *The Meaning of Meaning* (New York: Harcourt Brace Jovanovich, 1923), p. 18. I shall also refer to the following works by Richards: *Principles of Literary Criticism* (London: Routledge and Kegan Paul, 2nd ed., 1926; rpt. 1976); *Practical Criticism* (London: Routledge and Kegan Paul, 1929; rpt. 1976); *Speculative Instruments* (Chicago: The University of Chicago Press, 1955); hereafter cited respectively as *MM*, *PLC*, *PC*, and *SI*.

8. I cannot go into this at length here, but it is a crucial topic. For some sense of what is at stake, see John Fekete on Richards and Alvin Gouldner, *The Coming Crisis in Western Sociology* (New York: Basic Books, 1970), esp. pp. 313–20.

9. Michel Foucault, *Discipline and Punish*, trans. Alan Sheridan (New York: Pantheon Books, 1977); *The History of Sexuality:* volume I, *An Introduction*, trans. Robert Hurley (New York: Pantheon Books, 1978); hereafter cited respectively as *DP* and *HS*.

10. I am indebted to Barbara Jetton, a former graduate student of the eighteenth century at Columbia, for pointing out these parallels. In response to a presentation of part of this material at the MLA convention, Gerald Graff rightly objected that I had not explained how the revival of the lecture format "recentralized authority." The answer, of course, is, that it did not do it automatically, but as a close reading of the memoirs published by Richards' students makes clear, Richards consciously employed pedagogical techniques in the lecture hall that reinforced his own position of authority. As Bradbrook tells us, for example, Richards was not above using his authority in front of an overly crowded lecture hall to make a student feel his or her inadequacy as a reader—especially in comparison to his own sublimely developed skills at both discovering and controlling ambiguities. Discussing the spectacle of classroom performance is, of course, quite difficult, especially secondhand. No doubt many former students of Richards will object to my comment because they have their own stories to tell. There does, however, seem to be some evidence in all of our experience as teachers of what I am trying to get at here. Students admire their professors' and sometimes their colleagues' better developed skills as readers and writers, and the effect of this, in part, is that they will be moved to aspire to such higher sensibility and subtlety. In

316 2. A FREE, VARIED, AND UNWASTEFUL LIFE

other words, the fact that in some way we might "all" do something like what I am trying to suggest was central to Richards' method merely confirms the success and power of Richards' pedagogical and critical project. We are all to some extent his heirs.

11. See John Paul Russo, "A Study in Influence: The Moore-Richards Paradigm," *Critical Inquiry* (1979), 5:683–712.

12. See, e.g., Nikolas Rose "The Psychological Complex: Mental Measurement and Social Administration," *Ideology and Consciousness* (1979), No. 5:5–70.

13. I. A. Richards, *Coleridge on Imagination*, 3rd ed. (London: Routledge and Kegan Paul, 1962); first edition, 1934.

14. Murray Krieger, *The New Apologists for Poetry* (Bloomington: Indiana University Press, 1963), pp. 57 ff.

15. Edward W. Said, *Orientalism* (New York: Pantheon Books, 1978).

16. See Jonathan Arac, *Commissioned Spirits: The Shaping of Social Motion in Dickens, Carlyle, Melville, and Hawthorne* (New Brunswick, New Jersey: Rutgers University Press, 1979).

17. I say "might put it" since Said for reasons I shall explain in chapter 6, finds in Richards an exception to the "illiberality" of the Western representation of the Orient. See *Orientalism*, p. 254.

18. I. A. Richards, *Beyond* (New York: Harcourt, Brace, Jovanvich, 1974).

19. See, e.g., Harold Bloom, *A Map of Misreading* (New York: Oxford University Press, 1975).

20. Michel Foucault, "What Is an Author?", trans. Donald F. Bouchard and Sherry Simon, in Donald J. Bouchard, ed., *Language, Counter-Memory, Practice*, (Ithaca, N.Y.: Cornell University Press, 1977), p. 133.

21. Foucault, "What Is an Author?", p. 135.

22. See Jonathan Culler, *Structuralist Poetics* (Ithaca, N.Y.: Cornell University Press, 1976), and Gerald Graff, *Literature Against Itself* (Chicago: University of Chicago Press, 1979). See also Paul A. Bové, "The Poetics of Coercion: An Interpretation of Literary Competence," *boundary 2* (1976), 5:263–284, and Bové, a review of Graff, *Criticism* (1980), 22:77–81, and "Variations on Authority," *The Yale Critics*, ed. Jonathan Arac et al. (Minneapolis: University of Minnesota Press, 1983), pp. 3–19.

23. Fekete, *The Critical Twilight*, pp. 25–36.

24. John Brenkman, "Mass Media: From Collective Experience to the Culture of Privatization," *Social Text* (1979), No. 1:107.

3. LAST OF THE LATECOMERS, I

1. I refer to the following works by Auerbach throughout my text. They will be cited parenthetically as indicated: *Mimesis: The Representation of Reality in Western Literature*, trans. Willard R. Trask

(Princeton: Princeton University Press, 1953) (*M*); *Scenes From the Drama of European Literature*, trans. Ralph Manheim et al. (Gloucester, Mass.: Meridian Books, 1959) (*SD*); *Dante: Poet of the Secular World*, trans. Ralph Manheim (Chicago: University of Chicago Press, 1961) (*D*); "Philology and *Weltliteratur*," trans. Maire and Edward Said, *The Centennial Review* (Winter 1969), 13(1):1–17 (PW); and *Literary Language and Its Public in Late Latin Antiquity and in the Middle Ages*, trans. Ralph Manheim (Princeton: Princeton University Press, 1965) (*LL*).

2. A number of critics have commented on *Mimesis* as an "aesthetic object" to praise its beauties, to demystify its "historicism," or to "deconstruct" its metaphysics. See, for example, Timothy Bahti, "Vico, Auerbach, and Literary History," in Giorgio Tagliacozzo, ed., *Vico Past and Present* (Atlantic Highlands, N.J.: Humanities Press, 1981), pp. 249–66; Charles Breslin, "Philosophy or Philology: Auerbach and Aesthetic Historicism," *Journal of the History of Ideas* (1961), 22:369–81; Wilhelm Wolfgang Holdheim, "Auerbach's *Mimesis*: Aesthetics as Historical Understanding," *CLIO* (Winter 1981), 10(2):143–54; and David Carroll, "*Mimesis* Reconsidered: Literature, History, Ideology," *Diacritics* (Summer 1975), 5:5–12.

3. Edward W. Said makes precisely this observation in *The World, the Text, and the Critic* (Cambridge, Mass.: Harvard University Press, 1982), p. 8.

4. See Fredric Jameson, "Demystifying Literary History," *NLH* (Spring 1974), 5(3):605–12, where Jameson offers a reading of Auerbach's method as "mediation" able "to hold apparent antitheses together within the unity of a single thought" (p. 606). Jameson's characterization seems to overstate Auerbach's conclusions about the sort of synthesis his method can provide. "Mediation" suggests that synthesis produces "scientific" knowledge about the ontologically and socially "real." Auerbach, it seems to me, is much more tentative and anguished about the limited claims to truth and knowledge his modern perspectivism allows.

5. This appears to be a rather pathos-ridden, idealistic, humanistic vision, one whose effect is surely open to question. The ablest critical defender of this position on the scene today is Charles Altieri. See *Act and Quality* (Amherst: University of Massachusetts Press, 1981) and "An Idea and Ideal of a Literary Canon," *Critical Inquiry* (1983), 10(1):37–60.

6. For an account on how this process of specialization has continued and for an evocation of the critical diminishment that has resulted, see Wallace Martin, "Introduction," *The Yale Critics: Deconstruction in America* (Minneapolis: University of Minnesota, 1983), pp. xv–xxxvii, esp. pp. xxxvi–vii.

7. See especially Friedrich Meinecke, *Historism: The Rise of a New Historical Outlook*, trans. J. E. Anderson, revised H. D. Schmidt (Lon-

don: Routledge and Kegan Paul, 1972), hereafter cited parenthetically in my text as *H*.

8. See Carlo Antoni, *From History to Sociology: The Transition in German Historical Thinking*, trans. Hayden White (Detroit: Wayne State University Press, 1959).

9. See especially Max Horkheimer and Theodor W. Adorno, *Dialectic of Enlightment*, trans. John Cumming (New York: The Seabury Press, 1972).

10. Quoted in Harry Levin, "Two *Romanisten* in America," in Donald Fleming and Bernard Bailyn, eds., *The Intellectual Migration: Europe and America, 1930–1960* (Cambridge, Mass.: Harvard University Press, 1969), pp. 467–68. It is typical of the situation originally confronting Auerbach that in the following paragraphs Levin, warned by Auerbach of the ambition of his project, nonetheless comments on the specialized and antiquarian nature of Auerbach's ongoing research.

11. Helmut A. Hatzfield, review of *Mimesis, Romance Philology* (May 1949), 2:333–38; Ludwig Edelstein, review of *Mimesis, MLN* (June 1950), 65:426–31. In this section of my essay I rely heavily on reviews of *Mimesis* as a way of judging informed critical response to the work. I reject out of hand the idealizing and mystifying view that the reservations expressed by the reviewers are simply typical of the "carping" style of American reviewers (many of the reviews of Auerbach are very serious, indeed) and that, somehow, mysteriously, instantaneously upon its appearance, before it entered into the concrete and material networks for judging, distributing, interpreting, and translating academic books, *Mimesis* was recognized as a "classic." "Classics" are made, not born, despite how nice it would be to think the opposite. They do not appear like Minerva but are a function of real relations of interest, power, and needs. Of course, I am not claiming that the reviews and other published responses to Auerbach tell the whole story of his place in the academy and how it came about. There are the related matters of teaching, lecturing, gossip, patronage, and publication, as well as the efficacy of Auerbach's own strategies for positioning himself and his work, some of which I have glanced at in the previous pages. As a literary critic, however, I have an unfortunate predisposition to examine texts and so have taken the written material about Auerbach as a point of departure for my discussion.

12. Hatzfield, review of *Mimesis*, p. 333.

13. Edelstein, review of *Mimesis*, p. 426.

14. Hatzfield, review of *Mimesis*, p. 338.

15. Charles Muscatine, review of *Mimesis, Romance Philology* (May 1956), 9(4):448–57.

16. René Wellek, "Auerbach's Special Realism," *Kenyon Review* (1954), 16(2):306.

17. Muscatine, review of *Mimesis*, p. 455.

18. Wellek, "Auerbach's Special Realism," p. 299.

19. Harry Levin, *The Gates of Horn* (New York: Oxford University Press, 1966), p. 73.

20. Muscatine, review of *Mimesis*, p. 448.

21. Levin, "Two *Romanisten* in America," p. 484.

22. Frank Kermode, "Dante," *New Statesman* (January 7, 1966), pp. 15–16.

23. Wellek, "Auerbach's Special Realism," p. 299.

24. Muscatine, review of *Mimesis*, pp. 449, 456.

25. Breslin, "Philosophy of Philology," p. 381.

26. Ulrich Leo, review of *Mimesis*, *Comparative Literature* (Winter 1949), 1(1):95.

27. Wellek, "Auerbach's Special Realism," p. 300.

28. Wellek, "Auerbach's Special Realism," p. 305.

29. Muscatine, review of *Mimesis*, p. 456.

30. Levin, "Two *Romanisten* in America," p. 479.

31. Edward W. Said, *Beginnings: Intention and Method* (New York: Basic Books, 1975), pp. 68–69, 72–73, 76.

32. See Paul A. Bové, "R. P. Blackmur and the Job of the Critic: Turning from the New Criticism," *Criticism* (Fall 1983), 25:359–80.

33. Levin, "Two *Romanisten* in America," p. 476. Spitzer's letter to Levin is dated August 17, 1951.

34. Levin, "Two *Romanisten* in America," p. 483.

35. These two terms are central to a tradition of acclaim for Auerbach begun, as far as I can tell, by Wellek.

36. The ur-demonstration of this process is, of course, Marx's *Critique of Hegel's Philosophy of Right*, Joseph O'Malley, ed., trans. Joseph O'Malley and Annette Jolin (Cambridge, England: Cambridge University Press, 1970), esp. pp. 12–13, 20, 25ff., and 123.

37. For more on this, see my chapter 5 "Intellectuals at War" and Daniel O'Hara, "The Romance of Interpretation," *boundary 2* (Spring 1980), 8:259–84.

38. Fritz Ringer, *The Decline of the German Mandarins: The German Academic Community 1890–1933* (Cambridge, Mass.: Harvard University Press, 1969), hereafter cited parenthetically in my text as *GM*.

39. Gordon Craig, *Germany 1866–1945* (Oxford: Oxford University Press, 1978), pp. 479–80.

40. Peter Gay, *Weimar Culture: The Outsider as Insider* (New York: Harper and Row, 1968), p. 23.

41. Quoted in Klemens von Klemperer, *Germany's New Conservatism: Its History and Dilemma in the Twentieth Century* (Princeton, N.J.: Princeton University Press, 1957), p. 172.

42. See also Marx, *A Critique of Hegel's Philosophy of Right*, pp. 44f.

43. On the ideological and social contradictions of this moment, especially as they affect the professoriat, see George Lukacs, "The Ide-

ology of the German Intelligentsia in the Imperialist Period," in Rodney Livingstone, ed., *Essays on Realism*, trans., David Ferbach (Cambridge, Mass.: The MIT Press, 1981), pp. 78–90.

44. George Iggers, *The German Conception of History: The National Tradition of Historical Thought from Herder to the Present* (Middletown, Conn.: Wesleyan University Press, 1968), pp. 177–95.

45. Antoni, *From History to Sociology*, pp. 77ff.

46. Iggers, *The German Conception of History*, p. 191.

47. Iggers, *The German Conception of History*, p. 194.

48. See Bahti, "Vico, Auerbach, and Literary History," a fine reading of Vico in Auerbach that should perhaps be supplemented by further investigation into the influence of Meinecke, Troeltsch, and Croce on Auerbach's use of Vico.

49. Aristotle, "The Poetics," in S. H. Butcher, *Aristotle's Theory of Poetry and Fine Art, with a Critical Text and Translation of The Poetics*, fourth edition (New York: Dover, 1951), p. 35 (IX, 3).

50. Butcher, *Aristotle*, p. 192.

51. See W. K. Wimsatt, "The Concrete Universal," *The Verbal Icon* (Lexington: University of Kentucky Press, 1954), pp. 69–84.

52. Butcher, *Aristotle*, p. 150.

53. On the history of these affiliations, see George L. Mosse, *The Crisis of German Ideology: Intellectual Origins of the Third Reich* (New York: Grosset and Dunlap, 1964), and Fritz Stern, *The Politics of Cultural Despair* (Berkeley: University of California Press, 1961).

54. On their failure to contain the ideological contradictions of postwar Weimar society, see Lukacs, f.n. 43.

55. I am indebted here to Ringer's resonant interpretation of Mannheim's project in *GM*, pp. 426 ff. See also Theodor Adorno, "Sociology of Knowledge and Its Consciousness," in Andrew Arato and Eike Gebhardt, eds., *The Essential Frankfurt School Reader*, (New York: Seabury, 1982), pp. 452–65.

56. Of course, this is a very old and persistent idea. See, for example, Althusser's discussion of Montesquieu's claim that political scientists are alone able to bring legislation in line with the laws of human action, *Montesquieu, Rosseau, Marx: Politics and History*, trans. Ben Brewster (London: New Left Books, 1982), esp. pp. 17–30. For modern versions of theories privileging intellectual or "New Class" discourse and practice, see also Basil Bernstein's discussion of extended variants in "Elaborated and Restricted Codes," in J. J. Gumperz and D. Hymes, eds., *American Anthropologist* (1966), 6(2):55–69; and Alvin Gouldner's, *The Dialectic of Ideology and Technology* (New York: Seabury, 1976), pp. 23–66, and *The Future of Intellectuals and the Rise of the New Class* (New York: Seabury, 1979), passim.

57. Meinecke's *Historism* is perhaps only the most monumental and the best known.

58. See, for example, Mosse, *The Crisis of German Ideology;* and Stern, *The Politics of Despair.*

59. That the very success of the profession in the 1950s and 1960s led, in part, to such things as student revolts, which accelerate its later crisis, does not deny the sense of my argument.

4. THE LAST OF THE LATECOMERS, II

1. Erich Auerbach, "Vico and Aesthetic Historism," *Scenes from the Drama of European Literature,* p. 187. Hereafter abbreviated in my text as VAH.

2. George Iggers, *The German Conception of History,* p. 216.

3. Quoted in Iggers, *The German Conception of History,* p. 217; my emphasis.

4. See Said, *The World, the Text, and the Critic,* pp. 8ff.

5. For a study of how difficult it is to escape this structure of power/ interest, see my chapter 5, "Intellectuals at War."

6. For one example of such humanistic work, see Charles Altieri, *Act and Quality,* and footnote 5 above.

7. Of course, it is not possible to carry out such a full historical analysis. See Friedrich Meinecke, *Machiavellism: The Doctrine of Raison d'Etat and Its Place in Modern History,* trans. Douglas Scott, intro. W. Stark (New York: Praeger, 1965), rptd. from (New Haven, Conn.: Yale University Press, 1957); this text, like so much of Meinecke's work, constituted a large part of Auerbach's context in this essay. See also Antoni, *From History to Sociology;* and Iggers, *The German Conception of History,* pp. 174–228; and Ringer, *GM,* pp. 100–01, 341–49.

8. Meinecke, *Machiavellism,* pp. 10–11.

9. Meinecke, *Machiavellism,* p. 215.

10. Meinecke, *Machiavellism,* p. 11.

11. Meinecke, *Machiavellism,* pp. 11–12.

12. Meinecke, *Machiavellism,* p. 433.

13. Auerbach's unwillingness to carry out the philological and social analysis into Pascal's opposition between "mind" and "might," to probe, for example, the role of science in the political discourse of seventeenth-century France, is so untypical of Auerbach's usual methods that one can only conclude he was so interested in the allegorical possibilities a reading of Pascal's text provided him for an intervention into his own period that his usual historical procedures seemed superfluous. It might not be pointless to speculate if Auerbach's uncharacteristically historically imprecise and nonspecific intervention is not itself a sign of the developing malaise of humanistic work he so much laments, that is, the sacrifice of knowledge and exactness for occasional interventions.

14. I want to thank Joseph Buttigieg for sharing his work in progress on the "*contemptu mundi*" theme and attitude in modern literature and criticism; see his unpublished paper, "The Interest of Irony."

15. See my comments on Said's defense of Chomsky in chapter 5.

16. It is best to follow the translators' decision—in the note preceding the translation—to leave the term in German: "In our translation of Auerbach's article we have chosen not to put *Weltliteratur* into English. An expedient such as 'world literature' betrays the rather unique traditions behind the German word. It is, of course, Goethe's own word (which he used increasingly after 1827) for universal literature, or literature that expresses *Humanität*, humanity, and this expression is literature's ultimate purpose. *Weltliteratur* is therefore a visionary concept, for it transcends national literatures without, at the same time, destroying their individualities" (PW 1; Edward and Maire Said).

17. David Carroll, "*Mimesis* Reconsidered: Literature, History, Ideology," *Diacritics*, (Summer 1975), 5:5–12, "deconstructs" Auerbach's claims to being "nonideological" and "nonsystemic" by showing the undefined privilege Auerbach grants to notions of immediacy, vision, unity, and presence. Carroll concludes on an insight made possible by a certain reading of Derrida that Auerbach's *Mimesis* makes the claims to directness and naturalness it does because it exists within the logocentric metaphysical tradition that has become "natural" to a mystified West forgetful of *écriture*. Carroll's analysis can be supplemented by a somewhat different focus on the historical and tactical configuration of power and rhetoric throughout Auerbach's work.

18. For an absolutely essential demonstration of this desire's enduring power and its most capable modern defense, see the last chapter of Altieri's *Act and Quality*, esp. pp. 318–31.

19. For a brief discussion of the reestablishment in postwar Germany of many of the same traditional academic positions and patterns that existed before the war and for some sense of the increasing parallels to the American academy, see Michael Hays, "Tracing a Critical Path: Peter Szondi and the Humanistic Tradition," in Michael Hays, ed. and trans. Peter Szondi, *On Textual Understanding and Other Essays*, (Minneapolis: University of Minnesota Press, 1986).

20. See Burton W. Bledstein, *The Culture of Professionalism: The Middle Class and the Development of Higher Education in America* (New York: Norton, 1976), for some evidence of the fact that the American university was never particularly committed to humanistic research, except insofar as it was necessary to establish authority or to satisfy its "clients'" demands. Gerald Graff has recently suggested that it might be useful to understand modern American literary study in terms of our general consumerist ethic. See Graff's promised work on this topic. For a similar critique to that implied by Auerbach, see Karl

Kroeber, "The Evolution of Literary Study 1883–1983," *PMLA* (May 1984) 99(3):326–39, and also, for a similar critique of deconstruction, Edward W. Said, *The World, the Text, and the Critic*, pp. 191–93, 200–212.

21. For a powerful and convincing argument that "impotence" is the sign and manner of much of the most powerful contemporary criticism, see Donald Pease, "J. Hillis Miller: The Other Victorian at Yale," *The Yale Critics: Deconstruction in America* ed. J. Arac et al., (Minneapolis: University of Minnesota Press, 1983), pp. 66–89.

22. For one cast study of how this occurred in the United States, see Stuart Ewen, *Captains of Consciousness: Advertising and the Social Roots of the Consumer Culture* (New York: McGraw-Hill, 1976).

23. See Said, *The World, the Text, the Critic*, pp. 8ff.

24. See Erich Auerbach, review of Leo Spitzer, *Linguistics and Literary History*, *Comparative Literature* (Winter 1949), 1(1):82–84.

25. The attempt to transfer the modern humanists' remaining sphere of action from "myth" to "education," though preferable because active, remains essentially mandarin and is plagued by many of the same contradictions that Auerbach illustrates and acknowledges. For the strongest contemporary attempt I know to establish a humanistic pedagogy, see Charles Altieri, *Act and Quality*. For a naively direct statement of the ideology and interests involved in a reductive sense of humanism one needs only to consider Frank Kermode: "it must be obvious that the formation of rival canons . . . is very dangerous; that in allowing it to happen we risk the death of the institution. Its continuance depends wholly upon our ability to maintain the canon and replace ourselves, to induce sufficient numbers of younger people to think as we do." See Paul A. Bové, "Variations on Authority," *The Yale Critics*, pp. 3–19.

26. Edward W. Said, *Beginnings: Intention and Method* (New York: Basic Books, 1975), pp. 68ff. Said glosses *Ansatzpunkt* as "point of departure" in contrast to *Anfang* (beginning) in order, he claims, that "the constitutive, or constructive, sense of beginning could be stressed." To make that sense clearer it could perhaps be more precisely (if less elegantly) glossed as the point at, on, or from which one gets under way. The 1976 *Duden: Das grosse Wörterbuch der deutschen Sprache* points out that the term is used in methodological contexts and gives as an example the usage "*ein Ansatzpunkt zur Kritik*." Said suggests that Auerbach's choice of *Ansatzpunkt* over *Anfang* is deliberate. Since no *Duden* before 1976 lists *Ansatzpunkt* and it is not by any means frequently listed in any other earlier dictionary, Said's claim would seem to be correct; indeed, Auerbach may well be one of the first important critical figures to use *Ansatzpunkt* in this precise sense.

27. One likely instance of such an unschooled and insignificant assertion of synthetic order that is unescapably metaphysical is Cleanth Brooks's work on T. S. Eliot and W. B. Yeats in *Modern Poetry and the*

Tradition (Chapel Hill: The University of North Carolina Press, 1939), pp. 136–202. For an analysis of Brooks' work along related lines, see Paul A. Bové, "Cleanth Brooks and Modern Irony," *Destructive Poetics* (New York: Columbia University Press, 1980), pp. 93–130. It would be possible to show that Auerbach's objections to insignificant intuitions based on avowedly doctrinaire critical programs like the New Criticism are in large part an objection to the easy intuitions of order the American profession offered when it made the "grace," "complexity," and "comprehensiveness" of "close reading" the primary criterion for success.

28. *Beginnings*, pp. 72, 76. Said might now find his own formulation too ahistorical, too textual, and yet, that there is a continuity in Said's work that seems always to assert the primacy of the critic's revisionary will may be deduced from my comments on his work elsewhere in the book, especially in chapter 5.

29. *Beginnings*, p. 76. Said's comment is an apt warning for those who find themselves unable to write for this commitment to research.

30. *Beginnings*, p. 72.

31. *Beginnings*, p. 7.

32. Consider, for example, how enormously successful Jonathan Culler has been with his series of "guides" (the word is his): *Structuralist Poetics* (Ithaca, N.Y.: Cornell University Press, 1976); *In Pursuit of Signs* (Ithaca, N.Y.: Cornell University Press, 1981); *On Deconstruction* (Ithaca, N.Y.: Cornell University Press, 1982); and *Roland Barthes* (New York: Oxford University Press, 1983).

33. See Geoffrey Green, *Literary Criticism and the Structure of History: Erich Auerbach and Leo Spitzer* (Lincoln, Nebr.: University of Nebraska Press, 1982), p. 80.

34. M. H. Abrams' magisterial *Natural Supernaturalism* (New York: Norton, 1971), comes readily to mind as a recent effort that, I think must be acknowledged, has failed effectively to establish itself as a model of scholarly work in the profession of letters.

35. Erich Auerbach, review of Curtius, *Europäische Literatur und lateinisches Mittelalter*, MLN (May 1950), 65(5):348.

36. Auerbach, review of Curtius, *MLN*, 349.

37. Auerbach, review of Curtius, *MLN*, 349.

5. INTELLECTUALS AT WAR

1. See among the best of such studies, Dana Polan, "Fables of Transgression: The Reading of Politics and the Politics of Reading in Foucauldian Discourse," *boundary 2* (1982), 10(3):361–82.

2. Allan Megill, "Foucault, Structuralism, and the Ends of History," *Journal of Modern History* (1979), 51:451–503.

3. Megill, "Foucault, Structuralism, and the Ends of History," 496 ff. See also my chapters 3 and 4.

4. Lawrence Stone, Review of Jacques Donzelot, *The Policing of Families*, New Republic, Feb. 16, 1980, pp. 32–34. Paul Robinson, Review of *History of Sexuality*, New Republic, Oct. 28, 1978, p. 29.

5. Edward W. Said, *Raritan*, (1982), 1(3):41–67, hereafter cited parenthetically in my text as TT. Said has reprinted this essay, in slightly modified form, in *The World, the Text, and the Critic* (Cambridge, Mass.: Harvard University Press, 1983), pp. 226–47. I continue to refer to the original version because, not yet revised for book publication, it is somewhat more precisely focused on its own specific topic.

6. Edward W. Said, "The Problem of Textuality: Two Exemplary Positions," *Critical Inquiry* (1978), 4:673–714, revised and reprinted in *The World, the Text, and the Critic* as "Criticism Between Culture and Systems," pp. 178–225.

7. Frank Lentricchia, *After the New Criticism* (Chicago: University of Chicago Press, 1980).

8. For a recent example of the disruptive effects Said's work has caused among some orientalists and "humanists" see Bernard Lewis, "The Question of Orientalism," *The New York Review of Books*, June 24, 1982, pp. 49–56. See also Paul A. Bové, "Closing up the Ranks: Xerxes' Hordes Are at the Pass," *Contemporary Literature* (1985), 26:91–106, in which I analyze the nature of the political and intellectual response to Said's *The World, the Text, and the Critic*.

9. Edward W. Said, "Reflections on Recent American Left Literary Criticism," boundary 2 (1979), 8(1):11–30, reprinted in *The World, the Text, and the Critic*, pp. 158–77.

10. On the inevitability of such competition among intellectuals, see G. W. F. Hegel, *The Phenomenology of Mind*, trans. J. B. Baillie (New York: Oxford University Press, 1967), pp. 414ff; Regis Debray, *Teachers, Writers, Celebrities*, trans. David Macey (London: New Left Books, 1981); and Paul A. Bové, "Celebrity and Betrayal," *Minnesota Review* (Fall 1983), NS. 21:72–91.

11. Of course, Said's recognition that Foucault has "disciples" does not negate my claim that Foucault refuses to play the role of the leading intellectual. The point is that neither Foucault nor, as far as I know, any of those who take his work seriously suggest that intellectuals should play a prophetic role or offer an alternative vision of the future. Said and others implicitly recognize this reluctance on Foucault's part and often mark it as one of his limits. On the contrary, I think it is one of his peculiar virtues.

12. Michel Foucault, "Intellectuals and Power," in Donald F. Bouchard, ed., *Language, Counter-Memory, Practice*, trans. Donald F. Bouchard and Sherry Simon (Ithaca, N.Y.: Cornell University Press, 1977), pp. 205–17.

13. Michel Foucault, "The Confession of the Flesh," in Colin Gordon, ed., *Power/Knowledge*, trans. Colin Gordon, Leo Marshall, John Mipham, Kate Soper (New York: Pantheon Books, 1980), pp. 194–228.

14. Foucault, "On Popular Justice," *Power/Knowledge*, pp. 1–36; hereafter cited as PJ.

15. Foucault, "Truth and Power," *Power/Knowledge*, p. 131; hereafter cited as TP.

16. Above all, such a stance refuses, in advance, to engage seriously with Foucault's interpretation that the humanity to be liberated by revolution is itself a product of this regime of truth: "The man described for us whom we are invited to free, is already in himself the effect of a subjection much more profound than himself." Michel Foucault, *Discipline and Punish*, trans. Alan Sheridan (New York: Pantheon Books, 1977), p. 30.

17. Michel Foucault, "Power and Sex," trans. David J. Parent, *Telos* (Summer 1977), no. 32:160; hereafter cited as PS.

18. See chapter 1.

19. David Couzens Hoy, "Power, Repression, Progress," *Tri Quarterly* (Fall 1981), 52:48.

20. Hoy, p. 48.

21. I am, of course, supremely aware of the aporia confronting any intellectual critic of intellectuals. See Bové, "Celebrity and Betrayal."

6. CRITICAL NEGATION

1. Michel Foucault, *The Birth of the Clinic*, trans. A. M. Sheridan-Smith (New York: Pantheon Books, 1973), p. xvii, hereafter cited in my text as BC.

2. See, for example, "Entretien avec Michel Foucault," in Raymond Bellour, *Le Livre des autres* (Paris: Editions de l'Herne, 1971), pp. 135–44. The interview was conducted in 1966.

3. Immanuel Kant, *Anthropology from a Pragmatic Point of View*, trans. Victor Lyle Dowdell, revised and edited by Hans H. Rudnick (Carbondale, Ill.: Southern Illinois University Press, 1978), p. 6. Foucault translated this text, and in his preface "Notice Historique," promised a study of its relation to Kant's critiques. See *Anthropologie du point de vue pragmatique*, trans. Michel Foucault (Paris: J. Vrin, 1970), p. 10. Kant's text, in English translation, is cited in my text as A.

4. Edward W. Said, "Islam, Philology, and French Culture," *The World, the Text, and the Critic* (Cambridge, Mass.: Harvard University Press, 1983), pp. 278–79, hereafter cited in my text as WTC.

5. Michel Foucault, *The Order of Things*, trans. Alan Sheridan-Smith (New York: Random House, 1970), pp. 308, 311; see pp. 3–16. See also Hubert L. Dreyfus and Paul Robinson, *Michel Foucault*, 2nd. ed. (Chicago: University of Chicago Press, 1983), pp. 18–32.

6. Theodor W. Adorno, "Freudian Theory and the Pattern of Fascist Propaganda," in Andrew Arato and Eike Gebhardt, eds., *The Essential Frankfurt School Reader*, (New York: Continuum, 1982), p. 122.

7. I am stressing Kant's late reduced emphasis on the republican form of government in the face of Jürgen Habermas, for whom, as Thomas McCarthy's study makes clear, the republican form of government is a minimal necessary condition for meeting Habermas' goals: "that valid social norms incorporate . . . generalizable interests. . . . The criterion of rational consensus under conditions of symmetry retains the restriction specified in Kant's formula of the end in itself: that humanity be treated as an end and never as a means only, that it serve as 'the condition restricting all merely relative and arbitrary ends,'" "Practical Discourse," *The Critical Theory of Jürgen Habermas* (Cambridge, Mass.: The MIT Press, 1978), p. 330. Space does not permit a full consideration of Habermas here. He is by far the ablest continuer of the "anthropological attitude" in contemporary thought and, given his emphasis on "discourse" as the condition for rational social reorganization, perhaps he is its completion.

8. See Arno Mayer, *The Persistence of the Old Regime* (New York: Pantheon Books, 1981), p. 147.

9. Immanuel Kant, *Kants gesammelte Schriften*, ed. Königlich Preussiche *Akademie der Wissenschafter* (23 vols. 1–7, 14–16, Berlin: Georg Reimer, 1905–14; 9–13, 17–23, Berlin: Walter de Gruyter and Co., 1922–56), 20, p. 45. Cited in Frederick Van De Pitte, "Introduction," *Anthropology*, pp. xviii–xix.

10. Van De Pitte, "Introduction," p. xix.

11. See Irwin Ehrenpreis. "Three-Part Inventions," *New York Review of Books* (Jan. 19, 1984), 30(20–21):37–39. Ehrenpreis strongly disagrees with Said's characterization of Renan, arguing that Renan's biography shows he was left institutionally "unsupported." The point is, however, that Renan could make the sort of claims he did and attempt to acquire such authority he found only as a result of the operation of the institutions of modern humanistic discourse. Ehrenpreis' reading of Said is overly empirical. He misses the Nietzschean or Foucauldian dimension to Said's claim about how certain German/French cultural formations make possible certain types of intellectual practice and intellectual styles different than those typical, for example, of Arnoldian "declassé intellectuals."

12. Marshall Hodgson, *The Venture of Islam* (Chicago and London: The University of Chicago Press, 1974), 1; hereafter cited in my text as VI.

13. Michel Foucault, *Discipline and Punish*, trans. Alan Sheridan (New York: Pantheon Books, 1977); hereafter cited in my text as DP.

14. Indeed, in *Covering Islam* (New York: Pantheon Books, 1981), Said singles out Hodgson's work as a crucial example of the sort of historical scholarship Western Islamic scholars and Muslims must carry out. See esp. pp. 16 and 63. It is in the light of Said's claims for the political efficacy of such historical investigation and writing that his

recent essay, "Permission To Narrate: Edward Said Writes About the Story of the Palestinians," *London Review of Books* (Feb. 1984), pp. 16–29, 13–17, must be read.

15. Max Horkheimer, *The Essential Frankfurt School Reader*, pp. 412, 413, hereafter cited in my text as PT.

16. Ralph Waldo Emerson, in Albert R. Ferguson, ed., *The Collected Works of Ralph Waldo Emerson*, vol. 1, *Nature, Addresses, and Lectures* (Cambridge, Mass.: Harvard University Press, 1971), p. 7.

17. For an analysis of why pragmatism is attractive to left intellectuals and yet inadequate, see Frank Lentricchia, *Criticism and Social Change* (Chicago: University of Chicago Press, 1983), pp. 1–20.

18. I am thinking specifically of Barbara Johnson's as yet unpublished paper "Mallarmé as Mother," presented at the conference on "The Question of the Postmodern," Cornell University, April 1984.

19. See Walter J. Bate, "To the Editor," *Critical Inquiry* (1983), 10(2):365–66: "The Renaissance tradition of *litterae humaniores* has long served as a kind of hub to the wheel, giving a necessary center to the emerging spokes of more specialized approaches, which, without that center, lose their original purpose and function." It is precisely such unexamined and dogmatically "authoritative" assertions as this one that justifiably earn both Said's and Hodgson's scorn. Moreover, it is important to realize, as Bate's recent statements make plentifully clear, that often what is labeled as "major work" by the established academy rests on and emerges from essentially questionable assumptions about the role of the scholar and the nature of humanism in our era.

20. See Charles Altieri, "An Idea and Ideal of a Literary Canon," *Critical Inquiry* (1983), 10(1):51–52.

21. G. W. F. Hegel, *Hegel's Philosophy of Right*, trans. T. M. Knox (Oxford: Oxford University Press, 1952), pp. 20, 21, 22.

22. Hegel, *Philosophy of Right*, p. 22.

23. See Paul A. Bové, "Cleanth Brooks and Modern Irony," *Destructive Poetics* (New York: Columbia University Press, 1980), pp. 93–120.

24. For a specific example of Foucault's usefulness to one oppressed group's struggle, see Serge Livrozet, *De La Prison à la Révolte* (Paris: Mercure de France, 1973).

25. Michel Foucault, "The Discourse on Language," trans. Rupert Sawyer, *The Archaeology of Knowledge* (New York: Harper and Row, 1976), p. 219; hereafter cited in my text as DL.

26. For a general discussion of this imperial culture, see William Appleman Williams, *Empire as a Way of Life: An Essay on the Causes and Character of America's Present Predicament* (New York: Oxford University Press, 1980). A close reading of Williams' text reveals that

the political and academic leaders of the American empire, from Jefferson and Madison to the bright young men who brought us Viet Nam, fit precisely the mold and genealogy of the leading intellectual. This is no accident. As I have been suggesting throughout, the representative figure, the sublime, masterful figure so essential to bureaucratic professionalism, as well as heroic opposition, is always tinged with imperialism regarding the led or excluded "other."

Index

Adorno, Theodor, 96, 251, 252, 281, 307
Asthetics, 59–60, 122–24, 170. *See also*
Synthesis
After the New Criticism (Lentricchia), 219–20
Alienation, 175–78, 261, 272, 275. *See
also* Exile
Ansatzpunkt, 184, 186, 190–93, 202,
203, 206, 323n.26
"Anthropological attitude, the," 240,
247–48, 252, 257
Anthropological humanism, 10, 20,
41, 261, 267, 279–81; Auerbach and,
43, 262, 271, 275; and critical prac-
tice, 267, 273; Foucault and, 267,
307; Hodgson and, 263, 273, 275,
282–85, 290, 292–93; Kant and, 3, 43,
258–59, 301; and the leading intellectual, 258–259, 261, 265, 278–80;
Said and, 259, 271, 275, 282. *See also*
Humanism
Antoni, Carlo, 119–20
Arac, Jonathan, 69
Aristotle, 122–23
Arnold, Matthew, xvii, 273, 278
Asceticism, 9, 11–13, 16, 20, 32–36
Auerbach, Erich: alienation in,
175–77, 261, 271, 272, 275; and the
American critics, 79–80, 97–100,
102–8; and the American literary
institution, 79–80, 86, 100–109,
112–14, 119, 128–29, 142, 318n.11;
Ansatzpunkt, 184, 186, 188, 190–93;
202, 203, 206, 207; on the critic,
87–89, 103–4, 107–8, 110–11, 162,
189, 191–93, 195, 247–48, 287; on
Dante, 141, 166, 196, 198–99, 201,
203, 206; *Dante: Poet of the Secular
World*, 197–98; on education,
118–19, 168, 172–74, 177; and Foucault, 128, 207–8, 243, 247–48,
301–2; and the German tradition, x,
79, 92, 114–15, 128, 176, 194; and
historicism, 111, 119, 120, 131–132,
138, 143–44, 170, 204, 266; and historism, 93–96, 104–5, 111, 164–65,
169–72, 176–78, 186, 191, 203; history in, 79, 88–90, 105–6, 143–44,
168–70, 178, 205–8; and Hodgson,
263–64; 266, 269, 272, 291, 298–302;
and Horkheimer, 93, 96; and humanism, xv, xvi–xviii, 1, 35, 37,
72–73, 93, 95, 103, 105, 128–29,
140–41, 143–44, 152–53, 162–65,
168–71, 175–85, 193–95, 200, 206,
208, 298–99, 301–2, 323n.25; the individual in, 90, 91, 93, 105, 108–11,
128, 139–41, 143–44; and the institutionalization of literary studies,
172–73, 179, 192–93, 194, 247–48; on
the intellectual, 157–58, 160,
177–78, 180, 300; on language, 51,
131–32, 137–39, 142–43, 152, 300; as
leading intellectual, xiii, xvi, 80,
82–83, 91–92, 100–102, 105–6,
108–10; the leading intellectual in,
27, 112–13, 128–29, 132, 136–37,
142–45, 161–62, 170, 173–74, 179,
182–84, 195, 247–48, 259–60, 299;
*Literary Language and Its Public in
Late Latin Antiquity and in the
Middle Ages*, 81–82, 195, 196, 197,
200, 202, 203, 205, 206; and the mandarin tradition, 120, 126, 127, 128,

Auerbach, Erich (*Continued*)
131–32, 137, 138–39, 141–45, 153,
185, 208; and Meinecke, 92, 121,
133, 136, 152–56, 160–62, 166;
Mimesis, 81, 84–86, 88–89, 92–97,
99–101, 104–7, 112, 131, 141, 143,
153, 158, 163, 172, 177, 181, 182, 187,
189–90, 198, 203, 260, 271, 275, 302,
317n.11, 322n.17; modernity in,
84–86, 89–90, 99, 131, 137–39,
163–65, 167–68, 172, 175–77, 179–80,
182–83, 201–2, 204; on myth, 163,
169–70, 178–80, 186, 189; and oppositional criticism, 94–95, 126,
139, 142, 145, 179, 279; on Pascal,
43, 131–32, 152, 153–59, 160–62, 170,
177, 184, 321n.13; philology in,
87–90, 131, 163–64, 174, 177, 180;
"Philology and *Weltliteratur*," 79,
81, 134, 141, 143, 162, 163, 164–65,
177, 178, 180, 181, 182–84, 186, 188,
190–94, 195, 196, 202–6; "On the Political Theory of Pascal," 147,
152–53, 167, 183; and Said, xiii, 106,
142, 143, 144, 187–88, 190–91, 275,
287, 298–302; *Scenes From the
Drama of European Literature*,
154–55, 156, 159, 160–62; and specialization, 86, 89, 184, 193–94, 207;
and Spitzer, 85, 105, 107–8, 176, 186;
on the state, 151–53, 156, 167;
"synthesis," 81, 84–92, 96, 98, 108,
118–20, 127–28, 140, 144, 177,
186–88, 190, 195, 202, 203–8; on
Vico, 27, 131–32, 137–40, 144–46,
153, 169, 202, 264, 291, 317n.4,
323n.27; "Vico and Aesthetic Historism," 131–34, 136–38, 140–43, 192,
272; and Weimar, 82, 85, 86, 114,
118–19; *Weltliteratur*, 43, 91,
163–64, 170, 178, 180, 200, 262,
322n.16
"Author," the, 26–27, 30, 35–36, 74
Authority: in Auerbach, 70, 80, 86,
91–92; in literary studies, 80–81,
83–84, 116–17, 293–94; in Nietzsche,
11, 21, 23; in Pound's "Canto xiii,"
5, 7; in Richards, 52, 70. *See also*
Power

Babbitt, Irving, 39, 44, 261
Bacon, Sir Francis, 66, 77
Bate, Walter Jackson, xv, 261
Beckett, Samuel, 241
Benjamin, Walter, 256
Bentham, Jeremy, 44, 58
Bildung, 124, 135, 141, 148, 176
Blackmur, R. P., xvii, 106
Bradbrook, Muriel, 45, 64, 68, 75
Bradley, A. C., 66–67
Brenkman, John, 76
Breslin, Charles, 102–3, 109–10

Cambridge English, 40, 43–45. *See
also* Institutionalization of literary
studies, the
Canonization, 18, 26–27, 254, 256,
285, 286
Chomsky, Noam, 19, 221, 227–29,
230–31, 232, 235, 288
Civilization and Its Discontents
(Freud), 251
Coleridge, Samuel Taylor, 58, 60
Collins, Churton, 40–41
Conrad, Joseph, 27, 275
Conservatism, 117–18, 274; Auerbach
and, 132, 144; Kant and, 255, 256;
Richards and, 53, 55, 59, 64–65, 76
Contextualism: in Richards, 50, 52,
59, 67
Craig, Gordon, 113–14
Critic, the: in Auerbach, 87–89,
104–5, 107–11, 162, 168, 189, 191–92,
195, 247–48, 287; in Foucault, 218,
301; function of, xiv, 75; as function of discourse, 4; in Hodgson,
287, 295–96; and humanism, 2, 43,
74–75, 110–11, 128–29; in Kant,
281–82; as leading intellectual, x,
xiii, 2, 100–2; in Nietzsche, 22, 27;
in Richards, 62; in Said, 31, 189, 212,
214–15, 247–48, 276–77, 280–81,
281–82, 287–90, 295, 313n.27. *See
also* Intellectual, the; Genealogist,
the; Oppositional critic, the;
Scholar, the
Critical consciousness, 269, 281–82,
287, 289, 301
Critical humanism, xii, 2; Auerbach

and, xi, 247–48; Said and, xiii, 28, 30, 32–33, 247–48. *See also* Humanism
Critical practice, xi, xiii, 25, 55–56, 75, 272–73; Auerbach and, 80–81, 112–13, 267–68; Kant and, 252; Richards and, 59, 62, 67–68; Said and, 30–32, 274–75, 277–79, 288–89, 298–99
Critical Twilight, The (Fekete), ix
Criticism, *See* Critical practice
Culture: Hodgson on, 283–84, 293–94, 296–98; humanistic, 253–54; Kant on, 249–58, 293–94; Said on, 273–75, 284. *See also* Imperialism
Culture and Society (Williams), 276
Curtius, E. R., 114, 190, 205–6

Dante, 73, 82, 84, 87, 94, 95, 97, 100, 104, 141, 166, 196–203, 206
Decline of the German Mandarins, The (Ringer), 115, 116, 117, 125–27, 135
Deconstruction, 53, 95, 215, 278
de Man, Paul, 109
Derrida, Jacques, 50, 212, 278
Die Idee der Statsräson (Meinecke), 152
Disciplines: in Foucault, 300–308. *See also* Institutionalization of literary sudies, the
Discourse: "anonymous," in Nietzsche, 23; critic as function of, 4; critical, and the institutionalization of 2; critical, and the leading intellectual, 239–40; in Foucault, 24, 26, 213, 225, 242–44, 246–47, 300–303, 305; function of, in Kant, 249–50; in Hodgson, 293–94, 296; humanistic, 252, 260, 262; as power, in Said, 216–17; and truth, 309–10. *See also* Language

Edelstein, Ludwig, 97–98
Education: in Auerbach, 172–74, 177; as normalization, 254–55; and synthesis in Spranger, 124–25. *See also* Pedagogy
Edward VII, King, 41

Eliot, T. S., 27, 29, 48, 58
Emerson, Ralph Waldo, *Nature,* 267
Empson, William, 45, 75
"Eng. Lit.," x, 39, 40–41
Erlich, Victor, 109
European Literature and the Latin Middle Ages (Curtius), 205
Exile, 271, 275. *See also* Alienation

Facism, 251. *See also* Nazism
False Consciousness, 268
Fekete, John, ix, x, 76
Foucault, Michel: aim of, 23; as "antihumanist," xii, xv–xvi; and Auerbach, 128, 207–8, 247–48, 301–2; the author in, 30, 35–36, 74; *The Birth of the Clinic,* 240–41, 243–44, 246, 251, 299; and Chomsky, 221, 227–31; critics of, 210–12, 222, 231; *Discipline and Punish,* 26, 57, 68, 71, 229–30, 239, 262, 299, 302–3, 304, 306, 307–8, 309; on discourse, 24, 46–48, 213, 225–26, 242–44, 246–47, 300–301, 302–3, 305; *The Discourse on Language,* 300, 301, 302, 303; genealogy, 3, 13–14, 22, 25, 210–11, 225–26, 302–5; and Gramsci, 146, 221; *The History of Sexuality,* 57, 63; and humanism, xi, 23, 24–26, 32, 35, 37, 41–42, 241–42, 244–45, 247, 261, 267–68, 299, 300–301, 303; 305; and Kant, 227, 244, 250–51, 254, 258, 305; on knowledge, 46–47, 241–43, 247; on the leading intellectual, xvi, 23, 24, 35, 209–10, 222, 224–27, 229–30, 240, 305–6, 308–9; and Marxism, 225, 235, 304; and Nietzsche, 12, 20, 22, 24–26, 33, 36, 240–43, 300, 305; on the oppositional critic, 3, 25, 36, 146, 211, 225–26, 228–29, 314n.30; *The Order of Things,* 24, 46–48, 50, 246; "On Popular Justice," 226, 233; on power, 32, 57, 68, 71, 146, 210, 212–13, 220–22, 225–26, 276, 299–300, 302–3, 305–6; power/ knowledge, 23, 235–36, 248, 302, 307; *Power/Knowledge,* 225–26, 235; "Power and Sex," 232, 236;

Foucault, Michel (*Continued*)
"Powers and Strategies," xvi; and psychoanalysis, 225, 235; regime of truth in, 229–30, 233–34, 236, 303, 308, 326n.16; and Said, 26–27, 30, 33, 36, 212–14, 218–25, 227–32, 234–36, 246–48, 276–77, 299, 325n.11; the subject in, 3, 23, 35–36, 210, 299, 301, 308; "Truth and Power," 229, 235, 236; *La Volonté de Savoir*, 213; "What Is An Author?", 74; mentioned, 273, 288, 294
Freud, Sigmund, 169, 225, 247, 251

Gates of Horn, The (Levin), 100
Genealogist, the 17–18, 19, 20, 21, 22, 28; in Nietzsche, 10, 11, 14–17, 19–20, 31. *See also* Critic, the
Genealogy, 18, 34; and asceticism, 9–11; and Foucault, 3, 13–14, 25, 210–11, 225, 302, 303, 304–5; and Hodgson, 270, 285; and humanism, 10, 11, 17; and the leading intellectual, 11, 22; and Nietzsche, 3, 9, 12–14, 17, 23; and Said, 3, 216; the subject in, 22, 25
Geisteswissenschaften, 82, 86, 113, 115, 139, 185
German humanism, 114–18, 128–29, 132–34, 194; *See also* Humanism
Germinal (Zola), 90
Goethe, Johann Wolfgang von, 121, 164, 181–83, 261
Goldmann, Lucien, 217, 218
Gramsci, Antonio, 28, 30, 146, 221, 254, 277, 289

Habermas, Jürgen, 262, 327n.7
Hatzfield, Helmut, 97–98, 104
Hegel, G. W. F., 122, 135, 148, 149, 169, 190, 268, 281, 287, 288–89
Herder, Johann Gottfried von, 121; in Auerbach, 131–33, 142, 272; and the mandarin tradition, 131–34, 138; and Meinecke, 133, 135; philology in, 164; the subject in, 134, 190; and Vico, 138
Historian, the: and aesthetics, 122–23; and Aristotle, 122–23; in Auerbach, 206–8; Foucault as, 207–8; in Hegel, 122; in Meinecke, 122, 124, 149, 152; in Troeltsch, 122, 124
Historicism, 122, 125–26, 136, 193; in Auerbach, 99, 111, 120, 126, 131–32, 138, 144, 170, 204, 266; and the mandarin tradition, 131–32, 136, 144. *See also* Historism; History
Historicism and Its Problems (Troeltsch), 119
Historicist humanism, 297; in Auerbach, 131, 260, 283, 307; in Hodgson, 283–84, 290–91, 294; and power, 283–85, 296. *See also* Humanism
Historism: in Auerbach, 92–95, 104–5, 118–19, 139, 164–65, 169–72, 186, 191, 203; German, 92, 118–20, 123–24; in Vico, 138–39, 164. *See also* Historicism; History
Historism (Meinecke), 121–22, 133, 134, 152
History: in Auerbach, 88–90, 96, 105–6, 140–41, 143–45, 168–70, 172–74, 177–79, 205–6, 291; in Foucault, 210–11, 304–5; in Hodgson, 290–93, 296–97; Meinecke on, 151–52; in Troeltsch, 120–21. *See also* Historicism; Historism
History and Class Consciousness (Lukacs), 257, 305
Hitler, Adolf, 93, 126, 154, 260. *See also* Nazism
Hodgson, Marshall, 51; and Auerbach, 263–64, 266, 269, 271–72, 283, 285, 287, 290–91, 298–302; on culture, 263, 283–84, 293–94, 296–98; on disciplines, 290–93; on discourse, 292–93, 296, 300–301; genealogy in, 270, 285; and history, 293–94, 296–97; and humanism, xv, xvii, 1, 262–64, 269, 273, 275, 278, 282–87, 290–99, 301–2; on the individual, 293–96; and Kant, 240, 263, 269, 293–94, 301; on knowledge, 282, 292, 293; and the leading intellectual, 272–73, 278, 293–94; and Renan, 266–67, 293; and Richards, 284, 290–91, 293, 301–2;

and Said, xv, 246, 272, 273, 275, 281–83, 285–87, 290–92, 297–302, 327n.14, 328n.19; on scholarship, 2, 270–72, 290–97; scientism in, 282–84; on truth, 292, 296, 300; *The Venture of Islam*, 262, 263, 270–72, 284, 286, 290, 291, 293, 294, 295
Hölderlin, Friedrich, 35, 43, 245, 251, 260, 266, 267, 276
Horkheimer, Max, 93, 96, 265, 267–69, 281
Hoy, David Couzens, 234
Hugo of St. Victor, 177
Huis Clos (Sartre), 157
Humanism, x, xii, xv, 1–2; Auerbach and, x, xvi–xvii, 35, 37, 51, 70, 72–73, 91, 93, 95, 98–99, 102–5, 128–29, 140–41, 143–44, 152, 160, 162, 163–65, 168–72, 175–84, 193, 194, 195, 197, 208, 243, 276, 285, 295, 298–99, 323n.25; Foucault and, xi, 23, 25–26, 35, 37, 241–44, 247, 261, 302–7; Hodgson and, 264, 285–87, 293–98; Hölderlin and, 244–46, 267, 276; and the institutionalization of literary studies, 42, 74, 110–11, 145–46, 185, 194, 248; Kant and, 13, 240, 243, 245, 293–94; and knowledge, 14, 261, 292; and the leading intellectual, xiv, 11, 31, 52, 91–92, 128–29, 145–47, 193, 245, 256–57; Nietzsche and, 13, 19, 20–21, 34–35, 242; and the oppositional intellectual, 28, 276–77, 282, 298–99; and power, 66, 76, 296–98, 300; Richards and, x, 42, 51–52, 54, 58–59, 62, 68, 70, 72–74, 76, 298–99; Said and, xi, 28, 36–37, 215, 217, 261, 276–79, 286–87, 298–301; and synthesis, 86–87, 128–29. *See also* Anthropological humanism; Critical humanism; German humanism; Liberal humanism; Mandarin humanism; Western humanism

Iggers, George, 120, 136
Imperialism, 65, 73, 297–98, 313n.25, 328n.26. *See also* Culture
Individual, the: in Auerbach, 87, 90,

93, 105, 108–10, 139–41, 144–45; in the German tradition, 122, 132; in Hodgson, 293–96; in humanism, 293; in Kant, 293–94; and the literary institution, 105–6, 112–14. *See also* Subject, the
Institutionalization of literary studies, the, 39, 40, 42; in America, 103–6, 108–10, 322n.20; and Auerbach, 79–81, 86, 97–103, 105–10, 112–14, 128–29, 142, 179, 192–94, 248; at Cambridge, 43–44; in Germany, 83, 113–14, 117–18, 128–29; and humanism, 74, 106–7, 128–29, 145–47, 248; and the individual, 55, 105, 112–14; and the leading intellectual, 108–14, 128–29, 142, 145–47, 261; Levin on, 109, 110; Muscatine on, 110; and New Criticism, 103, 106–7, 129; and normalization, 76; and power, 42, 65, 80–81, 83–84, 100–102, 261; and revisionism, 142, 173; and Richards, 40, 43–44, 52–53, 76; Spitzer on, 107–8
Intellectual, the, xv, 2–3, 4, 8; in Auerbach, 157–58, 160, 177, 178, 180, 300; in Foucault, xvi–xvii, 23, 26, 221–22, 224–33, 235–37, 299–300, 303–4; in Gramsci, 28, 254; in Hodgson, 297, 300–301; in humanism, 279–81, 296–97; in Kant, 254; in Nietzsche, 9–10, 13, 300; in Said, 28, 214–18, 221, 223–25, 228, 281–82, 300–301; relation to truth, 299, 300. *See also* Critic, the; Leading intellectual, the; Oppositional critic, the; Scholar, the
Irony, 287, 289

Joyce, James 48, 84
Judgment: literary, in Richards, 66–67, 71–72
Justice, 134, 152, 154–56, 160–62

Kahler, Erich von, 117–18
Kant, Immanuel: "anthropological attitude," 240, 247–48, 250, 252, 257, 327n.7; anthropological humanism, 3, 43, 265; *Anthropology*,

Kant, Immanuel (*Continued*)
xiv, 240, 244, 246–50, 252–55, 258, 261, 265; and Auerbach, 307; on the critic, 281–82; on culture, 249–56, 293–94; and Foucault, 241, 243, 244, 250–51, 254, 258; function of discourse in, 249–50; and Hodgson, 240, 251, 263, 269, 293–94; and humanism, 13, 21, 240, 245, 248–50, 252–53, 258–59, 294, 307; and the leading intellectual, 245, 249, 251, 253, 254–59, 261, 265; and Nietzsche, 19, 251; and Said, 240, 281–82; on scholarship, 293–94; mentioned, 10, 18, 23, 149, 274, 279, 281, 301, 302, 304, 307
Kermode, Frank, 100
Kerschensteiner, George, 125, 139
Kierkegaard, Søren, 47, 287
Knowledge: in Foucault, 230, 241–44, 246–48; in Hodgson, 293; in Richards, 50–51; production of, 13, 14, 46–47, 258–59, 261, 267, 283–84, 292
Krieger, Murray, 61
Kulturstaat, 123, 127

Language: Auerbach on, 131–32, 137–39, 142–43, 152; as discipline, 48; and power, 49; as representation, 46–48; in Richards, 48–49, 61–62; status of, 46–48; theory of, and humanism, 51; Vico on, 138–39. *See also* Discourse
Langue, La (Saussure), 50
Leading intellectual, the, x, 8, 22, 24; Auerbach and, xiii, xvi, 80, 82–83, 91–92, 100–102, 108–10, 128–29, 131–32, 136–37, 139–45, 161–62, 170–71, 173–74, 179–80, 182–84, 195, 247–48, 260–61, 278–79, 299; and authority, 116–17, 293–94; Foucault and, xvi, 23, 24, 35–36, 146, 209–10, 222, 224–27, 229–30, 240, 245, 305–6; in the German tradition, 115–17, 124, 126–29, 134–37, 139–42, 150; Hodgson and, 272–73, 278, 293–94; and humanism, xiv, 11, 31, 52, 91–92, 128–29, 146–47, 193, 248, 258–59, 261, 265, 278–79, 299, 308;

and the institutionalization of literary studies, 108–11, 146–47, 239, 248; Kant and, 245, 250–52, 255–61, 281–82, 307; Lukacs and, 257, 261; Nietzsche and, 33–34; as oppositional critic, 28, 126, 146; and revisionism, 32, 145; Richards and, 52, 62, 299; Said and, 27, 222–25, 234, 247–48, 259, 277–79, 281–82, 289, 298–99; and the state, 256, 261, 302; and synthesis, 116–17, 126–27. *See also* Leading intellectual, the; Oppositional critic, the; Scholar, the
Lentricchia, Frank, 213, 219–20
Leo, Ulrich, 102–3, 107, 121, 144
Levin, Harry, 96, 100, 105–6, 108–9, 110
Liberal humanism, xiii, 240, 251, 293, 298. *See also* Humanism
Literature and the American College (Babbitt), 39
Lukacs, George, 83, 194, 217, 218, 257, 261, 268; *History and Class Consciousness*, 257, 305

Mandarin humanism, 131–32, 141–42, 254. *See also* German tradition, the, Humanism
Mandarin tradition, the, 116–17; Auerbach and, 120, 126–29, 131–33, 136–44, 152–53, 179, 185, 208; and the German state, 147–48, 155; Herder and, 134, 138; and historism, 123–24, 138–39, 144; and humanism, 124–26, 128–29, 131–32, 137; and *Kulturstaat*, 123, 127; and the leading intellectual, 124, 128–29, 135–36, 141–42; Mannheim on, 126–27; and Meinecke, 121, 133, 134, 148, 150, 151, 152–53, 155, 166; Ringer on, 115, 117–18, 125–27. *See also* German humanism
Mannheim, Karl, 114, 126–27
Marx, Karl, 47, 74, 126, 152, 247, 268
Marxism, 208, 225, 235, 304
Meaning of Meaning, The (Ogden and Richards), 48, 50, 64–65
Meinecke, Friedrich: and Auerbach, 92, 121, 133, 136, 152–53, 160–62,

166; *Bildung*, 135, 148; *Die Idee der Statsräson*, 152; and Herder, 132–133, 135; and historicism, 136; and historism, 92; the historian in, 122, 124, 149, 152; *Historism*, 121–22, 133, 134, 152; and humanism; 117, 151–52, 160; justice and power in, 155, 160; and the leading intellectual, 117, 124, 134–35, 150; *Machiavellism*, 134, 148, 151–52; and the mandarin tradition, 121, 133, 134, 135–36, 147–48, 150–53, 155, 166; and Pascal, 154–55, 160, 162; on the state, 149–55, 160; synthesis in, 122, 124; and Troeltsch, 121, 122, 124; mentioned, 211
Memory: in Auerbach, 111–12, 165, 173–74; cultural, 256, 263
Mill, John Stuart, 44, 58
Modernism, 29, 48, 88–89, 107; in Auerbach, 86–90, 93, 95, 98–99
Modernity: Auerbach on, 84–86, 99, 111–12, 131, 138–39, 163–65, 167–68, 172, 175–80, 182–83, 201–2, 204
Moment of Scrutiny, The (Mulhern), x
Mulhern, Francis, x
Muscatine, Charles, 98–100, 102, 105–6, 109, 110, 144, 145
Muse in Chains, The (Potter), 39
Muse Unchained, The (Tillyard), 39, 40, 43, 45
Myth: in Auerbach, 163, 168–70, 178–80, 186, 189

Nature (Emerson), 267
Nazism, 113, 132, 138, 154, 156. See *also* Hitler and Fascism
New Criticism, 46, 54, 69, 103, 106–7, 129, 172, 173
Nietzsche, Friedrich: and asceticism, 9, 11, 12, 20, 33–34; and Auerbach, 169, 172, 260; the critic in, 22, 27; on discourse, 23, 47, 300; and Foucault, 12, 20, 22, 24–26, 33, 211, 234, 240–43, 300, 305; and genealogy, 3, 9, 11, 12–14, 17, 20, 23; *On the Genealogy of Morals*, 9, 12, 13, 14, 15–16, 18, 19, 20, 21, 22–23, 33;

and humanism, 13, 19, 20, 24–25, 33–34; on the intellectual, 9–10, 13, 19, 300; and Kant, 19, 23, 251, 253; and nihilism, 9, 11, 16, 22, 24, 32, 35; and the oppositional critic, xiv, 3, 19–20, 22, 31–34, 312n.12; and Said, 20, 22, 23, 31, 32, 33; on the subject, 3, 22; "The Use and Abuse of History," 172; mentioned, 239, 247, 249
Nihilism: and humanism, 33–35; Nietzsche and, 9, 11, 16, 22, 32
Normalization: Auerbach and, 291; Brenkman and, 76; Foucault and, 68, 306; humanism and, 290–91, 296; Kant and, 254; the literary institution and, 76; Richards and, 67–68, 70, 71, 290–91

O'Hara, Daniel, 9
Oppositional critic, the: and Auerbach, 83–84, 94–95, 126, 139, 145, 179, 279; and Foucault, 25, 36, 146, 211, 213, 221, 225–26, 228–29, 314n.30; and humanism, 32, 36, 279–81, 297–99; and the literary institution, 83–84; and the mandarin tradition, 126; and Nietzsche, xiv, 19–20, 22, 31–34; and Richards, 55, 61; and Said, xiv, 29, 30, 31–33, 213, 221, 276–82, 298; and structures of power, 146; and Weimar, 83; See *also* Critic, the; Intellectual, the

"Panopticism": in Foucault, 69
Pascal, Blaise: in Auerbach, 43, 147, 153–59, 160–62, 321n.13; on justice, 155–56, 160, 161, 162; *Pensées*, 156; and Port-Royal, 154, 155–56; and St. Augustine, 154; mentioned, 152, 170, 177, 184
Pater, Walter, 47
Pedagogy: in Auerbach, 118–19; in the mandarin tradition, 124–26; and Weimar, 117–19, 315n.10. See *also* Education
Pensées (Pascal), 156
Perspectivism, 126, 211; in Auerbach, 88–89, 90–92, 99, 172, 189–90

Philology: in Auerbach, 85, 87–90, 137, 162–64, 174, 177, 178–80, 204; and German humanism, 115; myth and, 163; and professional specialization, 138

Philosophy of Right, The (Hegel), 135, 288

Plato, 58, 77

Pluralism, 8, 51, 76, 117–19

Potter, Stephen, 40–41, 42; The Muse in Chains, 39

Pound, Ezra: "Canto xiii," 3–11; mentioned, 27, 29, 48, 152, 215, 278

Power: Auerbach and, 82–83, 138–39, 152, 157–58, 161; and disciplines, 292–93, 305–6; in Foucault, 24–26, 32, 57, 68, 71, 146, 212–13, 218–22, 225–28, 230, 234, 241–43, 248, 276, 299–300, 303–6; in Hodgson, 282–84, 294, 296; humanism and, 66, 68, 76; and justice, 152, 154–55, 160, 161; in Kant, 253, 294; and the literary institution, 42, 64, 77, 101–2; in Nietzsche, 21, 24–25, 42; and the oppositional critic, 83–84; in Richards, 55, 64, 65, 70; in Said, 28, 212–14, 217, 221–22, 224; structures of, in Pound's "Canto xiii," 4, 5. See also Authority

Power/knowledge, 23, 235–36, 302, 306, 307

"Power, Repression, Progress" (Hoy), 234

Practical criticism, 41, 42–43, 45, 52, 53–55, 58, 63–64, 73, 215, 300

"Problem of Truth, On the" (Horkheimer), 265, 268–69

"Protocols": in Richards, 62–63, 65–66, 68

Psychoanalysis, 72, 75, 215, 225, 235

Punishment and Social Structures (Rusche and Kirchheimer), 304

Realism: in Auerbach, 84, 89, 90, 92, 98

Renan, Joseph Ernest, 245–46, 259, 260, 266–67, 278, 308, 327n.11

Representation: in Foucault, 46, 246–47, 299; in Hodgson, 292; language as, 46–48; and language theory in Richards, 48–49

Representative intellectual, See Leading intellectual

Revisionism: in Auerbach, 142, 143, 146, 173; and humanism, 117–18, 193, 257, 280; and the leading intellectual, 32, 145, 245; in Lukacs, 257; and the mandarin tradition, 124, 140; in Nietzschean genealogy, 12; and the oppositional critic, 145; in Pound's "Canto xiii," 6; in Said, 30

Richards, I. A.: and Auerbach, 300, 301–2; authority in, 51–52, 70; Beyond, 74; and conservatism, 57, 59, 64–65, 76; and contextualism, 50, 52, 59, 67; critical practice of, 62, 67; and empiricism, 49, 52; and Hodgson, 300–302; and humanism, x, xii, xvii, 42–43, 51, 54, 58–59, 61, 62, 70, 74, 76, 298–99, 301–2; and the institutionalization of literary studies, 40, 43, 45, 52–53, 76; intellectual fathers of, 58; Interpretation in Teaching, 50, 67; the leading intellectual in, 52, 62, 299; The Meaning of Meaning, 48, 50, 64; and New Criticism, 46, 69; "practical criticism," 42–43, 52–53, 58, 63–64, 73, 300; Practical Criticism, 44, 50, 65, 67, 68–69; Principles of Literary Criticism, 44, 60, 66, 67, 70, 72; "protocols," 62–63, 65–66, 68; relation to functionalism, x; and Said, 29, 32, 216, 276, 298–302; social order in, 53–54, 58–59; Speculative Instruments, 69–70; mentioned, 26, 254, 284, 307, 315n.10

Ringer, Fritz: The Decline of the German Mandarins, 115, 116, 117, 126–27, 135, 150; on the mandarin tradition, 113–15, 117–18, 126–27

Said, Edward W.; and Auerbach, xiii, 27, 106, 187–91, 271, 272, 275, 287, 298–302; on the author, 26–27, 30; Beginnings, 106, 276, 324n.28; and Chomsky, 221, 227–29, 232; on the

critic, 189, 212, 214–16, 247–48, 276–77, 280–82, 287–88; on critical consciousness, 281–82, 289, 301; critical practice of, 30, 216–18, 274–75, 277–79, 298–99; and criticism, 29, 214–15, 219–20, 297–98; on culture, 256, 274–75, 284, 297–98; and Foucault, 26–27, 30, 33, 36, 212–14, 218–25, 227–31, 235–36, 246–48, 273, 276, 277, 299, 325n.11; and genealogy, 3, 22, 28, 216; and Gramsci, 28, 30, 221, 287–89; and Hodgson, xv, 246, 272, 275, 281, 282–83, 285, 286–87, 292–93, 297–302, 327n.14, 328n.19; and humanism, xi, xiii, xiv–xv, 1, 28, 30, 32–33, 36–37, 214–15, 217, 247, 261, 271, 275–79, 281–82, 286–87, 297–98, 300–302; on the intellectual, 213–18, 221–23, 225, 228–29, 300–301; and Kant, 240, 247–48, 281–82; and the leading intellectual, xii, 134, 222–25, 247–48, 277–79, 281–82, 288–89, 298–99; and Nietzsche, 20, 22, 23, 26–27, 31, 32, 33; and the oppositional critic, xiv, 29, 30–33, 213, 276–81, 298–99; Orientalism, 26–27, 28, 29, 30, 31, 32–33, 65, 212, 216, 219, 234, 239, 298, 302, 314n.28; on Renan, 245–46, 259, 327n.11; and Richards, 29, 32, 215, 216, 276, 298–99, 301–302; "Secular Criticism," 27, 273, 274, 275; "Traveling Theory," 212–15, 217–23, 225; The World, The Text and the Critic, 245, 259, 262, 271, 273, 274, 275, 277, 278–81, 287–89, 298; mentioned, 19, 142, 143, 144, 208, 269, 273, 290, 295, 307, 308
Scholar, the: in Auerbach, 207–8, 272; in Hodgson, 270–72, 295–97; in Said, 272, 297. See also Critic, the; Intellectual, the
Scholarship: in Hodgson, 290–94; in Kant, 293–94; in Richards, 290–91; in Said, 292
Scientism, 41, 60–61, 282–84
Shelley, Percy Bysshe, 62, 260

Specialization: Auerbach and, 86, 89, 138, 185–86, 193–94, 207
Spitzer, Leo, 85, 105, 107–8, 176, 186
Spranger, Eduard, 124–25
State, the: Auerbach on, 152–53, 156, 160, 167; Foucault on, 226–27; and humanism, 261, 296; Kant on, 252–56; and the leading intellectual, 256, 261; Meinecke on, 148–56; Said on, 289
Subject, the: in Auerbach, 143–44, 189–90, 197–98, 299; in critical practice, 25; in Foucault, 3, 23, 24, 35–36, 210, 219, 289, 301, 308; in Herder, 134, 190; and the leading intellectual, 35–36; in the mandarin tradition, 134–35; in Nietzsche, 3, 22–23; in Richards, 299; in Said, 219; See also Individual, the
Synthesis: and American humanism, 81, 82, 98–99, 119, 128–29; Auerbach and, 81, 84–92, 96, 98–99, 108, 118–20, 127–28, 140, 143–44, 162–63, 177, 186, 187–88, 190, 195, 202, 203–7, 317n.4, 323n.27; and history, 119–20; 124; and German humanism, 116–20; and the leading intellectual, 116–17, 124; in the mandarin tradition, 126–27; Meinecke on, 117, 122, 124; and modernism, 87–89; Troeltsch on, 119–20, 122, 124; and Said, 187–88; and Vico, 140; and Weimar, 82, 86. See also Aesthetics

Thompson, E. P., 230, 276
Tillyard, E. M. W., 42, 44, 45; The Muse Unchained, 39, 40, 43
To The Lighthouse (Woolf), 88, 90
Trilling, Lionel, xvii
Troeltsch, Ernst, 119–24; Historicism and Its Problems, 119
Truth: and critical practice in Auerbach, 267–68; and criticism, 309–10; in Foucault, 232–34, 243–44, 300, 305, 306; Hodgson on, 283, 292, 300; Horkheimer on, 267–69; and the intellectual, 278, 299, 200; and

Truth (*Continued*)
knowledge in Nietzsche, 21; and
knowledge-production in humanism, 267–69; and power, 296, 300,
309–10; regime of, in Foucault,
229–31, 233–34, 236, 303, 308,
326n.16

Vico, Giambattista: in Auerbach,
131–33, 136–45; historicism in, 139,
144; and the mandarin tradition,
137–38, 140; as oppositional critic,
145; mentioned, 27, 146, 151, 153,
164, 169, 202, 291, 294
Vossler, Karl, 97, 114, 118

Ward, James, 43, 58
Weber, Max, 114, 116–18, 139
Weimar, 82, 83, 86, 113, 114–15,
117–19, 124–26, 155. *See also*
German humanism; Mandarin tra-
dition, the
Wellek, René, 98–100, 102, 104–5, 122,
211
Weltliteratur, 43, 91, 163–64, 170, 178,
180, 200, 201, 262, 263, 322n.16
Western humanism, 153, 296, 297,
301. *See also* Humanism
Will, 16–17, 23, 294, 300. *See also*
Power; Truth
Williams, Raymond, xvii, 217, 218,
230, 276, 328n.26; *Culture and Soci-
ety*, 276
Wimsatt, W. K., 45–46, 75
Woolf, Virginia, 84, 95; *To The Light-
house*, 88, 90

Zola, Emile, 82, 84, 87; *Germinal*, 90